Reading *Piers Plowman* and *The Pilgrim's Progress*

Reception and the Protestant Reader

Barbara A. Johnson

Southern Illinois University Press
Carbondale and Edwardsville

Library of Congress Cataloging-in-Publication Data

Johnson, Barbara A.
    Reading Piers Plowman and The pilgrim's progress : reception
and the Protestant reader / Barbara A. Johnson.
        p. cm.
    Includes bibliographical references and index.
    1. Langland, William, 1330?–1400? Piers the Plowman.
2. Bunyan, John, 1628–1688. Pilgrim's progress. 3. Protestants—
England—Books and reading. 4. Protestantism and literature.
5. Reader-response criticism. I. Title.
    PR2015.J6   1992
    821'.1—dc20   91-30326
    ISBN 0-8093-1653-6   CIP

To Wallace E. Williams (1926–1990)

Contents

Acknowledgments

In this work, when it shall be found that much is omitted, let it not be forgotten that much likewise is performed; and though no book was ever spared out of tenderness to its authour, and the world is little solicitious to know whence proceeded the faults of that which it condemns; yet it may gratify curiosity to inform it, that the *The English Dictionary* was written with little assistance of the learned, and without the patronage of the great; not in the soft obscurities of retirement, or under the shelter of academic bowers, but amidst inconvenience and distraction, in sickness and in sorrow.

Samuel Johnson, Preface to *The English Dictionary*

 It is not an accident that I call on the words of another to encapsulate all I feel about my own work, for this is a book about how reading the words of others can name our own experience. Unlike Samuel Johnson, however, I benefited enormously from the learned at all points during the writing of this study, especially from Barbara K. Lewalski, Suzanne Woods, and Joseph Wittreich, who provided valuable advice and encouragement. Mary Carruthers also provided a valuable reading at an early point. More recently, scholars such as John King and John Knott helped me define exactly what kind of book I was engaged in. My greatest debts are to my colleagues at Indiana University: first, to those who supported me "amidst inconvenience and distraction, in sickness and in sorrow," especially Susan Gubar and James Justus, and secondly, to those who also tirelessly read the manuscript as it evolved, especially Alfred

David, Lawrence Clopper, and Clifford Flanigan. I profited greatly from the reactions of other readers at various points, especially Eugene Kintgen, Paul Strohm, Katherine Flannery, Charles Forker, Anya Peterson Royce, Mary Burgan, and Judith Anderson.

Financial support in the form of an AAUW dissertation fellow-ship made possible the first trip to the British Library in 1979–80. An NEH summer stipend in 1985 for research in England helped me redefine the scope of the study. I wish to thank the staffs of the British Library, the Bodleian Library, the various college libraries at Cambridge, and the Lilly Library at Indiana University for their help. I also wish to thank the Lilly Library for permission to use two illustrations. A portion of chapter two has previously appeared in different form as "Falling into Allegory: The 'Apology' to *The Pil-grim's Progress* and Bunyan's Scriptural Methodology" in Robert Collmer's *Bunyan in our Time* (Kent State University Press, 1989) and is reprinted here with permission of The Kent State University Press. I owe a large debt to the staff at Southern Illinois University Press, especially Robert Phillips, who provided the initial contact, and my two editors, Curtis Clark and Carol Burns, whose support and patience were crucial. I also wish to thank my two copy editors, George Nicholas and Patricia St. John, for their forbearance.

Finally, the intellectual and emotional debt I owe to two people, Elizabeth D. Kirk and Robert S. Sturges, cannot begin to be acknowl-edged; without their support this book would simply not exist. The book itself is dedicated to Wallace E. Williams, whose cheerful, indomitable spirit was sorely missed during the final stages of this project, but who contributed much to its making.

1

Introduction
Tracing the History of Reading
Through the History of Books

In 1550 [Robert Crowley] printed the first edition of *Pierce Plowman's Vision,* but with the ideas of a controversialist, and with the view of helping forward the reformation by the revival of a book which exposed the absurdities of popery in strong satire, and which at present is only valuable or useful, as it serves to gratify the harmless researches of those peaceable philosophers who study the progression of antient literature.

Thomas Warton, *The History of English Poetry*

My intention was to deal with the venerable Bunyan as delicately as possible, and in no instance to deprive him of that beautiful simplicity, in which he will assuredly stand unrivaled to the end of the world. I admired his Pilgrim's guise, and wished only to adjust it in a few minute points, where it seemed to be inconsistent with the general decorum of his character. It appeared to me desirable, that he should be made to speak with a little more grammatical precision; that his extreme coarseness should be moderately abated; that he should be rendered less obscure in some passages, less tautological in others, and offensive in none.

Joshua Gilpin, preface to "a new and corrected edition" of *The Pilgrim's Progress*

This study explores the cultural transmission of the two texts described above. It argues for a historical connection between William Langland's *Piers Plowman* and John Bunyan's *Pilgrim's Progress* and charts the roles the two works played in the centuries following their composition, roles far more important and extensive than their modern critical reputations can explain. The story of what happens to these two works is a story about the part readers play in the way the meaning of a text is appropriated. It is also a story about changing ideas concerning the nature and status of books as well as the stature of authors. Tracing the reception of *Piers Plowman* and *The Pilgrim's Progress* provides a particularly graphic example of how literature and society intersect. The reception of these two works documents the means by which a culture shapes and is shaped by texts. The scope of this study, then, is not literary history but literature in history. And writ small, but perceptible in the transformations *Piers Plowman* and *The Pilgrim's Progress* undergo in terms of changing audiences, is the history of readers reading.

Thus, this is not a book about texts but about how and why readers read them in earlier periods. No attempt will be made to render an opinion on the meaning of either *Piers Plowman* or *The Pilgrim's Progress* except from the broader cultural perspective of reception. Nor will I assert a "literary" connection between Langland and Bunyan, for it does not matter whether Bunyan read Langland. Indeed, I will argue that our notion of the "literary" has prevented us from understanding the varied ways readers construed the meaning of texts in earlier periods. The historical connection between Langland's poem and Bunyan's narrative is not one of influence but of readership. They are linked here because they were seen as only marginally "literary," and as such, their receptions provide the best means of documenting the varied ways readers read what we label as "literature" in earlier periods. The two works were chosen not to advance theoretical models for reading but to document a way of reading that had its roots in the first stirrings of the Reformation, came to fruition in the phenomenon of *The Pilgrim's Progress*, and persisted well into the nineteenth century for some of Bunyan's later readers. A study of the reception of *Piers Plowman* and *The Pilgrim's Progress* in England from the fourteenth through the seventeenth century fleshes out a crucial chapter in the history of Protestantism and the Book.

In one sense, all readers in the English Renaissance were Protestant in their awareness of the way literature absorbed both the strategies and the politics of religion. The research of Barbara K. Lewalski, John N. King, David Norbrook, and others has documented the emergence of a Protestant tradition and its impact on the literature of the period, but I will focus here on a particular subset of those readers that needs to be acknowledged if we are to begin to understand the history of reading.[1] Although I frequently distinguish Protestant from literary or lettered[2] readerships, I use the term *Protestant reader* not in opposition to other kinds of readers, including the lettered, but to demarcate different ways and kinds of reading. As we will see when we survey the comments of readers on Langland's poem and Bunyan's narrative, the possible responses to texts in the period exist on a continuum, and the dividing line in terms of Protestant or lettered responses to texts is one of emphasis rather than division until the late seventeenth century. Nor do I use the term *Protestant* to denote any particular sectarian differences; this book considers what Protestant readers have in common in terms of their approach to reading rather than what divides them. These Protestant readers can be defined in a number of ways: they began to emerge at the point where there was a call to have the Scriptures in English; thus their orientation toward the written word marked them in ways other than those who were considered "literate" (i.e., educated in learning). Secondly, that orientation toward the religiously liberating written word marked their encounters with other texts also heralded as reformist in some sense. Texts seen in this light, as presented in John Foxe's *Book of Martyrs* and elsewhere, were thought of as divinely inspired and as forerunners for the new religious age. In order to reconstruct this kind of reader I will use *Piers Plowman* and *The Pilgrim's Progress* as crucial documents in the history of lay literacy as well as major landmarks in the way they embody the cultural matrix of the English Reformation movement. The development of the Protestant reader will be traced in the reception of *Piers Plowman* from its first explosive entry into the Peasants' Revolt of 1381 to the permutations of meaning it undergoes during the Renaissance, when its author is ultimately labeled a Protestant "by Prolepsis," and its printing in 1550 is seen as part of Reformation history. Finally, that Protestant reader emerges full-blown in the figure of John Bunyan and his book, *The Pilgrim's*

Progress. The work is often seen as eccentric and marginally "literary," although from the standpoint of conventional literary history, it represents the final flowering of medieval pilgrimage allegory as well as the starting point for the novel in England.[3] However, Bunyan's narrative emerges as a cultural phenomenon of unique import when its history, in terms of both its inception and its dissemination, is traced from the perspective of the Protestant reader rather than from the history of literary forms.

In fact, as we will see, the category of the literary itself is a historical construct, the contours of which can be traced in the reception of these two works. According to Raymond Williams, the word *literature* came into English in the fourteenth century and was linked to a sense of polite learning through reading. The emergence of the modern conception of literature and the literary occurs in the first half of the nineteenth century, when the word emerged as a label to be applied to imaginative writings.[4] But early signs, corresponding to a new sense of writing as a profession, occur in the late eighteenth century, a period succinctly circumscribed in the epigraphs from Thomas Warton (1774) and Joshua Gilpin (1811). In fact, when we speak of literature in history, we must acknowledge that we are reading backwards with modern expectations of the literary object as primarily an aesthetic experience. The two epigraphs from Warton and Gilpin document the phenomenon of reading backwards. Each critic registers his discomfort with what he considers to be the nonliterary characteristics of his chosen subject, and each attempts to recast the text into a more purely literary artifact. In the process, each discloses his own conceptual models for the nature of books and of authors, models that quite probably bear little resemblance to the original intentions of the authors, the editors, and the printers, or to the circumstances of transmission.

The epigraph from Thomas Warton can be seen as a palimpsest where an older way of reading is still visible even though it has been written over. Warton's orientation toward books and authors places him on the literary side of our continuum in his reaction to an earlier reading of *Piers Plowman*. Robert Crowley, who edited and printed *Piers Plowman* three times in 1550, comes under attack from Warton because his idea of what to do with Langland's poem violated Warton's own sense of what texts are for. Crowley's publication of the medieval poem was a political act. According to Warton, he should not have published a text with "the ideas of a controversialist." Antiquarians should be "peaceable philosophers" whose research is "harmless," unlike the product of Crowley's studies, which played a role in the Reformation. For Warton, a text like *Piers Plowman* has value and use, to use his terms, only insofar as it discloses its role in the "progression of antient literature."[5]

We should note as well Warton's description of *Piers Plowman*. The title appears to be incorrect; it is not Piers's vision, but the dreamer's. The description of the text's contents does not quite square with our twentieth-century perspective on the poem. Its dimensions of dream-vision and allegory are ignored here; instead, Warton sees it as a satire that exposed the "absurdities of popery," which represents quite a departure from our own sense of the poem's subject. At an earlier point, when he dealt with the poem itself and not with its Renaissance incarnation, he had labelled it a "satire on the vices of almost every profession; but particularly on the corruptions of clergy, and the absurdities of superstition." Warton's emphasis, then, is on the satirist and his targets. He goes on to say that these vices are "ridiculed with much humour and spirit, couched under a strong vein of allegorical invention."[6] Thus he sees the poem and its maker as particularly tied to a historical time; given this perception of the poem's topicality, the only possible literary genre to which it can be assigned is satire. It is worth noting, however, that despite the fact that he takes Crowley to task for politicizing the poem, he has ratified Crowley's presentation of it. Warton sees the poem less as an artifact to be admired and more as a polemic to be noted; he does not find the poem to be a pleasing literary specimen, for he faults its language, metrics, and obscurity.[7] Langland is more a critic of society than a poet proper because he attacks the religious and societal abuses of his own age, an age that Warton clearly feels holds no meaning for his own.

How a medieval Catholic poem came to be viewed in these terms will be a major focus of this study, as we trace patterns of reception from the poem's entrance in the fourteenth century to the seventeenth. As the example of Warton makes clear, the presentation of a work and the expectations we bring to a text shape our responses to it. Crowley shaped Warton's view of *Piers Plowman*, but Crowley's view was shaped by some of the work's earliest readers. One of them was John Ball, who co-opted the poem's central figure, Piers, and used the character to further the Peasants' Revolt of 1381. Other readers were the unknown authors of a substantial body of apocryphal plowman texts that argued for religious, political, and economic reform. The figure of the plowman played an important symbolic role in Protestantism and perhaps can help account for the rise of mechanick preachers (preachers who were also employed in a manual trade),[8] such as Bunyan, in the later seventeenth century. For Warton, however, texts are simply antiquarian byways or museum pieces. From his perspective, *Piers Plowman* played a quite negligible role in "the progression of antient literature," though it played a significant one in the culture.

Joshua Gilpin's epigraph is an eloquent witness to the divorce that occurred between Protestant and literary ways of reading; his place on our continuum is in the middle, with a dividing line drawn down the center of the chart. The editor of "a new and improved edition of an old and interesting work" shares similar assumptions about the value and use of literary artifacts, but his problem with *The Pilgrim's Progress* differs in kind. He too must grapple with the book's reception, but it is still a living text — and, in fact, one he admires — not an obsolete piece of literary history. The meteoric success of the *The Pilgrim's Progress* (Gilpin notes that "few religious works have obtained so much celebrity, or passed through so great a number of editions"[9]) demanded that the prose work be admitted to the domain of literature. But its author, a nonconformist minister who was once a tinker, hardly suited the role of a writer of "literature." Because of his own sense of the stature of authors, Gilpin saw a work that prominently displayed the lower class origins of its maker. As a result, he felt licenced to "adjust" the work and, in effect, to rehabilitate it, all in the interest of "decorum." The author of *The Pilgrim's Progress* is predictably damned with faint praise; he is not only "venerable," but his work also discloses his "beautiful simplicity" or, put another way, his lack of sophistication in the production of his text. The contents of the work are temporarily subordinated to considerations of its style, its "literariness." The specific features in need of adjustment include a "lack of grammatical precision" as well as coarseness, obscurity, tautologies, and offensiveness (xiv–xv).

Gilpin, however, has persuasive reasons for rendering a more "literate" and therefore "literary" version of *The Pilgrim's Progress*, and it is in his working out of his various motives for revising *The*

Pilgrim's Progress that we can best see the split that occurred between "Protestant" and "lettered" readings of texts. Despite the work's popularity, according to Gilpin, the "defects" of "language and style" enumerated above "have operated very powerfully against its influence among the more polished classes of society" (xiv). He "adjusts" Bunyan's prose to suit a particular audience with specific expectations and requirements for their reading matter. Thus, he claims that his attempt to refurbish *The Pilgrim's Progress* will enhance not only the work's reputation but also its mission as a religious book.

Joshua Gilpin's preface provides a barometer of the shifting fortunes of Bunyan's most famous book and his stock as an author in the nineteenth century. Information concerning its popularity and its readership has already come to light in the epigraph. It was spurned by the upper classes although, or perhaps because, it was so resoundingly embraced by the lower echelons of society. Gilpin's remark nicely dovetails with the assertion by E. P. Thompson that *The Pilgrim's Progress* emerged as "one of the two foundation texts of the English working-class movement."[10] But in addition to indicating upper-class responses to the text, Gilpin's comments touch on such matters as the category to which the work was assigned, patterns of readership, and views of Bunyan as an author.

Like *Piers Plowman, The Pilgrim's Progress* was seen as only marginally literary in the second century after its appearance. Having noted its celebrity as a religious work, Gilpin makes a sweeping claim about the success of the book's religious mission: "Had I not considered the Pilgrim's Progress as one of the most useful publications that ever appeared, or that is ever likely to appear, in the christian world, I should never have troubled myself about its form or fashion, nor felt any concern for its future fame in the world" (xv). The emphasis here is on *utile* alone, not *dulce*, which Gilpin tries to approach in his edition. What redeems *The Pilgrim's Progress* in Gilpin's eyes is its effect on the Christian reader. He defines this as the work's "important tendency," phrasing that suggests his grasp of Bunyan's motives in producing the work. Gilpin singles out for admiration Bunyan's "Pilgrim's guise," his fictive mask which barely conceals the writer's religious agenda: to awaken Christians to their spiritual state and to show them the way to salvation. To be sure, this view of the work is widespread throughout the nineteenth century, but it is not the only reason for the work's phenomenal success in the period.

What Gilpin has to say elsewhere about his encounters with *The Pilgrim's Progress* at different points in his life signals another appropriation of the text: what was a foundation text for the working class became a children's book for the upper-class family. The preface begins on a profoundly personal note that illustrates the generational pattern of readership of *The Pilgrim's Progress* among the upper classes. Gilpin opens with a moving account of the loss of his son, who, like his father, had been given Bunyan's work at a young age and who had asked his father to "adjust" it. Worth noting here is the fact that the editor, in articulating his relationship to *The Pilgrim's Progress* and justifying his endeavor, casts himself first in the familial role of a father fulfilling his dead son's wish. Unspoken, but palpable at this point, is his need to assuage the grief he feels over his loss by focusing on the redemptive vision of a progress through and out of this world and on to a better one. But this sentimental attachment to the text is immediately followed by more direct encounters with *The Pilgrim's Progress*, as Gilpin records both an early and more recent view of the work along with a critical assessment: "In early childhood, I perused this allegory with great delight, as an entertaining story: but, since that time, it has often excited my admiration, as an able and interesting delineation of the christian's progress from earth to heaven. But while the beauties of the Pilgrim's Progress are numerous and striking, its defects are conspicuous and offensive" (xiii). How can we account for the emergence of *The Pilgrim's Progress* as a children's book among the "more polished classes"? The convergence of two perceived "facts" about the text, its religious character and the simplicity of its matter and style (derived in part from the social standing of its author), rendered it an ideal choice as a book for children. Gilpin's comments bear witness to the efficacy of that choice; the child saw an entertaining story, the adult, its religious significance.

More revealing is the fact that Gilpin feels compelled to spell out what *The Pilgrim's Progress* has meant to him on a number of emotional and intellectual levels. His responses to Bunyan's work— as father, child, adult, and critic—provide a series of benchmarks over the course of his life, testifying to the multiple roles a text can play in the life of a reader. The rapid-fire way these comments come tumbling out delivers a picture of a reader struggling with competing views of *The Pilgrim's Progress* that evoke disparate emotions: affection for the delight the entertaining story afforded him as a child; admiration for the applicability of the story to one's own life; repugnance for an inferior literary production; and grief for the latest marker the book signifies in his life. What emerges here is a profile of a reader's evolving relationship to a text. Gilpin furnishes us with a spectrum of responses as he unfolds the layers of meaning a text can hold for a reader, some private and intimate, some public and distanced. Yet it is not the text that changes, but the reader; his stance shifts as he tries on different roles. It is worth noting is that no view is jettisoned in favor of any other, though they all are ultimately subsumed by the last mantle Gilpin cloaks himself in, that of editor of an insufficiently literary text, justifying his alterations of its "form and fashion" (xv). Finally, though Bunyan's work entertains, provides "an able and interesting delineation," and has "beauties," its "defects" cry out for adjustment. By undertaking this task, Gilpin literally becomes part of the transmission process not only in terms of his reading but also in terms of his rewriting of the text.

Proclaiming that "the Pilgrim of Bunyan comes abroad into the world under an improved experience" (xv) as a result of his efforts, Gilpin turns to the much maligned author of *The Pilgrim's Progress*. His remarks about Bunyan make it possible to gauge the mechanick preacher's literary and religious reputation as well as to measure the extent to which preconceptions about an author dictate a reader's orientation to a text. The "venerable" Bunyan has stood the test of time in terms of the publishing history of his most famous book, and the work's "beautiful simplicity," a simplicity of matter and style linked to the author's lower-class origins, has been singled out for praise, although it needs adjustment "in a few minute points, where it seemed to be inconsistent with the general decorum of his character." From our more egalitarian twentieth-century perspective, Gilpin, up to this point in the preface, appears to have done nothing but belittle Bunyan's achievement, appointing himself judge of what is fitting in Bunyan's presentation of himself as an author in *The Pilgrim's Progress*. But if we set his remarks in the context of his culturally determined expectations of the literary product as well as that of his religious mindset, we will see that Gilpin has consistently sought to enhance Bunyan's reputation by broadening his readership, even though it has meant sanitizing the work by removing the "coarseness" and "offensiveness" of Bunyan's lower-class style in order to render it more palatable to an upper-class audience.

Gilpin's final formulation of why he undertook this task, though jarring in its phrasing, documents the esteem in which he holds Bunyan as well as his colliding perspectives on the value and use of books: "But deeply convinced of its important tendency [usefulness as a religious work], and lying under the weight of many obligations to the author of this admirable production, both as to pleasure and to profit, I have thus endeavored to discharge a debt of gratitude to the excellent, though illiterate, Bunyan" (xv). Bunyan can be both "excellent" and "illiterate" as a writer because the reputation that Gilpin seeks to heighten (as well as the kind of "decorum" that he attempts to make consistent in *The Pilgrim's Progress*) is religious, not literary. In fact, his excellence as a religious figure is enhanced by his illiteracy, which in this case simply means that he is uneducated in letters or, translated into the radical politics of the later seventeenth century, that he has not been tainted by secular, "humane" traditions, literary or otherwise. In a characteristic flourish that we will encounter many times as we focus on the manipulation of the plowman figure by Langland's early readers and on how Bunyan situates himself as an author, Gilpin turns the disdain that people feel for Bunyan's origins to the preacher's advantage. He notes that Bunyan, like the "Prince of pilgrims," will always be exposed to the "sneers of the scorner" and that "the profane and the proud" will always agree "to hold his name in derision" (xvi). In the final paragraph of the preface, Gilpin states that Bunyan has been awarded an extraordinary honor by God. While he is participating in the glories of heaven, he is also active on earth through his book, where he is "the faithful conductor of way faring men from the City of Destruction to the city of the living God" (xvi). Bunyan emerges here and elsewhere as a Protestant version of a Christian saint; his miracle is the production of *The Pilgrim's Progress* and its effect on generations of readers. Like the members of the despised cult of Catholic saints, he is both in heaven and present on earth, but unlike them, what he has left behind is a book, not a bone. He is not an intercessor one prays to but a "conductor" who can lead the way to salvation if one embarks on his book.

At the close of the preface, Gilpin underscores how the book is to be used: "I feel a growing assurance, that thousands and ten thousands of the sincere and humble will sucessively travel, in his train, through the wilderness of this world to the Canaan of promise" (xvi). Gilpin echoes Bunyan's assertion in "The Author's Apology for his Book"[11] concerning the efficacy of *The Pilgrim's Progress*:

This Book will make a Travailer of thee,

If by its Counsel thou wilt ruled be;

It will direct thee to the Holy Land,

If thou wilt its Directions understand.

(lines 207–10)

However, Gilpin locates the authority to invite, counsel, and direct readers to heaven not in the book itself, as Bunyan had done, but in the author's presence in the book.

The stances that Thomas Warton and Joshua Gilpin respectively adopt toward *Piers Plowman* and *The Pilgrim's Progress* have been examined here with some care; the discussion forecasts the lines my argument will take to substantiate a historical relationship between Langland's poem and Bunyan's narrative. Moreover, Warton and Gilpin provide a foretaste of the larger theoretical and cultural issues such a study will raise. The analysis of the two passages represents a paradigm for how this study will proceed. First, we will focus on historical readers. Sometimes we will know them by name, sometimes only by their comments in the margins of a book, but we will find that there is much more historical evidence of how readers read in earlier periods than has been thought. Second, we will begin with the late reception of texts in order to frame what has happened to them over time. As the examples of Warton and Gilpin demonstrate, what is culturally transmitted is never just the work itself. It includes the vestiges of past readers' encounters with the text, traceable both in the way a given text is presented as well as in the way that presentation is received.

Recent theoretical studies of the reader's role in the production of meaning provide models for understanding the activities of readers such as Warton and Gilpin and, by extension, the Protestant reader that this book seeks to characterize.[12] Jonathan Culler, for example, posits a reader who is "competent," that is, one who has internalized a system of rules and conventions of interpretation.[13] Along similar lines, Stanley Fish puts forward a theory of "interpretive communities," which he defines as a bundle of strategies or norms of interpretation that we as readers hold in common and that regulate the way we think and perceive.[14] Culler and Fish, of course, are modern readers who see the act of reading within the context of a set of literary expectations that one brings to a text. Such terms as *rules, conventions,* and *strategies* imply a view of texts as artifacts that should conform to similar productions. As Jane Tompkins has pointed out, the stance of reader-response critics toward a text varies little from other twentieth-century brands of criticism; even though they locate meaning in the reader rather than the work, "they all share the assumption that texts are objects to be analyzed and deciphered."[15] She argues that earlier eras, such as the classical period, the Renaissance, and the Augustan Age, conceived of the value and use of books as means rather than ends in themselves, instruments of social and political power rather than objects.[16] This stance toward texts as objects for study was just beginning to take shape in the eighteenth century. Warton, viewing *Piers Plowman* as a literary specimen, assigns it to the generic category of satire and faults its chosen verse form as outmoded and unappealing. Similarly, Gilpin, though he admires *The Pilgrim's Progress*, struggles with the inadequacies of Bunyan's language as he attempts to make it over into a more literary production for an upper-class community of readers who will avoid its religious import if it is not made more pleasing.

We can best take the measurements of this approach toward the value and use of books and see what this kind of reader read for by focusing briefly on a remark Warton makes in the preface to his monumental *History of English Poetry* as he seeks to define the differences between "old" antiquarians and those of his own age. Old antiquarians "employed their industry in reviving obscure fragments of uninstructive morality and uninteresting history. But in the present age we are beginning to make ample amends: in which the curiosity of the antiquarian is connected with taste and genius, and his researches tend to display the progress of human manners, and to illustrate the history of society."[17] The work of old antiquarians (presumably he has men like John Bale, Robert Crowley, and John Foxe in mind)[18] will play a large role in helping to define the Protestant reader. Warton's description of their interests, though negative, will prove useful in defining the strategies for reading that regulated the ways this kind of reader made sense of texts. But for new antiquarians, as exemplified by Warton, "taste" and "genius" epitomize their agenda in approaching texts. These terms are conspicuously detached from the edification of the reader or the historical context out of which a given work arose, categories of experience that define the parameters of meaning for Protestant readers like Robert Crowley. Warton, however, only "revives" works if they conform to a standard of "genius" and are in harmony with the tastes of a lettered society.

Warton, of course, has a cultural project no less transparent than Robert Crowley's in publishing *Piers Plowman*. Crowley, according to Warton, had revived Langland's poem to forward the case for reformation in the church, and from Warton's perspective, he had specifically focused on "uninstructive morality" and "uninteresting history." Art, rather than the morality and history that an earlier generation of readers had seen as the basis of artistic production, dominates Warton's consideration of texts. But in *The History of English Poetry*, he defines his agenda in societal terms as well: "to develope the dawnings of genius, and to pursue the progress of our national poetry, from a rude origin and obscure beginnings, to its perfection in a polished age."[19] Crowley had used a document from antiquity to proclaim the validity of the reformers' cause; conversely, Warton uses texts of antiquity to promote the progress his own age has made. But more importantly, he views literature as a sphere of experience separable from all others, a social construct that reflects the progress his culture has made. His preface defines human society as the object of all art, and works of art as "the most picturesque and expressive representations of manners."[20] Little wonder that Warton finds antiquarians of the past curiously blind to the "genius" of earlier ages, for their agenda and their strategies for reading, as well as their conception of "genius," were conceived of in different terms than those described by Warton.

Terms such as *agenda* and *strategies for reading*, though useful in characterizing what different readers brought to texts, imply that readers like Crowley and Warton were entirely conscious of their cultural projects and that they deliberately made texts over to suit their "extraliterary" ends (a phrase that defines my own place on the continuum). On the contrary, they saw in texts what their surrounding culture had conditioned them to see, and what they saw was a reaction to the text itself. Too exclusive a focus on the reader obscures the text's role in the production of meaning. Reception theorists, most notably Wolfgang Iser and Hans Robert Jauss of the Konstanz school, place more emphasis on the text in their investigations of the interactions between work and audience. For example, Iser posits an "implied reader" that can be assembled from the structures of the text itself by focusing on the "gaps, blanks, and indeterminancies" that provoke varied responses.[21] But it is Jauss, in his quest to bridge the gap between historical and aesthetic approaches to the writing of literary history, who supplies the best model for understanding the text's role in the production of meaning and how that role evolves over time.

In "Literary History as Challenge to Literary Theory," Jauss proposes an "aesthetics of reception" that would require consideration of the "criteria of influence, reception, and posthumous fame" in order to judge the quality and rank of a literary work.[22] For Jauss, a literary work is not a "monument that monologically reveals its timeless essence"; rather it is "an orchestration that strikes ever new resonances among its readers."[23] Those resonances and their implications for a broader cultural understanding of how readers use books are precisely what this study will explore.

Jauss elevates the reader to a new status when he notes that in the "triangle of author, work and public the last is no passive part, no chain of mere reactions, but rather itself an energy formative of history."[24] In proposing to see "the history of literature . . . within the horizon of a dialogue between work and audience," he defines what he thinks the business of the writer of literary history should be: reconstructing a "horizon of expectations" (a notion ultimately derived from Gadamer)[25] that accounts for changing assessments of specific works of literature. Jauss describes ways to reconstruct this "horizon of expectations" in terms that define his and our modern approach to texts. In ways similar to Iser's, one deduces the first reception of a given work by noting how a text predisposes its audience to a very specific kind of reception by "announcements, overt and covert signals, familiar characteristics, or implicit allusions." Later reconstructions involve focusing on the "familiar norms or the immanent poetics of genre," implicit relationships to familiar works in the literary-historical surroundings, and (perhaps the most nebulous category) viewing the opposition of fiction and reality in assessing whether the "horizon of expectations" for a book's readers is "narrower" or "wider."[26]

Jauss, like Warton before him, views literature as a progression. However, what he seeks to illuminate is not the progress of human society as it is reflected in texts but the history of literature from the evolving perspective of its readers and critics. But his emphasis on the reader's role and his notion of how to construct a "horizon of expectations" that historical readers brought to texts is firmly anchored in literary history. Moreover, the terminology he uses inscribes a primarily literary landscape, as reflected in the use of such words as the "aesthetics" of reception, the "quality and rank" of a literary work," "influence," "fame," the "poetics of genre," and the like. Nevertheless, Jauss's concept of a "horizon of expectations" is an invaluable tool for charting the growth of a Protestant readership and the role *Piers Plowman* and *The Pilgrim's Progress* play in that development. Studies that have traced the emergence of a Protestant tradition have for the most part focused on works in the traditional canon such as Sidney, Spenser, and the devotional poets of the seventeenth century. John King's *English Reformation Literature* is a notable exception, but he too reads these Reformation texts in terms of the literary construct, as had lettered, educated readers of the time. What I propose is to explore the dimensions of a Protestant readership whose horizon of expectations concerning texts frequently diverged from, though sometimes overlapped, that of readers interested in works of literature as objects. A recent attempt to turn the writings of the later Puritan manifestation of this Protestant readership into literature, N. H. Keeble's *The Literary Culture of Nonconformity in Later Seventeenth-Century England*, underscores the problems inherent in canonization as we continually multiply the list of works that can be viewed as literary.[27] The writers and their readership that Keeble focuses on were not interested in the literary construct in itself but, in fact, set themselves up in opposition to it. If we are to understand the complex history of reading we must shed our preconceptions about what constitutes the literary act and focus on how that "act" was construed by various readers.

Although Jauss is somewhat vague on whether the text or the reader conducts in the production of meaning, the conception of the work as an "orchestration" is useful not only for studying literary history but also for charting the broader cultural dimensions of reception as we focus on how readers made sense of texts. Here we are not concerned with the quality and rank of a literary work but with the cultural interplay between *Piers Plowman* and *The Pilgrim's Progress* and their larger societies. Thus, ordinary readers rather than critics will be our primary focus as we attempt to trace not only how they made meaning but also the roles texts played in how they experienced their lives. Paul Fussell's *The Great War and Modern Memory* provides a twentieth-century example of how reading affects experience. He examines the World War I memoirs of soldiers and demonstrates that the works these writers had read determined the way they saw their experience of the war. A specific example pertinent to our concerns, *The Pilgrim's Progress*, a book almost all the soldiers knew, provided a means of processing and understanding what was happening to them. The trench experience called to mind for them the "Slough of Despond," the image of the soldier fully equipped with haversack and rifle found its original in the image of Christian with a burden on his back, and the experience of moving forward in position found its source in "the *Pilgrim's Progress* action of moving physically through some terrible topographical nightmare along a straight road."[28] Fussell's tentative thesis of reciprocity to explain this phenomenon, "life feeds materials to literature while literature returns the favor by conferring forms upon life," begs for a more sophisticated exploration of the relationship between books and society.[29]

Of course, our mission here is considerably more vexed than Fussell's, for the resources to gauge the impact of reading are far more limited for the period we focus on. But recent studies in the discipline that has come to be called *l'histoire du livre*, represented by the work of the cultural historian Robert Darnton and others, provide both the framework and the methodology for such an undertaking.[30] Historians such as Natalie Zemon Davis and Carlo Ginsberg have made inroads into the question of the impact of printing and Protestantism on popular culture. Davis, in her chapter entitled "Printing and the People," theorizes about the "complex ways in which printing entered popular life in the sixteenth century" and calls for evidence about audiences that can provide a "context for the meaning and the use of books."[31] Carlo Ginsberg, in *The Cheese and the Worms*, focuses on a peasant reader, one Mennochio, and his

trial for heresy. He claims that two events, printing and the Reformation, made the case of Mennochio possible, and he attempts to
explain the process by which Mennochio construed texts in developing his unorthodox views of creation.[32] Both Davis and Ginsberg
hover around a significant issue that will be pursued here in detail:
How did newly literate readers, readers who saw a strong tie between
the printed book and the new religion, see the role of books in their
lives, and how did this affect how they read them?[33] Or, put another
way, how did their relationship to Protestantism, the religion of the
Book, the Bible, orient their encounters with other books seen as
part of the same reformist tradition, such as Langland's poem and
Bunyan's narrative?

    In particular, the cultural historian Robert Darnton's attempts to
broaden intellectual history by creating a mixed genre, "the social
history of ideas," have influenced my own undertaking here to
expand the sphere of literary studies to include the cultural dissemination of texts.[34] Darnton defines the product of his research as
various explorations of "the book as a force in history."[35] My scope is
considerably more limited, but I will demonstrate that both *Piers
Plowman* and *The Pilgrim's Progress* played a greater role in their
respective societies than has hitherto been noted. Like Darnton in
*The Business of Enlightenment: A Publishing History of the Encyclo-
pedie, 1775–1800*, I plan to trace the "life story" of *Piers Plowman*
and *The Pilgrim's Progress* and the spread of their ideas in society. As
a historian, Darnton's investigations are more clearly oriented to
tracing a text's distribution and diffusion in a society, whereas my
own discipline of English leads me naturally to the more speculative
issue of a book's varied meanings for its readers. Nonetheless, one
aspect of his methodology, set out most clearly in *The Great Cat
Massacre and Other Episodes of French Cultural History*, is essentially my own: to view "opaque documents" and to attempt "to
unravel an alien system of meaning" that is reflected in them.[36] Only
by examining the responses of readers to texts, responses that at first
sight seem to be distortions or misreadings, can we begin to understand how works were read by earlier generations of readers. In an
article entitled "Towards a History of Reading,"[37] Darnton endorses
this kind of project by calling for a dual strategy of comparing implicit
readers of texts with actual readers of the past in order to develop "a
history as well as a theory of reader response."[38]

Darnton's definitions of both "reading" (not simply a skill, but a way of making meaning)[39] and "literature" (an activity rather than an established body of texts)[40] supply a much needed corrective to those who persist in seeing the meaning of literature as primarily stable and text-centered. Readers' orientation toward a text, their expectations about its value and its use, determine in part the outcome of their interaction with it. The truth of those definitions will become increasingly clear as we examine the fortunes of *Piers Plowman* and *The Pilgrim's Progress* in the centuries following their composition. A Protestant reader of *Piers Plowman* will locate prophecy in it; a lettered reader will find elements of satire. And these two readers can be the same person. Writing from a stance that evaluates the progression of literature in England, a lettered George Puttenham in *The Arte of English Poesie* (1589) labels Langland a bad poet; but Protestant Puttenham finds him a true prophet.[41]

Both *Piers Plowman* and *The Pilgrim's Progress* have long been perceived as marginal and eccentric works that fall outside the literary mainstream. But both works can emerge as mainstream productions in terms of their societal rather than their literary impact once we shift our frame of reference from the literary to the religious and posit readers different from ourselves. These readers are less interested in the aesthetic dimensions of texts but are vitally aware of the political, social, and religious currents that course through fictions as well as discursive texts. For their first readers, *Piers Plowman* and *The Pilgrim's Progress* were anything but marginal and were eccentric only in the degree to which they spoke out on the issues of their time to an audience that barely existed before their first appearance.

One of the more tantalizing facts about *Piers Plowman* and *The Pilgrim's Progress* is that their primary audiences were just coming into being when the works emerged. The circulation of both works corresponds to a phenomenon that has major implications for their unusual receptions: pronounced shifts in the literacy rate. And in each case the cause of religion was the motivating force. During the fourteenth and fifteenth centuries, lay literacy in the middle ranks of society expanded.[42] During Langland's time the shift to lay literacy was seen as a dangerous phenomenon allied with the Lollard movement, as the research of Margaret Aston and Anne Hudson documents.[43] Wyclif's call to English the Scriptures (incidentally, an issue that Crowley and others saw *Piers Plowman* addressing) threatened the clergy's hold over the middle class. In this highly charged atmosphere, new readers, readers who saw the Bible as a liberating force, read other books not just with their newfound skills but also with a revolutionary outlook that made all texts seem heretical, including *Piers Plowman*. And the explosive issue of religious reform spilled over into other areas. Some of Langland's first readers saw his work as calling for social as well as religious reform. As a result of their perceptions about the nature of Langland's poem, the radicalism of *Piers Plowman* was definitively and permanently established. It was a radicalism that in part brought to fruition the Reformation. The poem's insistence that the simple plowman knows the way to truth, without the mediation of priests, became a potent argument for religious reform in the sixteenth century. And in the next leap in literacy from 1500 to 1700[44] particularly associated with Puritan strongholds,[45] it enabled the mechanick preacher, John Bunyan, to produce a work based on the application of Scripture to the individual Christian and taking for its genre the dream-vision seen not as literary but as religious and reformist.

As we trace the history of these two books from the reader's perspective, we will see that the writing of books is an interactive process. The writer writes and the reader reads out of a context, though that context may not be the same for both. Assessing literary texts from the reader's perspective heightens our awareness of the volatility of texts. The writer's context, what Jauss would call the signals in the text that can help define the "horizon of expectations" for the book's first readers, can be ignored or "misunderstood," reactions that can provoke a writer to adjust his work after its first reception. Both Langland and Bunyan adjusted and reshaped their works in response to their first readers. Langland's reaction was perhaps an extreme one. Possibly in response to the pirating of his central figure by the leaders of the 1381 Peasants' Revolt, he produced the C-text, a much more conservative version of his dream-vision.[46] Bunyan's reaction was one of acquiescence. As we see in chapter 2, he expected to be condemned for writing a work that was "delivered under the Similitude of a Dream," a fiction, and thus a lie by Puritan standards for religious writings. In one of the most tortured defenses of fiction ever offered, he justifies his undertaking by appealing to a scriptural methodology as well as a tradition that he alludes to by announcing that not only is he not denied the use of this method but he has "leave" and "example"

> from them that have
>
> God better pleased by their words or ways,
>
> Than any Man that breatheth now adays.

("Apology," lines 172–74)

Bunyan's fears were unfounded. Far from considering the work "dark" and "feigned," his audience seems to have found it unambiguously clear and truthful. Conditioned to seeing their lives through the texture of Scripture, they saw that *The Pilgrim's Progress* contained "nothing but sound and honest Gospel-strains" (line 222). But contrary to Bunyan's original intent, they also saw that the work was about a particular life, his own, not allegorically but realistically conceived in terms of lived experience. They viewed his Everyman figure as a representation of the author rather than as a model of conversion. Thus, for example, by the second edition the "Denn" where the Dreamer dreams is glossed as the "Gaol," tying the work more closely to the biographical details of Bunyan's life. More dramatic evidence of this recasting can be seen in the addition (also occurring in the second edition) to the opening portrayal of Christian's despair, a passage in which he discusses his state with his family and tries to take them with him on his pilgrimage. The reception not only affected Bunyan's revisions of the original *Pilgrim's Progress*, but Bunyan's Everyman was so identified with its author and with individual lived experience in a community that when Bunyan published Part II in 1684, he felt compelled to produce an entirely different kind of allegory that describes what happens to the rest of Christian's family as they follow in his footsteps. For some of Bunyan's readers, Christian was a character in an episodic novel rather than a paradigm for them to follow. What has happened here is nothing less than a shift in the reader's sense of what fiction should do.

At the close of his "Author's Apology for His Book," Bunyan invited his readers to chart their spiritual progress through his vision of "Everyman," the developing Christian:

Would'st read thy self? and read thou know'st not what
And yet know whether thou art blessed on not,
By reading the same lines? O then come hither,
And lay my Book, thy Head and Heart Together.

(lines 233–36)

However, those readers were no longer interested in didactic instruction to develop that self but in models for living. In *The Pilgrim's
Progress's* relentless portrayal of an individual in pursuit of perfection in an imperfect world, they saw the nascent stage of what would
become a new genre, the novel. Those readers sought something
radically different from what an earlier readership had required of
texts. They did not see what earlier audiences had seen in *Piers
Plowman:* prophecy, reformist history, satire, moral doctrine gleaned
from imaginative scenes—perspectives that helped shape Bunyan's
agenda in his own narrative. What they saw and discovered was a
work that presented an individualized representation of a life, a
fictionalized biography that depicted Bunyan's individual but generic and hence universal encounter with the world.[47]

That interactive process can be seen on a much larger scale when
we see works surviving into a new context; the larger uses texts are
put to alter the horizon of expectations for the next generation of
readers. Thus *Piers Plowman* was seen over the shuttle of time as a
call to revolt, a prophecy, a history, a satire, and in the case of at least
one reader whose comments in the margin of a C-text manuscript
offer a unique record of a seventeenth-century reader's reactions to
the text, a spiritual autobiography. And *The Pilgrim's Progress* was
transformed by its readers into a spiritual autobiography of a Protestant saint, a children's book, a "foundation text" of the working-class
movement and, hauntingly, a mimetic picture of the soldier's experience in World War I, to name just a few of the ways the work was
appropriated by the culture.

Thus, the history of reading can be traced in the history of books.
In terms of how readers make meaning, it is literally written in the
books themselves, where we can catch readers in the act of reading in
their marginalia and indexing. What they ignore and what they
underscore demonstrates that readers read texts in varied ways and

for varied reasons. Much can also be deduced from the textual apparatus designed by editors and printers to guide (and sometimes divert) their readers to an understanding of the work's various meanings. We can learn about the context, degree of difficulty, targeted class of audience, and status of the author by viewing the textual machinery of later editions. For example, a 1561 edition of *Piers Plowman* attempts to turn Crowley's edition into an epic. The shifting reputation of both Bunyan and his book is reflected in the prefaces and notes appended to various editions. These are the kinds of "opaque" documents that we will use as we attempt to define the contours of meaning for Protestant readers.

Although the story of the development of a Protestant readership quite properly begins with the reception of *Piers Plowman*, *The Pilgrim's Progress* is the true focal point of this study. It represents the culmination of a theory of reading that began with the first stirrings for reform in the English church, and it inaugurates a new kind of readership hungering for similar novelistic productions. It is also the focal point because in its reception we can best see the collision of two different ideas about the nature and use of books as well as the origin and genesis of texts. Two competing horizons of expectation, the religious and the literary, have dominated the terms of the debate about Bunyan's narrative. We have already seen Gilpin articulating the inadequacy of Bunyan's status as an author ("the excellent, though illiterate, Bunyan"), but this view emerged almost immediately after the work's publication in 1678.

Bunyan himself provides evidence that ideas about what constitutes the literary act conspired to discredit his success. Some of his readers clearly felt that the caliber of the work far exceeded a mechanick's capabilities. "An Advertisement to the Reader," appended to *The Holy War* (1682),[48] documents that Bunyan felt called upon to defend himself against the charge that he did not write the book:

> Some say the Pilgrim's Progress is not mine,
>
> Insinuating as if I would shine
>
> In name and fame by the worth of another,
>
> Like some made rich by robbing of their Brother.
>
> (lines 1–4)

The "Advertisement" is a witness to the skepticism aroused by what appeared to be a sophisticated literary work. Some of the more lettered reading public must have felt that Bunyan had received help in writing it:

> Manner and matter too was all mine own,
>
> Nor was it unto any mortal known,
>
> 'Till I had done it. Nor did any then
>
> By books, by wits, by tongues, or hand, or pen,
>
> Add five words to it, or write half a line
>
> Thereof: the whole, and ev'ry whit is mine.
>
> (lines 15–20)

This careful disavowal of any assistance in the writing of *The Pilgrim's Progress* reveals the precise nature of the charges against him. Bunyan denies that someone else wrote the book. He then shifts to the manner (allegory) and the matter (the idea of an allegorical pilgrimage) and claims that he alone is responsible for these choices. Finally, he addresses the charge that he received assistance by reading (books) or by conversation (wits, tongues) or even in the editing of the work (hand or pen). He then goes out of his way to eliminate any possibility that the work was not entirely his own. We should bear in mind, however, that he is specifically responding to a charge of plagiarism and that his stance as a mechanick preacher precludes his addressing any other category, such as influence. In the "Advertisement" Bunyan injects the same naive report of the genesis of his book that he had given at the beginning of his "Apology":

> It came from mine own heart, so to my head,
>
> And thence into my fingers trickled;
>
> Then to my pen, from whence immediately
>
> On paper I did dribble it daintily.
>
> (lines 11–14)

Bunyan's readers were clearly responding to a problem about the book and its author that seemed insoluble. On the one hand, *The Pilgrim's*

Progress appeared to be a literary text, a fictive allegorical narrative about pilgrimage that had literary antecedents. On the other hand, Bunyan's statements about himself and about how his book came into being seemed far too simple to account for the sophisticated production that shone forth in the pages of *The Pilgrim's Progress*.

Why was Bunyan accused of plagiarism? For lettered readers like Thomas Warton, literature is an autonomous sphere of experience, separable from all other forms of discourse and viewed as a progression. The only explanation for the origin of a work is to cite other works, a procedure that is made quite difficult if the author in question sees neither himself nor his work in this restricted focus. Nonetheless, the persuasiveness of this concept of the origin of texts was clearly overwhelming in the eighteenth and nineteenth centuries. For instance, Boswell records Samuel Johnson's belief that *The Pilgrim's Progress* was influenced by other literary works: "It is remarkable, that it begins very much like the poem of Dante; yet there was no translation of Dante when Bunyan wrote. There is reason to think that he had read Spenser."[49] Johnson's comment arises not from any knowledge of Bunyan's life but from a reading of the work itself. *The Pilgrim's Progress* appeared to place itself so clearly in a literary tradition that it invited speculation about its sources and influences despite the testimony of the author.

This idea of the origin of *The Pilgrim's Progress* as a text with literary antecedents competed with an equally monolithic view of the inception of the work as a religious event. These two contexts for approaching the work are epitomized by Bunyan's two great nineteenth-century editors, George Offor and Henry Stebbing. Their editions appeared in the same decade (1850–60), but their attitudes toward Bunyan and his book are absolutely antithetical because they place the work in vastly different contexts. George Offor, who published a three-volume edition of Bunyan's works in 1856, saw *The Pilgrim's Progress* as a thoroughly divine achievement, proclaiming that "Bunyan's work comes nearer to the inspired poetry of the Hebrews in its character than any other composition."[50] In a section significantly entitled "Was Bunyan Assisted in the Composition of His *Pilgrim*?",[51] Offor surveys Bunyan's declarations on the subject, summarizes other critics on the question, lists, describes in detail, and analyzes fifty texts—including works of a literary nature, sermons, emblems, and lyrics that might conceivably be seen as similar in subject to *The Pilgrim's Progress*—before rejecting what he describes as attempts "to tarnish his fair fame."[52] As we saw in Gilpin as well, a literary reputation did violence to religious "fame." Offor's approach to the work placed major emphasis on Bunyan's life as the key to the achievement of *The Pilgrim's Progress*. Part of the power of *The Pilgrim's Progress* came from seeing it as the miraculous achievement of one of God's subjects, a poor tinker. Reading in the religious context, inspiration for the work originated with God.

Henry Stebbing subscribed to the literary explanation of the origin of texts. In his 1860 edition of Bunyan's works, he eagerly contemplated the prospect of what might have fired Bunyan's imagination, going over the same materials as Offor and generating even more highly improbable sources, such as Ben Jonson's masques and Shakespeare's plays.[53] In this context, the key to assessing the achievement of *The Pilgrim's Progress* was to find its likeness in hosts of other works of literature. Inspiration here is defined as contact with other "great" works of art, no matter how unlikely. For example, Stebbing believed that although Dante had not yet been translated, "Scores of men had heard, and could repeat, the best things of Dante in common, racy English." Stebbing has no illusions about Bunyan's background here; he argues that orally transmitted ideas were especially powerful to a mind as uneducated as Bunyan's and that in time they became "models of thought, or the groundwork of invention."[54] His explanation of Bunyan's possible indebtedness to Dante illustrates his overwhelming need to see its impact on the genesis of *The Pilgrim's Progress*.[55]

How do we harmonize these competing views of the origin of *The Pilgrim's Progress*? Tracing the growth of a Protestant readership provides the best means of moving beyond the narrow confines of the literary construct. One of the more unlikely literary sources that both Samuel Johnson and Henry Stebbing offer is Bunyan's contact with Dante. Though *The Pilgrim's Progress* "begins very much like the poem of Dante," would Bunyan have heard Dante's masterwork in "common, racy English"? No, but he would have known of Dante, and what he would have known about the author and his work would startle a modern reader's sense of the subject. John Foxe's *Acts and Monuments*,[56] a work we know Bunyan read, reflected a very different assessment of Dante's achievement: "Certaine of his writings be extant abroad, wherein he proveth the pope not to bee above the emperor, nor to have any right or jurisdiction in the empire. . . . In his canticle of Purgatorie, he declareth the pope to bee the whore of Babylon."[57] Like Crowley, Foxe is a Protestant reader, and the way he reads what we think of as a "literary" production underscores our impoverished sense of the relationship between literature and history. Here too we see a reader reading with an acute sense of the way the politics of religion courses through fiction as well as discursive texts.

In the Middle Ages literature and religion were not divorced spheres of experience. When the Biblical metaphor of pilgrimage first emerged in the fourteenth century as a central structuring device for long narratives, the distinctions between literary, religious, and polemical concerns were not drawn at all in theory nor with any sharpness in practice. Fictional works could, should, and did deliver doctrine that reflected the central issues of the time. The divorce between fiction and religious polemic was a seventeenth-century phenomenon, one that is closely allied to the extreme Puritan wing.

Accordingly, we must first define these special readers and their orientation toward texts. In order to do this, unfortunately, we must necessarily define them in opposition to other kinds of readers, especially those with literary expectations. But I am not arguing that these two poles of readership are mutually exclusive or monolithic. These two approaches toward texts can be categorized in terms of a set of expectations about the nature and status of books, their origin, and the stature of their authors. For the Protestant reader, texts are instruments rather than objects, and they are viewed in salvational rather than recreational terms. Inspiration comes from God, and specifically the Holy Spirit, rather than other works in a literary tradition. Finally, the stature of authors depends not on personal "genius," to use Warton's language, but on their function as God's servants. These are suppositions shared by all Protestant readers throughout the period, although sectarian differences account for variations within this readership. While the first examples of this kind of reader, the Lollards, can be seen as a community of readers, later manifestations of this readership are far more diverse.

We will find no better example than Bunyan in his stance toward his work as reflected in his "Apology" for *The Pilgrim's Progress*, which I discuss in chapter 2; here we see the tensions between fictional models and religious experience played out in Bunyan's reading of his own work. Chapter 3 examines the early reception of *Piers Plowman* by focusing on apocryphal texts that reflect some of the ways the poem and its major figure were "read" in the fifteenth and sixteenth centuries. The importance of Robert Crowley's three editions of Langland's poem in defining how Protestant readers read is explored in chapter 4, while the reception of the edition itself is the subject of chapter 5. In chapter 6 I explore the differences between these unusual productions. Not only does the lens of the Renaissance *Piers Plowman* provide a re-vision of Bunyan's agenda in *The Pilgrim's Progress*, it allows us to locate in these two convenient landmarks the key shift in religious perspective that began to take place in the late Middle Ages and that found its final expression in the later seventeenth century. In the concluding chapter I examine the immediate afterlife of *The Pilgrim's Progress* itself. I argue for a new kind of reader coming into being at the time of the work's inception who conditioned its reception in the centuries following its publication. Here I briefly suggest ways the work has entered our consciousness, although its cultural transmission has now been reformulated in secular terms, by focusing on its appropriation by readers. We must now turn to Bunyan himself in order to see through his "Apology" how revolutionary his approach to fictive expression really was.

THE
Pilgrim's Progress
FROM
THIS WORLD,
TO
That which is to come:

Delivered under the Similitude of a

DREAM

Wherein is Discovered,
The manner of his setting out,
His Dangerous Journey; And safe
Arrival at the Desired Countrey.

I have used Similitudes, Hof. 12.10.

By *John Bunyan.*

Licensed and Entred according to Order.

LONDON,
Printed for *Nath. Ponder* at the *Peacock*
in the *Poultrey* near *Cornhil,* 1678.

Title page of the 1678 edition of The Pilgrim's Progress. (Courtesy of the Lilly
Library, Indiana University, Bloomington, Indiana.)

2

Bunyan as First Reader
of *The Pilgrim's Progress*
Puritan and Protestant Paradigms
for Reading

This Book will make a Travailer of thee.
John Bunyan, *The Pilgrim's Progress*

 The first readers of John Bunyan's *Pilgrim's Progress* must have been startled by the title page of the 1678 edition, for it both announces and attempts to conceal the true nature of the volume.[1] The first few lines are, of course, fairly straightforward: "The / Pilgrim's Progress / From / This World, / To / That which is to come." But what follows is anything but predictable for a Puritan audience: "Delivered under the Similitude of a / Dream." The word *dream* is in heavy black type, by far the largest lettering on the page. "Delivered under the Similitude of a," positioned above it, is in the smallest lettering, perhaps in the hope that it could almost be overlooked. A description of the dream's contents comes next, emphasizing that what will be revealed is the journey of a character: "Wherein is Discovered, / The manner of his setting out, / His Dangerous Journey; And safe / Arrival at the Desired Countrey." And finally this summary is followed, above the author's name, with what must have seemed an admission of guilt if not effrontery: "I have used Similitudes, Hos. 12.10." The dynamics of the title page thus underscore the surprise for the book's first audience. John Bunyan, the dissenter, the mechanick preacher, has produced not a "plain tract" but a fictional work that depicts its subject through a similitude.

29

The skittishness about his enterprise reflected on the title page is played out in full in "The Author's Apology for His Book," prefixed to the first and all subsequent editions of *The Pilgrim's Progress*. The "Apology" is one of the most puzzling statements ever offered about a work of fiction. Far from a conventional introduction, it is instead a strenuous defense. One measure of its contradictory nature appears as soon as we turn from the title page to the opening statement. For while the title page has used language that indicates intentionality, Bunyan begins by proclaiming that he didn't mean to make a fictional work at all; it just happened that he "fell suddenly into an Allegory" (line 9). That falling requires an elaborate and complicated defense that begins with a naive proclamation that the work was an accident, includes a debate with a reader about the style and method, and ends with a comprehensive and radical statement about how his book is to be read. Toward the close of the "Apology," Bunyan insists that although *The Pilgrim's Progress* employs the similitude of a dream to portray the journey of a character, it nonetheless can give counsel and directions:

> This Book will make a Travailer of thee,
>
> If by its Counsel though wilt ruled be;
>
> It will direct thee to the Holy Land,
>
> If thou wilt its Directions understand.
>
> (lines 207–10)

Bunyan's goal in the "Apology" is to make the case that an allegory can, in fact, deliver religious instruction. We can deduce from the "Apology" the particular features and strictures of Bunyan's Puritan audience with respect to books and to ideas about their value and use by examining the strategies he uses to defend his activity as well as the models he cites for sanction. First, however, we must return to the question of the book's first readers and their potential reaction to the declaration on the title page of *The Pilgrim's Progress*.

The Horizon of Expectations for Bunyan's First Readers

In order to reconstruct the horizon of expectations that Bunyan's first readers brought to the title page of *The Pilgrim's Progress*, we need to borrow Jauss's methodology, though not his literary frame of reference. We have already examined the "announcements" and "overt and covert signals" Bunyan employs both to reveal and conceal the nature of his unorthodox production. We need to turn now to what Jauss calls the "poetics of genre" and the "implicit relationships to familiar works in the literary-historical setting," though in our case the context is religious, not literary. The first half of the title would have startled no one. Its evocation of the metaphor of pilgrimage to define the religious life was perfectly standard in the period; between 1577 and 1678 countless tracts and sermons evoked the metaphor in their titles as a hook to draw in their audience. But these works emphatically insisted in the second half of their titles that plain doctrine rather than metaphorical expression would turn their readers into heavenly travellers. Titles of such works as Thomas Tuke's *Highway to Heaven: Or the Doctrine of Election, Effective Vocation, Justification, Sanctification, and Eternal Life* (1609),[2] Christopher Lever's *Holy Pilgrime, Leading the Way to Heaven: Or a Divine Direction in the Way of Life* (1618),[3] one J. M.'s *Soul's Pilgrimage to Celestial Glory: Or a Perfect Way to Heaven and to God* (1634),[4] and John Reading's *Guide to the Holy City: Or Directions and Helps to a Holy Life* (1651)[5] illustrate that the pilgrimage metaphor had become the common property of religious discursive works in the plain style.[6] Using the metaphor as bait, these works define themselves as guides that give counsel and direction on how to enter the religious life as they prescribe various formulas for salvation, such as election, regeneration, baptism, and prayer. Implicit in this series of religious writings is the notion that the journey promised in the first half of the title will be one of education for readers as they advance in their understanding of religious doctrine.

The exceedingly full title page of George Keith's *Way to the City of God Described* (1669) provides an interesting counterexample to Bunyan's:

The Way to the City of God Described, or a Plaine Declaration How any Man may, within the day of visitation given him by God, pass out of the unrighteous into the righteous state: As also, how he may go forward, in the Way of Holiness and righteousness, and so be fitted for the Kingdom of God, and the beholding and enjoying thereof.

Wherein Divers things, which occur to them, that enter into this way, with respect to their inward trials, temptations and difficulties, are pointed at, and directions intimated, how to carry themselves to the works and exercises of Religion as to find acceptance with God. With divers other weighty Particulars, which may be of service to inquirers and beginners.

Written by George Keith, in the year 1669.

In the time of his being a close Prisoner in the Toll-booth in Edinburgh.[7]

Like *Pilgrim's Progress,* Keith's text is a "prison" book, but unlike Bunyan's production, it insists on defining itself as a "Plaine Declaration" that will give directions and describe the difficulties for those readers willing to "enter into this way." *A Way to the City of God Described* was reissued, with additions the author made during his second imprisonment, in 1678, when the first edition of Bunyan's narrative was published. In this second edition, Keith included a preface that demonstrates just how central the metaphor of pilgrimage had become in exploring the religious life. Keith's language is saturated with the metaphoric possibilities of a journey as he attempts to justify his work. Citing Heb. 13.14 ("For here have we no continuing citie, but we seeke one to come"), he declares that

the whole aim and scope of it was to help and assist such, who desire sincerely to live a godly life in their *journey and travel,* as the title of it imports, which is, *A Description of the Way to the City of God,* for thither all our endeavors and labors tend, for we have here no abiding city. And, seeing, without holiness, none can see God, and unless a man be born again, he cannot enter into the Kingdom of God, therefore this whole treatise doth hold forth divers necessary and useful things, concerning the Nature of Regeneration, how, after what manner it is begun and carried on. *So that the various steps of the Spiritual Traveller* are set down from the beginning, un-

til a good growth and *progress* be attained in the new birth or life of
holiness itself; And who are thus far advanced, they are more safe,
and more out of danger to miscarry and *miss their way*, than beginners are: and therefore it is mainly intended for beginners, and
such, as have made no great *progress in this divine travel.*[8] (emphasis added)

Like Keith's, Bunyan's mind was steeped in the metaphor of pilgrimage. He tells us in the beginning of his "Apology" that he too was
writing of divine travel, "of the Way / And Race of Saints in this our
Gospel-Day" (lines 7–8). Unlike Keith, however, he found himself
"falling" into allegory, depicting rather than defining the "steps of
the Spiritual Traveller," envisioning rather than describing what
constitutes "progress" in the religious life.

No other work in this series of religious writings "falls" into
allegory so definitively. Several of these texts extend the topos of an
allegorical journey beyond the confines of their titles, but only to use
allegorical imagery for section headings that expound religious
doctrine.[9] In David Lindsay's *Godly Man's Journey: Containing Ten
Several Treatises* (1625),[10] the titles of the treatises mimic the stages
of an allegorical journey, but the treatises themselves explicate rather
than flesh out the figures used. For example, the first two treatises
are named "The Heavenly Chariot," parts I and II; the two sections
define the chariot as the love God has bestowed on man. The third
treatise is labelled "The blessed Chariots man"; this turns out to be a
figure for the Holy Spirit. Samuel Denny's *Pelecanicidium: Or the
Christian Advisor Against Self-Murder. Together with a Guide, and
the Pilgrim's Pass to the Land of the Living* (1653)[11] also uses an
allegorical landscape to define the "Dangerous Path to Self Murder"
and a way out of it. The allegorical landscape, "the pilgrim's pass to
the land of the living," consisting of such categories of experience as
the "Den of Idleness," the "Cell of Humility," the Grotto of Repentance," and the "Farm of Self-Resignation," is confined to a "divine
Poem" for each section. What follows the poem is a "Perspective,"
which gives a prose paraphrase and an explication of the poem; a
"Moral" buttressing its meaning with authorities; a "Prospect" that
delivers moral counsel in verse; and a "Consolatory Essay" designed
to provide comfort for the reader as he moves through the stages of

despair and repentance. The tracts by Lindsay and Denny epitomize the marked tension in the seventeenth century between indulging in allegory and speaking plainly about religious experience.

This divorce between allegorical fiction and religious polemic is paradoxically attested to by the one work in this series that is even remotely fictional, the Anglican Bishop Simon Patrick's *Parable of the Pilgrim: Written to a Friend* (1665).[12] This work is a pilgrimage narrative in only the most limited sense, for its fictional structure is minimal and subordinated to discursive ends. Patrick's protagonist is called Philotheus (lover of God) and also Theophilus (loved by God). The plot is comparatively simple. One day Philotheus, who is weary of travelling, suddenly imagines that an angel has flown past and touched him with his wing. The experience reminds him of Jerusalem and kindles a desire to go there. He is counselled at interminable length by a guide, a venerable old man, and he then sets out. After many weeks his resolution fades and he becomes ill, but a letter from his guide restores him to health. The guide becomes his constant companion, and they set out for Jerusalem. Finally they arrive at the top of a hill where a group of pilgrims is straining to see something that turns out to be Jerusalem. The bulk of the narrative consists of conversations between the pilgrim and his guide; there is no attempt to mirror psychological states through either personification or an allegorical landscape. For example, Philotheus's guide tells him to take Charity and Humility as companions on his journey, but these virtues are never given the status of characters. When Philotheus sets out, he travels alone. The fiction here exists only as the barest of frameworks on which to hang overt, didactic discourse about the religious life.

In a revealing preface addressed to a friend, Patrick declares that he is reviving the allegorical narrative about pilgrimage, implying that it is no longer current:

> That I send one to wait on you in the habit of a Pilgrim, which hath been so long out of Fashion, and quite worn not only out of use, but out of our knowledge, may seem a thing very strange and be surprising to you. But when you consider that old fashions are wont to come about again, and that we are much in love with Antiques, and that eyes are drawn to one that appears in an unusual or foreign dress, who else would not be observed; it may abate the wonder.[13]

But in reviving this "antique" idea of a fiction based on the metaphor of pilgrimage, Patrick distinguishes his own work from that which has come before it:

> As to the dress of it, I know that you will not expect this *Pilgrim* should come to you in fine Apparel and like some Gallant; but rather judge it more decent that he is attired plainly according to the quality and condition of his person and profession. This made me the more careless in what clothing I set him out, and to take such trimmings as come next to hand: having a far weightier care upon me, to make him speak such clear and perspicuous language as you might readily apprehend. And indeed if there be anything said here that is not plain and easie it is very much against my will.[14]

Using the figure of the pilgrim as a synecdoche for his book, Patrick distinguishes his own work from any predecessors in terms of *dress*, or the manner in which the work is presented. Patrick's work will be "plain" and "easie" and its language "clear and perspicuous," unlike previous treatments of the theme.[15]

The distinction between works that are "plain and easie" and those that are "dark" and hard to understand is a central one for Bunyan as well:

> Art thou offended? dost thou wish I had
>
> Put forth my matter in another dress,
>
> Or that I had in things been more express?
>
> ("Apology," lines 160–62)

Bunyan chose the more complex dress of allegory, but Patrick deliberately detached the idea of a fiction based on the metaphor of a pilgrimage from its natural mode of the allegorical and the metaphorical. He eschews the "fine Apparel" of allegory because it was more important to be "plain and easie." In an aside from the "Advertisement" that follows his address to his friend, Patrick demonstrates the extent to which he is willing to jettison the fictional base of his work in deference to the doctrine of plainness. He tells us he will write "in plain words (for those I most affect; and if you meet with so much as any Metaphorical expressions in the Book, it is but seldom, and only to comply with the Title)."[16] As this passage makes clear, *The Parable of the Pilgrim* is only marginally fictional, only enough to meet minimally the requirements of its title. Patrick's work and the others surveyed here exemplify what happened to the idea of an allegorical pilgrimage in the seventeenth century. The metaphor is increasingly used merely as a context for direct didactic expression, and not as a basis for a fiction that communicates experientially. Ultimately, these kinds of texts serve to underscore the radical nature of Bunyan's narrative. Although Bunyan shared a common goal with these tracts, to turn the reader into a heavenly traveller, he chose to render an imaginative picture rather than a "plain" and "easie" exposition of the pilgrimage of life.

Patrick had chosen the word *parable* to define his fiction, aligning his work with the New Testament sense of story. Bunyan, on the other hand, had announced (admittedly in the smallest of print) that his story of the pilgrim would be discovered through the similitude of a dream, a far more radical and dangerous enterprise than telling a parable. We need only think of the biblical pronouncement in Jer. 23.32 ("Behold, I am against those who prophecie false dreames, sayeth the Lord, and doe tell them, and cause my people to erre by their lyes and by their lightnesse, yet I sent them not, nor commanded them: therefore they shall not profite this people at all, sayth the Lord")[17] to be reminded that dreams that do not come from God are suspect for the members of Bunyan's Puritan audience. We should also be reminded that the biblical sanction on Bunyan's title page for the use of similitudes (Hos. 12.10) was perceived to be the province of biblical writers inspired by the Holy Ghost.

Bunyan as First Reader in the "Apology"

Thus, given the audience's horizon of expectations for the particular genre of religious writings we have just surveyed, Bunyan's pronouncements on the title page literally require an apology to his readers. He begins his defense of his work at the point where his own conventional expectations and those of his Puritan audience most nearly converge, and he becomes in effect the work's first reader, registering all the objections he expects to encounter from his audience as he maneuvers them into accepting the validity and efficacy of his choice of dress. Within the "Apology," Bunyan evokes the paradigms for reading of three kinds of reader: his own audience of seventeenth-century Puritan readers who find fiction immoral, a lettered readership who have no ideological objections to fiction, and an earlier Protestant tradition of reading that he was aware of but guarded about, where certain kinds of fiction are sanctioned by biblical models and the religious, reformist tradition. But before he can substantiate the claims of his title page by appealing to this earlier understanding of the role of books and of reading, he must find a way to cushion his audience and assuage their fears that he has committed an unpardonable act. He must initially modulate their response to his effort by denying that he ever consciously intended to produce a work of this kind:

> When at the first I took my Pen in hand,
>
> Thus for to write; I did not understand
>
> That I at all should make a little Book
>
> In such a mode; Nay, I had undertook
>
> To make another, which was almost done,
>
> Before I was aware, I this begun.
>
> (lines 1–6)

The "Apology" falls into four distinct units. In the first and second units (lines 1–34, 35–60), devoted to *The Pilgrim's Progress*'s origins and publication history, Bunyan focuses on his own and his audience's potential reactions to the work. The third unit (lines 61–192) turns to the defense of his style and method. He dramatizes a debate with a "Man of God" in which all the charges are brought out and answered. Bunyan appeals to and then rejects a lettered readership's defenses for fiction before finally endorsing an earlier Protestant readership's orientation toward texts and a way of reading. In the fourth section (lines 193–236), Bunyan declares that he will "shew the profit of my Book," and in the process he delivers instructions to his readers on how the book is to be read.

Bunyan's denial of conscious intention as well as his careful delineation of how the work came into being and the steps leading up to publication testify to the gravity of what he has done. His story of the genesis of the text, with its emphasis on falling into allegory while he was writing a more conventional kind of work, signals that he recognizes it as an offence that he must answer for. He describes this falling as a process with a will of its own, a spontaneous generation of ideas that multiply "Like sparks that from the coals of Fire do flie" (line 14). Ideas "breed" in him until he removes them and sets them apart for fear they will swallow up the book he was originally writing. The next two verse-paragraphs take up the question of why, in that case, he continued to write the book. Here Bunyan begins to tell how he justified the activity to himself. He claims that he never intended "To shew all the World my Pen and Ink / In such a mode" (lines 20–21) and that he still didn't quite understand what he was doing: "I only thought to make / I knew not what" (lines 21–22). Claiming that "I did it mine owne self to gratifie" (line 24), he continues to write, though he assures his readers that he did not spend "vacant seasons" in this "Scribble" (lines 25–26) because the process of writing the book diverted him from "worser thoughts." Having justified his writing to himself, Bunyan can then go on to describe how the book grew to its full length. In simple but highly significant terms, he tells us his technique: "For having now my Method by the end; / Still as I pull'd, it came" (lines 31–32) until the book was finally finished. However, having finished it, he had to decide what should be done with it.

In the second section, Bunyan turns to the book's fate as an independent creation. Even after the book was written, his doubts caused him to show it to friends who disagreed heatedly about what should become of it:

> Well, when I had thus put mine ends together,
>
> I shew'd them others, that I might see whether
>
> They would condemn them, or them justifie:
>
> And some said, let them live; some, let them die:
>
> Some said, *John*, print it; others said, Not so:
>
> Some said, It might do good; others said, No.
>
> (lines 35–40)

The first set of terms in which the book is assessed is moral:

"condemn" or "justifie" (line 37); the second is judicial: "let them live" or "let them die" (line 38); the third is literary: to print or not to print (line 39); the last is didactic: will the book do good or not (line 40)? This sequence of frames through which to view the book provides a paradigm of the Puritan response to the world. We begin with the ethical issue of whether the book can be justified intrinsically, in itself, apart from any good it might do. The didactic question is not the first issue of importance but the last.

Throughout this second section Bunyan's naive persona remains. He has decided to publish the work, he says, only because his friends could not decide for him: "To prove then who advised for the best, / Thus I thought fit to put it to the test" (lines 47–48). He hopes it may give delight to readers who thought it should be printed. Those who thought it should not be printed are asked to withhold judgment until they see what happens. Those readers who do not like it do not have to read it: "If that thou wilt not read, let it alone; / Some love the meat, some love to pick the bone" (lines 57–58). No other introduction to a fictional work offers quite such a defensive account of the steps leading to publication, but then no other fictional work has had to contend with quite the strictures of Bunyan's Puritan audience. Critics have often taken this opening statement to substantiate their view of Bunyan as an unconscious artist.[18] On the contrary, this version of the story of how his book came into being underlines just how conscious he was of what he had done. It is a strategy designed to disarm his audience's initial objections, whatever else it has to say about the creative process.

With the third and longest section of the "Apology," however, Bunyan's tone changes sharply. Gone is the naive persona.[19] A significant shift in strategy occurs; a comparatively elaborate defense of style and method takes the form of a debate between the speaker and an unspecified objector he calls both a "Man of God" and a "Carper." He introduces the debate as part of the history of the steps leading to the publication of *The Pilgrim's Progress*: "Yea, that I might them better palliate, / I did too with them thus Expostulate" (lines 59–60). But the past event becomes mightily present as Bunyan chooses to create a reader and dramatize their dispute about the legitimacy of a work like *The Pilgrim's Progress*. His tone throughout this section betrays his profound anxiety about the reception of this work. His strategy is to move through a number of defenses until he can locate one that can withstand the objections of his persecutor. He

begins, albeit half-heartedly, with the standard Renaissance justifica-
tions for fiction, shifts to a biblical defense of style and method, and
finally in desperation refers to three models that provide sanction for
his fiction. Bunyan's style in verse conspicuously lacks the simple
clarity for which his prose style has always been admired. As a result,
the sheer difficulty of following the shifts in his argument has
prevented due appreciation of how drastic a position he is taking and
how sophisticated is his articulation of it.

Bunyan begins the section by taking up the question of what
good the work can do a reader, shifting the emphasis away from the
issue of whether he should have written the work at all. He focuses
specifically on the issue of whether the style and method chosen can
legitimately be used to instruct as well as delight the reader:

> May I not write in such a stile as this?
>
> In such a method too, and yet not miss
>
> Mine end, thy good? why may it not be done?
>
> (lines 61–63)

After an appeal to nature ("Dark Clouds bring Waters"), his first real
answer is to repeat the standard Renaissance view of imaginative
writings. The Horatian dictum of *dulce et utile* claims that literature
instructs by delight because it entices and draws the reader toward
truth through fictional means. Here Bunyan dwells upon entrap-
ment. The way a fisherman catches fish or a fowler snares game is
analogous to the way the writer must approach the reader:

> You see the ways the Fisher-man doth take
>
> To catch the Fish; what Engins doth he make?
>
> Behold! how he ingageth all his Wits;
>
> Also his Snares, Lines, Angles, Hooks and Nets:
>
> Yet Fish there be, that neither Hook, nor Line,
>
> Nor Snare, nor Net, Nor Engin can make thine;
>
> They must be grop'd for, and be tickled too,
>
> Or they will not be catcht, what e're you do.
>
> (lines 73–80)

Just as the fisherman must "tickle" some fish in order to catch them, the writer must "tickle" with a decorative surface fiction in order to bring the reader to truth. John Steadman has noted that the notion that poetry should delight through its fictions and instruct through its allegorical meaning was "a commonplace, if not an axiom, of both medieval and Renaissance criticism."[20] However, the Puritan attitude toward the use of a simile or metaphor, as Kenneth Murdock has noted, was fairly straightforward. "The method was dictated by the purpose. If a simile or metaphor made truth more intelligible and rationally more convincing it was good; if it simply tickled the senses and gave pleasure, or if it distracted the reader's attention from the doctrine, it was clearly bad."[21] It is not an accident that Bunyan begins with this commonplace, even though like Puritans in general he then rejects it except as an interim argument.

Bunyan points to other fictional models that are sanctioned by a literary readership and that provide, with careful qualification, a model for his own work:

> If that a Pearl may in a Toads-head dwell,
>
> And may be found too in an Oister-shell;
>
> If things that promise nothing, do contain
>
> What better is then Gold; who will disdain,
>
> (That have an inkling of it,) there to look,
>
> That they may find it? Now my little Book,
>
> (Tho void of all those paintings that may make
>
> It with this or the other man to take,)
>
> Is not without those things that do excel,
>
> What do in brave, but empty notions dwell.
>
> (lines 89–98)

The reference to the "pearl" in an "oister-shell" demonstrates that Bunyan is aware of literary models that "promise nothing" because they are fictions but that may contain "What better is than Gold" under their decorative surfaces. Nonetheless, Bunyan emphatically separates his narrative from these other models. His "little Book" is the "void of all those paintings" although it too contains "those things that do excel." The fact that he himself ultimately calls these "brave" "paintings" "empty notions" indicates how half-hearted this defense is. One of the reasons the meaning is murky here is that Bunyan's guise as an unlettered preacher is being compromised. How does he know of these other works to which his work is an alternative?

Given a voice in the "Apology" through italicization, his Puritan reader answers this defense by shifting the grounds on which the book is to be judged. The central question, he argues, is not what good the work can do—potentially good results of an act are no defense if the act is intrinsically immoral—but rather whether the book can stand in itself. Is it ethically justifiable to write a work of this kind?

> *Well, yet I am not fully satisfy'd,*
> *That this your Book will stand, when soundly try'd.*
> Why, what's the matter? *It is dark*, what tho?
> *But it is feigned*, what of that I tro?
> Some men by feigning words as dark as mine,
> Make truth to spangle, and its rayes to shine.
> *But they want solidness:* Speak man thy mind:
> *They drown'd the weak; Metaphors make us blind.*
>
> (lines 99–106)[22]

All the major charges have here been brought together in this dramatic interchange. The work is dark, hard to understand; feigned because it is based on a lie, the dream; and, because of its allegorical mode, lacking in solidity. The standard Renaissance formulation that truth can be delivered through a decorative fiction is not acceptable in the Puritan aesthetic precisely because the feigned nature of any given work cannot be ethically justified however benevolent its intention. "Metaphors make us blind" because what the implied comparison adds to truth is a distraction from truth, which should be delivered plainly.

In Puritan discussions of literature, as Lawrence Sasek notes, the word "'feigned' appears regularly as a pejorative term" indicating simple falsehood.[23] Indeed, even recourse to the language of other kinds of readers who sanctioned fictional expression provided little comfort. Renaissance poetic theory used terms like *dissimulation* and *duplicity* in discussing the relationship of form and content, especially in metaphor and allegory. George Puttenham's *Arte of English Poesie* (1589) epitomizes the Renaissance definition of Allegoria, "which is when we speake one thing and thinke another, and that our wordes and our meanings meete not,"[24] thus amounting to "a kinde of dissimulation."[25] Puttenham finds allegory and metaphor to be closely allied: "But properly and in his principall vertue *Allegoria* is when we do speake in sense translative and wrested from the owne signification, nevertheless applied to another not altogether contrary, but having much conveniencie with it as before we said of the metaphore . . . and this manner of inversion extending to whole and large speaches, it maketh the figure *allegorie* to be called a long and perpetuall Metaphore."[26] Puttenham thus emphasizes the gap between word and meaning: "For what els is your *Metaphor* but an inversion of sense by transport; your *allegorie* by [but?] a duplicitie of meaning or dissimulation under covert and darke intendments."[27] The justification for the use of allegory offered by Renaissance theory was that truth unpalatable to those not yet attuned must be made attractive by pleasing language, that metaphor and allegory are a protection from the intrusion of those not morally or intellectually qualified, and that the difficulties train the capacities of mind and heart so that the reader can understand more truth. Edmund Spenser, the foremost Protestant poet of the previous century, had proclaimed that the difficulty of his work could fashion the reader. Yet even he felt apprehensive enough about his enterprise to append a letter to Raleigh that admits "how doubtfully all Allegories may be construed" and provides a key unlocking the meaning of the work.[28] Little wonder that these defenses for allegory had not been accepted by Puritan writers and readers of the seventeenth century.

To counter the charge that his work is feigned, Bunyan begins by replying that other writers by feigning words have in fact revealed truth: "Some men by feigning words as dark as mine, / Make truth to spangle, and its rayes to shine" (lines 103–4). Here too, however, he declines to name an example. But against the formidable charge that metaphoric language lacks solidity and makes us blind, Bunyan invokes a more authoritative model, a model that his reader will have a difficult time dismissing:

> Solidity, indeed becomes the Pen
> Of him that writeth things Divine to men:
> But must I needs want solidness, because
> By Metaphors I speak; was not Gods Laws,
> His Gospel-laws in older time held forth
> By Types, Shadows and Metaphors? Yet loth
> Will any sober man be to find fault
> With them, lest he be found for to assault
> The highest Wisdom. No, he rather stoops,
> And seeks to find out what by pins and loops,
> By Calves, and Sheep; by Heifers, and by Rams;
> By Birds and Herbs, and by the blood of Lambs;
> God speaketh to him: And happy is he
> That finds the light, and grace that in them be.
> Be not too forward therefore to conclude,
> That I want solidness; that I am rude.
>
> (lines 107–22)

With this statement, the whole tenor of the "Apology" changes. The speaker becomes much more explicit about what he is doing and argues more forcefully for the validity of his work, although the repetitiousness with which he points to Scripture as a model signals both his discomfort with what the comparison implies and his frustration at being debarred from naming other models. He begins by agreeing with his critic that solidity is necessary when writing "things divine to men," thus announcing that his purpose is to write of divine reality. The word *solidity* clearly refers to the content of his work and implies that its vision will be substantial and meaningful. But can metaphoric language be solid? Can it encapsulate truth? The answer to that question is contained in the rest of the verse-paragraph. Scripture uses "Types, Shadows, and Metaphors" to deliver divine truth to readers. God himself speaks through symbols: "By Birds and Herbs, and by the blood of Lambs." Thus, metaphoric language is capable of delivering divine reality to readers, and Bunyan is justified in using it, but that language must be derived from Scripture. Scripture's metaphors, unlike the ones the objector attacks, have solidness because God himself uses them. Bunyan thus transposes the very idea of metaphor from the realm in which Puttenham located it, the realm in which the tenor and the vehicle are in opposition, to the realm of scriptural truth. There tenor and vehicle are intrinsically connected, because God has made the world in such a way that these connections exist. In the Bible, word and meaning meet. Unlike the traditional rhetorician's metaphor, which links disparate things, these "Types, Shadows and Metaphors" are available for discourse because they embody an intrinsic connection built into the creation itself. Even God has no more direct mode of discourse in which to speak of major truths. No words can convey divine truth as adequately as concrete things used metaphorically: "By Birds and Herbs, and by the blood of Lambs."

But the Bible in this passage functions as a model for reading as well as for writing as Bunyan seeks to disarm his critic. He first points out that no "sober man" would dare "assault / The highest Wisdom" by criticizing God's elected style for Scripture. Then he turns to how readers must read the Bible; they must "stoop" and seek "to find out what by pins and loops" God is saying to them. Bunyan's point is that no one objects to this reading program for unlocking the meaning of Scripture because it results in light and grace. In citing Scripture as his model for both writing and reading, Bunyan instructs the reader on how he wishes his own work to be read and promises the result of such reading. He announces that his work, like Scripture, can deliver truth: "My dark and cloudy words they do but hold / The truth, as Cabinets inclose the Gold" (lines 127–28). After this bold assertion, the critic is heard no more, although Bunyan continues to address his remarks to him throughout the rest of the section, at one point calling him a "Carper" and directing him to look to his own life to find "darker lines" than those contained in *The Pilgrim's Progress*. The appeal to the scriptural model is buttressed in a number of ways. He cites the actual practice of the prophets, the apostles, and Christ in the use of metaphorical language (lines 129–32). He reiterates that although Scripture is full of "Dark Figures, Allegories," it delivers light that "turns our darkest nights to days" (lines 133–38). And he notes that St. Paul forbids fables but allows parables in which "lay hid" "That Gold, those Pearls, and precious stones" that are "Worth digging for" (lines 153–58).

In the course of his argument, Bunyan elaborates on his understanding of the relationship between form and content, dark figures and truth. He develops a theory of reading based on the Bible and far more sophisticated than the argument for moral benefit with which the "Apology" began:

> Come, Truth, although in Swadling-clouts, I find
>
> Informs the Judgement, rectifies the Mind,
>
> Pleases the Understanding, makes the Will
>
> Submit; the Memory too it doth fill
>
> With what doth our Imagination please;
>
> Likewise, it tends our troubles to appease.
>
> (lines 147–52)

The surface fiction is like "Swadling-clouts" that enclose divine truth. The term *Swadling-clouts* suggests a biblically based conception of form and content. In Luke 2.12, an angel tells the shepherds, "And this shall be a signe unto you; yee shall find the babe wrapped in swadling clothes lying in a manger." Swaddling clothes are a sign by which to know Christ. They do not conceal to reveal, nor are they like the surface *delight* of Renaissance theory; they are not chaff or shell. They ready a living truth to reveal itself and make recognition of it possible. Bunyan's metaphors, like the "Swadling-clouts," contain divine truth that cannot be conveyed in any other way. The base things of this world become the means of apprehending the divine. Judgment, mind, understanding, and will are all exercised and informed. The vision of truth retained by the memory is one that has pleased the imagination. Finally, this reading experience tends to appease other troubles.

Yet not even the biblical model, a sophisticated theory of reading, and the explicit sanction of New Testament writers allay Bunyan's uneasiness completely:

> Let me add one word more, O Man of God!
>
> Art thou offended? dost thou wish I had

Put forth my matter in another dress,

Or that I had in things been more express?

Three things let me propound, then I submit

To those that are my betters, (as is fit.)

(lines 159–64)

That Bunyan still feels the final judgment should be left to others reveals how severe the strictures are against which he is ranging himself. He asks himself yet again whether "another dress," another mode, might still be preferable to the fictive and the allegorical. Would eliminating the fictional frame, even if it is marginally licit, be more appropriate? Are "Dark Figures," even defensible ones, inferior to "more express" language?

The last part of this section again takes up the question of fictional models, as Bunyan points to other writers who have used a metaphorical method to deliver truth:

1. I find not that I am denied the use

Of this my method, so I no abuse

Put on the Words, Things, Readers, or be rude

In handling Figure, or Similitude,

In application; but, all that I may,

Seek the advance of Truth, this or that way.

(lines 165–70)

The writer may use allegorical methods so long as he does not "abuse / Put on the Words, Things, Readers," that is, force more meanings than legitimately exist upon his contents or his audience. Nor must he do violence ("be rude") to figures and similitudes in their handling. Neither will happen as long as his principle is to "Seek the advance of Truth, this or that way." Then Bunyan interjects a curiously cryptic passage claiming that his use of allegory is not merely allowed. Writers in the distant past offer sanction and examples of this kind of work.

Denyed did I say? Nay, I have leave,

(Example too, and that from them that have

God better pleased by their words or ways,

Than any Man that breatheth now adays,)

Thus to express my mind, thus to declare

Things unto thee that excellentest are.

(lines 171–76)

Here, Bunyan seems to be referring to other imaginative works that employ the same strategy as *The Pilgrim's Progress*, specific models of non-scriptural religious writings in the past, from which he derives either his method or support in using it. To late seventeenth-century readers, *The Pilgrim's Progress* may have appeared to be an unusual production for a religious writer. But Bunyan wants his reader to regard the work as part of a larger tradition more pleasing to God than any discourse, Puritan or non-Puritan, being produced "now adays."

For wayside support he cites another kind of model, the dialogue, whose didactic purpose is widely accepted as justifying its fictitious character:

2. I find that men (as high as Trees) will write

Dialogue-wise; yet no Man doth them slight

For writing.

(lines 177–79)

Presumably he is referring to works like Arthur Dent's *Plain Mans Path-way to Heaven* (1601), another example of the religious genre that we surveyed at the beginning of the chapter, in which four characters debate Christian doctrine through the course of a day.[29] Bunyan's point is that writers of dialogues are not criticized for creating a fictional situation unless "they abuse / Truth" (lines, 179–80). Next, he harks back to the opening of the "Apology":

let Truth be free

To make her Salleys upon Thee, and Me,

Which way it pleases God. For who knows how,

Better than he that taught us first to Plow,

To guide our Mind and Pens for his Design?

And he makes base things usher in Divine.

(lines 181–86)

Bunyan is saying that he did not willfully choose his mode of writing; the event was by divine will. Truth makes "Salleys" upon a writer as well as a reader. Here again, his model is the Bible and its author, the Holy Spirit who first taught us "to Plow." By the seventeenth century, plowing had become a common metaphor for preaching. A secondary meaning plays on the metaphorical possibilities of plowing, breaking open the "earth," the scriptural text, and turning it over to bring to the surface scriptural truth. Such plowing, such reading, is done with "Mind" and "Pens." God himself is working his "Design," whether the writer or the reader has one or not.

A third statement returns to Scripture as the model for his method:

3. I find that holy Writ in many places,

Hath semblance with this method, where the cases

Doth call for one thing to set forth another:

Use it I may then, and yet nothing smother

Truths golden Beams; Nay, by this method may

Make it cast forth its rayes as light as day.

(lines 187–92)

Bunyan's need to reiterate the point reflects a quite accurate sense that it is a revolutionary one for some readers. He respects and shares his objector's conviction that a metaphorical language can be justified only if it is not really feigning at all, that is, if it reveals truth—and not just any truth, but truth of a particular kind. Citing the Bible is a far safer course than citing any other model of metaphorical discourse, especially if you define yourself as an unlettered "mechanick preacher."

The speaker has journeyed a long distance from his initial assertion that he had never intended to make a book in such a mode; that mode has now been identified as biblical practice. That he "fell suddenly into an Allegory" has now been traced to God's guiding his pen and mind. The specious excuse that he wrote only to divert himself from worse thoughts has been replaced by explaining Truth's "Salleys" upon both the writer and the reader. And finally, "Still as I pulled it came" has been superseded by aligning the method with that of holy purpose even where man has none: "He makes base things usher in Divine." These are precisely the presuppositions of the Protestant reader about the genesis of religious texts and the role of the author as God's servant. When Bunyan notes that God makes "base things usher in divine," he is evoking one of the core biblical texts, 1 Cor. 1.27–28, used for justification of their practices first by the Lollards and later the mechanick preachers: "But God hath chosen the foolish things of the world, to confound the wise: and God hath chosen the weake things of the world, to confound the things which are mighty. And base things of the world, and things which are despised, hath God chosen, yea, and things which are not, to bring to nought things that are." Bunyan's claim, finally, is that his very baseness in terms of class, his foolishness and his weakness as an uneducated man, results in his empowerment by God to write a work of this kind. As we will see in the next chapter, it was the same attitude about God's purpose, growing out of a call to have the Scriptures in English for all classes, that resulted in the Lollard movement.

Having made his case for this kind of fiction, Bunyan, in the last section of the "Apology," turns away from his objector and toward the general reader. The critic has been defeated, an event signaled when Bunyan commits his readers and his book to God:

And now before I do put up my Pen,

I'le shew the profit of my Book, and then

Commit both thee, and it unto the hand

That pulls the strong down, and makes weak ones stand.

(lines 193–96)

That final line, of course, is yet another allusion to the scriptural passage just cited. The critic was a strong figure in articulating his objections, but God provided the will to make the weak one, the unlettered tinker, stand up to his "Carper."

In the final section of the "Apology," attempting to "shew the profit" of a book written in this way, Bunyan defines its contents more precisely. He singles out the particular readers he is trying to reach and asks questions to entice them into reading it. The description now offered for his book is a broad one:

> This Book it chaulketh out before thine eyes,
>
> The man that seeks the everlasting Prize:
>
> It shews you whence he comes, whither he goes,
>
> What he leaves undone; also what he does:
>
> It also shews you how he runs, and runs,
>
> Till he unto the Gate of Glory comes.
>
> It shews too, who sets out for life amain,
>
> As if the lasting Crown they would attain:
>
> Here also you may see the reason why
>
> They lose their labour, and like fools do die.

(lines 197–206)

He will portray not just the history of one Christian soul but of many, some of whom will fail in the journey, thus setting the conversion experience of one man in a world peopled with other Christian seekers. His metaphor emphasizes the visual: the work "chaulketh" a winning runner. It relies on a succession of images to tell a funda- mental truth about human experience (which is not like those other "painted" works he had mentioned earlier) that requires revising the established Puritan prejudice against imaginative writing. Because the book rests upon a commonplace—life as a journey and the Christian as a traveller—Bunyan can dare to develop that metaphor to aid the reader's own life:

> This Book will make a Travailer of thee,
>
> If by its Counsel thou wilt ruled be;

It will direct thee to the Holy Land,

If thou wilt its Directions understand:

Yea, it will make the sloathful, active be;

The Blind also, delightful things to see.

(lines 207–12)

The fictional representation can deliver doctrine, and perhaps do this better for the slothful and the blind, because it contains "Truth within a Fable" (line 214). For a less strict audience, Bunyan needs no scruples about the word *fable* and can reincorporate standard Renaissance views on the connection between *utile* and *dulce*.

In a final summing up Bunyan terms *The Pilgrim's Progress* "rare, and profitable" (line 213), "Truth within a Fable" (line 214), and full of "Riddles" (line 225). It is a book that can make one laugh and weep (line 230), a book where one can lose oneself and find oneself again (lines 231–32), and finally a book where one can dream and not be asleep (line 229). Because his audience has clearly changed, he shifts back to the playful aspects of fiction, which, after the preceding wrenching exposition, can now be acknowledged.

Bunyan singles out those readers who could not be reached in any other way as his target audience:

This Book is writ in such a Dialect,

As may the minds of listless men affect:

It seems a Novelty, and yet contains

Nothing but sound and honest Gospel-strains.

(lines 219–22)

The allegorical mode is a dialect, a variation of language used within a subgroup. Its value for that group is its ability to affect the minds of "listless men" who are unmoved by the plain, exhortative language of the tracts surveyed earlier. Thus its unusual mode can communicate to an audience that has not yet awakened to religion. Though this strategy makes the book a "Novelty,"[30] it introduces no novel content, for it represents scriptural truth as it is applied to the individual Christian whose life is altered by grace.

That some subjects by their very nature require allegorical treatment while others do not is confirmed by the contrast between *The Pilgrim's Progress* and another of Bunyan's works, *The Life and Death of Mr. Badman* (1680), the preface of which indicates that the two books are companion pieces: "As I was considering with my self, what I had written concerning the *Progress* of the *Pilgrim* from this World to Glory, and how it had been acceptable to many in this Nation: it came again into my mind to write, as then, of him that was going to Heaven, so now, of the Life and Death of the Ungodly, and of their travel from this world to Hell."[31] Use of the same metaphorical language about pilgrimage underlines the similarity: "Here therefore, courteous Reader, I present thee with the Life and Death of Mr. *Badman* indeed; Yea, I do trace him in his Life, from his Childhood to his Death; that thou mayest, as in a Glass, behold with thine own eyes, the steps that take hold of Hell; and also discern, while thou art reading of Mr. *Badmans* Death, whether thou thy self art treading in his path thereto."[32] Here the invitation to watch Mr. Badman's steps leads the reader to expect another allegorical journey. *Mr. Badman,* however, is not an allegory. It adopts a different form, the dialogue, and has two figures, Mr. Attentive and Mr. Wise, who discuss Mr. Badman's sins in realistic detail. These include swearing and cursing in childhood, followed by drunkenness, dishonest business practices, and cruelty toward his wife. We can infer that Bunyan's choice of a narrative form rests on his belief that the experience of a life without grace does not call for allegorical representation. Allegorical representation is called for in *The Pilgrim's Progress*, however, because the world it portrays has been altered by the Christian's changed perspective.[33] In short, Bunyan means exactly what he says when he argues that the subject he was treating when the idea for *The Pilgrim's Progress* took hold of him, "the Way / And Race of Saints in this our Gospel Day," (lines 7–8), is one of a specific and limited group of subjects "where the cases / Doth call for one thing to set forth another" (lines 188–89) so that "similitudes" are not just licit but necessary.

Finally, Bunyan closes the "Apology" by indicating that readers can chart their spiritual progress by finding themselves in the work:

Would'st read thy self, and read thou know'st not what

And yet know whether thou art blest or not,

By reading the same lines? O then come hither,

And lay my Book, thy Head and Heart together.

(lines 233–36)

To read the book will be to read oneself and learn whether one is of the elect or not. In other words, Bunyan asks that the book be read like Scripture; the reader must take responsiblity by gleaning doctrine and applying it to the self. "My Book, thy Head and Heart" must come together so that the reader, not the writer, must perform the final step.

It is worth noting what the "Apology" does not say in assessing just how revolutionary a position Bunyan takes with respect to his Puritan audience. The title page word that is given the most emphasis is *Dream*. The most logical defense of the book, given Puritan attitudes, would have been to claim that it records an actual dream. Bunyan himself had already done this in *Grace Abounding*, where he describes a vision in which he sees the members of Bedford congregation on the sunny side of a mountain, cut off from him by a wall. He then interprets the dream: "Now, this Mountain and Wall, &c., was thus made out to me; the Mountain signified the Church of the living God . . . the wall I thought was the Word that did make separation between the Christians and the world."[34] But Bunyan did not choose such a strategy for *The Pilgrim's Progress*. Instead, he seems to have wished to describe what life within that wall is like and to have felt that no usual mode of discourse was adequate. To do justice to the world within the wall, he must use the wall itself, the Bible, and must also make his reader fully conscious that he is doing so, even at the risk of incurring the disapproval of the very people whose transformed mode of life he is depicting. He must call attention to the book's status as a made thing, not gloss over it. When Bunyan modifies traditional literary defenses of art, he is driven to a much more radical claim. Since it is God who guides the pen and the mind, *The Pilgrim's Progress* not only resembles Scripture but is an extension of the very process which produced Scripture in the first place. Such an understanding about the origin of religious writings is, as we have noted, one of the central features of an earlier Protestant readership.

Bunyan as a Reader of the Bible and of Foxe

Generations of readers of *The Pilgrim's Progress* have assumed that its author worked outside the literary and religious traditions of earlier ages and was influenced by other thinkers only enough to have absorbed the evangelical thought of his dissenting milieu. The "Apology" makes evident a more sophisticated relationship. Bunyan is quite aware of, though uncomforted by, traditional Renaissance theories about imaginative literature. He insists that he knows of models from an earlier time, models he defends while clearly regarding them as either too provocative to be named directly or too incompatible with his "mechanick preacher" stance to be specified in detail. And in his aesthetic, the Bible is seen not merely as a source of doctrine or a catalyst for self-examination but as a model for and example of metaphorical discourse.

As radical as this stance toward Scripture is, Bunyan did not intuitively stumble upon it. Rather, he is knowingly extending the implications of contemporary views of the Bible as asserted by Protestant theorists in the debate between Anglicans and Puritans over the nature of a plain style in preaching. In the seventeenth century, as Barbara K. Lewalski has pointed out, the Bible was viewed not only in terms of salvational history but as a rhetorical work. Poets and rhetoricians found in the Bible "a literary model which [the Christian poet] can imitate in such literary matters as genre, language, and symbolism, confident that in this model at least the difficult problems of art and truth are perfectly resolved."[35] Such a view of the Bible was pervasive enough to have laid the groundwork for one of the most creative periods in English religious poetry.

Four seventeenth-century treatises seem especially pertinent for understanding Bunyan's attitude toward Scripture as reflected in the "Apology." John Smith, in *The Mysterie of Rhetorique Unvailed* (1657), presents a survey of traditional tropes and figures. His book differs from other rhetorics, however, in that he illustrates his prescriptions not only with literary examples in both English and Latin but also with examples from the Bible:

Lastly, For that the Holy Scripture is not barren of but abounds with Tropes and figures of all sorts, as containing the most excellent and sublimist eloquence, and is like a pleasant garden, bedecked with flowers; or a fruitful field, full of precious treasures; I apprehended it a work worthy the undertaking to dig into those sacred Minerals for the better finding out the Metaphors, Synecdoches,

&c. which lie hid there, and have given Scriptural Examples pertinent to each of the Tropes and Figures.[36]

His end is to redeem rhetoric by aligning it with right understanding
of Scripture: "Rhetorique, where it is reduced to a blessed subor-
dination and conformity to the teachings of the Spirit of Truth, is a
good gift of God, proceeding from the Father of lights, and very
conducent to the unfolding and right understanding of the Figurative
and Tropical Elegancies of that blessed Book, which abounds with
the most excellent and divinest eloquence."[37] Similarly, John Prideaux's *Sacred Eloquence: Or, the Art of Rhetorick, As it is layd down
in Scripture* (1659) argues that study of the Bible can improve
rhetoric. For Prideaux, "*Sacred Eloquence* is a Logicall kind of
Rhetorick, to be used in Prayer, Preaching, or Conference; to the
glory of God, and the convincing, instructing, and strengthening of
our brethren."[38] Both men would redeem rhetoric from the charge
that it is an inherently amoral science.

A more radical defense can be seen in Robert Ferguson's essay,
The Import and Use of Scripture-Metaphors (1675), published only
three years before *The Pilgrim's Progress*. Ferguson proclaims that
"God by his unfolding himself and his Mind to us in several kinds of
Metaphorical Terms, hath not only allowed, but sanctified our Use of
the like."[39] This argument comes closest to Bunyan's. It is therefore
important to note that Ferguson, like Bunyan, was a nonconformist
and that his tract is intended as

the vindication of the *Non-Conformists*, who are publickly charged
for *turning Religion into unaccountable Phansies and Enthusiasm's,
drest up with empty Schemes of speech; and for embracing a few
gawdy Metaphors & Allegories instead of the substance of true and
real Righteousness.* So that if you believe a late Authour, *herein lyes
the Material difference between the sober Christians of the Church
of* England, *and the Modern Sectaries, that while those express the
precepts & Duties of the Gospel in plain and intelligible Terms,
these trifle them away by childish Metaphors and Allegories, and
will not talk of Religion but in barbarous and uncouth Similitudes.*[40]

For Ferguson, as for Bunyan, religious doctrine is inextricably wed to metaphoric expression: "Metaphors are not used to impregnate our Minds with gawdy Phantasms, but to adjust the Mysteries of Religion to the weakness of our Capacities."[41] When God speaks in metaphors "he condescends to lisp those Mysteries to us which would never be so well understood by any other way of expressing them."[42] Ferguson's language makes clear that the very features of Bunyan's title page that seem the most startling—his emphasis on presenting *The Pilgrim's Progress* as not only a dream but a feigned dream, and his choice of "I have used Similitudes" as an epigraph—are features that demand understanding in the context of a particular attitude toward Scripture. In short, Bunyan's title page allies him with those nonconformists Ferguson's treatise was intended to defend.

On the other hand, we must remember that Ferguson means by "metaphors" only the verbal figures we encounter in the individual sentence. A tract by John Smith, "Of Prophecy" (1660), which contains a view of Scripture similar to Ferguson's, develops it in a direction more oriented toward narrative elements and therefore sheds further light on Bunyan's justification of narrative allegory. Smith, of course, is speaking exclusively about biblical prophecy. But his analysis of how biblical prophecy works resembles Ferguson's description of the function of biblical metaphor:

> *Truth* is content, when it comes into the world, to wear our mantles, to learn our language, to conform it self as it were to our dress and fashions: it affects not the State or *Fastus* which the disdainfull Rhetorician sets out his style withall, *Non Tarentinis aut Siculis haec scribimus;* but it speaks with the most *Idiotical* sort of men in the most *Idiotical* way, and becomes all things to all men, as every sonne of Truth should doe, for their good.[43]

Truth wears our "dress" and "learn[s] our language," but Smith goes even further by widening the conception of metaphorical discourse from verbal trope to dramatic action:

> But for a more distinct understanding of this business, we must remember what hath been often suggested, *That the Prophetical scene*

or S*tage upon which all apparitions were made to the Prophet, was
his Imagination;* and that there all those things which God would
have revealed unto him were acted over *Symbolicallie,* as in a
Masque, in which divers persons are brought in, amongst which the
Prophet himself bears a part: And therefore he, according to the exigencie of this Dramatical *apparatus,* must, as the other Actors, perform his part, sometimes by speaking and reciting things done,
propounding questions, sometimes by acting that part which in the
Drama he was appointed to act by some others; and so not only by
Speaking, but by Gestures and Actions come in in his due place
among the rest; as it is in our ordinarie *Dreams.*[44]

He even goes so far as to say that "it is no wonder to hear of those
things done which indeed have no *Historical* or *Real* veritie; the
scope of all being to represent something strongly to the Prophets
Understanding."[45] This description of prophecy bears considerable
similarity to the action of *The Pilgrim's Progress,* especially Smith's
understanding that such prophecy included a projection of the
prophet-narrator himself acting a part among the other characters
and offering commentary and explanation. If such strategies are
inherent in biblical prophecy, they could offer a model for writers
concerned to create a vision—or a re-vision—of the Bible from the
point of view of the individual Christian.

However, commentators like Ferguson, Prideaux, and John Smith
in "Of Prophecy" are concerned strictly with improving the reader's
grasp of the Bible itself and with using it as a rhetorical model for
religious instruction at the level of the individual verbal trope or
figure. Ultimately, their argument underlines the uniqueness of
Bunyan's enterprise. Bunyan took the Bible as a model not just on the
level of the sentence but at the level of an entire plot in which a
complete narrative, generated out of whole cloth, is accorded the
status of a biblical similitude.

The paradoxes of Bunyan's title page call attention to the central
point his "Apology" defends discursively and his plot enacts in
practice. Bunyan means exactly what he says when he asserts that
Scripture was one of his models. But there were others, as an
examination of the "Apology" has revealed. Though he cannot men-

tion them directly, he clearly knows of a tradition of writings that present "leave" and "example" for doctrine that can be "delivered" under the "Similitude of a Dream." We should pause for a moment to consider what we know, apart from the "Apology," about Bunyan's reading. We have a certain amount of information from Bunyan himself and from a contemporary source about the works he did read, as well as references in his tracts to other works.[46] If we consider the implications of the reading we do know about more carefully than has previously been done, we will find our sense of what Bunyan knew drastically revised.

The common assumption that Bunyan's reading was minimal and does not explain the genesis of *The Pilgrim's Progress* is a natural response to some of Bunyan's own statements. For example, in the preface to *Solomon's Temple Spiritualized* (1688), he says, "True, I have not for these things fished in other men's waters; my Bible and Concordance are my only library in my writings."[47] He makes a similar pronouncement in *Light For Them That Sit In Darkness* (1674): "I have not writ at a venture, nor borrowed my doctrine from libraries. I depend upon the sayings of no man. I found it in the Scriptures of truth, among the sayings of God."[48] But these statements must be interpreted in the context of Bunyan's status as a mechanick preacher, as Tindall shows: "The enthusiast, who appeared to speak with the tongue of God, was compelled by the character of his office to maintain his spiritual distinction by denying the influence of man. The simple audience of the inspired would have turned in sorrow from the politic prophet whose admission of literary assistance had proved the imperfection of his gift."[49] The impression that Bunyan read very little is not his fault alone; others contributed to this perception. Charles Doe, who visited Bunyan in prison, reported that "there also I saw his library, the least but yet the best that e're I saw—the *Bible* and the *Book of Martyrs*."[50]

To generations of readers unfamiliar with the scope of John Foxe's book and thinking of it as a compact and highly colored account of Protestant martyrdoms, Doe's comment has seemed to reinforce a picture of Bunyan as working outside any literary or historical tradition, in jail, with only a Bible and the stories of other martyrs who suffered for their faith. This juxtaposition of Foxe with the Bible as the two central texts would have pleased Foxe. In recommending that someone compile a history like Foxe's, John

Bale, the Tudor antiquarian and Protestant polemicist, had written, "I can not thynke a more necessarye thynge to be laboured to the honour of God, bewtye of the realme, erudicyon of the people, and commodite of other landes, next the sacred scriptures of the Byble, than that work wolde be."[51] John Foxe's book, just as Bale had in mind, is considerably more than a Protestant *Lives of the Saints*. The title of the 1632 edition delivers a more accurate description of its contents:

> Acts and Monuments of Matters Most speciall and memorable, happening in the Church, with an universall Historie of the same. Wherein is set forth at large the whole race and course of the Church, from the primitive age to these later times of ours, with the bloudy times, horrible troubles, and great persecutions against the true Martyrs of Christ, sought and wrought as well by heathen Emperors, as now lately practised by Romish Prelats, especially in this Realme of *England* and *Scotland*.
>
> Now againe, as it was recognised, perused, and recommended to the studious Reader, by the Author, M. *John Fox*, the seventh time newly imprinted.
>
> Whereunto are annexed certaine Additions of like persecutions which have happened in these later times.

The 1632 edition consists of three folio volumes containing not only narrative but such documents as letters, papal bulls, trial records, statutes, sermons, tracts, and prophecies relating to ecclesiastical and national history.[52]

The stories of martyrdom of such figures as William Tyndale are, of course, given center stage, but they are buttressed with meticulous documentation. Along with historians, theologians and philosophers, to say nothing of legal documents and tracts, Foxe discusses a number of poets as if they were equally good proof that the Reformation was not "new" but had its roots in antiquity. Among these writers are Dante (as we have seen), Petrarch, Gower, and Chaucer. In his treatment of the whole fourteenth century, both before and after 1360, Foxe gives an account of writers and works that exemplify the first stirrings of the spirit of the Reformation. He is the quintessen-

tial Protestant reader in terms of his understanding of the role of
books and authors in God's intervention in history to reform his
church. Foxe's survey is set in a time frame derived from the Book of
Revelation and covering much of Western history. Of particular
interest for our concerns, given the date of *Piers Plowman*, Foxe
chose the year 1360 as a turning point and gives as his heading to the
section: "The Fifth Book, containing the last Three Hundred Years
from the loosing out of Satan."[53] He goes on:

> These things thus premised for the loosing out of Satan, according to
> the prophecie of the *Apocalyps* now let us enter (Christ willing) to
> the declaration of these later times which followed after the letting
> out of Satan into the World. Describing the wondrous perturbations
> and cruell tyranny stirred up by him against Christs Church; also the
> valiant resistance of the Church of Christ against him and Antichrist,
> as in these our books here following may appeare.[54]

As we will see in the next chapter, Chaucer and the apocryphal
plowman texts are part of the "valiant resistance," although Foxe
nowhere mentions *Piers Plowman* itself. Under 1360, Foxe notes

> we are come now to the time wherein the Lord, after long dark-
> enesse, beginneth some reformation of his Church, by the diligent
> industry of sundry his faithfull and learned servants. . . .
>   Now to these (the Lord willing) we will adde such other holy
> martyrs and confessors, who following after in the course of yeeres
> with like zeale and strength of Gods Word, and also with like dan-
> ger of their lives, gave the like resistance against the enemy of
> Christs religion, and suffered at his hands the like persecutions.[55]

These pre-Reformation figures are portrayed as servants of God and
part of his divine plan to restore his church. God himself empowers
these men to resist the tyranny of the established ecclesiastical
authorities.

What does all this have to do with Bunyan's reading? Bunyan tells
us himself in *Grace Abounding* what he found in Foxe.

By this text [1 Cor. 16.15–16] I was made to see that the Holy Ghost
never intended that men who have Gifts and Abilities should bury
them in the earth, but rather did command and stir up such to the
exercise of their gift, and also did commend those that were apt and
ready so to do, *they have addicted themselves to the ministry of the
Saints*: this Scripture in those days did continually run in my mind,
to incourage me, and strengthen me in this my work for God: I
have also been incouraged from several other Scriptures and examples of the Godly, both specified in the Word and in other ancient
Histories. *Act* 8.4; & 18.24, 25 &c. I *Pet*. 4.10; *Rom*. 12.16; Fox. *Acts
and Mon*. (86)

Notice that here too Scripture and Foxe's book are seen as comparable texts and that it is the Holy Ghost that produces readers who
become writers. Note as well that he admits to reading other "ancient
Histories" where he found sanction for his writing, his "work of
God."[56] Foxe provides Bunyan with "examples of the Godly" who
seem to be especially pertinent to the question of Bunyan's educating
himself to become, though a plain working man, a preacher and
writer.[57] Bunyan would have found in Foxe two examples of the
plowman tradition that developed from *Piers Plowman* itself, as well
as accounts of Lollard preachers and martyrs with no clerical credentials or conventional educations. Charles Doe's comment tells us at
least this much: Bunyan was exposed to the pre-Reformation tradition of which *Piers Plowman* was a part and had an active interest in
and knowledge of Reformation history. We also know he read the
documents in *Acts and Monuments* carefully.[58] Bunyan's interest in
ecclesiastical history, and specifically a pre-Reformation English
tradition, is shared by his contemporaries. But it is now time to turn
to the fourteenth-century Lollard origins of this particular way of
reading.

3

Whom God Hath Chosen
Lollards, Reformers, and the Figure of Piers Plowman

> But God hath chosen the foolish things of the world, to con-
> found the wise: and God hath chosen the weake things of the
> world, to confound the things which are mighty.
>
> 1 Cor. 1.27

 In *The History of the Worthies of England* (1662), Thomas
Fuller, a near contemporary of Bunyan, has the following
entry under "Learned Writers . . . Since the Reformation":
"Robert Langeland. Forgive me, Reader, though placing him (who lived
one hundred and fifty years *before*) *since* the Reformation: for I
conceive that the *Morning-star* belongs rather to the *Day*, then to the
Night. On which account this Robert (regulated in our Book not
according to the Age he was in, but Judgement he was of) may by
Prolepsis be termed a *Protestant*."[1] Fuller's assessment of Langland's
role is remarkable. In its use of the imagery of darkness and light to
characterize the history of the Reformation, it evokes John Foxe's
distinctive reading of ecclesiastical history, and it appropriates the
image of the morning star, one usually associated with Wyclif.[2] As we
will see in chapter 4, Robert Crowley's editions of *Piers Plowman* help
to explain the perception of Langland as a proto-Protestant, and the
revival of the work in the mid-sixteenth century justifies Fuller's
placement of Langland in a Reformation time frame. But Crowley did
not bring the perception of the poem as a Protestant work into being; he
merely reinforced a reading that had begun almost before the poem was

completed. Langland came to be seen as a primarily Protestant writer and his book emerged as part of the history of the Reformation because of its reception by one specific group of readers, the Lollards. The way in which these readers read texts and its continuity with the Protestant readings of texts in the sixteenth and seventeenth centuries, as well as the cultural effects that followed from the adoption of the poem and its major figure by various segments of the society, will be our focus in this chapter. But before we can turn to these issues, we must set in place the nature of the "opaque documents" at our disposal for documenting the Lollard reception of Langland's *Piers Plowman* and its impact on the culture. These consist of a series of reformist texts subsequent to Langland that appropriate the figure of Piers himself or of a generalized plowman to articulate the need for religious, social, or political reform.

That a *Piers Plowman* tradition existed has been known for a long time, but it has always been approached from a literary horizon of expectations.[3] Two questions about the relationship between Langland's poem and these plowman texts have been framed in terms of a literary construct. One has to do with Langland's possible exposure to the ideas of Wyclif and his followers as they are reflected in *Piers Plowman*, and the other concerns the literary indebtedness of the writers in this tradition to *Piers Plowman* itself. The varied answers to both questions are governed by literary rather than cultural assumptions about readers and reading.

Several recent essays epitomize the literary response to these two issues. On the first question, Pamela Gradon, in "*Piers Plowman* and the Ideology of Dissent," succinctly summarizes the literary dimensions of the problem: "Any study of the relationship between Langland and Wyclif invites three questions: firstly, is what we know of the chronology and dissemination of Wyclif's work compatible with such a relationship? Secondly, does the text of *Piers Plowman* supply any evidence of such a relationship? Thirdly, how important is such a study to our understanding of the poem as a whole?"[4] All three questions emerge out of a perspective that is focused exclusively on the author and on the text itself. Taking up each question in turn, Gradon separates the ideas of Langland from those of Wyclif and concludes: "But in the last resort, *Piers Plowman* is less concerned with the inculcations of theories, orthodox, heterodox, or heretical, than with a prophetic vision of a corrupt society and its eschatological doom."[5] Responding to critics who have noted that the Wycliffite writings were being produced around the same time as Langland's last two versions of *Piers Plowman*, Christina von Nolcken argues that they "have brought Langland too close to the Wycliffites."[6] She concludes that recent evidence about the dating of Wycliffite texts makes it likely that they were written after the C-version of *Piers Plowman*, and she endorses David Lawton's perspective that the Lollards had "Langlandian sympathies" rather than the reverse.[7] For von Nolcken, it is a question of doing an injustice to both Langland and the Wycliffites by linking the two.[8]

For both Gradon and von Nolcken, the question of Langland's relationship to the Wycliffite movement is one that violates their notion of Langland as an author and *Piers Plowman* as a literary production distinct from reformist propaganda. The cases they make for distinguishing between Langland's and Wyclif's ideas are persuasive if our object is to establish the meaning of *Piers Plowman*, but our focus here is exclusively on reception of the poem from a cultural perspective. For our purposes, it does not matter whether Langland is heterodox or orthodox.[9] The point is that the existence of the plowman texts, in appropriating the figure of Piers Plowman, testifies that some readers read *Piers Plowman* from a Wycliffite perspective.[10]

As to the second issue, concerning whether these unknown authors of the plowman texts actually responded to *Piers Plowman* itself, the question again revolves around how we define reading. Anne Hudson, in "Epilogue: The Legacy of *Piers Plowman*" surveys the plowman material and concludes that "*Piers Plowman* in the two and half centuries after its composition was more honoured in the name than in the reading."[11] Though she finds it "tempting" to suggest that Langland influenced the Wycliffite texts, she dismisses the possibility, noting that these writers "were drawing upon a common tradition."[12] Those works that specifically appropriate the figure of Piers, such as *Pierce the Ploughman's Crede*, provide a literary case for reading but not for influence; their range of interests is "tiny" in comparison to Langland's poem.[13] She doubts that those texts that evoke a generalized plowman figure, such as *The Praier and complaynte of the plowman unto Christe*, even belong in a survey concerning the legacy of *Piers Plowman* because they lack "direct allusions" to the poem even though "there is an evident similarity of concern and some comparable phraseology."[14] For Hudson, reading here involves the question of literary influence. Did these writers specifically respond to the fabric of *Piers Plowman* by taking it as a model, and is that influence inscribed in their texts in the form of allusions? But from a cultural perspective, the question of reading must be reconceived. Some of Langland's first readers read the poem from an entirely different set of expectations about its value and use. The phenomenon of the plowman texts is an eloquent testimony to *Piers Plowman*'s impact on its own society and subsequent ones. These "opaque documents" provide readings of the hold that *Piers Plowman* had on the imagination of a Lollard community of readers.

What can we find out about who Langland's early readers were? Manuscript evidence provides a clue to their social class. There is an unusually large number of manuscripts extant not only from the fourteenth century but from the fifteenth and occasionally the sixteenth centuries as well.[15] It is also a fact that the *Piers Plowman* manuscripts, by comparison with, for example, the Chaucer manuscripts, are generally the product of much less fashionable and expensive scriptoria, and many bear signs of having been written for clients of lesser social and economic standing.[16] Working from evidence in terms of ownership and dating as well as the poem's relationship to other works in the manuscripts, J. A. Burrow concludes that the poem's intended audience was the clergy.[17] Working from roughly the same kind of evidence, Anne Middleton notes that the three versions of Langland's poem "achieved a virtually nationwide distribution within a generation of their production."[18] She argues that the audience consisted of both clerical and lay readers, "an audience interested, by virtue of social location and experience, in the foundations of Christian authority, and right relations as well as faith within the Christian community."[19] But manuscript evidence of this kind can supply information only about ownership, not readership.[20] Janet Coleman speculates that Langland's audience consisted of the orthodox middle class,[21] but the existence of the plowman texts attests to the poem's popularity among the Lollards and the lower echelons of society.[22] It is to the nature of that readership we must now turn.

The Lollard Textual Community, the Peasants' Revolt of 1381, and *Piers Plowman*

As Janet Coleman has noted, "Fourteenth-century Christians were becoming more aware of their heritage as people of The

Book."[23] Two beliefs about the Book emerged in the period. The first was that the Bible, as God's book, contained all that was necessary for salvation, and the second was that God intended that all people should have access to his Word. Wyclif's call to have the Scriptures in English had a profound effect on the literacy rate. According to Margaret Aston, "Heretics (like later Protestants) regarded the acquisition of literacy as part of a religious vocation."[24] Out of that sense of reading as religious vocation the Lollard community of readers was forged.[25] They spread the Word abroad by making available Scripture and other works that promoted their cause and embodied their understanding of the way to salvation. Their sense of reading as a vocation was what ultimately defined them; as Margaret Aston notes, "It was as a vernacular literate movement that Lollardy had gathered momentum and it was as a vernacular literate movement that it was suspected and persecuted."[26]

Brian Stock has described what he calls "textual communities" of the eleventh and twelfth centuries. Textual communities, according to Stock, tend to be reformist in character, centering on authoritative texts that in the community's view serve as more authentic manifestations of divine truth than the corrupt oral tradition of the mainstream. Members of these communities need not be literate themselves; their experience of texts may be mediated by a literate minority within the group.[27] Stock uses this fact to document the historical interaction between the "rise of literacy" and the "formation of heretical and reformist groups."[28] The fourteenth-century Lollard movement bears considerable resemblance to this earlier phenomenon. Not only the Bible but other books as well were accorded a more authoritative status than the traditions of the church.

It is difficult to work our way back to what the call to English the Scriptures meant to that community, but we must acknowledge that the issue was perceived as one of human freedom and class struggle. Though Lollardy began at Oxford, the university quickly shut its doors to the heretical movement.[29] By the 1520s the community of Lollard readers no longer included university men, but clerks and tradespeople, for the issue had become one of class.[30] As the author of the "General Prologue" to the Lollard Bible had remarked, "god both can and may, if it liketh him, speed simple men out of the university, as much to know holy writ, as masters in the university."[31] Thus, the anti-intellectual bias was built into the premises of the

Lollard textual community almost at its outset. God himself would make sure that his people could understand Scripture without a mediator. The notion that God cared desperately about the fate of his Book resulted in the belief, among Lollards at least, that God emboldened others to write books to promote his aims for reformation of the church.

In *The Drama of Dissent,* Ritchie Kendall has focused on four hallmarks of Lollardy: the invocation of inspired perception, the belief in the priesthood of all believers, the adoption of Old Testament models of the biblical prophet, and the appropriation of New Testament models of living the "simple life of the gospel."[32] These characteristics may explain why *Piers Plowman* was embraced so enthusiastically by a later Lollard community of readers; its prophetic stance and its central figure placed it emphatically in their tradition. And its distinctive use of Scripture to define issues also contributed to this effect. As Hudson has noted, "The Wycliffites would have regarded all their writing as in some sense biblical exegesis—exegesis of the biblical words, or exegesis of the world around them in the light of biblical words."[33]

Unfortunately, much of what we can find out about Lollards as readers can be learned only from the vitriolic comments of their enemies. One such critic, Bishop Reginald Pecock, thought there were two kinds of Lollard readers. One embraced only the New Testament and rejected all other books as redundant. The other set of readers read other books which, according to Pecock, "they cherished as rich jewels, to be 'embraced, loved and multiplied' abroad among all Christian people."[34] Anne Hudson's meticulous research documents the extremely high value that Lollards placed on their books.[35] Not only did they with painstaking care make available their own works, they also appropriated existing orthodox works and made distinctly Lollard interpolations as part of a bid "to win a wider circle of readers."[36] The appropriation of the figure of *Piers Plowman* may well represent another kind of attempt to broaden the boundaries of their textual community. If so, their effort was enormously successful, for the Lollard books, in turn, were embraced by sixteenth-century reformers as "jewels" to be made available to all readers as evidence of the rightness of their cause.

But as Margaret Aston has noted, "Sedition and dissent [came] of age together" in the late fourteenth century.[37] *Piers Plowman* participated in both of those aspects of the period and, in each case, the growth in lay literacy was an integral factor in the unusual reception of the poem. Janet Coleman, attempting to assess the consequences of the growth of lay literacy and social mobility in the fourteenth century, speculates that the literature that was produced was written "as an encouragement to critique and change" the ecclesiastical and social institutions.[38] Perhaps this is so, but we can state more reliably that, whatever the intentions of the author, newly literate readers certainly saw the function of writing in these socio-political terms and acted upon those perceptions. The link between *Piers Plowman* and the Peasants' Revolt of 1381 is perhaps the most telling witness to the emergence of a new kind of reader, one whose attitude toward the nature and use of books was very different from that of an educated audience.

The fact that the poem exists in three distinct versions is a possible indication of an uneasy relationship between author and audience over the meaning of the text. It has been suggested that the C-text, a more conservative rendition of the poem, was written to tone down the B-text's radical political overtones.[39] We know that the leaders of the Peasants' Revolt saw the poem as a political statement. The texts of six letters by John Ball and other organizers of the revolt have been preserved in several contemporary chronicles. These consciously evoke associations with the poem and employ symbolic names derived from it. One letter by a one-time priest, John Ball, to the Commons of Essex, reads: : "Johon Schep, som tyme Seynte Marie prest of York, and now of Colchestre, greteth wel Johan Nameles, and Johan the Mullere, and Johan Cartere, and biddeth hem that thei bee war of gyle in borugh, and stondeth togidre in Godes name, and biddeth Peres Ploughman go to his werk, and chastise wel Hobbe the Robbere, and taketh with yow Johan Trewman, and alle hiis felawes, and no mo, and loke schappe you to on heved, and no mo."[40] In this first appropriation of the elements of Langland's poem, its major symbol was perceived to be a code word for class struggle. R. B. Dobson speculates that the names used, rather than designating the recipients of the letters, are more likely "masonic," and that the correspondence "reveals two essential characteristics of the author and his audience—a strong sense of personal identification with the ideal of a social brotherhood, and a deeply personal devotion to the most simple and literal truths of the

Christian religion."[41] Another letter by "Jakke Carter" refers to Do-Well, Do-Better, and Do-Best, and thus definitely alludes to the B-version, the one Crowley was to print:

> Jakke Carter prayes yowe alle that ye make a gode ende of that ye
> have begunnen, and doth wele and ay bettur and bettur, for at the
> even men heryth the day. For if the ende be wele, than is alle wele.
> Lat Peres the Plowman my brother duelle at home and dyght us
> corne, and I will go with yowe and helpe that y may to dyghte youre
> mete and youre drynke, that ye none fayle; lokke that Hobbe robby-
> oure be wele chastysed for lesyng of youre grace for ye have gret
> nede to take God with yowe in alle youre dedes. For now is tyme to
> be war.[42]

The great editor of *Piers Plowman,* W. W. Skeat, reading with a sense that literature and politics were separate spheres of experience, saw John Ball and the other organizers of the revolt as perverting Langland's "bold words . . . into watchwords of insurgency,"[43] but Ball clearly had a different sense of books and their uses. Dobson speculates that Langland's notion of the relationship of the king and the "commune" "was not too far removed from that of the rebels of 1381."[44] Our concern here is not with Langland's intentions, what-ever they may have been, but with how his poem was perceived: John Ball and other organizers of the revolt read *Piers Plowman* not as literature in our modern sense but as a social manifesto (perhaps especially in the prologue's depiction of the Rats' Parliament)[45] that spoke to their condition.

The letters were included in a number of chronicles. One, that of Dieulacres Abbey, actually lists "per plouman" as one of the conspira-tors.[46] This link between *Piers Plowman* and the Peasants' Revolt may explain why Foxe does not allude to it in *Acts and Monuments* and also why the publication of the poem ceases after Elizabeth I assumes the throne. Thus, from its very inception and even after the C-text revisions, the poem may have been seen by some as a subversive poem that advocated the overthrow of the established hierarchical order.

Overlapping with this reading of the poem in terms of the politics of class was another that saw *Piers Plowman* as participating in the politics of religion. The poem was seen as embodying John Wyclif's call for radical changes in religious institutions, changes that had social and political implications.[47] As Janet Coleman has noted, "*Piers Plowman* is itself a victim of the contemporary social and religious crisis and a record of a confrontation."[48] Thus, for its extreme criticism of the social, political, and ecclesiastical structure, *Piers Plowman* somewhat anachronistically came to be associated with the revolutionary religious views of Wyclif and his Lollard followers as well as with the political views of the Peasants' Revolt.[49] Furthermore, even though the critique of abuses was common in the later Middle Ages and did not necessarily imply rejection of the institutions being criticized, successive generations of readers naturally assumed that Langland's diatribes were of a piece with those of later writers whose intentions truly were revolutionary. The radical associations the poem picked up in the Renaissance were no new or sudden phenomenon.

This is not the place to assess whether *Piers Plowman* is or is not a truly radical poem, in either a social or a theological context. My concern at this point is solely with its reception and the reputation it acquired over two centuries. Nonetheless, it is useful to set forth briefly some reasons why it acquired a radical reputation. Though twentieth-century readers perceive *Piers Plowman* as a theologically orthodox poem, its orthodoxy would not have been readily apparent to many readers from its own time well into the nineteenth century. *Piers Plowman* delivers a portrait of a society riddled with corruption in both church and state. The tone of the poem is harsh and vitriolic and its sentiments anticlerical. Thus it is not at all surprising that the poem was co-opted by the leaders of the Peasants' Revolt and the Lollards of the fifteenth century. To take one example out of many: the poem is against going on literal pilgrimages—it proposes making only "pilgrimages" to truth, as in the passage in passus 5 in which Piers gives the pilgrims directions to Truth. His allegorical language makes it clear that such a journey involves not physical movement but the reformation of the self.[50] This issue became a distinctively Lollard one.

But *Piers Plowman* really is a radical poem in at least one respect. As Elizabeth Kirk has demonstrated, Langland's treatment of the plowman figure is a far more radical departure from tradition than has generally been appreciated.[51] Attempts (like that of Jill Mann)[52] to show that the idealized plowman of Chaucer's General Prologue is a conventional figure are mistaken. According to Kirk, picturing the wage-earning plowman as a type of the ideal Christian marks a major departure from traditional biblical symbolism in which the shepherd is the ideal Christian and the plowman or non-nomadic farmer is his antithesis (Abel and Cain are the most obvious instance of this). Kirk argues that Langland's presentation of the plowman reflects major social and economic changes in the Middle Ages and concomitant changes in the context of theological thought. She suggests that "the plowman, in history as in Langland's model, is the force on which the whole system rests; the plowman is responsible for the existence of the economically, socially, and ethically complex world probed by Langland as he tries to reconcile it with traditional models, structures, and norms."[53] What is new about Langland's use of the plowman image is not its traditional symbolic association with preaching, which Stephen Barney has demonstrated, but its literalness. Piers is more than a symbol; he functions on the poem's literal level as a moral exemplar. The effects of this radical presentation of the plowman continue throughout the sixteenth century, as some use the symbol and others attack it.

This adoption of the figure of the plowman ignites what has been described as the *Piers Plowman* tradition. It is therefore worth asking what aspects of the figure proved attractive enough to these writers to provoke appropriation. To do so, we must examine the traditional image of plowmen and peasants before the advent of Langland's Piers. As Barney has pointed out, a positive image of the plowman did exist before Langland. However, Barney cites only references that use agricultural labor purely as a symbol or metaphor. Kirk has shown that literal representations of peasants are far more negative and that as a way of thinking about the lives of real laborers this tradition was more widespread and influential than the positive symbolic one.[54] Peasants in general and plowmen in particular were seen in the dominant tradition as dissolute, irresponsible, wasteful, and insubordinate. The classic picture is that offered by Langland's contemporary, John Gower, in *Le Mirour de l'omme* and in his account of the Peasants' Revolt in *Vox clamantis*.[55] It is summed up in the comment of a near contemporary, the Franciscan Alvarus Pelagious, in the early fourteenth century: "For even as they plough and dig the earth all day long, so they become altogether earthy; they lick the earth, they eat the earth, they speak the earth; in the earth they have reposed all their hopes, nor do they care a jot for the heavenly substance that shall remain."[56] Another text that illustrates the low esteem in which plowmen were held is "How the Ploughman Learned his Paternoster—a lytell geste."[57] It was printed in the sixteenth century but reflects the older tradition. This fabliau tells the story of a plowman in France who has all the riches he can acquire through hard labor but who cannot learn his paternoster. A priest tells him that he will be unable to have his heavenly reward and offers to teach him the prayer if he will give wheat to and will remember the names of forty people that the priest will send to him. The priest offers to pay the plowman double the price for the wheat he gives away. The forty people turn out to be named the forty words in the prayer. When the plowman remembers them, the priest refuses to pay, saying that the plowman has bought his heavenly reward by feeding the poor. The case winds up in court, and everyone laughs at the plowman who vows never to trust a priest again. Occupational stereotypes are common in the fabliaux; that this plowman is a bumpkin and miser whose salvation is at the mercy of the clergy suggests the nature of the plowman image that Langland's figure seeks to replace.

The emergence of *Piers Plowman* shifts the emphasis decisively. After Langland, the alternate, more positive conception of the plowman predominates. Piers is a simple man, a plain man who can direct pilgrims to truth, a model of honest living through hard labor. These qualities have earned him an authority that comes directly from God. But that religious symbol had political overtones, as its adoption by the leaders of the Peasants' Revolt testifies. Suddenly that image catches fire and ultimately exerts an influence over two centuries, with at least an indirect effect as late as the seventeenth century. What in Langland's own exposition of the character accounts for its long life?

E. Talbot Donaldson provides a partial answer to that question:

The curious paradox that caused Langland, a political moderate, to become associated with the Peasants' Revolt and, among literary historians, with the more radically democratic elements of his age . . . is exactly paralleled by another one, which caused Lang-

land, a religious moderate, to become associated with the most drastic
of ecclesiastical events, the Reformation. The explanation for both of
these paradoxes lies in the quality of the poet's thought. Christianity
points out that the path to spiritual salvation lies through the heart of
the individual—*cor hominis*. Saturated with Christian thought, the
poet saw everything in terms of it and, as I have just said, found that
the path to political salvation lay through the same country as the path
to spiritual salvation. Even though the details and formulas of his religious and political thought are conservative and traditionalist, his doctrine of the individual tends inevitably toward the radical. . . . In his
emphasis on the individual, Langland was in advance of his own
church and of his own nation—and, indeed, of himself.[58]

Langland's proto-Protestant emphasis on the individual results in the
elevation of the layman to a new status. Piers knows how to work out
his own salvation unmediated by the clergy. The poem also confronts
the old paradigm of the shepherd and his flock who depend upon him
for spiritual food; in its place we have Piers, a worker among workers,
who knows the way to truth and can define it for others. Salvation as
reflected in the poem comes about in part through inward reformation; the way to truth is through the Ten Commandments, not
through outward sacraments. Needless to say, *Piers Plowman* as a
whole does not take so absolute a position, and the liturgy and the
sacraments play an important role, as we will be noting. But though
Piers Plowman is strictly speaking an orthodox Catholic poem, it
does in another sense shift the emphasis from the clergy to the
individual and therefore was correctly perceived as a harbinger of the
Reformation, if one read with an idea of the nature and use of books
radically different from our own. How the Lollards read Langland's
poem and how the later sixteenth-century reformers read those
Lollard texts will be the focus of our next section.

The *Piers Plowman* Apocrypha

In order to understand the Renaissance publication of *Piers
Plowman* and the form in which readers subsequently encountered
it, we must situate the event in a series of late medieval Lollard texts

and later Renaissance reconstructions of them that laid the groundwork for the rediscovery and interpretation of *Piers Plowman* itself.
These texts will here be termed "*Piers Plowman* apocrypha" because
through their adoption of the plowman figure they clearly align
themselves with the authority of *Piers Plowman* itself. The early
Lollard texts clearly reflect and register the ways in which *Piers
Plowman* was being read. The apocrypha that sprang into being after
the original poem was written were injected into the Reformation by
sixteenth-century reformers eager to legitimize their railings against
the church by pointing to the antiquity and, therefore, the validity of
their claims. The reformers also created new texts that use the
character of Piers to denounce church and state. These texts, which
were directly or indirectly derived from Langland's text, were put
into print before *Piers Plowman* itself was printed by Crowley and
explain his reading of it. The texts represent expansions of the figure
of the plowman that develop the attributes of the character, pursue
the issues with which he is associated, and extend and emphasize the
symbolic connotations that had developed as the figure was appropriated by various groups. They must be set into place in order to
reconstruct the horizon of expectations the Protestant reader brought
to the text of the 1550 editions of *Piers Plowman*.

For our purposes, the essential questions are these: how did the
Lollards read and spread their understanding of the import of *Piers
Plowman*? How and why did the sixteenth-century reformers employ
the apocrypha to advance the cause of the Reformation? And finally,
what were the immediate and the long-term cultural effects of
adopting the plowman as an advance guard for the Reformation?

Judith Anderson, in a study of Langland and Spenser, observes:
"*Piers Plowman* reentered the literary and religious experience of
English readers in the decade of Spenser's birth."[59] But in one sense,
Piers Plowman really never left the consciousness of the English
Protestant reader. Though *Piers Plowman* itself, according to John N.
King, was "prohibited by the heresy and treason statutes of Henry
VIII" until the repeals act under Edward VI,[60] Lollard readings of it
surfaced in the apocryphal plowman texts to keep its revolutionary
ideas about God's relationship to "lewd men" alive.

The two earliest Lollard texts that respond to the fabric of *Piers
Plowman* focus on the comparison between religious and lewd men.
The first, *Pierce the Ploughman's Crede*, aligns itself with Langland's

work by using alliterative verse.[61] The poem was written about 1394, printed in 1553, and reprinted in 1561 as a companion piece to *Piers Plowman* itself. It is largely an attack on the friars. The narrator looks for someone to teach him his creed and works through all four orders of friars without success. He finally finds a plowman who teaches him his creed and denounces friars for their corruption and their persecution of Wyclif and the early Lollard Walter Brute. The portrait that is painted of Piers is remarkable. He wears ragged clothes and labors in the field with his wife while their children weep with hunger and the baby sleeps in rags. Yet when the plowman sees the narrator's distress he offers to share some food with him. The picture is obviously meant to present the opposite of the friars' denial of religious poverty, but it also reflects both a reading of Langland's character and an embellishment of it. In contrast to the plowman in the paternoster poem, this one can teach the creed. The figure of Piers is quite consciously being set up as an alternative to the clergy, for the friars are presented only as the preeminent example of the failure of the contemporary clergy in general.[62]

Pierce the Ploughman's Crede reflects the first stage in the development of the plowman figure. In Langland's poem, Piers is the ideal Christian, but he is not the spokesman for anticlericalism; the dreamer, not Piers, is the polemicist. In *Pierce the Ploughman's Crede*, the two roles are combined and located in one figure: the plowman. It is a logical step. If Piers is the ideal Christian who can direct the reader to truth, he must also have the authority to denounce those who were appointed for that role and have not fulfilled it. The accrued image of the plowman—with his plainness, poverty, and rude speech, and with his special relationship to God (he is Truth's servant)—is redefined in this anticlerical context. The plowman is elevated above the clergy and has leave to criticize them.

A second early text that reflects an opposition to the traditional clergy is *The Praier and complaynte of the plowman unto Christe*. The date of this poem is unclear. According to Hudson, it probably dates from the early fifteenth century,[63] and is said to have been put into print by William Tyndale in Antwerp in 1531.[64] It was reprinted in Foxe's *Acts and Monuments*, the quintessential text for defining the contours of meaning for the Protestant reader, under 1360, the year in which he considers that the era of the English Reformation really begins:

Which booke as it was faithfully set forth by William Tindall, so I have as truly distributed the same abroad to the Readers hands: neither changing any thing of the matter, neither altering many words of the phrase thereof. Although the oldnesse and age of his speech and tearmes be almost growne now out of use; yet I thought it so best, both for the utility of the booke to reserve it from oblivion, as also in his owne language to let it goe abroad, for the more credit and testimony of the true antiquity of the same. Adding withall in the margent for the better understanding of the Reader, some interpretation of certaine difficult tearmes and speeches, which otherwise might perhaps hinder or stay the Reader. The matter of this complaining prayer of the Ploughman thus proceedeth.[65]

Like the Lollard readers before him, Foxe wants to make the poem available to a wider circle of readers, but he respects its power to speak on its own terms, so he glosses what he fears the reader will not understand. The *Praier and complaynte* is a prose tract attacking the abuses of the church. It rails against the pope, the clergy (especially friars), the venerating of relics, the lack of preaching, and auricular confession—all typical Lollard issues. It deliberately evokes the contrast between the plain plowman and the clergy who sell prayers for money:

And Lord, we lewed men han a beliefe, that thy goodnesse is endlesse: and gif we keepen thine hestes, then ben we thy true servants, And though we preyen thee but a little and shortlich, thou wilt thinken on us, and granten us that us nedeth, for so thou behited us sometime. And Lord I trow, that pray a man never so many quaint prayers, gif hee ne keepe not thine hests, hee is not thy good servant. But gif hee keepe thine hests, than hee is thy good servant. And so me thinketh, Lord, that praying of long praiers ne is not the service that thou desirest, but keeping of thine hests: and then a lewd man may serve God as well as a man of religion; though that the ploughman ne may not have so much silver for his prayer, as men of religion. For theye kunnen not so well preisen their praiers as these other chapmen: but lord, our hope is, that our praiers be never the worse, though it be not so well sold as other mens prayers.[66]

The layman pleads with God to accept his prayer which, in its way, is as good as a man of religion's. The tract asserts—as had *Piers Plowman* for its Lollard readers—that lewd men can serve God better than religious because they are not corrupt; they take no silver and their prayers are not "quaint." The *Praier and complaynte* also repeatedly evokes the shepherd / sheep paradigm: "But Lord, there commeth hired men, and they ne feden not thy sheep in thy plenteous lesew, but feden thy sheepe with suevens, and false miracles and tales. But at thy truth they ne comen not: for Lord, I trow thou sendest them never. For have they hire of thy sheepe, they ne careth but little of the feding and the keping of thy sheepe."[67] The tract rejects the paradigm, reflecting instead the newfound voice of the layman who is unwilling to allow priests to mediate for him in his relationship with God.

The reformers of the sixteenth century made use of the new-found status of the plowman and expanded the dimensions of the image. Aston discusses ways the reformers seized upon Lollard texts to "prove that new reformers were but old reformers writ large."[68] She does not discuss the plowman texts in these terms, but they were clearly used in exactly the same ways.

A perfect example of this recasting process can be seen in the preface to the 1531 edition of the *Praier and complaynte*.[69] This preface contains all the significant features the image of the plowman takes on in the sixteenth century. The preface begins by describing the Crucifixion as an event that happened as a result of the hostility of men to Christ's message. It was "new lerninge," and Christ and his disciples were "men nother of authorite nor reputation / but laye men / ydiotes fyschers, / carpenters and other of the rascall sorte." Therefore, how could God "open that unto such rude sorte"? The writer then points to the Resurrection and says, "His disciples have ever had the victory apon the crosse and testified unto the world the wisdome of God in these pore ydiotes / and veray foolishnes and wisdome of the flesh in these gret lerned aunciente fathers." The writer then turns to his own time, where he sees the same situation occurring: "Oure holy byshops with all their ragmans rolle" are of the same breed as those that put Christ to death and now put martyrs like Thomas Hilton to death because of their "new learning." The bishops, the author says, persuade the people that the work of God is heresy and the men who preach it heretics. But, he adds, the martyrs will rise up in truth again. Having set up the context through which we are to view the text, he turns to the text itself as a witness that what the martyrs espouse is not new learning but had its roots in the past. The writer says specifically that he has changed nothing in printing the text, presumably because he wants its antiquity to be perceived, adding that if he comes across any other "holy reliques" he will print them as well.[70]

In the term *new learning* lies a partial clue to the motives of the reformers in reviving the apocryphal plowman texts. As Alan G. Chester notes, the phrase *"new learning* was a term of opprobrium used by the religious conservatives against the teachings of Martin Luther and his English disciples."[71] To counter the charge that the issues of the Reformation were new and therefore heretical, the reformers turned to antiquity to show that the Reformation was no sudden development but rather the culmination of a long process.

The *Praier and complaynte* represented to the reformers a way to legitimize their complaints about the abuses of the church. By calling the very text a holy relic they use religious language to undermine the church itself. But the appeal to antiquity, though the strongest motive for printing this text, is only part of the story. The plowman figure as such, because it seemed to stand outside the usual channels of religious authority, offered the reformers a useful vehicle through which to criticize the church. The preface evokes all the significant motifs of the Reformation. Looking back to the Crucifixion is supposed to provide light on the current scene, a stance typical of Protestant preoccupation with primitive Christianity and the attempt to recreate it. The plowman figure is set in the context of primitive Christianity. He, like the "lay men and ydiote fyschers," the disciples of Christ, is most nearly the servant of God. At the base of this comparison is 1 Cor. 1.27–28. The plowman, like the "ydiots" at the Crucifixion, is one of the rude sort that God imbues with wisdom; he is the perfect vehicle to articulate the abuses of the church because he is untainted by human traditions and human learning.

One tract that shows the reformers explicitly linking the plowman both with antiquity and with Lollardy is *A Proper Dialogue Between a Gentilman and a Husbandman eche complaynyng to the other their miserable calamitie, through the ambition of the clergy. An ABC of Spirituality*[72]).] The text begins with a warning to the clergy: "How longe have ye the world captyved / In sore bondage of mennes traditions?" Again we have the church as the corrupter of primitive Christianity. The husbandman and the gentleman complain about the clergy and their demands. Then the husbandman introduces a fragment of a Lollard text that discourses on the illegality of the clergy.[73] He does so, he tells us, to show that complaints against the clergy are not "a newe work of heretiques" but rather an issue of antiquity and therefore legitimate. It is, of course, the husbandman who knows the text; he is linked with religious reform and with antiquity. The dialogue is followed by another text arguing for the availability of the Scriptures in English.[74] The plowman image is thus also linked to translation of the Bible, another element in the nexus of typically Lollard concerns. The plowman ought to have Scripture available, for he can work out his own salvation by studying it instead of depending on priests.

The reformers not only reproduced plowman material, they reworked other Lollard texts to fit into the plowman tradition. And to further legitimize their claim of antiquity, they attributed some of these works to Chaucer. *Jack Upland, Friar Daw's Reply and Upland's Rejoinder,* printed in 1540 and reprinted in Foxe's *Acts and Monuments* is a prose attack on the friars.[75] Jack says of the friars: "The selliest folke, that ever antichrist found, beene last brought into the church and in a wonder wise, for they been of divers sects of antichrist, sowne of divers countries and kindreds. And all men knowne well, that they be not obedient to bishops, ne leegemen to kings: neither they tillen, ne sowen, weeden, ne repen, wood, corn, ne grasse, neither nothing that man should helpe: but only themselves their lives to sustaine."[76] We see here how the symbol of the plowman has established itself. Because plowmen contribute the food that is the basis for society, they have become the metaphorical measure of all other roles in society. This is even clearer when we note that although the text calls Jack Upland merely a countryman, when Foxe prints it he describes Jack as a plowman. He attributes the treatise to Chaucer:

So now to annexe also to the same a certain other ancient treatise compiled by *Geffrie Chaucer* by the way of a dialogue or questions, moved in the person of a certaine uplandish and simple ploughman of the countrie. Which treatise, for the same, the author intituled *Jacke Upland*, wherein is to be seene and noted to all the world, the blinde ignorance and variable discord of these irreligious religions, how rude and unskilfull they are in matters and principles of our Christian institution, as by the contents of this present dialogue appeareth, the words whereof in the same old English wherein it was set forth in this wise do proceed. Wherein also thou mayest see, that it is no new thing that their blasphemous doings have by divers good men in old time beene detected, as there are many and divers other old bookes to shew.[77]

Here again Foxe articulates the Lollard position on the antiquity of books that have been written by "divers good men" to expose the "blasphemous doings" of the Roman church.

Another text attributed to Chaucer was actually called the "Plowman's Tale," since it was taken to be the missing tale of the plowman described in the General Prologue to *The Canterbury Tales*. The poem is a debate between the Pelican (true religion) and the Griffon (the church) on the issue of ecclesiastical authority. It is the plowman who is deemed the appropriate speaker for a fable that heaps invective on the church.[78] Thynne included this work when he printed his second edition of Chaucer (1542). His son Francis Thynne relates in his *Animadversions*[79] that the book was almost banned by Parliament as a result. It was saved only by the argument that Chaucer's work was fiction, not religious polemic,[80] an early sign of the impending divorce between lettered and religious readings of texts. Foxe has an extensive entry on Chaucer, following one on Gower, which takes for granted that the "Plowman's Tale" is his. Speaking of the importance of Chaucer's works being generally known, Foxe observes:

This I mervaile to see the idle life of the priests and Clergy men of that time, seeing these lay persons shewed themselves in these

kindes of liberall studies so industrious and fruitfully occupied: but
much more I mervaile to consider this, how that the Bishops, con-
demning and abolishing all manner of English bookes and treatises
which might bring the people to any light of knowledge, did yet au-
thorise the Works of Chaucer to remaine still and to be occupied.
Who (no doubt) saw in Religion as much almost as even we do now,
and uttereth in his Works no lesse, and seemeth to be a right Wick-
levian, or else there never was any.[81]

Unlike the censors, he makes no distinction between fictional text
and religious polemic. For Foxe, books exist to "bring people to the
light of knowledge," and the knowledge that he is interested in as a
Protestant reader is the truth of the Reformation. Against the
marginal gloss "Men brought to Truth by reading Chaucer's Works,"
Foxe continues:

So it pleased God to blinde then the eies of them, for the more
commodity of his people, to the intent that, through the reading of
his treatises, some fruit might redound thereof to his Church, as no
doubt it did to many. As also I am partly enformed, of certaine
which knew the parties, which to them reported, that by reading of
Chaucer's Workes, they were brought to the true knowledge of religion: And not unlike to be true. For to omit other parts of his volume, whereof some are more fabulous than other, what tale can be
more plainly told than the tale of the ploughman? or what finger
can point out more directly the Pope with his Prelats to be Antichrist, than doth the poor Pelican reasoning against the greedy
Griffon? Under which *Hypotyposis*, or poesie, who is so blinde that
seeth not by the Pellican the doctrine of Christ, and of the Lollards
to be defended against the Church of Rome? Or who is so impu-
dent that can deny that to bee true which the Pellican there affir-
meth in describing the presumptuous pride of that pretensed
Church? Againe, what egge can be more like, or Figge, unto another, than the words, properties, and conditions of that ravening

Gryph resembleth the true Image, that is the nature and qualities, of that which wee call the Church of Rome, in every point and degree. And therefore no great mervaile if that narration was exempted out of the copies of Chaucers Workes: which notwithstanding now is restored againe, and is extant for every man to read that is disposed.[82]

The distinction between the other "fabulous" tales and the "Plowman's Tale" appears to be one of content. Rhetorical figures are put in the service of advancing God's truth by defending the Lollards and revealing the nature of the corrupt Roman church. Note that God not only opens the eyes of his servants to see the truth and write about it, he closes the eyes of those who could prevent the spread of that truth.

In fact, according to Foxe, God's role in promoting the reformation of his church extended beyond opening and closing the eyes of participants in the disputes over reform; he intervened in history even more directly by inventing printing. In a section entitled "The Benefit and Invention of Printing," Foxe briefly discusses the history of the invention, but he ultimately proclaims that the human inventors were mere instruments in God's plan to reform the church: "Notwithstanding, what Man soever was the Instrument, without all doubt God himself was the ordainer and disposer thereof, no otherwise, than he was of the gift of Tongues, and that for a singular purpose. And well may this gift of Printing be resembled to the gift of Tongues: for like as God then spake with many Tongues, and yet all that would not turn the *Jews*; so now, when the Holy Ghost speaketh to adversaries in inumerable sorts of Books, yet they will not be converted, nor turn to the Gospel."[83] Foxe's comparison of printing to the gift of tongues provides a succinct formulation of how a Protestant readership viewed books; the Holy Ghost spoke directly to readers through many different kinds of writings. Human authors were only agents of God's will.

Foxe discusses God's "end and purpose" in bestowing printing on the world. He claims that God chose a dark moment when the Pope had condemned John Hus and Jerome of Prague to death as heretics and had turned all Christians into "vassals": "in this very time so dangerous and desperate, where Mans power could do no more, there the blessed Wisdom and Omnipotent Power of the Lord began to work for his Church, not with Sword and Target to subdue his exalted adversary, but with Printing, Writing and Reading to convince darkness by light, error by truth, ignorance by learning. So that by means of this Printing, the secret Operation of God hath heaped upon that proud Kingdom a double confusion."[84] For Protestant readers, books are God's weapons against Rome. Remarking that the Pope must "abolish Printing" or "Printing doubtless will abolish him," Foxe proclaims "That through the Light of Printing, the world beginneth now to have eyes to see, and Heads to judge."[85] The Pope may have managed to silence John Hus and Jerome of Prague "yet instead of *John Hus* and others, God hath opened the Press to preach, whose voice the Pope is never able to stop with all the puissance of his Triple Crown. By this Printing, as by the Gift of Tongues, and as by the singular Organ of the Holy Ghost, the Doctrine of the Gospel soundeth to all Nations and Countries under Heaven, and what God revealeth to one Man, is dispersed to many, and what is known in one Nation is opened to all."[86] Foxe's understanding of the phenomenon of printing is an eloquent witness to the charged meaning of books for a Protestant readership. God speaks through the Holy Ghost in "tongues," that is, in different kinds of books, to spread the gospel and defeat his adversary. Human authors are part of God's plan for his church, and they preach directly on the issues through their written works despite their date or their use of fiction and rhetorical figures.

For example, the "Plowman's Tale" remained a living part of religious and political polemic into the seventeenth century. It was republished separately in 1606, after the Gunpowder Plot of November 1605.[87] Its title page indicates an expectation that its readers will be comparatively uneducated and that it will be seen as pertinent to recent events: "The Plowman's Tale. Showing by the doctrine and lives of the Romish Clergie, that the Pope is Antichrist and they his Ministers. Written by Sir Geoffrey Chaucer, Knight, amongst his Canterburie tales: and now set out apart from the rest, with a short exposition of the words and matters for the capacitie and understanding of the simpler sort of Readers."

The final stage of this manipulation of the figure of the plowman is reflected in three texts that were probably composed in the first half of the sixteenth century (before Crowley published his edition) and that also use Piers to articulate criticism of church and state. Two of them, *A godlye dyalogue and dysputacyon betwene Pyers Plow-*

man and a popish preest / concernyng the supper of the lorde and *I playne Piers*, seem to have been printed in Antwerp between 1530 and 1550.[88] Each text projects a different image of the plowman, but the two together exemplify the dimensions of the image that had become important to the Reformation. The first, the dialogue between Piers and a priest, evokes the banquet scene in *Piers Plowman* and projects an image of Piers as an innocent: the plain, uneducated man. The narrative begins thus:

> It chanced that this simple Pyers Plowman com to a certeyne house
> where as was a daner, prepared for the neyghbors dwellyng there
> aboute, at the which dynner were iiii Prests amongest whom was
> muche resoning concerning the sacrament of the Aultre, to be
> shorte one amongest these iiii (to make the symple people beleve
> that he was better learned than all hys fellowes) sayde and declared
> ther that the sacrament was the very body and bloud of Chryste Al-
> leagynge further that great daunger yt was to receyve yet un-
> worthely &c. where uppon Pyeers plowman, encouraged hym selfe,
> yea was rathere boldened and encouraged by the secret motyon of
> the holy goost.[89]

Piers, through the workings of the Holy Ghost within, asks a series of questions of this priest, finally refuting the priest's assertion about transubstantiation. The title page of the work underscores the role in which the writer employs Piers by citing as its epigraph 1 Cor. 1.26–27: "God hath chosen the weake thinges of the worlde to confounde thynges whiche are myghtye. yea thynges of no reputacyon for to bryng to nought thynges of reputacion, that no flesh shuld presume in his sight." A manuscript directly related to the *godlye dyalogue* shows that the presentation of the plowman as an early reformer did not go unchallenged: *The Bankett of Johan the Reve, Unto piers ploughman / Laurens laborer / Thomlyn Tailyor / And Hobbe of the hille / with other.*[90] The *Bankett* attempts to enlist Piers in the Catholic cause. Here we have the same dinner setting, but this time Piers argues for the doctrine of transubstantiation. The fact that this text survives only in manuscript documents its lack of success in dismantling the reformist status of the figure.

Another work published before Crowley's edition, *I playne Piers*,[91] evokes a version of Piers that contrasts sharply with the innocent who figures in the *godlye dyalogue*. Its title page, too, underscores certain specific aspects of the plowman figure:

I playne Piers which can not flatter

A plowe man men me call

My speche is fowlle / yet marke the matter

howe thynges may hap to fall.

Piers is still the plain man, but here the emphasis falls not on his innocence but on his inability to lie or flatter because he is unlettered. His speech is rude, but it is also prophetic in a way that harks back to the prophetic character of *Piers Plowman*. The work is by far the most radical critique of both church and state we have yet seen. It attacks the existing church as papistical, the king as protecting the Antichrist, and all those in authority as accountable for the ills of the poor. Often ironic and always enigmatic, the work is written in both verse and prose, though the verse is not set out as verse in the text. (It does rhyme, however.) It is the first of the plowman texts that not only defends the working classes but makes a laborer into their political spokesman, calling for drastic social change and a reversal of the existing order. For the first time since the reception of *Piers Plowman* itself, the figure of Piers is used as a call for revolt, and the voice more clearly represents the concerns of the poor. The plowman figure, which the apocrypha embellished with anticlericalism, is also combined with prophecy for the first time since Langland's poem.

I playne Piers takes up most of the issues usual in these texts, such as the need to have the Scriptures in English, but it offers a striking contrast to the other plowman apocrypha. Its style is deliberately dense and allusive as it denounces the existing order and prophesies a new one:

As it is written, for thy sake are we kylled, all the day longe we are counted, as shepe to the slaughter, the tyme shall come and even nowe it is at hande, when the righteous shall stande in great stedfastnes against suche as have delt extremely with them, and hath

taken away thyr labourers, when thei se it thei shal be vexed wyth
horryble feare, & shall wonder at the hastynes of so soden health
gronynge for very distres of mynde, and shal say within them selves,
these are they whiche sometime we had in derysyon, and jested
upon, we fooles thought theyr lyves very madnes, and theyr ende to
be without honour, but lo, how they are counted amonge the
chyldren of God And their porcion is amongees saintes.[92]

In the new order, those who have been among the poorest and most
despised, whose lives were perceived as madness and their end to be
without honor, will be recognized as the children of God, a sentiment
that harks back to the passage in 1 Corinthians with which this
chapter began.

Piers the plowman in Langland's poem represented the ideal
Christian who knew the way to truth. The earliest apocrypha use the
image of the plowman as ideal Christian but combine it with strong
anticlericalism and align the figure with Lollard issues, invoking the
authority of *Piers Plowman* itself. The reformers in the sixteenth
century saw in the plowman an antique figure who could lend
authority to their claims. And finally, in *I playne Piers*, the plowman
emerges as prophet and speaks for the poor.

I playne Piers presents an interesting variation on the theme of
"new learning": "Christ unto Peter his sinnes forgave, and Mari
Magdelyn prest never shreve, yet must we new doctryne learne, is
neither the old testament good, nor yet the new in Christes blod, but
we must fear lawes of oure owne making."[93] The new learning is here
equated with traditions of the church such as confession. The work
also rails against celibacy for priests, the burning of martyrs, and the
persecution of printers. It is primarily addressed to the clerical
orders, and most of its bitterness is directed toward them. The tract
closes on an exceedingly bitter note:

God save the kynge & speede the ploughe.

And send the prelates care ynoughe.

Ynoughe, ynoughe, ynoughe.[94]

The final apocryphal text composed in the sixteenth century was issued in the same year as *Piers Plowman*. It may even have been written by Robert Crowley, because it articulates concerns associated with him. In *Pyers the plowmans exhortation, unto the lordes, knightes and burgoysses of the Parlyamenthouse* (1550),[95] the rude rustic addresses Parliament to speak against enclosure and complains that, since the monastery lands were appropriated entirely by great landowners instead of common people, these lands no longer provide the poor with even the jobs they had under monasticism. The rich are attacked and the disastrous effects of unemployment are spelled out by Piers, the simple man. Though economic ills are the subject, Piers's rebuke is based on moral and biblical grounds:

> For these injuries that we do unto the poore members of Christ / we do unto him / sayth he. Therefore after such evident knowledge of the scripture: & after so manifest admonition by the preachers: what can folowe but the just vengeance of God: if reformation be not had. If youre Children hadde so much understanding to forsee the plage and vengeance of God / ready to be powred doune uppon the whole realme / for this cruell oppression of the pore which so frely is suffered here to reyne amongest us / wolde they not altogether knele uppon their knees with the teares running doune by their chekes / rufullye loking towardes you of the parlyament house/ and holding up their handes, desire you altogether with one voyce / that you with all diligence and hast possible would se to the reformacion hereof, that the dredefull wrath of God myght be spedely turned from them.[96]

Piers Plowman had criticized and called for reforms in society as well as in the church, but by now the figure of Piers himself had become exclusively identified with issues of religion by the Lollards and the later reformers. With the publication of *Pyers plowmans exhortation*, the figure is once more put to use for social causes. He is in fact asking that the Reformation spill over into the social and economic spheres, something that the next regime would not have regarded kindly.

The composing of major plowman texts ends with the *Pyers plowmans exhortation*. But there is one last and highly significant development in the tradition: the reprinting in 1590 of a portion of *I playne Piers* as a Marprelate tract.[97] Just as the reformers recast materials to advance the cause of Reformation, so in this instance an early Reformation work is recast to suit later ends. Any references that would have marked it as an earlier text are eliminated. For instance, references to burning martyrs are replaced by references to jailing them. The title page, by its additions to the old title, registers the significant aspects of the reprint:

Read me, for I am of great Antiquitie.

I plaine piers which

    can not flatter

A plouhman men me call

My speech is fowlle, yet marke the matter

How things may hap to fall,

But now another Ile have for me

    I think it as fit to say, if any my name do craave,

I am the Grandsier of martin marprelitte.

Compiled afore yeasterday, for the behoofe and over

-throw of all Parsons, Vikars, and Curats, who have

learned their Catechismes and can not yet understand

them, although they be past their grace.

    Newly corrected, you will say it was by a greene

head, but Ile tell thee true,

    My head is neither greene nor blew,

        You are deceived bum fay,

My head is either white or gray.

        So Beneado so

    Printed either of this side or of that

    side of some of the priestes.

The headnotes of the pages reflect how the figure of Piers is here being used; they read, alternately, "Read me for I am of great Antiquity" and "Read me for I am the annointed." Clearly, the figure of Piers as prophet and reformer has been enlisted in the extreme Puritan cause.

This work marks the end of the plowman tracts. The tradition had begun with the image of the plowman being used as an antique figure who saw the truth and could legitimize current criticisms of the Roman church; it ends with a similar manipulation of text and figure, and for similar reasons. But the object of the attack is now the English reformed church. Piers emerges at the end of the tradition as a scathing critic of a reformation that has not gone far enough.

The Cultural Effects of the Appropriation of Piers the Plowman

We have seen the issues that became attached to the figure of Piers the Plowman, but what implications for the society as a whole, as opposed to the reformers alone, emerged as a result of this appropriation of the figure? From a cultural perspective, the *Piers Plowman* apocrypha had considerable impact. Three specific cultural effects can be charted in the realms of class perceptions, religious symbolism, and spiritual empowerment.

The author of the *Bankett* written in response to *A godlye dyalogue* was not the only reader to use the figure of Piers while diverging from the tradition of the reformers. George Gascoigne, in *The Steele Glas*,[98] a satire on the estates, responds to the tradition by treating Piers favorably while dissenting from the idealization of plowmen as such. He begins by singling out Piers as a worthy representative of his class: "Therfore I say, stand forth *Peerce* plowman first, / Thou winst the roome, by verie worthinesse" (H2r). He then explains why Piers ranks first, beginning with a long disclaimer of any idealization of peasants:

Behold him (priests) & though he stink of sweat

Disdaine him not: for shal I tell you what?

Such clime to heaven, before the shaven crownes.

But how? forsooth, with true humilytie.

Not that they hoord, their grain when it is cheape,

Nor that they kill, the calfe to have the milke

. . . .

Nor for because, they can both crowche & creep

(The guilefulst men, that ever God yet made)

When as they meane, most mischiefe and deceite.

(H2r)

The reason turns out to be the importance of the plowman's role as the base on which society rests:

But for they feed, with frutes of their gret paines,

Both King and Knight, and priests in cloyster pent;

Therefore I say, that sooner some of them

Shal scale the walles which leade us up to heaven.

(H2v)

Gascoigne's ambivalent treatment of Piers documents the class hatred that had changed little from the days of John Gower. He recognizes the value of the symbol and articulates its importance in the religious sphere, but he is clearly separating religious iconography from what he perceives to be the reality of the lower classes.

The figure of the plowman remained a popular folk character associated with religious and political reform and with the aspirations of the lower classes, at least to the end of the seventeenth century. An indication of this is its presence in ballads and broadsides. Two examples of this genre can be found in the Bodleian Library. (It may be significant that one is printed in a kind of imitation black letter, suggesting antiquity.) The first, dated 1678, is called "The Plow-Mans Complaint, The Free-Holder's Proposition, And, The High-shoes Resolution."[99] It is an exhortation to Parliament to pass laws to strengthen the national defense, especially the navy, for protection against "Papist blood-hounds, Rogue and Whore," to pursue the Popish Plot, to reform the tax laws, and to repeal laws against Protestant dissenters:

> To Protestant Dissenters be kind, and do'em Right
>
> Repeal those Laws that now in Force against them Fight
>
> 'Gainst which there's none will be, but th'Ignorant-Clergie-Mite,
>
> Or he who is, or is to be a Romanite.

The choice of the plowman for a spokesman to Parliament when the issues have nothing to do with farming shows the persistence of the tradition in which the plowman represents social justice and the Protestant cause, including its more extreme wing. The other ballad, to be sung to the tune of "Cock Laurel, Or, The Country Miss," is called "The Plow-mans Prophesie, Or, The Country-mans Calculation."[100] It begins:

> By this you may perceive when it will be,
>
> None will be covetous, but all men free;
>
> When these things come to pass you'll find it plain,
>
> No Covetousness in England will remain.

After some twenty-four quatrains that list impossible conditions, ranging from men bearing children to lawyers pleading without fees and poets endowing free hospitals for the poor, the ballad ends:

> And when you do find all these things come to pass,
>
> Then do not you say the Plowman's an Ass;
>
> But you may conclude he hath very well sung,
>
> When Covetousness out of England is run.

Clearly, the reforming, prophesying plowman remained a live figure in popular culture in Bunyan's time.

But it is in the religious sphere that the adoption of the plowman as symbol has the greatest effect on the culture as a whole. A Lollard letter dated to the early fifteenth century by Foxe and printed in his *Acts and Monuments* may reflect the influence of Langland's plowman and his symbolic activity. It evokes the symbolic dimensions inherent in the plowing image:

Forasmuch as no man that putteth his hand to the plough and looketh backe is meete for the kingdome of God, as our Saviour Christ
saith: what marvell is it, although master Nicolas Hereford, which
at the first (by the visitation of the spirit of God peradventure) put
his hand, that is, gave his diligence unto the plough, that is, to the
sowing of the Word of God and holy Scripture, as well in preaching
as in doing good workes, is now so blind and unskillfull to expound
the Scripture, that hee knoweth not what is understood by the kingdome of heaven?[101]

As one aspect of the shift in emphasis in the use of the plowman
figure, the metaphor of plowing comes more consistently to mean
sowing the word of God, doing good work, and preaching and
expounding the Scriptures. This symbolic dimension is present in
Piers Plowman, in which Piers plows a symbolic half-acre, working
out his salvation. As a result of the plowman tradition, the figure of
the plowman is made into a religious image for a new kind of priest.
Hugh Latimer, in 1548, writes a sermon proclaiming that preachers
are plowmen. In "The sermon of the Plow," according to Robert
Kelly, Latimer places himself within the plowman tradition:[102]

I told you in my first sermon, honorable audience, that I purposed
to declare unto you two things: the one, what seed should be sown
in God's field, in God's plowland; and the other, who should be the
sowers, that is to say, what doctrine is to be taught in Christ's
church and congregation, and what men should be the teachers and
preachers of it. . . . And now I shall tell you who be the plowers, for
God's word is a seed to be sown in God's field, that is, the faithful
congregation, and the preacher is the sower. And it is in the Gospel:
Exivit qui seminat seminare semen suum, "He that soweth, the husbandman, the plowman, went forth to sow his seed" (Luke 8.5). So
that a preacher is resembled to a plowman; as it is in another place,
*Nemo admota aratro manu, et a tergo respiciens, aptus est regno
Dei*, "No man that putteth his hand to the plow and looketh back is

apt for the kingdom of God" (Luke 9.62). That is to say, let no preacher be negligent in doing his office.[103]

Catholic priests are shepherds; Protestant preachers are plowmen. The change in emphasis signals a more fundamental change in religious experience for the congregation.[104] The shepherd leads a flock and gives spiritual sustenance, the sacraments. But the plowman image and the activity of plowing signal an interior and individual action. Preachers are plowmen because they have dug for meaning in the Scriptures, as well as having planted the seeds of the gospel in individual souls.

This metaphoric exposition, with its shift in emphasis from the negative to the positive image of the plowman, persists into the seventeenth century. Book III of Benjamin Keach's *Tropologia, or, a Key to Open Scripture-Metaphors* is devoted, according to the title page, to "several of the most Frequent and Useful *Metaphors, Allegories,* and express *Similitudes* of the Old and New Testament." Keach compares professing the gospel with plowing in ten "particulars," a passage to which we will return in chapter 6. Keach's co-author, Thomas Delaune was responsible for Book I. The title page describes that book as concerned with "Sacred *Philology*, or the *Tropes* in Scripture, Reduc'd under their proper Heads, with a brief Explication of each."[105] It lists aspects of plowing and their metaphorical meanings with some comments on what it is about plowing that makes it an apt metaphor. We see Delaune's awareness of the violent nature of plowing as compared with the traditional metaphor of "sowing" the word. Plowing

is a preparation of the Field for Sowing; by which calamity and affliction is sometimes noted. . . . The reason is taken from the cutting or (as it were) wounding of the Field, by the Plow-share. . . . by the term plowing true Repentance, and the culture or dressing of piety is understood: The Reason is taken from the end and effect of plowing, which is to pluck and destroy Thorns, Bryers, and the Roots of bad Herbs, and rightly to dispose the Field to bear good fruit.[106]

A less obvious but striking use of the image emphasizes the importance of inward and individual experience. To plow "is properly to turn the divided Earth, so as that the inner or under part may be heav'd up to the superficies, or top; and metaphorically . . . denotes a search or thorough inquisition into secret or inward things."[107] The emphasis on laborious and sustained discipline of the mind is also clear: *This is the most arduous and chief business* (viz. *of my discipling and Gospel Preaching) that he which once enters into a profession, is concerned by continual care and study.* . . . This metaphor is taken from husbandmen, who are obliged to a continual and uninterrupted care and study, in tilling and plowing their Fields."[108]

Perhaps the strangest and, for our purposes, most revealing metaphorical use of the verb *to plow* is Bunyan's own in his "Apology" for *The Pilgrim's Progress*:

> For who knows how,
> Better then he that taught us first to Plow,
> To guide our Mind and Pens for his Design?
> (lines 184–86)

Only the tradition that had come to equate plowing with preaching and teaching could account for this usage. In the context, "he that taught us first to plow" is God. For the earlier reformers, this kind of plowing was an overtly public role. But for later Puritans, plowing is a more individual activity, as the Holy Scriptures direct the reader to find its meaning.

But these societal and religious consequences of appropriating the figure of Piers had a third major impact that included both spheres of experience. The stance and attitudes embodied in the figure did not disappear; they survived and were employed by the mechanick preachers of the seventeenth century. As Tindall notes, "Inspiration, example and opportunity united after 1640 to call tradesmen of all radical sects to the ministry of the word."[109] These mechanicks, like the writers of the apocryphal plowman texts, used the example of the apostles as justification for their preaching:

> These works of Satan's party gave voice with various emphasis to
> three objections to mechanicks: their want of ordination, their illit-

eracy, and their lowly social position. Concentrating upon these objections, the mechanicks and their friends met attack with attack: they assailed ordination as antichristian, they decried learning as an impediment to inspiration. and they made of social obscurity a virtue: for the Almighty, as Scripture affirms, had chosen not the proud and noble but the poor and low.[110]

The appeal to 1 Cor. 1.27–28 was of course a central tenet in the elevation of the plowman in the century before, and the plowman tradition must be counted among the factors contributing to the movement.

The best exponent of the tenets of the mechanick preaching movement was a learned man, William Dell, who was master of Gonville and Caius College in Cambridge during the Interregnum. Dell was castigated for his support of the movement, and his association with Bunyan himself was a factor in the upsurge of feeling against Dell. A petition for Dell's removal from his office states that "he hath declared in the public congregation that he had rather hear a plain countryman speak in the church, that came from the plough, than the best orthodox minister that was in the country; upon Christmas day last one Bunyan, a tinker, was countenanced and suffered to speak in his pulpit to the congregation, and no orthodox minister did officiate in the church that day."[111] Dell's acquaintance with Bunyan is highly significant. Dell's championship of the movement echoes the central positions taken by the reformers a century before in the plowman texts. Throughout his writings, the argument that we first saw put forth in those texts reappears: "For Antichrist could not deceive the world with a company of foolish, weak, ignorant, prophane, contemptible persons, but he always hath the Greatest, Wisest, Holiest, and most Eminent in the visible Church for Him, and by These he seduces and subjects to Himself, even the whole World."[112] These men are like the "Byshopes with their ragman rolle" in the preface to the *Praier and complaynte*; the mechanicks are like the "poor ydiotes" at the Crucifixion. Dell specifically attacked the validity of books. In the preface to the 1652 edition of his *Sermons*, he writes: "We are almost at the end of Books; these Paper Works are now preaching their own Funeral."[113] Like the reformers before him who pointed to Piers, Dell points to the mechanicks as evidence of the workings of God. Once again, the example of the Apostles was a presage to succeeding ages of how God was to choose his ministers: "Wherefore when Christ chose his ministers according to his Father's counsel, he chose not the wise and learned, but plain, simple men; that it might appear how infinitely able the unction of his Spirit alone is, without any addition of anything else, for the ministry of the New Testament."[114] The meanness and lowness of the mechanicks were evidence of their elect status as ministers of God. Dell, like Bunyan and others, must have seen in the apocryphal plowman texts a vindication of their position. In "A Testimony From the Word Against Divinity Degrees in the University," Dell selects a plowman tract to substantiate his thesis: "In Edward the Third's Time, there was an excellent discourse set forth, called the Plowman's Complaint, &c. which testifieth against the Divinity Degree in these words: 'Antichrist maketh Masters too many, who teach the people with their own teaching, and leave Gods teaching, which is needful, and hide it with quaint glosses from the mean people.'"[115]

Dell was not the only defender of mechanicks to cite this kind of evidence. In *The Poor Mechanick's Plea Against the Rich Clergy's Oppression*, J. B. Bockett uses evidence found in Foxe to buttress his discourse against tithes. As a mechanick, he includes the predictable disclaimer. "Although the Style therein may seem to some to be in a mean and plain Manner: But let such know, I am no learned *Academick*, but a poor Mechanick, and have endeavored to be intelligible unto all."[116] Bockett uses *Praier and complaynte*, along with such figures as Hus, Swynderby, Brute, and John Wyclif, to show that his case against the clergy is nothing new but has its roots centuries before: "And in the Prayer and Complaint of the *Plowman*, which is thought to be the said John Wickeliff's, 'tis said, 'But Lord there cometh hired Men, and they ne feeden not thy Sheep in thy plenteous Lesew, but feeden thy Sheep with Dreams, and false Miracles, and Tales, but at thy Truth they ne come not; for Lord I throw thou sendest them never.'"[117]

The tradition that had been embodied in the plowman texts of the fifteenth and sixteenth centuries was more alive than ever, though in a different form, in Bunyan's world of the seventeenth. Furthermore, those who spoke for the mechanick preacher movement were quite aware of the connection, to the point of citing not only Wyclif and other Lollards and reformers as part of their justification, but some of the plowman texts themselves. For all of them, the key to the connection lay in the very books that made up Bunyan's "least" but "best" library in prison, the Bible and Foxe. But there were other books that were accorded equal status by the Protestant reader. We must now turn to the Crowley edition of *Piers Plowman* to see how a Protestant reader reads.

4

The Holy Ghost Is the Author of Books

A Protestant Reader Reads *Piers Plowman*

> Loke not upon this book therfore, to talke of wonders paste or
> to come, but to emende thyne owne misse, which thou shalt
> fynd here moste charitably rebuked.
>
> Robert Crowley, preface to *The Vision of Pierce Plowman*

 Piers Plowman established itself in the consciousness of the
Renaissance for one reason: it was seen as part of the development that connected the fourteenth-century Lollard
movement with the emergence of an English Protestant church under
Henry VIII. *Piers Plowman* was originally printed as part of the plowman tradition surveyed in chapter 3 and played a role in legitimizing the
aims of the English reformers. Robert Crowley printed *Piers Plowman*
three times in 1550,[1] when restrictions on publishing Wycliffite material were lessened under Edward VI.[2] He included a synopsis of the
poem in the second and third editions. All three editions contain
marginal glosses, but each successive edition incorporates more notation. All these changes reflect a progressive attempt by Crowley to shed
more light on the text as he reads the poem according to the strategies
he learned as a member of a Protestant readership. Our focus here will
be on the editions of *Piers Plowman*, for they are a witness to the fact
that the transmission of texts must always involve interpretation.

Crowley's presention of the poem exercised a great influence on
subsequent attitudes. John King has stated that Crowley "kidnapped
this orthodox medieval demand for reform of monasticism and society,

converting it . . . into a powerful revolutionary attack against monasticism and the Roman Catholic hierarchy."[3] However, the word "kidnapped" defines our present readership, not the one I have been tracing. We have seen that earlier readers had in effect already "kidnapped" it by reading it in a way that was very different from our own. These Protestant readers used its major figure to articulate the need for reform, and what a later reader, Robert Crowley, saw when he approached the text was what he had been conditioned to see by the apocryphal plowman texts. Crowley certainly underscored those parts of *Piers Plowman* that applied to the issues of his own time. But he saw them in the text; he did not create them. For Crowley, the work was another "holy relique" that evoked the mantle of antiquity and legitimized the reformer's claims. In fact, he modernized and altered the text very little, so that modern editors accord his editions some textual authority.[4] Yet in spite of all his detailed knowledge of the text, Crowley misread (from our literary perspective) the action of the work in precisely the way suggested by the works that had preceded *Piers Plowman* into print.

A survey of all this material makes it clear that, for the Protestant reader, Langland's poem appeared as a quest for individual reformation unmediated by external assurances bestowed by the church. The text defines true pilgrimage as a quest for truth and pictures the human condition as suspended not between heaven and hell but between truth and falsehood. The quest for Do-Well, Do-Better, and Do-Best places in the foreground the ethical question of how to live in this world and still gain the next. Finally, "having" Piers Plowman is defined as reforming the self into the image of the ideal Christian who knows the way to Truth. Crowley's presentation of the poem throws these elements into relief. But he is seldom pointing to anything Langland himself did not say, however drastically he may shift the emphasis. The fact of the matter is that Langland is more radical and Crowley more conservative than has been appreciated, as the evidence of readers who saw the poem in manuscript, not in Crowley's edition, will make clear in chapter 5. Crowley was convinced, as he tells us in his preface, that though the poem was difficult, it was not inaccessible to readers like himself who were willing to make an effort: "the sence [is] somewhat darcke but not so harde, but that it may be understande of suche as will not sticke to breake the shell of the nutte for the kernelles sake" (°2v). In his edition he attempts to crack the shell enough that the reader can get to the kernel, but not so much as to make what seemed to him actual changes in the nut itself.

The Crowley rendition of the work made a difficult poem accessible to a Renaissance audience. The interpretive acts contained in the preface, synopsis, and marginal glosses direct a reading of the poem that has important implications for an understanding of Bunyan's agenda for *The Pilgrim's Progress* because it takes the contours of meaning for the Protestant readership into account. The first edition contained a preface and some marginal glosses. Crowley added to the second and third editions a synopsis of the poem, "A Briefe Summe of the principall poyntes that be spoken of in thys boke," and a greatly expanded set of marginal notations. Each edition included a new typesetting, correction of errors, and further "emendation."[5] Crowley modernized the text to make it easier for a contemporary reader by employing sixteenth-century standards of usage and orthography, changing the syntax of many lines to introduce the modern subject-verb-object word order, and modernizing Middle English verbs and pronouns.[6] On the other hand, Crowley introduced only a very small number of substantive alterations in the text. For instance, he substituted the name of Christ for Mary in one passage, omitted a reference to transubstantiation in another, and altered a reference to the doctrine of purgatory at another point. His most significant alteration was the omission of a thirteen-line passage in praise of the monastic ideal.[7] The book's printing history testifies to the poem's popularity in 1550; the expansion of the editorial apparatus bears witness to Crowley's progressive effort to illuminate the poem's meanings for the reader. Our concern in this chapter is not with Crowley's text in the strict sense but with the implications of the preface, summary, and glosses through which he transmitted his interpretation to his readers.

The Preface

In "The Printer to the Reader,"[8] Crowley sets out what he knows about the author and discusses his own motives for putting the work into print. He calls it a "most worthy worke" and describes how he went about his research, gathering as many manuscripts as he could find and consulting with others who were familiar with the study of antiquities: "And by some of them I have learned that the Autour was named Roberte langlande, a Shropshere man borne in Cleybirie, aboute viii myles from Malverne hilles" (°2v). He then recounts the deductions by which he discovered that the poem was written about two hundred years before (1350) during the reign of Edward III. Up to this point Crowley has presented himself, from our perspective, as a literary historian carefully collecting information.

Having established his credentials as an authority on the text, Crowley introduces a Protestant reader's assessment of how the text should be read in terms of history. Citing the reign in which the work emerged, he claims that in that period:

> it pleased God to open the eyes of many to se hys truth, geving them boldenes of herte, to open their mouthes and crye oute agaynste the worckes of darckenes, as did John Wicklefe, who also in those dayes translated the holye Bible into the Englishe tonge, and this writer who in reportynge certaine visions and dreames, that he fayned hym selfe to have dreamed: doeth moste christianlye en-struct the weake, and sharply rebuke the obstinate blynde. There is no maner of vice, that reigneth in anye estate of men; whiche this wryter hath not godly, learnedlye, and wittilye rebuked. (°2r)

Crowley does not proclaim that the text is a "holy relique" as the author of the preface to *Praier and complaynte* does, but by invoking antiquity Crowley seeks to invest the text with greater meaning for his own time. He shifts the focus from literary antiquarianism to the issues of the day, the break with Rome and the overthrow of monasticism. God is portrayed as intervening at a specific time to open the eyes of some to see his truth; he gives them boldness of heart to speak out against the corruptions of society and religion. John Wyclif and the writer of *Piers Plowman* are the men who were moved by God to speak out.

More importantly, Crowley sets side by side as related events Wyclif's translation of the Scriptures into English and Langland's writing of *Piers Plowman*. Linking Langland with Wyclif and juxta-posing the translation of Scripture with the composition of *Piers Plowman* makes the context into which Crowley is placing Langland's work unmistakable. For Crowley, *Piers Plowman* is not a literary product but a religious exhortation for the reform of the individual and society. He views the text as having quasi-biblical authority because of its prophetic character; *Piers Plowman* furthered the cause of reform just as the translation of the Bible into English had done. Crowley's focus on Langland as an author who reported "certaine visions and dreames, that he fayned hym selfe to have dreamed" demonstrates that he understood Langland's adoption of the dream-vision form as a means of crying out "agaynst the worckes of darckenes" by veiling his criticisms in an allegorical form. He considers the work not a decoratively crafted product but rather a persuasive exhortation designed to instruct the weak and rebuke the blind. As Crowley perceived it, Langland's purpose was to rebuke all manner of vice "godly, learnedlye, and wittilye." Thus the poem, for Crowley and his first readers, was a document demonstrating that their claims for reform were not "new learning" but part of antiquity and therefore legitimate. Wyclif and Langland were forerunners of the struggle that was still being played out in Crowley's and his readers' own time, and they were therefore to be seen as Christian heroes who had made possible what had recently taken place, the break with Rome and the overthrow of monasticism.

But Crowley does not print *Piers Plowman* simply as evidence of the antiquity of the English reformer's claims. After talking about the meter of the poem in ways that demonstrate his understanding of alliterative verse,[9] he goes on to discuss features such as its allegorical mode, as in the passage quoted above. There he evokes a traditional conception used to define allegory; the shell is the literal level, the kernel, its allegorical meaning. For Crowley, the poem's difficulty is not a limitation but part of its function, and he challenges the reader to search out the poem's true subject, the corruption of the times.

Crowley then turns to the work's prophetic cast, calling the reader's attention to illustrative passages. Significantly, he rejects as inauthentic the prophecy of passus 6, the foretelling of a famine, because "diverse copies have it diverselye," citing two examples. However, he does not reject but rather underscores the prophecy of the suppression of the abbeys in passus 10: "Nowe for that whiche is written in the. l. leafe, concerning the suppression of Abbaies: the Scripture there alledged, declareth it to be gathered of the juste judgement of god, whoe wyll not suffer abomination to raigne unpunished" (°2v). Crowley's criteria are significant. In addition to his judicious use of manuscript evidence, he considers this passage a prophecy not only because it has come to pass but because the passage from Scripture that Langland cites (the Nineteenth Psalm) can be said to foretell the same events. In Crowley's eyes, the fact that Langland has used Scripture to substantiate his meaning reinforces the seriousness of the work. Scripture and the direction and content of the work are seen to be in agreement.

Having demonstrated the prophetic character of Langland's work, Crowley then turns to the uses to which the reader might put it. It is noteworthy that at this point he subordinates the prophetic aspect of *Piers Plowman* to the didactic and asks readers to look to their own lives and behavior when approaching this book: "Loke not upon this boke therfore, to talke of wonders paste or to come, but to amende thyne owne misse, which thou shalt fynd here moste charitably rebuked. The spirite of god gyve the grace to walke in the waye of truthe, to Gods glory, & thyne owne soules healthe. So beit" (°2v). So while Crowley clearly identifies Langland as a figure analogous to Wyclif and presents the work as "Tudor prophecy" (in John King's terms) he also demands above all that readers use the book to amend their own lives. Thus the poem is not simply printed to legitimize the goals of English reformers but has a meaning that transcends its historical context. That meaning is in no way invalidated by a recognition that the dreams it records are "fayned." Similarly, at the close of the "Apology," Bunyan directs readers to look at their own lives and defines the readers' responsibilities in reading the text.

No less important in reconstructing what the Protestant reader encountered in the printed edition of the text was Crowley's selection of a title. Crowley called the work *The Vision of Pierce Plowman*, a somewhat ambiguous formula. It suggests that Crowley made no differentiation between the dreamer and the figure the dreamer sees in various sections of the text. This notion about Crowley is confirmed by other evidence. When we turn to his synopsis of the text for passus 8, directly after the Visio, we find "It declareth howe Pierce went to seke Dowel, How he reproveth the fryers for saying that dowel dwelte wyth them," and he closes by describing Thought as one "Of whom Pierce desiered to learne what Dowel, Dobet, and Dobest were" (°5r and °5v). This is clear evidence that from our perspective Crowley misread the text, for it is the dreamer, not Piers, who goes in search of Dowel, Dobet, and Dobest. This conflation of the dreamer and Piers accounts for the title identifying the vision with Piers rather than with its author or narrator. But how could an editor who knows the poem as well as Crowley does, and whose synopsis and glossing show him to be an astute observer in most respects, fall into so obvious a misreading? The answer is that he was not misreading, given his horizon of expectations about the text and his understanding of how the work was to be read.

The confusion between the dreamer-narrator and the figure of Piers is a direct result of the impact of the apocryphal plowman texts surveyed in the previous chapter. Those texts, working from Langland's poem, combined the figure of the plowman with the biting invective of the dreamer-narrator who criticized religious abuses and society as a whole. By 1550, the image of Piers had developed several aspects beyond Langland's representation of the rude, plain man who knows the way to Truth. Piers had become throughout the poem what Langland's Piers becomes only in the final passus, a scathing critic of religious abuses and a prophet as well as a potential aspect of every Christian. As a result, when Crowley turned to the text, he assumed a relationship between the dreamer and Piers very different from our own ideas. This view is not entirely wrong in its assumption that a relationship of complementarity and would-be identification exists between the two, as Judith Anderson has pointed out.[10]

The presentation of Chaucer's works in the Renaissance provides a contrasting model by which to assess the context in which Langland's poem is placed. Thynne's edition of Chaucer's works in 1532 contains a preface written by Brian Tuke and addressed to the king, whereas Crowley addresses his remarks to the reader. The Chaucer preface begins solemnly with a history of languages and describes the author's devotion to Chaucer and his search for authentic texts. The writer of the preface claims that Chaucer's works are being presented as "so precious and necessary an ornament of the tonge of this your realme." The view of Chaucer presented in this preface is exclusively literary:

The bokes of that noble and famous clerke Geffray Chaucer / in whose workes is so manyfest comprabacion of his excellent lernying in all kyndes of doctrynes and sciences / such frutefulnesse in wordes / wel accordynge to the mater and purpose / so sweet and pleasaunt sentences / such perfectyon in metre / the composycion so adapted / such freshnesse of invencion / comendyousnesse in narration / suche sensyble and open style / lackyng neither majeste ne mediocrite convenable in disposycion / and such sharpness or quicknesse in conclusyon / that it is moch to be marvyled / howe in hys tyme / whan doubtlesse all good letters were layd aslepe throughout the worlde / as the thynge which either by the disposycion and influence of the bodies above / or by other ordynaunce of God / semed lyke and was in daunger to have utterly peryshed / such an excellent poete in our tonge / shulde as it were (nature repugnyng) spryng and "aryse."[11]

Set against Crowley's "Printer to the Reader," this preface helps to define the very different presentation accorded a literary production. Crowley everywhere asserts that the poem he is setting into print has historicity, that its author is a religious figure, and that the poem has a direct meaning and relevance for his time. The Chaucer preface, on the other hand, clearly defines its role as bringing a man of letters the stature and attention he deserves. The Thynne edition of Chaucer's works is also decorated with woodcuts, whereas Crowley decorates his text with marginal notes designed to emphasize the immediacy of Langland's meaning. Chaucer is being presented in the Thynne edition in an artistic and literary context; Crowley presents Langland in a prophetic and historical one.[12] Finally, the quotation above focuses on Chaucer's works as objects to be admired; Crowley's preface presents *Piers Plowman* as an exhortation, not an object of study.[13]

Crowley's Synopsis and Glosses

Important though Crowley's preface is (and, as we will see, its influence on Renaissance readings of the poem can be nothing less than decisive), his more detailed annotations are the element of his edition that directly affected his readers' progress through the poem. His passus-by-passus summary of the action shows, much more decisively than the preface, how he actually perceived the poem.

What he implies about the proper perception of the poem and what he passes over in silence are as crucial as what he actually says. Similarly, his emphases in the marginal notes offer the best test of what the generalizations in the preface really meant to him in practice.

Before we examine these aspects of his editions, we must consider what Crowley's role in the English reform movement tells us about his interest in the poem. Crowley's controversial works, especially *The Voyce of the Last Trumpet . . . calling al estats of men to the right path of their vocation*,[14] published in the same year as *Piers Plowman*, shows that he was a militant, millenarian Protestant, so much so that he was obliged to seek asylum in Frankfort on the accession of Queen Mary. An understanding of his role in the English Reformation, as John King has demonstrated,[15] is invaluable for the light it sheds on his motives for resurrecting *Piers Plowman*; without it, the phenomenon of the edition would remain a historical anomaly. King's thesis is that Crowley deliberately transformed *Piers Plowman* into something alien to Langland's concerns, a text prophesying the Protestant millennium of the sixteenth century.[16] King asserts that the Crowley glosses, especially toward the end of the work, directed his readers to see the poem as predicting that the Second Coming was at hand and put forth Edward VI as "the just and pious Christian ruler who is to precede the Second Coming of Christ."[17] King's view that Langland did not intend the kind of reading Crowley brought to *Piers Plowman* is, of course, correct in terms of literary history.[18] But in terms of the Protestant history of reading, it may be more correct to suggest that in his editions of the poem Crowley merely emphasized those characteristics actually present in it that a specific way of reading had conditioned him to look for.

Certainly Crowley held millenarian views and expressed them elsewhere, and his preface shows that he associated Langland with Wyclif and presented the text as a prophecy of the English Reformation. But did he also exploit the poem's apocalyptic vision to suggest future events, to promote the idea that the millennium was at hand? Surprisingly enough—in view of Crowley's radical position in other respects—the central emphasis of his apparatus is ethical, directed toward the personal reformation of the individual reader. Crowley's preface emphasizes that Langland instructs the weak and rebukes the blind; Crowley does not say that he prophesies the Second

Coming. Where he does talk about prophecy he restricts himself solely to the "prophecy" concerning the suppression of abbeys and feels it necessary to justify even that by appealing to Scripture. Crowley sees *Piers Plowman* as a way to legitimize what has come to pass; he is less concerned with what will come. Indeed, he closes his preface with an admonition against seeing the work primarily as prophecy: "Loke not upon this boke therfore, to talke of wonders paste or to come but to emend thyne owne misse, which thou shalt fynd here moste charitably rebuked." Crowley's warning underscores what he feels is important about the work: not its prophetic character but its ability to instruct and rebuke, bringing about the individual reformation of the reader. His understanding of the value and use of *Piers Plowman* can be understood only in the context of the Protestant readership that we have been exploring.

The bulk of the marginal glosses either encapsulate (correctly) the moral of a given passage or provide an index to the action. Comments that might seem to reflect an apocalyptic perspective actually reflect the radical elements already present in Langland's poem. For example, in passus 15 where Anima issues a warning that reform must take place, Crowley records in the margin "How covetise of the cleargy will destroy the church" (Y1r). Outside the context of the passage, the comment may seem to be radical. But the passage to which Crowley's comment applies shows that his note is totally appropriate to it:

> For covetise after crosse, the crowne standes in golde
>
> Both rych and religious, that rode they honour
>
> That in grotes is graven, and in golde nobles
>
> For covetous of that crosse, men of holy kyrke
>
> Shall turne as templers did, the time approcheth nere
>
> Wyt ye not ye wyse men, how tho men honoured
>
> More treasure than trouth.
>
> (Y1r)

Crowley's gloss is a literal summary of the passage, where Langland himself uses the future tense. Crowley's comment certainly reflects the fact that he is responding to and glossing those parts of the poem

that speak immediately to him, and his other works make clear why
they did so. But he is not forcing a reading of the poem that is not
immanent. His glosses do not subvert the text but shed light on it
from the perspective of a Protestant readership. They represent his
attempt to index Langland's argument for his readers.

In general, Crowley is cautious in his treatment of the prophetic
elements in the poem. For example, he singles out as important
Conscience's vision in passus 3 of a Utopian future:

And kinde love shal come yet, and conscience togyther

And make of lawe a labourer, such love shal arise

And such a peace amonge the people, & a perfit truth

The Jewes shal wene in their wit, & waxe wonders glad.

(D4r-v)

But he is at pains to point out that any prophecy in the passage is a
prophecy already present in the Bible and reflects no special prophetic insight on the part of the poet: "Thys is no prophecy but a
resonable gathering" and "Thys is no prophecye—but a truth gathered out of scriptures" (D4r-v). Crowley is generally quite accurate,
if somewhat selective, in indexing the actual statements made in a
poem whose balance between orthodox theology and radical, even
millenarian hopes for reform has always been hard to assess. Only
occasionally does Crowley go outside the terms Langland himself
suggests. For example, when Lady Mede is confessing to a friar, she is
given no penance because she bribes him; Crowley comments, "The
fruites of popish penaunce" (C4v). This is clearly anachronistic, since
Langland is certainly not attacking the Catholic practice of confession as such, as the term "popish penance" suggests. But even this is
not as great a distortion of the text as it first appears. Langland is
objecting to many of the problems that would eventually lead the
reformers to reject auricular confession. As a Protestant reader,
Crowley believes, like Lollard readers before him, that texts are
evidence provided by God to support their understanding of the
right way to salvation in terms of reforming the church.

However traditional Langland's theology may be and however
common critiques of abuses in the church were in the fourteenth

century, Langland himself is a millenarian. Indeed, he ends his poem with an apocalytic vision of Antichrist.[19] Langland himself inveighs against the abuses of the church and deplores the effects on the ordinary Christian of many Catholic practices, the very practices Crowley saw threatening to continue in the Anglican church. Even in his synopsis of the poem, he does not put the action in a more radical frame of reference than Langland. He does translate Langland's concerns into Reformation terms, but with considerable restraint. Whatever may be true of Crowley's other writings, his apparatus for *Piers Plowman* does not use any of the prophetic exhortations or direct contemporary applications attributed to him by King. If Crowley printed the poem as a "Tudor prophecy," he did so by allowing the work to stand on its own terms. No millenarian readings can be found in the critical apparatus, and it is doubtful that he could have published the work if he had included any.

This can most clearly be seen in Crowley's synopsis of the last passus, in which the coming of Antichrist is portrayed, where we would most expect to find millenarian commentary. Here Crowley summarizes Langland's action in terms that remain firmly didactic and downplay any direct historical application except to the past (note the shift to the past tense where specific abuses are concerned):

It declareth what a manne may do when nede compelleth hym, That temperaunce is the chiefe vertue, who receyved Antichrist fyrst, How Antichrist doth seduce many good men, The manner of gods visitation The maner of men whan plages cease That covetise and simony make prelats, That Life & fortune beget Slouth, That Slouth marieth dispaire, That Age killeth both phisitian & surgion, That Nature wolde have us to love, That the .vii. capital sinnes besieged Conscience. The answere of an Irysh prieste, That Curates ought to have a compotent livinge certaine That friers have no numbre, That such as went to the fryers to shrift, be like saintuary men, That Hypocrisy woundeth many prechers, The negligence of patrons and bishops. And what penaunce gostly fathers were wont to enjoye [enjoyne?] their gostly children. Finis. (*8r)

Much of the language merely uses Langland's own terms. The statement "That Hypocrisy woundeth many prechers," which occurs in the synopsis and stands as a marginal notation next to the passage it refers to, merely indexes Langland's terms and summarizes the author's meaning:

> Hypocrisy and he an harde assaute they made
>
> Hipocrisy at gate hard gan to feight,
>
> And wounded well wickedlye many a wyse teacher.
>
> (Ff4r)

Thus, despite his millenarian tendencies, Crowley does not subvert the text into a prophecy of the millennium at hand. He nowhere attempts, in the preface, synopsis, or marginalia, to give the apocalyptic vision of the poem a contemporary historical application.[20] Crowley does not shape the text into reformist propaganda, though he does provide an excellent seismograph for assessing the poem's impact on a Protestant reader.

Crowley's belief in *Piers Plowman* as a prophecy fulfilled in his own time led him to call attention in the margins of the first edition to the clerical abuses of an earlier age. This concern, however, becomes more muted in the second and third editions. The marginalia increasingly direct readers to look to their own lives and situations more closely. Crowley's attention shifts from a description of past abuses to warnings about present ones. For instance, in passus 10, Wit is speaking about the wrong use of tithes and is contemplating an age when that abuse will be eliminated: "Sholde no chrysten creature crie at the gate / Ne fayle payne ne potage & prelats dyd as they shuld" (L3r). In the first edition, Crowley's marginal gloss on that passage transmits his radical interpretation of Langland's attack on abuses: "against priests." In the second and third editions, that comment is replaced by two others that are directed more explicitly to his reader's own time. The first occurs when Wit claims that Holy Church should support the helpless: "I finde that holie churche / Shulde fynde hem that faute and fatherles children" (L2v). Crowley comments: "Wo be to you that tarn the tithes to private use." Next to the passage quoted above, in place of "agaynste priestes" we find "Bestowe youre tythes as you are bounde to do." In this passage,

Crowley's attention has clearly shifted from the text's illumination of an earlier age to the poem's ability to rebuke his own time.

The second edition, with its addition of a synopsis and greatly expanded marginal notes, is as a whole a witness to that change. In the first edition, the marginal notes had been scarce and stopped altogether after the beginning of passus 11. They stood largely as an index to the poem's action. For instance, in the first passus, where Holy Church lectures the dreamer, the marginal notes index what is under discussion: "the tour," "the dungeon," "Judas," "David made Knightes," "Lucifer was caste out of heaven because of hys pride," and "Truth is the greatest treasure." In the second edition, while many of the marginal notes remain the same, there is a significant addition. Langland's Latin scriptural passages are identified in the marginal notes so that the reader who reads no Latin can look them up. Identifying scriptural passages also underscores the religious and ethical significance of the text. Similarly, Crowley's "Briefe Summe of the principall poyntes that be spoken of in thys boke" represents a major change in his approach to the work. The poem was not just a record of antiquity but a tract whose points had to be brought out for the reader.

This synopsis is of great interest in itself and is an instance of practical criticism in action. It stands in marked contrast with Crowley's initial focus on the writer in his "The Printer to the Reader," which spoke of the author and his method of feigning dreams and stressed the prophetic character of the work. The summary, in contrast, does not mention the feigned dreams or single out the author as the deliverer of the vision or underscore the prophetic element. Rather the synopsis for the most part sets out the "poyntes," the doctrine engaged by the text.

The synopsis to passus 1 epitomizes the function of Crowley's summaries:

> And in the person of a woman whom it calleth holy church: it open-
> eth the meanynge of the Turret mentioned in the fyrst leafe, Com-
> mandeth measure in all thyngs. Forbiddeth excesse by the example
> of Loth, Wylleth all men to pay tribute to their princes, and labour
> diligently for their living, Expoundeth the meanynge of the dun-
> geon, Declareth truth to be the best treasure, Prayseth charitie,

Telleth knightes office, Telleth Lucifers fal, Exhorteth men to love and do as they wold be done by, Declareth that worckes muste sprynge out of our fayeth: and that if wee be liberall to the pore, God wyll be liberal to us. (°3v)

The summary of passus 1 ignores the interplay between the dreamer and Holy Church and reduces the passus to a series of ethical commands. Crowley underscores the role of the personification— "in the person of a woman whom it calleth holy church"—as a means of articulating doctrinal, ethical issues. More importantly, the focus is no longer on the author but the book. It opens and commands; it has evolved an independent existence of its own, apart from its author's historical witness of an earlier time. When Crowley refers to the work as "it," he confers on the text a status and authority independent of its author, almost analogous to the independence of Scripture from the particular human authors used by God to write it. Such a view, of course, is one of the defining characteristics of the Protestant readership. In singling out "poyntes" that are spoken of in the book, Crowley invites the reader to see the text as a religious tract exhorting reform of both the society and the individual.

The summaries for each passus undercut and obscure the literary dynamics of the fictional setting. Crowley's synopsis of the prologue ignores the figure of the dreamer entirely in recounting his initial dream of the tower of truth, the dungeon of falsehood, and the fair field of folk in between. His synopsis of that passage is as follows: "The vision begynneth the fyrste leafe, and continueth to the fourth, declaryng fyrste the diverse studies that menne folowe. Some gyve them selves to tyllage. Some to be gallant Some to contemplation and straighte lyfe, Some to solitary lyfe, some to Marchaundice and all kynd of biynge and sellinge, Some to jesting, Some to beggyng, Some to wandryng, as Pilgryme, Hermets, Fryers, and Pardoners" (°3r). The visual impact of that initial scene and its use of the dreamer's perspective are absent from the summary. The very existence of the dream frame is ignored. Instead, Crowley substitutes what the "vision" declares. Langland's diatribe against religious abuses, with its vivid figure of the pardoner, is translated by Crowley in the same way: "Than it declareth the great wyckednes of the byshoppes, that spareth not to hange their seales at every Pardoners proxes, and what shameful Simony reigneth in the church" (°3r). The coronation procession in which the king sets up law is also abstracted in a similar fashion: "Nexte it declareth some what of the powre and office of Kinges and Princes, and than secretly in latine verses it rebuketh their cruelnes and tyranny" (°3r). The justly famous "Rat Parliament" episode is described as a parable that rebukes "the foly of the commune people" and "lamenteth the state of that realme, wherein the kinge is childishe." At this point, Langland's vision leaves the field and returns to the dreamer and his thoughts. But the summary does not acknowledge the shift at all. Instead, Crowley merely abstracts the moral of the passage: "Finally it rebuketh the fautes of men of lawe, and Byshoppes, Barons, and Burgeses, and to conclude of all artificers, And this parte is as an argument to the whole boke" (°3r). Crowley's summation of the prologue to *Piers Plowman* makes it clear that he was a good enough reader to see that the prologue is an "argument" and that it analyzes and judges society while calling for its reform. But he takes little notice of the literal level of the poem, assuming that it can be easily reduced into a series of "poyntes." In general, as a Protestant reader, his mind seems to function at a level so detached from the actual drama of the poem that he can be seen to moralize or allegorize even where the poem does not, or even where Langland's own apparent concern runs in quite a different direction from the particular piece of edification Crowley manages to extract from a given passage.

The Impact of Crowley's Presentation

The effect of all these highlightings and explanations is much greater than the sum of the parts and must be looked at as a whole if we are to understand the course of subsequent discussion of *Piers Plowman*. What sort of work does the poem, as packaged by Crowley, become in the eyes of its Renaissance readership? Out of the many issues addressed in the poem, Crowley seizes on those that he considers the most significant, identifying (for the most part correctly) the religious abuses Langland focused on, precisely because they are the very ones that pushed the Reformation into being. First and foremost, Crowley seems to have presented for his readers a view of the poem as a whole as being against the Catholic institution of pilgrimage and in favor of a form of religious life for which a transformed conception of pilgrimage can be a successful metaphor. At two points in the marginal notes Crowley defines "true pilgrimage." He labels the point in passus 5 where Reason proposes a journey to Saint Truth as true pilgrimage: "And ye that seketh saint James, & saintes at Rome / Seke saynt truth, for he may save you all" (F1r). The same phrase occurs again in passus 15 where Charity is described as going on pilgrimage:

And other whyle he is wonne to wend on pilgrymage

There pore men & prisoners ligged, her pardon to have

Though he bear hem no bread, he bear sweter livelod.

(T4r)

Crowley's marginal note at this point in the text indexes the action: "going on pilgrimage." The journey to Truth and the picturing of Charity's action as one of pilgrimage define for Crowley the correct reading of the concept of pilgrimage. Crowley's definition and transformation of the image is of great significance for its use by later writers.

There are three distinct kinds of pilgrimage built into the structure of *Piers Plowman*. All three implicitly ridicule the institution of going on pilgrimage. The first, of course, is the idea of seeking Saint Truth as the only hope of salvation. The poem as a whole can be seen as the record of a mind in quest of that truth. And this conception of pilgrimage militates against the idea of miracles and intercession by the saints and calls for an examination of the self. The second kind of pilgrimage is the search for Do-well, Do-Better, and Do-Best; being on pilgrimage is defined in ethical, behavioral terms. The third kind is the search for Piers himself, announced at the end of the poem.

We first see Piers at the close of passus 5, where he claims to know the way to Truth and sets forth a landscape made out of the Ten Commandments. Piers promises the people that he will lead them to Truth if they help him plow his half-acre. In passus 7 he receives a pardon from Truth and tears it in half, vowing "Of praiers & of penaunce, my plowe shal be hereafter" (K2r). Piers disappears after passus 7 and does not reappear until passus 16, where he is seen caring for the tree of Charity. In passus 19 the Crucifixion is portrayed through the image of Christ jousting in Piers's armour. Finally, at the close of the poem, Conscience sets out to look for Piers:

> By Christ quod Conscience tho, I wol become a pilgrime
>
> And walken as wyde as the world lasteth
>
> To seke Pierce the plowman, that pride may destroy
>
> And that fryers had a finding, that for no nede flatteren
>
> And contrepledeth me Conscience, now kind me aueng
>
> And send me hap & heale, til I have Piers the plowman
>
> And syth he grad after grace til, I gan awake.
>
> (Gg1r–v)

The plowman figure has developed over the course of the poem so that at the end Piers has become a metaphorical condition. Conscience wants to "have" Piers Plowman, and thus he wishes to become him.

If we assume this pattern to be correct, one of the structural features of the poem is the developing image of Piers and a concurrent development in the other characters' relationship to him. If so, it becomes important to try to imagine what Protestant readers thought when they began — as Crowley's summary of passus 8 tells them to do (and, as we will see, as subsequent Renaissance readers did) — with the assumption that Piers *was* the dreamer. For such a reader, the poem becomes a spiritual record written by a visionary about his own spiritual growth. This scenario, though wrong-headed, becomes credible if we remember that it is Conscience, not the dreamer, who announces at the end that he will seek Piers. If the reader were taking the literal action at all seriously, these final lines must have been seen as Piers himself waking, having seen Conscience vow to take him as a model of what Conscience wishes to become. No contemporary commentary demonstrates that readers did arrive at this conclusion about the ending. But as we will see in the next chapter, there are marginalia demonstrating similar interpretations of other passages. In any case, the general tendency of Protestant readers to allegorize all sorts of texts in terms of Reformation history would make it the most natural thing for a reader to worry less about the literal relationship between characters and more about the possible significance of the action, taking the complementary roles of different speakers for granted. But by whatever means they arrived at their view, they may have seen *Piers Plowman* as structured around the connection between a narrator-pilgrim and the idealized plowman whose gradual transformation into a model Christian he observes. We must assume that the Renaissance reader either had no sense at all of the literal action of the poem, or saw it in this way.

Like *The Pilgrim's Progress*, *Piers Plowman* depicts the state of Christians in this world and attempts to chart a way to heaven. Both works ask the question "What shall I do to be saved?" But in *Piers Plowman* we essentially never get out of Interpreter's House. The way to Truth in Langland's poem has two aspects: first a journey into what can be known, involving Thought, Wit, Study, Clergy, Nature, Reason, and finally Imagination, which takes up the middle portion of the book; and secondly the recreation of Old and New Testament history, which dominates the last part of the book. *Piers Plowman* attempts to educate the reader in spiritual truths. At the close of the poem, Conscience and we as readers have seen what we must become: Piers. But the poem stops there. There has been no attempt to move outside, from education to the world. In *The Pilgrim's Progress*, however, Christian leaves Interpreter's House having been initiated into spiritual truths. Bunyan's text moves from initiation to action as he portrays Christian's route back into the world.

Both works, however, put forward the thesis that Christians must work out their own salvation. At least, Crowley's reading of the pardon scene demonstrates that he believed that to be the scene's meaning.[21] In passus 7, Truth sends Piers a pardon that states that those who do well will go to eternal life, while those who do evil will burn in eternal fire. A priest looking over Piers's shoulder proclaims that it is not a pardon at all. At that point Piers "for pure tene" tears the pardon in half. Is it a pardon or not? The pardon scene has generated more critical argument than any other passage in the poem; yet Crowley seems confident that the meaning is clear. He glosses the pardon itself in the margin as coming from Matthew, chapter 25, where Christ sits in judgment and sends the sinner either to eternal life or eternal fire. Significantly, Crowley cites a general biblical source rather than the precise source of the words themselves, which is the Athanasian Creed. Crowley feels that the plot needs no further explanation. Indeed, later in the passage, when the priest chides Piers about his presumption in claiming to know Scripture, Crowley labels the passage "A blinde priestes taunt." The priest is blind because he neither recognizes the pardon nor realizes that the plowman, poor and unlettered as he may be, can and does understand Scripture.

The dreamer's ambivalent reflections on the pardon scene are similarly cast into Protestant terms by Crowley as he accents whatever in the passage fits with his interpretation of the poem. Langland's dreamer is openly confused by the pardon scene; he is torn between seeing pardon as the reward for doing well and seeking pardon from the institution of the church:

And how do wel at the day of dome, is dignly underfoungen

And passeth al the pardon of s. Peters church

Now hath the Pope power pardon to graunt the puple

Without any penaunce to passe into heven,

This is our beleve, as lettered men do us teach.

(K4r)

Crowley discounts the dreamer's confusion, believing the narrator to be Piers, and assumes that the reference to "our beleve" is meant satirically: "Note how he scorneth the autority of Popes." Crowley must have seen this passage as suggesting a new order where Do-Well will surpass the power of Rome that is current before the Reformation: "Now hath the Pope power . . ." At the close of the Visio, the dreamer concludes that all the pardons in the world will not help the sinner if Do-well does not speak on his behalf. He ends with a prayer:

That god give us grace here, or we go hence

Suche worckes to worcke, while we be here,

That after our deathes day, do wel rehearse

At the day of dome, we dyd as he hyght.

(K3v)

The dreamer asks for grace to do good works so that having done well he may enter heaven. Crowley's translation of this scene in the synopsis seems to reverse Langland's relative valuation of faith and works by taking Langland's reference to grace in Reformation terms, thus focusing the scene on a major Reformation issue: "And to truste for salvation in workes, is but a vayne thing" (°5r). Crowley rephrases Langland's rebuke against religious abuses in Reformation terminology and here aligns Langland's call for "grace . . . Such worckes to worcke" with the Reformation dictum of salvation by faith, not works.

This easy shift from literal scene to Reformation perspective can be readily seen in Crowley's summary of the Lady Mede episodes. When Holy Church in passus 2 shows the dreamer Lady Mede, Crowley's synopsis of the passus strikes an even balance between plot summary and abstracted meaning:

> And styll under the name of holy church [the second part] openeth abuses, And fyrste it describeth Mede, and declareth hyr progenye. Telleth how she is maryed unto false, Reherseth the charter graunted to that mariage, Telleth how the true preacher rebukith this mariage, Telleth howe Mede worcketh by brybes, Describeth the trayne that Mede rydeth wythall towardes Westmynster, Howe Trueth ranne before secretely, & tolde the kinge of all, Howe false fleede for feare: and how he was receyved and entertained of marchauntes and many other sortes of men. (°3v)

Crowley again calls attention to the use of the personification ("under the name of holy church"). More importantly, he sees the scene's whole reason for being as a means to open abuses. While the synopsis is faithful to the plot, he shifts Langland's balance by emphasizing certain actions and figures here and in the marginal notes. For instance, the figure of Theology, a minor one (and morally ambiguous at that) in Langland, is glossed both here and in the marginal comments as the "true preachar." On the other hand, most of Crowley's annotations are true to Langland's meaning, as when Crowley points out that Falsehood and Mede are in alliance. Mede works by bribes, and the train of people following Mede winds up at

Westminster, a natural image of power and corruption in politics. When False has to flee to the merchants, Crowley glosses the passage: "False can lack no master" (°3r).

In passus 3 Crowley again turns the episode into a speaking picture of Catholic abuses and Reformation correctives. When Lady Mede makes a confession to a friar, Crowley's summary observes "What abuse was in auricular confession" (°4r), and he notes in the margin of the passage "the fruits of popish penance." The closing scene of the passus receives another distinctly Reformation comment. Mede, defending herself from Conscience, quotes a passage from Scripture: "He that maketh presents shall purchase victory and honor" (Prov. 22.9), but Conscience rebukes her for quoting only half of the line, which ends "but he carrieth away the souls of the receivers." Crowley's summary directs the reader to a major issue for the Lollards, the sixteenth-century reformers, and maybe even Langland himself: "howe scripture muste be reade whole" (°4r).

It is clear that Crowley does not force meanings on the poem. But he does heighten and translate into Reformation terminology the issues that, as a Protestant reader, he thought—seldom without reason—were actually in the text. Conversely, he plays down those issues that appear to his eyes contrary to Protestant belief either by not commenting on them at all or by warning the reader. For instance, in passus 15, Langland quotes from the *Legend of Saints*. Crowley does not eliminate the passage nor does he denounce it, but he does point to it and caution the reader: "The Legend of sayntes, beleve it if ye luste" (Xlv). In general, Crowley makes a real effort to guide the reader rather than force a meaning that would distort the text. Sometimes, rather than commenting directly, he underscores a passage he thinks is particularly fine. In passus 10, next to the following lines:

And nowe is religion a rider, a romer by streate

A leder of love dayes and a loude begger

A prycker of a palfrey from Maner to Maner.

(N2r)

Crowley merely remarks "Reade thys," as if its turn of phrase were particularly apt and its rebuke of clerics manifestly clear.

The shift in Crowley's attitude to the text represents a fundamental reorientation on his part. The poem was seen not just as a
historical witness to an earlier time but as a text whose meanings
could be applied to the individual reader. He invites his readers to
read the text according to the common practice of interpreting
Scripture according to doctrine and use. A century later, William
Perkins in *The Art of Prophesying* sets out the principles of this
approach in terms of preaching, but it is equally applicable to
individual reading: "1) To reade the Text distinctly out of the Can-
onicall Scriptures. 2) To give the sense and understanding of it being
read, by the Scripture it self. 3) To collect a fewe and profitable points
of doctrine out of the naturall sense. 4) To apply (if he have the gift)
the doctrines rightly collected to the life and maners of men in a
simple and plaine speech."[22] This program for reading Scripture is
similar to Crowley's method in his annotations; he gives his sense of
the meaning of a scene, locates doctrine at points in the passus, and
applies the doctrine, or moral of the scenes, to "the life and manners
of men." Not surprisingly, Crowley approached Langland's work as
he did because of the strategies employed by the readership to which
he belonged. *Piers Plowman* is obviously not Scripture, but Crowley's approach to interpreting the poem in these terms signals how
important he considers the efficacy of the text.

These Reformation perspectives on the poem did not make it a
tame work in the eyes of those in authority. The firm association of
Piers Plowman with events long past, and its final apocalyptic vision,
may well have been construed as dangerous. There is some evidence
that the issuing of *Piers Plowman* was seen in the Renaissance as a
subversive act. One indication is the character of Owen Rodgers's
1561 edition of the poem. This edition has been described by Skeat
and others as a messy and inaccurate reprint of Crowley's work,
which in fact it is.[23] What has been obscured by discussion of
Rodgers's small changes is what he eliminated from the text. He
removed Crowley's preface and his marginal notes, all the material
that guided the reader to see the work as a prophecy. He retained the
synopsis of the poem's action but broke it up into passus-by-passus
units, printing each before the relevant section. This format was
exactly what one would find in a printed text of a classical or Italian
epic, with the argument appearing before each section. In any case,
the summaries merely explain the action; their primary emphasis is

on moral instruction, and they would therefore be less inflammatory. It is likely that under Elizabeth I, who disliked Puritan apologetics, the only way the text would be allowed into print was if its prophetic character had been toned down. Finally, Rodgers eliminated the name of Langland from any association with the work. His title page declares the work to be "*The Vision of Pierce Plowman*, Printed from the author's olde copy." Is Piers the author, or is Crowley the presumed author? Piers had already assumed an identity in the period, and it is likely that Rodgers, like others after him, simply thought Piers was the author. In any case, this too distances the poem from historical ferment. Rodgers's behavior suggests that the poem had been seen as subversive in its first three printings. Indeed, the very fact that Crowley ceased printing Langland's poem himself, even though there had been enough demand for it that three editions had been produced in one year, is indicative of the same thing. In other words, the prophetic and historical character attributed to the poem was anything but a dead issue, and the work was far from being regarded as of primarily literary interest. Its author's role in a struggle that continued into the present, which made the poem a holy relic to some, made it dangerously unsettling to others. Its dream-vision form was seen as a means to instruct and rebuke the corruptions of the time and to prophesy a future that had only partially come to pass. Langland's vision was perceived as not completely fulfilled; that was why Crowley set it into print. The figure of Piers himself as a critic and spokesman for economic and social issues, as seen in his address to Parliament, reinforced the belief that the work as Crowley set it forth was subversive. Thus Rodgers had to find a way to print it without evoking those associations. Rodgers's presentation of the poem probably accounts for the some of the changes in its reception in the later sixteenth and seventeenth centuries.

Robert Crowley and John Bunyan as Protestant Readers

What would a work like the Crowley *Piers Plowman* have meant to a reader approaching it from the context that Bunyan embodies? We cannot know ultimately if Bunyan read *Piers Plowman* or even knew of it (although he might have been exposed to it through his contact with William Dell), but the speculation is worth pursuing in order to establish the attitude toward the value and use of books that the Protestant readership shared. If Bunyan did encounter *Piers Plowman*, he would have found a literary model, the dream-vision, that was perceived in a historical and religious tradition rather than a literary one. He would have found the deliberate "feigning" of a dream justified so long as the writer's intention was to instruct and rebuke. He would have seen a work that projects a figure who is unlettered and working-class, but who knows the way to truth and announces that the unlettered plowman will get to heaven first. He would have encountered a poem that is openly hostile to the clerical order. And finally, he would have discovered a poem that represented to an audience of Protestant readers a spiritual record of individual reformation. Above all, it is an example of how to declare truth through a dream-vision and an allegorical mode. This would not have been apparent without the help of Crowley's apparatus. Behind Crowley's preface, synopsis, and marginalia is a theory of reading and of what one does with a text in which a reader like Bunyan would have felt secure. Crowley's invitation to read the poem in the same way Scripture was being read, according to doctrine and use, would have provided Bunyan with a model for fiction that could convey truth. First, in the preface, Crowley announces that the feigned dream is a means of crying out and that the work's purpose is to instruct the weak and rebuke the blind. Bunyan sees his work in similar terms in his "Apology":

> This Book will make a Travailer of thee,
>
> If by its Counsel thou wilt ruled be;
>
> It will direct thee to the Holy Land
>
> If thou wilt its directions understand:
>
> Yea, it will make the sloathful, active be;
>
> The Blind also, delightful things to see.
>
> (lines 207–12)

The book, though in one sense fictional, can nonetheless give counsel and directions. Crowley makes precisely that claim at the close of the preface when he bids the reader of the book "to emend thyne owne misse." The work in each case claims to locate the reader in the text.

Bunyan says: "Would'st read thy self, and read thou know'st not what /
And yet know whether thou art blest or not" (lines 233–34). In each
work, the reader is the true focal point of the fiction, and the dream-
vision is a means of communicating the truth about him- or herself to
the reader.

Crowley's approach to the allegory of *Piers Plowman* in his
summary of "poyntes" would have allayed Bunyan's fears about the
use of the allegorical mode. His synopsis of the passus moves easily
between plot summary and abstracted doctrine. It totally ignores the
fictional, literal level of the poem and turns the scenes into speaking
pictures that instruct and rebuke. For Crowley, the literal level does
not just deliver a general sense of life or even a historical witness to an
earlier time; rather, he sees it as delivering a series of *dos* and *don'ts*, a
catalogue of instruction. In his reading, the visual action on the
literal level provides direct rules for the amendment of life, in a way
that a twentieth-century reader finds hard to fathom. Bunyan's
"Apology" shows a similar confidence in the visual picture of action:

> This Book it chaulketh out before thine eyes,
>
> The man that seeks the everlasting Prize:
>
> It shews you whence he comes, whither he goes,
>
> What he leaves undone; also what he does:
>
> It also shews you how he runs, and runs,
>
> Till he unto the Gate of Glory comes.
>
> It shews too, who sets out for life amain,
>
> As if the lasting Crown they would attain:
>
> Here also you may see the reason why
>
> They loose their labour, and like fools die.
>
> This Book will make a Travailer of thee.

> (lines 197–207)

Bunyan is sure, just as Crowley appears to be, that the literal level of
the fiction can and does speak directly to the reader.

Finally, Crowley's marginal notations—which index the plot,

abstract doctrine, and identify scriptural passages—provide further proof that the reader could be guided and alerted to the meaning contained in the fiction. The physical characteristics of the Crowley marginalia are similar to those found in *The Pilgrim's Progress*. If we set side by side the early editions of *Piers Plowman* and *The Pilgrim's Progress*, we can easily see the shift in how Protestant readers read and what they required from their reading. Crowley indexes topics by putting key words in the margins, commenting upon them, and citing scriptural passages, but his most significant editorial decision is his synopsis of the "principall poyntes that be spoken of in thys boke." The synopsis moves from passus to passus almost never mentioning the literal level of the fiction. From our perspective, he reduces imaginative scenes to "speaking pictures" from which a specific moral can be gleaned and set down. We find the same kind of marginalia in the first edition of Bunyan's narrative, where the writer translates the meaning of the scenes and reinforces the work's scriptural underpinnings by citing passages from Scripture.

Thus, the Crowley *Piers Plowman* would have provided the example Bunyan needed to convey religious truth in a fictive, allegorical mode. But Bunyan tells us his mysterious model provided "leave" as well as "example." This curious distinction can be explained by Langland's overt preoccupation with the ethics of being a poet. Both Langland and Bunyan in their respective works feel an intense need to justify their fiction-making. Indeed, one of the most striking features of *Piers Plowman* is the dreamer-poet's recurrent doubts as to the legitimacy of writing the poem as well as about the value of intellectual learning in general. Bunyan confines his fears about his enterprise to the "Apology," but Langland includes his questioning of the process in many places throughout the whole work. Especially in passus 12, in the dreamer's encounter with Imaginatif, we see Langland overtly addressing the question and explicitly answering it.[24] Imaginatif rebukes the dreamer for writing the poem: "And thou medlist with makings & mightist go sai thi psalter" (P4r). The dreamer counters this rebuke at first by saying that he did it for solace. He claims that holy men "pleyden." Crowley heightens this excuse in the margin: "Holy men used recreation." Bunyan himself, in the "Apology," claims that this was the work's first reason for being: "I did it mine own self to gratifie" (line 24) and to divert his mind from "worser thoughts." Next, Langland's dreamer states that if any man could tell him "What were Dowel & Dobet, & Dobest at the last / Would I never do werke, but wend to holy church" (P4r). The writing of the poem is a necessary process toward learning something that cannot be known till afterwards. Bunyan states in similar fashion: "I only thought to make / I knew not what" (lines 20–21). For each writer, the writing of the work is a process of discovery.

This exchange between Imaginatif and the dreamer launches Imaginatif into a discourse on learning (Clergie), natural understanding (Kynd Wyt), and their relationship to books. Imaginatif first discusses how learning and understanding are "mirrours" to amend the self:

> Therfore I counsel the for christes sake, clergy that thou love
>
> For kynd wyt is of his kin, & nygh cosins both,
>
> To our Lord leve me, therfore love hem I read,
>
> For both ben as myrrours, to amend our defautes,
>
> And leaders for lewde men, and for lettred both.
>
> (Q1r)

Learning and understanding are "myrrours" to see the self and "leaders" who show the way to correct oneself. The passage is very like Crowley's attitude toward the text and its relationship to the reader. Imaginatif goes on to describe this relationship as a means of seeing and relates it to the value of books:

> For as a man may not see, that misseth hys eyen,
>
> No more can no clarke, but if he caughte it firste by boks
>
> And s. Spirite the samplare & sayd what men should wryte
>
> Right so leadeth letture, lewde men to reason
>
> And as a blinde man in battel beareth wepen to fight
>
> And hath no happe wyth hys axe hys enemy to hytte
>
> No more can a kind witted man, but clarkes him teach
>
> Come for all his kinde wyt, to christendome & be saved.
>
> (Q1v)

Without learning, even natural understanding cannot save the sinner. The value of "boks" is that they contain truth; the clerk "caught" his learning from books. There is a reason why books have truth value. The old commonplace that comes from St. Paul, "All that is written is written for our doctrine," is given a rationale: this is so because the Holy Ghost is a "samplare," the example, the instructor who tells men what to write, a central tenet of the Protestant readership. Crowley, in his marginal note, singles out and emphasizes that point: "The holy ghost is the autor of bokes." He does not say Scripture in particular; he says books, and it is clear from his preface that he believed that God had inspired Langland to write *Piers Plowman*.

The discussion in passus 12 of the truth value in writing moves from the idea that one writes for amusement, through the idea of writing as a process of discovery, and finally to the conclusion that the inspiration and content of what one writes come from God. That is precisely the movement we find in Bunyan's "Apology." Bunyan began with the idea that the book was an intentionless activity, but he concludes by arguing that the intention came from elsewhere:

> but yet let Truth be free
> To make her Salleys upon Thee, and Me,
> Which way it pleases God. For who knows how,
> Better then he that taught us first to Plow,
> To guide our Mind and Pens for his Design?
>
> (lines 181–85)

Bunyan claims that truth made "Salleys" upon him in the writing of the work, that God himself guides both the pen and the mind, and that as a result the work itself will convey truth to the reader. Whether Bunyan knew Langland's poem or not, both he and Robert Crowley are quintessentially Protestant in their sense of the origin of texts as well as their understanding of the value and use of books. And *The Pilgrim's Progress* owes a considerable debt for its existence to the growth of a Protestant readership, a readership inaugurated in part by Lollard "readings" of *Piers Plowman*.

5

"Peres became a protestande"
Renaissance Readings of *Piers Plowman*

Conscience ys a sleppe till he come againe [.] Consience will
not come into this lande till the proude Prelotes and the
[va?]nitous lawyers be swept awaie which will not be longe to
Amen So be it.

Anonymous marginal notation in
a seventeenth-century manuscript of *Piers Plowman*

It is one thing to note the implications of the Crowley *Piers
Plowman* in and of itself. It is quite another to demonstrate
that Crowley's presentation actually had the effect on
readers that the apparatus seems to imply. We must now turn to a
much more elusive question, though one of even greater importance
for my larger argument concerning the existence of a Protestant
readership. To what extent, with what degrees of understanding, and
with what resulting conclusions were readers actually reading the
poem? Although *Piers Plowman* was not discussed in great detail in
print, two kinds of evidence are available. First, there are direct
commentaries on *Piers Plowman* and demonstrable instances of its
influence on later works. Second, and in some respects more significant for our purpose, in the marginalia inscribed in copies of the
Crowley edition (and, perhaps still more revealingly, in manuscripts),
there exist records of the responses of readers in the act of reading
that indicate that the work was being read thoroughly and perceptively throughout the period.

Such evidence reveals a view of the poem that differs radically
from modern interpretations. From our twentieth-century perspec-

tive, readers of the poem in the sixteenth and seventeenth centuries misread the content and action of the text. But their perception of the poem's meaning and their grasp of the issues reflected in the work yield interpretations of the poem no less pertinent than our own. We must now turn to the shifting reputation of *Piers Plowman* in sixteenth- and seventeenth-century England and provide an overview of how the work as a whole was perceived.

No single monolithic view of the poem existed in the Renaissance and seventeenth century. Rather, there were multiple perceptions of the poem and its problems, including such questions as authorship, generic category, and verse form. All these references, however brief, yield partial perceptions about the poem, indicating that there were three basic frames through which it was viewed: prophecy, satire, and history. At different stages and for different kinds of readers, one or more of these perceptions dominated; sometimes they overlapped.

During the first stage of the poem's reputation, the work and its author were perceived primarily as powerful symbols of the Reformation. *Piers Plowman* was received by its readers as a prophecy fulfilled in their own time. The poem was thought to be both difficult and dangerous because of its prophetic cast. The second stage of the poem's reputation was less volatile and had two aspects. Readers of the poem in the late sixteenth and early seventeenth centuries viewed it as a literary product and a historical document. Literary theorists attempted to place it in a generic category, though they were somewhat dubious about its artistic merits;[1] historians took the work to be a true description of an earlier time. During the final stage, extending from the mid-seventeenth century to at least the beginning of the eighteenth century, the work emerged as part of Reformation history. Thomas Fuller proclaimed that Langland was by prolepsis a Protestant, William Prynne alluded to the work as sacred and serious, and historians began to include it in histories of the Reformation.

The First Stage: *Piers Plowman* as Prophecy and Polemic

The primary text exemplifying this view of *Piers Plowman* is the Crowley preface itself, which links the poem with Wyclif's translation of the Bible. Crowley tells us that his information comes not only from consulting a variety of manuscripts,[2] but "such men as I know to be more exercised in the studie of antiquities, than I myselfe have ben." It is generally believed that Crowley's primary authority was John Bale, who presents this view of Langland in his monumental catalogue of British writers. Bale's earlier work lists the title *Petrus Agricola* under "Wyclif."[3] But the larger 1557 version assigns it to Langland and uses the same language as that in Crowley's preface, though Bale assigns the poem a slightly later date:

> Robertus Langelande, sacerdos, ut apparet, natus in comitatu Salopie, in villa vulgo dicta Mortymers Clibury, in terra lutea, octavo a Malvernis montibus milliario fuit. Num tamen eo in loco, incondito & agresti, in bonis literis ad maturam aetatem usque informatus fuerit, certo adfirmare non possum, ut neque, an Oxonii aut Cantabrigie illis insudaverit: quum apud eorum locorum magistros, studia praecipue vigerent. Illud veruntamen liquido constat, eum fuisse ex primis Joannis Wiclevi discipulis unum, atque in spiritus fervore, contra apertas Papistarum blasphemias adversus Deum & eius Christum, sub amoenis coloribus & typis edidisse in sermone Anglico pium opus, ac bonorum virorum lectione dignum, quod vocabat *Visionem Petri Aratoris*, Lib. I. *In aestivo tempore cum sol caloret*. Nihil aliud ab ipso editum novi. In hoc opere erudiso, praeter similitudines varias & jucundas, prophetice plura predixit, que nostris diebus impleri vidimus. Complevit suum opus anno Domini 1369, dum Joannes Cicestrius Lodini praetor esset.[4]

Bale reinforces the connection between Wyclif and Langland by claiming that Langland was a disciple of Wyclif. He also gives a view of the poem that celebrates Langland's mission in even stronger terms. The author is portrayed as being "in a fervent spirit against the open blasphemies of the papists." At the close of the section, Bale underscores the prophetic character of the work by asserting that the prophecies have been fulfilled "in our days."

For Bale, as for Crowley, the allegorical mode that Langland adopted was a valid and necessary means of rebuking religious abuses and prophesying what was to come. The poem's difficulty, its artifice, its use of "fayned" dreams are clearly no obstacle for the reformers of religion. Nor is Langland's method justified primarily as a device for evading ecclesiastical censorship. Langland, in a fervent spirit, spoke out under the veil of "delightful embellishments" and "figures." By doing so, Langland produced a work worthy of reading by good men.

Piers Plowman continued to be cited in polemic justifying the Reformation, though less and less often as the poem came increasingly to be perceived as too radical for mainstream Protestants (in part because of its connection with a Marprelate tract) and as Elizabethan fears of revolt and dissent grew. "Piers Plowman" is cited along with a revealing selection of other writers, for example, in an anonymous work published about 1590.[5] The reference to *Piers Plowman* comes under the writer's final point in the title and table of contents:

A Petition directed to her most excellent Majestie, wherein is delivered

1 A meane howe to compound the civill dissention in the church of England.
2 A proofe that they who write for Reformation, doe not offend against the stat. of 23.Eliz.c. and therefore till matters bee compounded, deserve more favour. . . .
16 Lastly, many have written both against the state of the Church and common wealth as it was & is fenced by law who were never accounted diffamers of our Princes.

First he cites writers who have attacked features of English law. Then he proceeds to those who attack the state of church. The first of these many to be cited is "Wicleve" for his declaration that clerics may not *"rule like civill Lordes"* nor may the king *"impose uppon"* any cleric in *"any secular matters"*. The writer comments: "although the Archbishop of *Cant.* and the Bishop of *London* did put Wicleve to silence for this doctrine (as their successors do at this day) yet they did not call him *a diffamer of the King.*"[6] Other writers cited are the early Lollard William Swynderby and reformers like Tyndale, Barnes,

Hooper, and Latimer. Among these spokesmen we find "Piers Plowman" who, like Wyclif and Swynderby, "wrote against the state of
Bishops, and prophecied their fall in these wordes":

> If Knighthood and Kindwite and Comone by conscience
>
> Together love Lelly, leveth it well ye Bishopes
>
> The Lordship of Landes for ever shall ye lese,
>
> And live as Levities as our Lord ye teacheth.[7]

A marginal gloss next to this passage reads "A prophecy of the fall
of Bb."

Chaucer, who was more often presented as a literary figure than
as a figure in Reformation history, is cited here as well: "*Geffrey
Chaucer* also in *Henry* the forths time wrote effectually against the
state of Bb. in this maner." After quoting two stanzas of the apocryphal "Plowman's Tale," the writer adds:

> Thus wrote this famous Poet against the English Bishops, and yet
> was never accounted diffamer of the Kinge, though the Bb. in his
> time did hold their Lordships of the Kinge as they do nowe in En-
> gland. *Sir Geffrey Chaucers* his workes were in K. *Henry* the eight
> his daies authorized to bee Printed by an Act of Parliament, to
> which that glorious king would never have condescended, if hee
> thought that the diffamation of the Bishops had bin a diffamation of
> him selfe."[8]

The writer is calling for radically Puritan reform of the English
church and hopes, like Wyclif himself and just as unrealistically, that
the Crown can be enlisted against the established power of the
church. In such a context, he thinks the authority of "Piers Plowman"
will carry a weight comparable to that which the Reformation had
given to Wyclif. Nothing could more clearly show that *Piers Plowman*
was considered a major landmark of historical and prophetic tradition. But this writer's argument indicates, as did the Marprelate tract
we cited earlier, that *Piers Plowman* was being co-opted by the
radical Protestants.

The Second Stage: Satire and History

Once the text was distanced from its initial turbulent introduction into the struggle for religious reform, the reputation of *Piers Plowman* in the late sixteenth and early seventeenth centuries changed significantly. No longer used as ammunition in a bitter dispute, the poem began to receive attention as a literary work and a historical document. But the two ways of reading overlapped. Its previous reception conditioned those new perceptions about the work and produced some interesting results. Literary theorists were clearly uncomfortable with its qualifications as literature and therefore saw it exclusively as satire. Chroniclers cited the work for its historical witness, but confusion remained as to its author.

PIERS PLOWMAN AS LITERATURE: THE SATIRIC LANGLAND

In general, *Piers Plowman* receives comparatively little attention from literary theorists, however eager to affirm a native tradition. That is not altogether surprising considering its earlier polemical role. Commentators do not discuss its dream-vision form or allegorical mode, aspects that were important to Bale and Crowley. Its salvational quest structure went unnoticed. Because the distinction between the dreamer-narrator and the figure of Piers was all but obliterated, the basic movement of the poem, the dreamer Will's quest for salvation, was obscured. The biting invective the dreamer directs at religious abuses and a corrupt society were seen as originating from Piers himself. Thus, the satiric aspects of the poem were seen as its fundamental thrust by lettered readers who viewed texts as at least partly "recreational." As we have seen, George Puttenham, though a Protestant, epitomizes that way of responding to *Piers Plowman*. Puttenham, like William Webbe, Francis Meres, and others, attempts to locate a native tradition comparable to the classical one and places Langland's work in a clearly defined generic category in *The Arte of English Poesie* (1589): "There was yet another kind of Poet, who intended to taxe the common abuses and vice of the people in rough and bitter speaches, and their invectives were called *Satyres,* and them selves *Satyricques.* Such were *Lucilius, Juvenall* and *Persius* among the Latines, and with us he that wrote the booke called Piers Plowman."[9] For Puttenham, the "rough and bitter speaches," the invective directed against religious abuses and society as a whole, is the defining characteristic of *Piers Plowman*. Puttenham also clearly does not know or does not accept Crowley's designation of Langland as the author of the work. In chapter 31, "Who in any age have bene the most commended writers in our English Poesie, and the Authors censure given upon them," Puttenham delivers his view of the literary history of the time: "And those of the first age were *Chaucer* and *Gower* both of them I suppose Knightes. After whom followed *John Lydgate* the monke of Bury, and that nameles, who wrote the *Satyre* called Piers Plowman, next him followed *Harding* the Chronicler, then in king *Henry* th'eight times *Skelton*, (I wot not for what great worthines) surnamed the Poet *Laureat*."[10] Puttenham not only does not mention Langland as author, he places the writing of the poem in the fifteenth century, along with the works of Lydgate. Why this confusion in chronology? It is quite possibly caused by the profusion of apocryphal plowman texts that date from the fifteenth century. Puttenham might well have seen some of them and *Piers Plowman* itself as all of a piece and therefore may have rejected Crowley's designation and dating of the text.

Puttenham's censure on the writers of antiquity gives first place to Chaucer for his learning. As we have seen in chapter 1, Puttenham delivers a mixed review of Langland's poem: "He that wrote the Satyr of Piers Ploughman, seemed to have bene a malcontent of that time, and therefore bent himselfe wholy to taxe the disorders of that age, and specially the pride of the Romane Clergy, of whose fall he seemeth to be a very true Prophet, his verse is but loose meetre, and his termes hard and obscure, so as in them is litle pleasure to be taken."[11] This passage makes clearer the effect the apocryphal plowman texts had on the reception of *Piers Plowman* itself. Puttenham's description of the author as a malcontent in the very same sentence that acknowledges him an accurate prophet of the Reformation indicates that the development of the plowman image had fed into his view of the work. His description of the author as a malcontent may also be a reaction to the poem's radical social criticism, an element underlined by its association with the Peasants' Revolt of 1381.[12] Puttenham's remarks indicate that the poem was still too unsettling to evoke unmixed admiration. As late as 1589, he uses language that suggests ambivalence toward the work's prophetic context. Langland is a malcontent, which is bad; but he seems to have been a true prophet, which is good.

Puttenham's designation of satire as the generic species to which the work belongs reveals another facet of the poem's reception in the Renaissance. One feature of satire that differentiates it from other literary kinds is that the relationship between writer, work, and audience is perceived as being especially close. Satire, as opposed to a genre like epic, is not perceived as standing in isolation, to be judged on artistic grounds. Puttenham does not see it as a made thing in the way that Chaucer's *Troilus and Criseyde*, for example, would be perceived. Rather, the author is elevated as a focal point, especially after the targets of his satiric attack are no longer an issue. Satiric works demand to be assessed according to three criteria: the author (in Puttenham's terms a malcontent); his target (the disorders of his age, particularly the pride of the clergy); and the audience (those who are being chastised and those who should be aware of the contemporary situation). The result of this generic distinction is a heightened emphasis on the figure of the author, since the Juvenalian pose of righteous indignation is perceived as central to satire. The work tends to be approached in terms of the critic's conception of the author as a man, rather than as a craftsman. Langland receives exactly this kind of attention in Puttenham's discourse. At the end of this Protestant tradition of reading, when Bunyan mentions in his "Apology" that he had "leave and example," he too gives a similar emphasis to the figure of the author who is portrayed as having an active role in his work, effecting change by "words" or "ways."

But Puttenham is not alone in seeing a close relationship between author and text. William Webbe's *Discourse of Englishe Poesie* (1586) shows that the tradition exemplified by Puttenham had also been picked up by less sophisticated theorists. Webbe sees an even stronger identification between writer and work. After discussing Gower, Chaucer, and Lydgate, he goes on to describe *Piers Plowman*: "The next of our auncient Poets that I can tell of I suppose to be *Pierce Ploughman*, who in his dooinges is somewhat harshe and obscure, but indeede a very pithy wryter, and (to hys commendation I speake it) was the first I have seene that observed the quantity of our verse without the curiosity of Ryme."[13] Puttenham is unclear who the author is; Webbe clearly thinks that Piers is the author. He underscores the writer's active role by describing the poem as "his dooings." The terms *harsh* and *obscure* may refer to the poem's difficulty and the abrasiveness of its satire. But since Webbe goes on to comment, however erroneously, on the poem's meter, he is more likely to be referring to style and versification. Nevertheless, Webbe finds Piers a "pithy" writer, one who is worth reading. Curiously enough, in his zeal for classical imitation, Webbe mistakes the alliterative line for quantitative verse, perhaps because the question of whether English poetry ought to become quantitative had received so much attention in the 1580s. Like Puttenham, he places the work in the fifteenth century, after Lydgate but before Skelton. Like Puttenham, too, Webbe seems to be rejecting Crowley's research as well as being confused about where the other plowman texts fit in. It is interesting to note that the other apocryphal texts are not included in his summaries of notable books. Perhaps the fact that Piers is the presumed author simply implies that they are included in these discussions. Webbe may be merely ignoring them because he perceives the texts, correctly of course, as of a lesser literary quality, or he may simply be, as he often is, confused.

Francis Meres in *Palladis Tamia* (1598) also attempts to place *Piers Plowman* in a native English tradition. He believes, perhaps because he is following Webbe, that the author was using a quantitative verse line: "As Homer was the first that adorned the Greek tongue with true quantity: so *Piers Ploughman* was the first that observed the true quantitie of our verse without the curiositie of rime."[14] More importantly, he too believed that Piers was the author. In assessing the great writers of satire he says: "As Horace, Lucilius, Juvenall, Persius, and Lucullus are the best for Satyre amonge the Latines: so with us, in the same faculty, there are chiefe, *Piers Plowman*, Lodge, Hall of Immanuel Colledge in Cambridge, the Author of *Pigmalion's Image* and *certain Satyrs*, the Author of *Skialetheia*".[15] Piers is named along with other known authors rather than listed among the anonymous works. Clearly, sixteenth-century readers of the poem not only thought of Piers as the narrator of *Piers Plowman*, as Crowley did, but saw Piers as the work's author as well. Why this belief in Piers as the author came about and what its implications are for reconstructing sixteenth-century perceptions of the poem are important but elusive questions.

The apocryphal plowman texts, some written in the fifteenth century and some in the sixteenth century, used the mask of the plowman to articulate religious, social, and economic issues. Though initially, in the fifteenth century, the writers of these texts were responding to the fabric of *Piers Plowman* itself, they expanded and redefined Langland's plowman to the point where the image had a life of its own apart from any specific work. The character of Piers could be brought into any text; its nexus of meaning would be implicit. When Robert Crowley approached the text in search of its meaning, he simply assumed that the narrative voice was Piers's because he could not imagine it emanating from any other source, based on what he knew about other works that used the mask of the plowman. However, he had enough sense of the work's fictional status to assume that author and narrator were separable, and his research bore him out.

The response of the literary theorists, on the other hand, was one of ambivalence. Crowley's designation of Langland as author was for the most part rejected because it did not square with the critic's sense of what the work was doing. Critics like Puttenham viewed the work as a satire and therefore perceived it as having a more immediate and less artistic relationship to its age. The central emphasis was placed on its author, a malcontent, who castigated his times, whereas Crowley clearly saw the author as a Christian hero along with Wyclif. Literary theorists, unpersuaded by its role in the religious struggle and uncomfortable with the effect other plowman texts had on their own age, saw it in a somewhat different light. Its author wrote satire because he was a malcontent, a maker of discord. As a result, the work was not seen as a literary triumph whose author should be set next to Chaucer and Gower as a "maker" of poems. Rather, the question of authorship was not seen as important. Critics felt that the case for a historical author separable from the assumed speaker, Piers, was an unnecessary one. The distinction between author and narrator implies a more complex relationship between author, work, and audience. Literary theorists, electing satire as the genre to which the work belonged, chose Piers as its author because doing so emphasized and articulated what they thought the work was about.

PIERS PLOWMAN AS HISTORY

Chronicle references to *Piers Plowman* in the late sixteenth and early seventeenth century display no comparable ambivalence about the nature of the work. For Renaissance historians the poem's significance resided in its historical dimensions and its prophetic character. The poem's truth value is continually affirmed. However, historians had their own political problems with the poem. As we saw earlier, the association between *Piers Plowman* and the Peasants' Revolt of 1381 persisted into the sixteenth century. The letters by John Ball, the leader of the revolt, and others, which use language and symbolism from *Piers Plowman*, were still current and appeared in many histories. Thus, the work still had negative connotations for many because of its assumed link with the overthrow of society. Perhaps as a result of this association, an alternate tradition of authorship was put forth. This other theory of authorship surfaced first in John Stowe's *Annales of Englande* (1580). Stowe cites one John Malverne as the author of *Piers Plowman* and dates the text somewhat earlier than Crowley and Bale: "This year, 1342, John Malverne, Fellow of Oriel College, in Oxford, made and finished his booke, entitled The Visions of Pierce Plowman."[16] It is not known where this tradition began. Why would an earlier date and a different author be put forth at so late a stage? The most obvious reason, though the most difficult to substantiate, is that this explanation appealed to readers who wanted to save the work from being rejected out of hand because of its similarities to other plowman texts. The earlier date distances it from the fifteenth-century texts and removes it and its author from any possible associations with the Peasants' Revolt, a matter of increasing concern in view of Elizabethan fear of revolt. Also, the new attribution, "fellow of Oriel College," sets the writer securely in a learned tradition. The role of *Piers Plowman* in the Marprelate tract and the 1590 *Petition* certainly lends credibility to this explanation. Stowe's attribution also places the author in a scholarly context, eliminating any associations with the lower classes. The name "John Malverne" seems an obvious fabrication based on the fact that Malvern Hills, according to the poem itself, was where the vision took place. One final interesting dimension of Stowe's notation is that he does not feel called upon to explain what the text is. He assumes that all know of it; he is simply recording who its author was.

As a matter of fact, Stowe was quite a careful reader of the text. It is interesting to note that he changes the title of the work from "Vision" to "Visions." This is a more correct reflection and description of what *Piers Plowman* actually is; eight visions can be located in the poem. Stowe also regards the text as if it were pure history. In *A Survey of London* (1603), Stowe cites a detail from Langland's work to shed light on his subject: "Moreover in the 44 of Edward the third *John Chicester* being Maior of London, I read in the visions of *Pierce Plowman*, a booke so called as followeth. There was a careful commune, when no Cart came to towne with baked bread from Stratford: tho gan beggers weepe, and workemen were agast, a little this will be thought long, in the date of our Dirte, in a drie Averell a thousand and three hundred, twise thirtie and ten, &c."[17] This passage comes from the Vita de Dowel, passus 13 (lines 265 and following), one of the more difficult sections in the poem. Stowe reads the poem as a historical document, a primary source in which one can find hard evidence. Whatever else Stowe thought about the poem, he clearly read it with great care and found its description of at least some events purely factual. This response to the historicity of the poem was not confined to specific details; it extended to its larger content. Nor was Stowe the only historian to use the poem in this way. William Camden, in *Remains Concerning Britain*, accepts *Piers Plowman* as an accurate report of the age: "Neither was the clergy free from pride, as you may perceive from Pierce Plowman."[18] Clearly, Camden believes his readers will find it self-evident that *Piers Plowman* is a historical document.

John Selden in his notes to Michael Drayton's *Polyalbion*, a work that attempts to make an epic of the landscape of Britain, discusses the area of Malvern Hills and relates it to Langland's poem. His comments, though brief, demonstrate that the work's historic dimensions are at the forefront of his mind: "Upon these / the Malvern Hills / is the supposed vision of Piers Ploughman, done (as is thought) by Robert Langland, a Shropshire man, in a kind of English meter: which, for the discovery of the infecting corruptions of those times, I prefer before many more seeming serious invectives, as well for invention as for judgment. But I have read that the author's name was John Malverne, a fellow of Oriel College in Oxford, who finished it 16 Edward III."[19] Here too we find Piers conflated with the dreamer, as well as a sense that the supposed vision really occurred in a particular place. It is also significant that the poem's factitious or artificed strategy ("supposed vision," "more seeming serious invectives") does not seem to Selden to be in any way in conflict with its historicity or authoritative status. Selden registers as well the confusion about who the author was. This indicates that both traditions of authorship were still alive. His praise of the poem underscores its historic validity; he prefers it over "more seeming serious invectives" because of its method, the reporting of dreams to uncover the "infecting corruptions of the times." Selden likes the poem for its invention as well as its judgment. He praises Langland for his method of dreaming dreams that reveal truth and applauds his choice of subject matter, as well as preferring it before other polemical works because of the historic justice of its indictment against the clergy.

But what were these other "seeming serious invectives"? *Piers Plowman* is not alone in being seen in this category. John Weever, in *Ancient Funeral Monuments* (1631) cites other works as ones he prefers to Langland's.

> In this Kings raigne [Edward III]; *Robert Longland*, a secular Priest, borne in Shropshire, at Mortimers Cliberie, writ bitter invectives against the Prelates, and all religious orders in those dayes, as you may reade throughout this book, which he calls, The vision of Piers Plowman.
>
> *Chaucer*, who was contemporarie and companion with *Gower*, in the Plowmans tale, the Romant of the Rose, and in his Treatise which hee intitles, Jacke Upland, writes as much, or more, against the pride, covetousnesse, insatiable luxurie, hypocrisie, blinde ignorance, and variable discord amongst the Church-men, and all other our English votaries. As also how rude and unskilfull they were in matters and principles of our Christian institutions; to whose workes, now commonly in print, I referre my Reader, for further satisfaction.[20]

Two of the three works that Weever cited for Chaucer were, of course, not his but plowman texts. His comment registers exactly how far that tradition went beyond *Piers Plowman* in a direct polemical attack on social and religious abuses. Observe as well that these works are said to be still in circulation; this implies that Langland's work is also current. Chaucer, in particular, fares better in

Weever's view because he was seen as being harsher than Langland. But the other work Weever cites as Chaucer's turns out to be his supposed translation of a highly satirical allegory. Clearly, the historicity and satiric dimensions are what is important about their inclusion in his work—they are not cited for artistic or literary reasons. Weever claims on the title page to intermix and illustrate his work with a "variety of Historical observations, annnotations, and briefe notes, extracted out of approved Authors, infallible Records, Lieger Bookes, Charters, Rolls, old Manuscripts, and the Collections of Judicious Antiquaries." Thus the texts cited above and many others as well fell into the category of "approved" because of their historical witness to an earlier time. This is one more indication of the curious second life of Langland's work in the Renaissance.

So even when distanced from Crowley's polemical introduction, the reputation of *Piers Plowman* in the late sixteenth and early seventeenth centuries still carried its reformist associations, its historical and prophetic contexts. Chroniclers and historians included it in their works and treated it as a historical document. Literary theorists, searching for a genre to which to assign it, selected satire precisely because of the work's historic and prophetic role as well as its "rough" meter. This inevitably undercut the fictional status of the work. Its author was portrayed as a figure in the poem, Piers, who attacked historical abuses. Thus, *Piers Plowman* was presented as a curious hybrid, literary only in a strict sense; its prophetic and historic dimensions were defined as its *raison d'être*.

SPENSER AND DRAYTON: POETS ON *PIERS PLOWMAN*

The question of how other poets—as distinct from critics, historians, and reformers—viewed *Piers Plowman* is both more elusive and, ultimately, more illuminating. Two writers in particular, Edmund Spenser and Michael Drayton, can help us document the poem's literary reputation. They also demonstrate that Langland had played a part in defining the role of the Protestant poet. Spenser's allusions to the poem shed a great deal of light on the typical Renaissance conflation of the dreamer and Piers. Drayton paraphrases a portion of the poem in one of his historical legends. Both writers respond to the fabric of *Piers Plowman* in ways that might have been expected, given the permutations of its reputation that we have been documenting; but by doing so they remove these attitudes from the realm of the abstract and the historical and make their meaning more accessible and intelligible.

What has been taken as Spenser's only direct allusion to *Piers Plowman* is a passage at the close of *The Shepheardes Calendar*:[21]

> Goe lyttle Calender, thou hast a free passeporte,
>
> Goe but a lowly gate emongste the meaner sorte.
>
> Dare not to match thy pype with Tityrus hys style,
>
> Nor with the Pilgrim that the Ploughman
>
> played a whyle.

Much has been written about this passage, which has often been interpreted as representing a view of the relationship between the author, the pilgrim or dreamer-narrator, and the character Piers that is contradicted by the poem itself. Skeat, typical of most subsequent literary historians, interprets it as revealing a misunderstanding of the poem so complete as to be incompatible with direct knowledge of the text.[22] If that were the case, it would preclude any serious engagement with the poem on Spenser's part and would reduce any influence by Langland to the trivial and external. But we have already seen that readers who had a deep and thorough acquaintance with the poem did not find a conflation of Piers and the dreamer incompatible with the text. On the contrary, they found this a natural way of reading, especially in view of the Crowley annotations. But it is by no means clear that Spenser is conflating Piers and the dreamer in this line. Skeat's view reflects an assumption that a rigid distinction exists between the voices of the poem, an approach to its complex structure that has been increasingly abandoned by modern critics. Judith Anderson, especially, in her excellent study of Langland and Spenser, remarks that the line indicates "that Spenser not only knew Langland's poem but also knew it well enough to understand Piers as an aspect, a face, of Langland's narrator, which in fact Piers turns out to be."[23] Spenser's own practice as an allegorist indicates that he thought naturally in terms of figures who are complementary in the sense that they extrapolate varying possibilities of a role or concept and contribute to a cumulative exploration of that element in the narrative. He has the kind of literary imagination that could quite credibly be supposed to have understood Langland better than his contemporaries in a matter of this kind. In the context of the *Shepheardes Calendar* in particular, he may be thinking of Langland and his surrogate the Dreamer as playing the plowman just as Spenser himself, as Colin Clout, plays the shepherd.[24] After all, the entire pastoral tradition is accustomed to seeing rural figures not as literal subject matter but as projections embodying the various concerns of city dwellers in general and poets in particular. But even if the line is interpreted as literally conflating the Dreamer and Piers, that does not prove Spenser's ignorance of Langland, since such a reading of the poem would do no more than reflect the views of most serious readers in the sixteenth century.[25]

Whether or not Spenser read Langland more perceptively than Crowley, there is no ambiguity about the view of *Piers Plowman* reflected in Michael Drayton's "Legend of Thomas Cromwell,"[26] which provides further insight into the Renaissance view of the poem. Drayton paraphrases closely a portion of the last passus of the poem, the culminating attack of Antichrist on Unity, the last remnant of Christendom, which is destroyed by the Friars in spite of Conscience. In Drayton's poem, Cromwell is set up as the narrator who describes his own role in history; as narrator, he elects to use Langland's poem and its major figure Piers to help him tell his story. The fact that Drayton follows Langland's text so closely is significant. But it is the opening and closing references to Piers that deserve our special attention. Cromwell introduces the paraphrased material as follows:

> The Church not willing others should her praise,
>
> That shee was leane, when as her Lands were fat,
>
> > Her selfe to too much libertie did give,
> >
> > Which some perceiv'd that in those times did live.
>
> Pierce the wise Plowman, in his vision saw
>
> Conscience sore hurt, yet sorer was afraid
>
> The seven great Sinnes to Hell him like to draw.
>
> > (lines 781–86)

After recapitulating the whole tragedy of Unity, Cromwell concludes, "This the wise Plowman shew'd me from his sleepe." For Drayton, the vision belonged to Piers: he was the dreamer, and he articulated it in his vision. Here we find a poet familiar with Langland's text and convinced that it offers him a useful approach to his own concerns, and he clearly shares some of the suppositions of the Protestant readership we have been examining. He brings together two major points about the Renaissance perception of *Piers Plowman*. Piers is designated as author (the "wise plowman" speaking "from his sleepe" is the "faithful and industrious Pen"). His role is a dual one; he is both satirist cataloging and rebuking faults and prophet diagnosing the major ills of his time and prescribing their cure.

Having established that conflating Piers and the dreamer is no evidence that a poet is not well acquainted with *Piers Plowman*, we may go on to several other points about Spenser. Spenser uses Piers's name in the May eclogue of *The Shepheardes Calender*, in which he sets up the shepherd Piers as the ideal Protestant minister.[27] And in Book I of *The Faerie Queene* we find out that Redcross was found by a "Plowman in a furrow" and was raised by him "in ploughmans state to byde" (FQ, I. x. 66, 3–6). Redcross's education must begin in the ploughman's state. It is striking that a chivalric figure should be given such a rustic background, and it can be accounted for by pointing to Langland's poem and the tradition it created. Clearly the association with the plowman is an important part of Redcross's quest for holiness. Spenser found the religious associations of *Piers Plowman* important and used them; Drayton, by invoking and paraphrasing an apocalyptic section of the work, evoked the poem's prophetic and historical dimensions. For both writers, Piers was both author and participant in the poem, and both make allusions to the poem's historical and prophetic contexts. Spenser's and Drayton's readings of Langland's poem represent the full coming of age of the attitude to *Piers Plowman* we have been tracing, the point where major poets searching for a way to relate their Protestant witness and their poetic function turn to *Piers Plowman* for an established image of the two roles fused in one.

The Final Stage: The Later Seventeenth Century

One other writer's response to Langland's poem should be recorded because it demonstrates that *Piers Plowman* was still being read in the seventeenth century and that its literary dimension was not forgotten. John Milton, in the *Apology for Smectymnuus,* places *Piers Plowman* in the same category as the Latin and Italian satirists and implies that no one should attempt so ambitious a literary task as satire without knowledge of Langland's work: "Who might have learnt better among the Latin, and Italian Satirists, and in our tongue from the *Vision and Creed of Piers Plowman*, besides others before him."[28] Milton seems to have held the poem in high esteem and assumed its currency at least among serious readers. Like Puttenham and Webbe, Milton clearly is most interested in a consideration of the poem according to its generic category and its role in a native tradition. The title Milton cites differs from that recorded in Puttenham; *The Vision and Creed of Piers Plowman* is the title used in the 1561 edition of the poem, the edition that was toned down by Owen Rodgers.[29] Rodgers's edition contained Langland's poem and an apocryphal plowman text, *Piers Plowman's Creed.* One final note about Milton's reference: it is singularly ambiguous what notion Milton held regarding the authorship of the poem. He mentions Latin and Italian satirists but then speaks of *The Vision and Creed of Piers Plowman* as if he were either unsure of the author or thought the author was Piers himself. Whatever the case, it seems clear that Langland's poem still exercised an effect on readers well into the seventeenth century.

Finally, in confirmation, we should note some later evidence that *Piers Plowman* was specifically excepted from Puritan strictures against imaginative writing in general and an even more rigid taboo against playwriting. William Prynne in his *Histrio-mastix* (1633), a diatribe against "playpoems," describes works that it is lawful to read:

I shall here approve & not condemn, the ancient Tragedy stiled, *Cristus passus* (falsly *attributed to Nazianzen*) wherein Christs passion is elegantly descyphered, together with *Bernardinus Ochin* his *Tragedie of Freewil*, *Plessie Morney* his *Tragedie of Jeptha his daughter*, *Edward the 6 his Comedie de meretrice Babilonica, John Bale his Comedies de Christo & de Lazare, Skelton's Comedies, de Virtute, de Magnificentia, & de bono Ordine, Nicholaus Grimoaldus*

de Archipropheta & Tragedia, &c. which like *Geffry Chaucers &*
Pierce the *Plowmans tales* and *Dialogues*, were penned only to be
read, not acted, their subjects being al serious, sacred, divine, not
scurrilous wanton or prophan, as al modern Play poems are.

Thirdly, as it is lawfull to pen, so likewise *to recite, to read such*
tragicall or comicall poems as these.[30]

Prynne's description of these works as all "serious, sacred, and
divine" provides an indication of how he views *Piers Plowman*.
Observe as well that he talks about multiple works of Chaucer's and
Langland's, referring almost certainly to the entire plowman tradition in which Chaucer was thought to play a part. These tales and
dialogues are in a select company with biblical history and morality
plays. The reason seems clear: they are important because they
played a role in Reformation history and told a version of the truth
about those times.

As we have seen, Bunyan's contemporary, Thomas Fuller, in his
Histories of the Worthies of England (1662), delivers the strongest
statement up to this point about the worth and meaning of Langland's
work to the later seventeenth century. In the section on Shropshire,
under the category of learned writers, and dated "Since the Reformation," Fuller discusses Langland:

Robert Langeland. Forgive me, Reader, though placing him (who
lived one hundred and fifty years *before*) *since* the Reformation: for
I conceive that the *Morning-star* belongs rather to the *Day*, then to
the *Night*. On which account this Robert (regulated in our Book not
according to the Age he was in, but Judgement he was of) may by
Prolepsis be termed a *Protestant*.

He was born at *Mortimers-Clibery* in this County, eight miles
from Malvern-Hills; was bred a Priest, and one of the first followers
of John Wickliffe, wanting neither Wit nor Learning, as appears by
his Book called "The Vision of Pierce Plowghman."[31]

Fuller's designation of Langland as a Protestant is in part a recognition of and a response to the second life the book assumed in the

Renaissance. Langland is designated as one of Wylcif's priestly followers. Fuller's conviction about the centrality of Langland's poem is attested by his placing Langland among writers after the Reformation though he knows that this is, on a factual level, incorrect. Fuller also connects "The Complaint of the Plowman," a work Bunyan certainly knew from Foxe, to *Piers Plowman*: "There is a Book first set forth by Tindal, since exemplified by Mr. Fox, called "The Prayer and Complaint of the Plowghman," which, though differing in title and written in prose, yet be of the *same* subject, at the *same* time, in the *same* Language, I must refer it to the same Author." Fuller is the first explicitly to connect these two works in print, but it is clear from previous comments that readers had long assumed they were written by the same person. We should note as well that Fuller, as a Protestant reader, makes the case for authorship on the grounds of similar subject matter rather than style, unlike the literary critics discussed in chapter 3.

Another historian, William Greaves, in *The History of the Church of Great Britain* (1667), clearly conflates *Piers Plowman* and the Tyndale-Foxe "Complaint." His title is that of the "Complaint," his attribution of authorship is to Langland, and his description of the book's contents, given Crowley's interpretation of *Piers Plowman*, could be applied to either:

About that time a Book was written in English, called The Complaint and Prayer of a Ploughman. The writer of it is said have been Robert Langland, a Priest. After a general complaint of the Iniquity of the Time, the Author wrote zealously against Auricular Confession, as contrary to Scripture, and profit of the publick, and as a device of man: against the Simony of selling Pardons: against the Pope as an adversary of Christ. He complaineth of the unmarried Priests committing wickedness and by example provoking others; of Images in Churches as Idolatry; of false Pastours, which feed upon their flocks, and feed them not, nor suffer others to feed them. He wrote also against Purgatory.[32]

Greaves and Fuller, distanced from the work's polemical introduction in 1550 and past the initial grappling with a generic category, define *Piers Plowman* as a significant part of Reformation history. Their works are nearer to the kinds of writing that Bunyan might have read, and their conclusion about the similarities between the plowman texts is one that Bunyan would have been led to as well. Fuller acknowledges the problems presented by the language, referring to "a few of his strange words and their significations." But it is noteworthy, in assessing the difficulty of the poem's language for a reader like Bunyan, that Fuller lists (and translates correctly) a mere sixteen words. The language in Crowley's edition was simply not so great an obstacle as one might think.

That the tradition was by no means dying out in the late seventeenth century is indicated by an early eighteenth-century work that offers a similar perspective on *Piers Plowman*. John Strype's *Ecclesiastical Memorials* (1721) defines itself on the title page as "Relating chiefly to Religion, and the Reformation of it" during the reigns of Henry VIII, Edward VI, and Queen Mary. He tells us in his preface that he has "noted the various Books that came forth from year to Year, as I had seen, or met with them, of what Sort soever they were; but chiefly, such as concerned Religion."[33] Under the year 1550, Strype lists the Crowley edition of *Piers Plowman* ("Now was The *Vision of Pierse Plowman* the second time printed by the foresaid Crowley") and summarizes the contents with material taken directly from the preface.[34] By the time Strype is writing, Crowley's edition itself, as distinct from the features of the poem, is being interpreted as an important contribution to the struggle for reform.

In short, it is clear that Crowley's three editions of *The Vision of Pierce Plowman* still had an impact on readers in the seventeenth century. Its reputation had journeyed quite a distance from its initial publication, but the poem remained rooted in a prophetic, historical context, not a purely literary one. Whether it was called a "holy work" (Bale) or a "Satyre" (Puttenham), it remained a "true" utterance about an earlier time and was therefore not a fictional structure. The work's contexts were clear: it involved itself with historical issues and participated in Reformation history. It was both readable and widely read.

Renaissance Readers of *Piers Plowman*

None of the more or less public statements that we have just surveyed answers directly the question of whether ordinary readers really were reading the poem in the later sixteenth and seventeenth centuries. If so, what did they make of it? The evidence we can bring to bear on this question is necessarily slim but more revealing than one can normally expect from so early a period: marginalia in surviving copies of the Crowley and Rodgers editions and a few manuscripts. The majority of the printed copies have some marginal annotations revealing careful reading and clear comprehension.[35] For example, the reader of one second edition, probably the Nicholas Smith who signs his name in a number of places in a late sixteenth-century hand, has made a long list of biblical quotations and the leaves on which they are cited, along with a complete table of Anima's names.[36]

The Huntington Library first edition "is heavily underscored, with emphasis on the abuses of the clergy, the doctrine of simplicity, and an apparent millenarianism."[37] Most of these notes, however, are of little intrinsic interest, since they merely point out the subject matter or comment "nota bene" or "a goodlye note." Some merely have owners' signatures at intervals throughout, and some have doodles, drawings of heads or pen exercises, suggesting that even readers far from spellbound by the contents were reading their way through the book.

Three copies, however, deserve more detailed attention. John King examined one of these and used it to show that Crowley infuriated at least one reader who was not a part of the readership we have been describing. This is the copy signed "Andrew Bostock, 1613" which has notes objecting vehemently to Crowley's Protestant reading of the poem.[38] King notes that "Bostock returns to the traditional interpretation of *Piers Plowman* as an orthodox appeal for reform within the established church."[39] As an educated Roman Catholic, Bostock specifically castigates Crowley's view that the poem included a prophecy of the overthrow of monasticism. But Bostock's reading of the poem, judging by the survey of the reputation of the poem cited in this chapter, was clearly a minority view. *Piers Plowman*, in the two centuries after the publication of Crowley's edition, was still seen as a forerunner of the Reformation. Most of the marginalia inserted by readers in other copies of the poem show no like inclination to dispute Crowley's interpretation.

Of all the editions I have examined, the one that best demonstrates the thoroughness with which the poem was read by someone displaying no specialized historical or literary knowledge is in the British Library.[40] The copy is well marked and has comments in a later sixteenth-century hand. The reader blocks out particularly important passages and adds sketches of hands that point to certain lines. The comments are extensive enough to show a whole range of responses to the fabric of Langland's poem and to the Crowley annotations. The reader of this copy of the poem is unknown, but his thinking about the poem characterizes him clearly. His annotations demonstrate that he approached the work in exactly the terms Crowley had intended.

The poem's prophetic character was clearly an important feature of the poem for this reader. On the second page of the preface, the reader displays dissatisfaction with the sketchy treatment accorded this element in Crowley's preface by listing other "prophecies" he had located in the text:[41]

xvi lefe

By six sons-a shype false-a sheaf of arrowes

an other prophety of dissolving of abays in the xlx life

where he speakythe of a mydyell of a mon

nother prophecy to begin

in a day will apear.

Although this annotation is difficult to untangle, two lines, the first and the third ("By six sons-a shype false-a sheaf of arrowes" and "where he speakythe of a mydyell of a mon"), refer to a passage in passus 3 in which Conscience evokes a time when reason will reign and govern the land, and prophesies the conversion of the Jews:

And or thys fortune fall, fynde shall men the werste,

By six sones and a shippe and halfe a shefe of arowes

And the mydle of a mone shall make the Jewes to turne.

(D3v)

The second line ("an other prophety of dissolving of abays in the xlx life") refers to a passage in passus 10 that Crowley glossed in the second edition as being another prophecy about the suppression of the abbeys. The reader simply records the page ("xlx life") without citing the lines. The passage in question is the following:

And ther shall come a king & confesse you religious

And beat you as the byble telleth for breking of your rule

And amend monials monkes and chanons

And put hem to her penaunce.

(N2r)

But these are not the only passages the reader has spotted.[42] The marginal notes indicate that he has carefully gone through the text and marked out those passages that are prophetic and gnomic. For instance, in the prologue to the Visio, Langland issues a warning for reform in religion that the reader glosses as "the fyrste prophecy":

For sith charitie was chapman and chere to shrive lordes

Many ferleis have fallen in fewe yeres

But holy churche and I hold better togyther

The most mischiefe on molde is mountinge welfast.[43]

(A1v-A2r)

His most interesting comment about prophecy illustrates his ability to think independently of Crowley, though in sympathy with his approach. It occurs in the latter part of the "Rat Parliament" where the rat quotes the scriptural text: "Woe the land were the king is a child." Crowley, as King notes, had taken great pains in his Latin comment on this passage to say that it means "when the king is childish" not "when he is a child," in order to eliminate a possibly derogatory allusion to the child king Edward VI.[44] The reader— clearly writing at a later date—rejects this quibbling remark and comments succinctly: "prophycy paste."

The reader's marked interest in the "prophetic" passages illustrates that the poem was clearly perceived as a prophecy. But the marginal comments about prophecies are restricted to the gnomic sayings and the passages about suppression of the abbeys. Only once does the reader point out a prophecy that refers to events still in the future. In passus 3, when Conscience makes a long speech about Reason reigning over the land and making law a laborer, the reader announces "This is to come" (D4v). But his comment must be set against Crowley's own note for the passage: "This is no prophecye, but a truth gathered out of scriptures." Both the editor and the reader point to a time near the end of the world. Crowley, in his synopsis, translates that scene and defines that time in the following way: "What perfite state the worlde shall be in the tyme of renovation." Neither Crowley nor his reader announces that time is at hand. One further point of interest about the reader's interpretation of the text as a prophecy: his copy is heavily annotated, but only up to a point. He stops abruptly in passus 19 before the advent of Antichrist. No signal is given as to why he stopped, but he clearly did not include the closing passages of the poem in his catalogue of prophecies.

Marked as his interest in the prophetic character of the work was, this reader, like Crowley, treated it as a religious tract that exhorted reform. His comments are in general remarkably like Crowley's. They are an amalgam of plot summary, translation into doctrine, and warning to those who will read the work after him. He often indexes particular scenes. For instance in passus 5 when Envy makes a confession, he draws a line down the page to single the passage out and labels it "the confessyon of Envye" (F2r). More often he marks the passages he perceives as particularly important; he constantly remarks "note" or "a goudly note." Next to the passage where Conscience debates with Lady Mede about the two kinds of Mede, the reader draws a hand and writes "Note here the diversyty of Mede" (D3v). The reader's comments move easily from the scene to its meaning: "a special note preachers wyll doo as they say" (F1r), "here ys wedloke commendyd" (L3v), "how we sholde be maryed" (M1v). The literal level of the fiction is not a barrier; the moral is gleaned and recorded in the margin.

For all the reader's attention to the "prophecies" in the work, he, like Crowley, views it as a reformist Protestant reader, seeing the text's primary thrust in its ability to instruct and rebuke. The reader, like Crowley, insists on the poem's immediacy and relevance for his own time. Even the simplest statement is reworded with a reflection. When Imaginatif introduces himself—"I am Imaginatif quod he, idle was I never" (P3v)—the reader remarks "be ocup 'ed in good workes." When Imaginatif warns the dreamer to amend his own life: "Amende the while thou may, thou hast ben warned oft" (P4r), the reader's remark totally ignores the fictional interplay between the dreamer and Imagination. His comment directs the reader outside the text and to himself: "Preacharys amend ye selfe and then ye may saffly correcte other." This comment provides a further illustration that the fictional frame is totally obscured by the search for correction. Yet nothing could more convincingly demonstrate that the poem was not too hard or too theologically alien to seem vividly contemporary to Renaissance readers. The marginal notes by the reader record his personal response to a difficult work, yet he seems totally secure in moving from scene to abstracted meaning. *Piers Plowman* is a poem filled with rebuke for religion, society, and most specifically the dreamer himself. But Crowley and his reader view the work as continually moving outward to the reader.

In some ways the most significant copy for the literary historian is one of Rodgers's edition which bears the signature of Richard Harvey, brother of Gabriel Harvey, dated 1585.[45] The date is significant in itself, both as being long after the last publication of the poem in 1561 and as being only a few years before Gabriel Harvey published two polemical works that attempted to mediate between the Marprelate writers and their opponents.[46] Here we have a reader who, given his connection to his brother, is more "lettered" than those we have discussed so far, but whose reading demonstrates that even educated Protestant readers read very differently from us in terms of their approach to the literal level of the text. The copy is heavily underscored—as many as half the lines on the page in most instances—and bears a variety of marks to call attention to lines Harvey has found important. While most of the verbal annotation merely indexes the action, several features of Harvey's commentary are important for the light they shed on Spenser's milieu as well as for their witness about how Langland's poem was perceived by a more learned and literarily sophisticated reader. The first point is that, in a long note on the first page, Harvey immediately situates the work in the context of Reformation polemics, differing from other works of its kind primarily in its greater literary artistry: "More art & lesse vanity in this vision than in the Traunce of Pasquin: yet both are against the Romish Glory &. Chaucers plowman & this pm much alike in final end and effect." "Chaucers plowman" is, of course, the apocryphal "Plowman's Tale." "The Trance of Pasquin" is probably a reference to a work published in 1566:

> Pasquine in a Traunce A Christian and learned Dialogue (containing wonderfull and most strange newes out of Heaven, Purgatorie, and Hell) wherein besydes Christes truth playnely set forth, ye shall also finde a numbre of pleasaunt hystories, discovering all the crafty conveyaunces of Ante-christ, Whereunto are added certayne Questions then put forth by Pasquine, to have bene disputed in the Councell of Trent. Turned but lately out of the Italian into this tongue, by W. P. Seene (and) allowed according to the order appointed in the Queenes Majesties Injunctions.[47]

This work is not only polemical but satiric and ironic, and it shares a number of features of the works we surveyed in chapter 3 such as history, the genre of dialogue, and an insistence that, although it is a dream, "Christes truth" is "playnely set forth."[48] Harvey's reference to "The Trance of Pasquin" signals his assumption that earlier Catholic works attacking the abuses of the Church were automatically to be considered in the same category as post-Reformation anti-Catholic polemics. For him, this aspect of the poem's content and its satiric mode were the leading characteristics of *Piers Plowman*. Harvey also cites on the first page the John Malverne theory of authorship (which we have seen in Stowe), apparently feeling at home with the idea of a donnish author.[49] In view of Harvey's concern with Reformation controversy, it is important to note that, in contrast to the reader of the preceding copy, he shows almost no interest at all in the prophetic aspects of the poem, taking note of them only to the extent of writing "ecce" next to the gnomic prophecy at the end of passus 6 (K2r) and placing a cryptic sign next to the "Abbot of Abbington" passage, beside "beate you as the bible telleth" (O1v).

A second revealing point is that Harvey begins by assuming, apparently as a matter of course, that the narrator is Piers. Opposite "Al this I saugh slepyng" at the end of the prologue, he writes "Pierce asleepe" (A4v), and after the waking interlude in passus 5, notes "Pierce asleepe agane" (F1r). Opposite "By Peter, quod a plowman," when Piers is first introduced in passus 5, he merely notes "truth" (H2r), even though his normal practice is to mark the appearance of new characters by putting their names in the margin. Guided by the Crowley plot summary—which, in Rodgers's edition, is printed at the head of each passus—he probably began the *Vita de Dowel* with the same assumption. But as soon as he encounters passages in which Piers is mentioned or quoted to the Dreamer by other characters as a third person, he begins to write "Pierce" in the margin as if the distinction were clear (e.g., S3r and Y3r). He also manifests a particular interest in the passage associating Piers, rather than the clergy, with Christ: "Petrus id est Christus" (Y3r). He then starts keeping track of the dream-waking pattern, calling attention to "I waked" (Dd1r) at the end of a passus. But he no longer identifies the sleeper as "Pierce." In general, he is alert to the changing roles of characters on which so much of the poem's structure depends, noting, for example, at the end of the poem, "conscience is becom a pilgrim" (Ii2v). It is therefore worth noting that, although he was attentive enough a reader to figure out eventually that Piers and the Dreamer are not literally the same character, he does not seem to regard this discovery as a matter of any major importance, or one that significantly alters his perception of the poem's structure or meaning. He sees characters as having complementary roles, so that they are in a literal sense distinct but in a more fundamental way parts of the same thing. This seems to him so natural an aspect of a story that the degree of separateness between characters is a minor matter.

The most illuminating marginalia of all, however, occur not in a Crowley edition but in a British Museum manuscript of the C-text that was annotated at intervals from the early sixteenth century to the seventeenth century by five or possibly six different hands and signed by four owners.[50] These comments provide a sequence of thinking about *Piers Plowman* itself, with implications about literature in general over one hundred and fifty years, that deserves extensive study in its own right. For our purposes, the comments of the 1603 and later hands are of special value in demonstrating how readers considerably nearer to Bunyan's time than to Crowley's approached *Piers Plowman*. It is clear from the extent and detail of these comments that at least some seventeenth-century readers were quite undeterred by medieval handwriting or by the lack of linguistic and other glossing from following the poem at least as well as modern readers.

Some of the marginalia in the manuscript demonstrate that Crowley's interpretation of the poem was not idiosyncratic but had caused and may also have reflected widely held assumptions which maintained their ascendancy into the seventeenth century. These assumptions include conflating the dreamer with Piers, reading the pardon scene as anticlerical and antiprelatical, and believing that the poem's critique of the church was an integral part of the movement leading to the Reformation. The resemblance is the more striking in that this manuscript, being a C-text version of the poem, contains many passages unparalleled in the B-text that, therefore, were never commented on by Crowley.[51] Perhaps the most famous of these is the so-called "autobiographical" confession of the dreamer which the C-reviser placed at the beginning of passus 5 as a preface to the confession of the seven deadly sins. One of the annotator's most significant comments is provoked by this passage.

The "autobiographical" section opens with the dreamer waking from his dream:

Thus y awakede, woet god, whan y wonede in Cornehull,

Kytte and y in a cote, yclothed as a lollare,

And lytel ylet by, leveth me for sothe,

Amonges lollares of Londone and lewede ermytes,

For y made of tho man as resoun me tauhte.

(C. passus 5, lines 1–5)

The commentator, in a seventeenth-century hand, remarks, "Piers dwelled in Cornwall with his friend Christopher or his wyf cotte in there bede had a vision" (fol. 28v).[52] There could be no better indication that Piers is identified as the dreamer and that the work itself is seen as his vision. More striking still, opposite "Amonge lolleres of Londone" the commentator inserts "peres became a protestande and loved his lyke" (fol. 28v). Thus, the poem was perceived as a record of Piers's individual reformation; the commentator assumes that Piers is a Lollard.[53] Moreover, he sees the vision as the story of how Piers breaks with Catholicism as a post-Reformation thinker would define it and joins a movement that the commentator regards as part of Reformation history. This is made even clearer by his gloss on "lollere" in a subsequent passage that reflects normal fourteenth-century derogatory use of the term. There Reason accuses the dreamer of being a lollere, a lazy person:

'Thenne hastow londes to live by,' quod Resoun, 'or lynage ryche

That fynde the thy fode? For an ydel man thou semest,

A spendour that spene mot or a spille-tyme,

Or beggest thy bylyve aboute at men hacches

Or faytest uppon Frydayes or feste-dayes in churches,

The whiche is lollarne lyf, that lytel is preysed

There ryhtfulnesse rewardeth rhyt as men deserveth.'

(C. passus 5, lines 26–32)

Opposite line 30 the annotator comments, "lowlars regarded not fridaies fast" (fol. 29r). interpreting the term in its later Reformation sense. It is clear, then, that his identification of Piers and the dreamer is compatible both with detailed knowledge of the poem and with extensive acquaintance with Reformation history.

In fact, the seventeenth-century commentators go far beyond Crowley in the radicalness of their religious and social critique and in their millenarian expectations. The passage about the suppression of the abbeys is still being seen as a prophecy of events that have since come to pass; opposite that section of the text a seventeenth-century annotator comments, "A prophecye trulye fulfilled by kinge henrye the viii" (fol. 31v). But the annotations also point out "prophecies" of more radical change in the future. One comment labelled "script 1603" remarks on Reason's program of reform in passus 4,[54] "Thus farr of prophises yet to come all the reste followinge are past saving the fall of the lawe and byshoppis nowe at hande" (fol. 26r). This comment has particular reference to the following lines: "That lawe shal ben a laborer and lede afelde donge / And love shall lede thi land as the leef lyketh" (C. passus 4, lines 144–45). Thus at least one annotator is caught up in the prophetic contexts of the work, and the fact that he dates his comment shows his awareness of placing prophecy within a consciously considered pattern of historical development. The commentators frequently abstract moral lessons in the same way that Crowley does: for example "bishops should have no more than Christe had" (fol. 57r), and "Theologie is no seyence but a sothfaste beliefe and teacheth us to love" (fol. 62v). Some comments concern doctrinal issues: "gods body under the elliment of brede not transsustan" (fol. 116r). But the radical critique remains the dominant refrain. At least three hands take the pardon scene as anticlerical, and as antiprelatic as well since bishops are responsible for ignorant priests. Langland's corrupt "doctour" at the banquet is glossed in fol. 77r: "Doctor Robinson, Dr. Baresons of Lincoln with many mor." Some of the terms used are typically seventeenth-century radical Protestant ones. For instance, the priest that interprets the pardon for Piers was called "blinde" by Crowley but in this manuscript is termed "a hirelinge" (fol. 53v).

The marginalia in the C-text manuscript, unlike Crowley's annotations, which are directed toward individual reformation, continually attempt to relate the work to the annotator's own historical time. In the C-text prologue to the Visio, the line "conscience cam and cused hem" (C. prologue, line 95) is glossed by an annotator, "This conscience is now supposed to be Kinge James ye Sixt." Langland's poem is being accorded the same power as the prophetic books of the Bible to sustain new interpretations as history unrolls. The most moving and radical of all the comments comes at the close of *Piers Plowman*. Langland ends:

> "By Christ," quod Consience tho, "y wol bicome a pilgrime,
>
> And wenden as wyde as the world regneth
>
> To seke Peres the plouhman, that Pruyde myhte destruye,
>
> And that freres hadde a fyndynge, that for nede flateren
>
> And contrepledeth me Consience Now Kynde me avenge,
>
> And seende me hap and hele til I have Piers plouhman.'
>
> And sethe he gradde aftur Grace tyl y gan awake.
>
> (C. passus 22, lines 381–86)

The commentator remarks: "conscience ys a sleppe till he come againe [.] Consience will not come into this lande till the proude Prelates and [va?]nitous lawyeres be swepe awaie which will not be longe to Amen So be it" (fol. 124r). Here we find full-blown the apocalyptic reading of the text that Crowley, in spite of his millenarian concerns, never directly imposed on it, yet that is the logical outcome of the perspective the early reformers brought to Langland and his poem. In those lines, we see illustrated more graphically and poignantly than in any formal analyses the fascination *Piers Plowman* continued to exercise on the imaginations of radical seventeenth-century Protestants and the urgency with which the poem seemed to speak to them about struggles and hopes for their own time, a time in which the Reformation was still seen as tragically incomplete. The annotators' comments go far toward corroborating the impression suggested (as we noted in chapter 3) by the use of a plowman text as a Marprelate tract at the end of the sixteenth century; by the seventeenth century, *Piers Plowman* had become too radical to be held up as a model by mainstream Protestants.

Frontispiece of Robert Southey's 1832 edition of The Pilgrim's Progress. *(Courtesy of the Lilly Library, Indiana University, Bloomington, Indiana.)*

6

"The excellent, though illiterate, Bunyan"

Reconfiguring Bunyan and His Book Within a Protestant Paradigm for Reading

> How can we think of one without being reminded of the other? Some distant relationship seems to exist between the Ploughman's *Dowell* and *Dobet,* and *Dobest,* Friar *Flatterer, Grace* the Portress of the magnificent Tower of *Truth* viewed at a distance, and by its side the Dungeon of Care, *Natural Understanding* and his lean and stern wife *Study,* and all the rest of this numerous company, and the shadowy pilgrimage of the "Immortal Dreamer" to the Celestial City. Yet I would mistrust my own feeling, when so many able critics, in their various researches after a prototype of that singular production, have hitherto not suggested what seems to me so obvious.
>
> Isaac D'Israeli, *The Amenities of Literature*

 Readers do not create the texts they read, but they do see them through specific lenses that determine the outcome of their interaction with texts. If we isolate the reactions of Robert Crowley and George Puttenham to the fabric of *Piers Plowman*, we can see how the very different lenses forged by their horizons of expectations about the nature of books and authors defined what they saw when they encountered Langland's poem and conditioned their experience of it. Reading from a religious perspective on the nature and value of books, Crowley saw a historical and prophetic document written by one of God's servants, a book that was still capable of playing an active role in promoting reform for both society and the individual reader. The lens Crowley looked through magnified the book's designs on the reader. Reading from a literary perspective, Puttenham saw a particular literary form, the satire. His attention gravitated to the figure of the author rather than to the book's impact on readers. The writer was a "malcontent," although he seems to have been a "true Prophet." Crowley saw an exhortation; Puttenham, an artifact. The lenses through which *The Pilgrim's Progress* was seen also magnified different aspects of the text. As we saw in chapter 1, in the example of Joshua Gilpin we have a reader who brings multiple lenses to bear. His perception of the importance of *The Pilgrim's Progress*'s effect on the Christian reader testified to his allegiance to the Protestant perspective on the nature and value of books. But superimposed on that lens was another, created from literary assumptions about books that demanded that he alter the fabric of the work. The form and fashion, the aesthetic dimensions of the work, needed to be rehabilitated if the "excellent, though illiterate" author was to garner the fame he deserved.

D'Israeli's wistful comment above about a possible relationship between *Piers Plowman* and *The Pilgrim's Progress* succinctly circumscribes the kind of lens an exclusively lettered reader brought to Bunyan's narrative. Such a reader processes texts in terms of generic categories, searches for a "prototype," and speculates about what the author had read. As we have seen, Samuel Johnson's experience of reading *The Pilgrim's Progress* shows a similar interest in the author and his literary activity when he muses to Boswell about whether Bunyan knew Dante or Spenser. Implicit in D'Israeli's and Johnson's comments is a sense that literature is a distinct classification with its own taxonomy, separable from all others. that books beget other books, and that a writer's appropriation and manipulation of a literary tradition is of paramount interest.

Those suppositions about the literary product and its author have provided the lens through which modern critics have perceived the fabric of *The Pilgrim's Progress*. As critics, we have approached the work in terms of a literary taxonomy, using the structures of various genres, both literary and quasi-literary, to assess Bunyan's achievement. But our understanding *The Pilgrim's Progress* must be reconfigured to yield, not a view of the author's "literary" activity, but an understanding of the role of the book and its author in actively engaging the minds and hearts of its readers. It is in terms of a specific kind of readership that Langland's poem and Bunyan's narrative are connected. Without the readership that *Piers Plowman* initiated, *The Pilgrim's Progress* would not exist.

We cannot know whether Bunyan read, or even knew of, the texts that comprised the *Piers Plowman* tradition, but what we can know for sure is that Bunyan was a product of the growth of a Protestant mode of reading that I have been tracing, and that *Piers Plowman* and *The Pilgrim's Progress* stand at the beginning and the ending of this phenomenon. Ultimately, however, the religious, reformist model Langland's poem offers in its Renaissance incarnation throws into relief aspects of *The Pilgrim's Progress* that differ markedly from *Piers Plowman*. Setting the two works side by side magnifies fundamental cultural changes that began to take place in the Middle Ages and found their final expression in the late seventeenth century. Those changes are a direct result of the adoption of the Bible as the one sure way to salvation, and they can be explained by the growth of a Protestant readership encountering Scripture in the intervening centuries. But before we can reconfigure *The Pilgrim's Progress* within a Protestant paradigm for reading, we must begin with its reception by a lettered readership in order to frame what has happened to the text up to our own time. We may then understand why we have been unable or unwilling to see this text through the lens its author brought to it.

Bunyan and the Politics of Being "Literate"

As we noted in chapter 1, the category of the literary is a historical construct, and its contours can be traced in the changing reputation of *The Pilgrim's Progress*. Ideas about authors and about where books come from, using both a literary and a religious perspective, have dominated the debate over Bunyan's achievement in *The Pilgrim's Progress*. Despite the fact that Bunyan's work had an audience second only to the Bible, or perhaps because of it, *The Pilgrim's Progress* has always fit uncomfortably in the literary canon; it has been regarded both as a primarily literary and as a primarily religious text. From the seventeenth century to the twentieth, both aspects of its reputation developed at least partly in terms of the author's and the reader's class. Joshua Gilpin's assessment of Bunyan as "excellent, though illiterate" epitomizes the competing perspectives on Bunyan and his book. These two perspectives about authors and about where books come from are foregrounded in the work of the two nineteenth-century editors of Bunyan's works, George Offor and Henry Stebbing. Both editors use Bunyan's lack of education as a key piece of evidence. For Offor, Bunyan's claim not to have read literary works was evidence of his religious purity, while Stebbing tried to show that Bunyan could have come in contact with works such as Dante's through an oral tradition appropriate to an uneducated writer.

Class expectations of authorship and readership, then, produced differing categorizations of Bunyan's book as a literary or a religious event. But it is *The Pilgrim's Progress*'s status as a literary phenomenon that we will be concerned with in this section. The bewildering spectrum of responses to Bunyan and his book document the difficulty *The Pilgrim's Progress* has presented to a lettered readership whose attention naturally gravitates toward the figure of the author and the formal characteristics of the work to explain its origin. The truth of Robert Darnton's definition of literature, "an activity rather than an established body of texts,"[1] can be discerned in the practices of various critics who see *The Pilgrim's Progress* through the lens of literary expectations.

A survey of the editions of *The Pilgrim's Progress* would be a monumental task, but some knowledge of its printing history can shed light on the question of its reception by a lettered audience. The editions of *The Pilgrim's Progress* in the first two centuries after its publication fall into two basic categories that John Brown in his biography of Bunyan labels as "inferior" and "more ambitious."[2] Perhaps a clearer way to categorize them is in terms of the class of their audiences, popular versus lettered. "Inferior" editions were a result of the great demand for the work.[3] As these editions multiplied, according to Brown, "the get-up of the book deteriorated, till at last . . . it was often printed on tobacco paper, and the illustrations became coarser and more smirchy."[4] "More ambitious" editions were printed on a higher quality of paper and were replete with embellishments of various kinds.

Unfortunately, the poor quality of the popular editions and the practice of collecting the best and cleanest copies of rare books by research libraries make it impossible to guess how it was read by a popular audience, although the proliferation of cheap editions testifies that it was widely read. But the marginalia of that readership, who viewed *The Pilgrim's Progress* as an instrument rather than an object, have not been preserved. We do not have recourse to those "opaque documents," but we can deduce what a lettered readership saw in *The Pilgrim's Progress* by examining the textual machinery of several later editions of Bunyan's work for that audience. The first "more ambitious" attempt, according to Brown, was the twenty-second edition, published by J. Clark in 1725,[5] and the first modern edition was that by Robert Southey in 1830. Both editions advertise themselves as literary objects in their prefaces and illustrations, and the Southey edition in particular represents the first full-scale attempt to turn *The Pilgrim's Progress* into literature.

The 1725 edition of Bunyan's work was reprinted numerous times until 1800.[6] The title page, after giving the title and author, focuses on the illustrations: it is "Adorned with curious Sculptures," engraved by J. Sturt. This phrase succinctly signals the audience the publishers were trying to reach, as does the unsigned preface, presumably by J. Clark. It closes by locating an audience willing to pay more for better editions:

> The Universal Good, which this incomparable Treatise hath done to Mankind, and the Desire of its farther public Benefit, is the Occasion of this present Edition; for the former Impressions being, on Account of the Poorer Sort, published at *so cheap a Rate,* it was out of their Power to purchase a *Better;* so that a great many worthy Christians, thro' Age or other Infirmities, were unhappily deprived of the Benefit of it, which some Persons of Distinction and Piety duly weighing, in order to remedy that Inconvenience, very generously and highly becoming their character and good Intentions, proposed that it might be sent into the World, in the handsome Manner it now appears. Great Care has been taken, not only in the Correct Printing, but in the Engraving of the several Copper-Plates, which adorn it: so that it is not in the least doubted, but the Whole will give such entire Satisfaction to the Public in general, as well as those Worthy Gentleman in particular who have so handsomely and generously contributed to this beautiful Edition, by their large Subscriptions, as will fully answer their Expectation.[7]

"Age and other Infirmities" required better paper and clearer printing, but class expectations about books also demanded a "Correct"
text as well as fine illustrations. The "Public" is clearly a lettered
readership that views books as artistic objects first; the edition must
be produced in a "handsome Manner" if it is to be read. Just as we
saw in the example of Gilpin's edition, the "Universal Good" that *The
Pilgrim's Progress* can deliver must be "dressed" in the appropriate
garb in order to reach that audience.[8]

The preface to this edition provides a clear example of the lens a
lettered readership brings to a work, for the issues of genre, previous
models, and execution are at the center of the reader's interest. The
preface begins by defining the work in terms of its literary kind:
"This Manner of Allegorical Writing, by way of Parable, hath ever
been esteemed by Men of the brightest and most refined Genius,"[9]
and it cites Plato, the writers of Scripture, and Christ himself as
evidence for this point. After evoking these models for writing
parables, the writer of the preface praises Bunyan's handling of the
allegory: "Mr. *Bunyan* hath been very Happy in his Idea of the
Pilgrim: It is a delicate and familiar Topick, and wonderfully natural
to represent, in all its Degrees and Circumstances, the Life of Every
Man, who is a *Stranger and Sojourner, and a Pilgrim, as all his
Fathers have been*: And he hath so happily executed his Design, that
no Performance of this Kind hath ever come up to it."[10] The
emphasis here falls on Bunyan's choice of idea, its aptness, and his
skill in executing his design, terms that are slanted toward the artistic
aspects of Bunyan's production. He next cites two other models of
this kind of work, St. John Damascene's story of Balaam and Jehosa-
phat and Simon Patrick's *Parable of the Pilgrim*, in order to show how
much more accomplished Bunyan's effort is:

Such tedious Pieces as they, are wholly void of Life and Spirit, so
they are very unapt to stir up those warm Affections and Religious
Fires, which the Nature of so eminent and important a Subject essentially requires.

It fares otherwise with our Author, thro' whom there reigns a
wonderful Simplicity of Diction, attended with Sentiments the most
surprizingly Touching. The *Allegory* is admirably well continued

and interwoven, the Transitions easy and natural, and all the Images
are lively, strong and nervous; mixed with such a Spirit of true Piety, as hath not its Equal, but in the Holy Scriptures.[11]

Bunyan's "Piece" is superior because of its diction, sentiments,
transitions, and images. The argument for moral improvement is not
jettisoned, but it is temporarily subordinated to a consideration of
the work as an aesthetic object. What redeems the work most of all is
the "Spirit of true Piety," which is without equal except for the Bible,
a perspective on Bunyan that will be repeated innumerable times as
we chart the reception of *The Pilgrim's Progress* in chapter 7. But
finally, the writer of the preface must confront the fact that *The
Pilgrim's Progress* was written by a mechanick preacher and was
embraced by the lower classes.

The comparison of Bunyan's style to the "Holy Scriptures"
provides him with the reason why *The Pilgrim's Progress* could appeal
to all readers, both lettered and unlettered. The fact that Bunyan had
thoroughly studied the Bible and had in *The Pilgrim's Progress*
"almost everywhere expressed himself in their Style and Language"
made it possible that "the Simple and Illiterate" could "learn Improvement and Instruction, and even the Learned finds Matter
wherewith to employ his Speculation."[12] The reader then acknowledges that the work itself bears none of the earmarks of a lettered
production, both in terms of its style and its author, although it has a
power that goes beyond them:

And one Thing particularly is observable in this Work, that a Man
can scarce take it in his Hand, but he is tempted to go through with
it, it so agreeably engages the Attention by its Narration, which in
some Places contains such Moving Circumstances of Human Mis-
ery and Distress, in its plain Garb, as we no where find in the finest
Pieces of Art, however set off with all the Pomp and Glitter of accurate Phrase and Rhetoric: And I believe no one in the World, of
what Sect, Party, or Profession soever he be, can read several of the
Episodes especially the *Passing of the River,* in the Conclusion,
without some sort of Religious Emotion and Affection.[13]

This eloquent tribute to the power of *The Pilgrim's Progress* has both a heartfelt sincerity and a dash of impassioned pleading in it. The writer of the preface contrasts the "Pomp" and "Glitter" of the "finest Pieces of Art," defined in terms of the right use of language, and the "plain Garb" of Bunyan's narrative. Essentially, he is asking this specific audience to accept the work even though the author's credentials and the text itself fall short of their expectations of a literary production.

Having raised the issue of the "illiterate" author by speaking of the work's power over the reader, the writer of the preface next turns to what is represented by Bunyan's achievement. And here, there is more than just a touch of envy evident in his praise of Bunyan:

> All these Things considered, Is is [it?] not wonderful that a plain, simple Man, and unlearned, as Mr. *Bunyan* was, should notwithstanding, have composed so useful and admirable a Treatise? But alas! from the *Mouths of Babes and Sucklings* GOD is sometimes pleased wonderfully to manifest his Glory; and the Poor and Unlearned gain Heaven, while (to use S. *Augustin's* Expressions) *the Great Ones of this World, with all their mighty Stock and Boast of Learning, sink into Perdition.* So true is it, that the Spirit of GOD is unconfined: And he ordereth its *Salutary Influence where he listeth.*[14]

God is the only explanation of how the unlettered tinker could have written such a useful book. We find in this quotation a perspective on 1 Cor. 1.27 from the side of the "Great Ones," and the "alas" has a certain wistfulness in it.

A century later, Robert Southey is willing to claim Bunyan as a major literary figure, and the textual machinery of the 1830 edition of *The Pilgrim's Progress*, in which his "Life of Bunyan" appears, bears all the signs of a serious literary endeavor. Instead of the woodcut of Bunyan sleeping, we find an engraving of the Sadler portrait of Bunyan (an illustration of it is placed at the beginning of this chapter). The title page opposite prominently features Southey's name and title as poet laureate and refers to the text's embellishments: "The / Pilgrim's Progress. / with / a Life of John Bunyan, / by

Robert Southey, Esq. LL. D. / Poet Laureate, &c. &c. &c., / Illustrated with Engravings / London: / John Murray, Albemarle-Street / and / John Major, Fleet-Street, M. DCCC.XXX." Southey's "Life of Bunyan" follows next, but before we reach the narrative itself, there is a poem by Bernard Barton entitled "Lines on Seeing the Portrait of John Bunyan engraved for this Work" and a "List of Embellishments" divided into two parts (copper plates and wood engravings) with the names of the craftsmen.[15]

The engraving of the Sadler portrait and the lines by Bernard Barton provide one register of the ways the publishers are trying to promote Bunyan as a major author.[16] The crude woodcut by Robert White of Bunyan asleep, dreaming out his dream, with Christian leaving the City of Destruction and moving to the Celestial City, had been a standard feature since the third edition of *The Pilgrim's Progress*.[17] The Sadler portrait, which Barton footnotes as an authentic likeness of Bunyan, depicts Bunyan as a serious author with a book in his hand, without any visual clues about the narrative itself. Barton begins "Lines on Seeing the Portrait of Bunyan Engraved for this Work" by extolling the virtues of its appropriateness to an edition of *The Pilgrim's Progress*:

And this is BUNYAN! How unlike the dull

    Unmeaning visage which was wont to stand

His PILGRIM'S Frontispiece,—its pond'rous skull

    Propped gracelessly on an enormous hand;—

    A countenance one vainly might have scann'd

For one bright ray of genius or of sense;

    Much less the mental power of him who plann'd

This fabric quaint of rare intelligence,

And having rear'd its pile, became immortal thence.[18]

The "Sleeping Portrait" was inadequate because it did not depict the "genius" and "mental power" of the author of *The Pilgrim's Progress*. The Sadler portrait, on the other hand, depicts an author of incomparable genius:

But here we trace, indelibly defined,

> All his admirers' fondest hopes could crave,

Shrewdness of intellect, and strength of mind,

> Devout yet lively, and acute though grave;

Worthy of Him whose rare invention gave

To serious Truth the charm of Fiction's dress,

> Yet in that fiction sought the soul to save

From earth and sin for heaven and happiness,

And by his fancied dreams men's waking hours to bless.[19]

The emphasis is on Bunyan as a great author rather than God's servant. The next four stanzas depict the poet's rapturous vision of the episodes of *The Pilgrim's Progress*, which occurs while he is staring at the portrait, and the final two stanzas applaud Bunyan's achievement in terms of its appeal to people at all stages of life and its ability to trace each stage "Of the rough path thy holy Travellers trod, / THE PILGRIM'S PROGRESS marks to glory, and to God!" Barton's "Lines" on Bunyan's portrait and the engraving of the portrait itself as a frontispiece provide a visual illustration of Bunyan's journey from sectarian preacher to august author, but it is Southey's "Life of Bunyan" that best exemplifies the goals of the edition in terms of audience.

Southey's "Life" offers a detailed illustration of Darnton's notion of literature as an activity and not a particular kind of text. It is divided into two parts, Bunyan's biography and a discussion of "the work that made Bunyan famous."[20] In order to rehabilitate Bunyan's status as an "author" and promote the artistic qualities of *The Pilgrim's Progress*, Southey must grapple with the issue of Bunyan's class in both parts, as well as that of the primary audience of *The Pilgrim's Progress*, and he must do it so as to appeal to his own audience of lettered readers.

Southey begins by confronting directly the issue of Bunyan's popularity among the lower classes and the attendant hostility of a more lettered readership. On the page facing the biography, he places William Cowper's encomium on Bunyan, which registers the contempt earlier lettered readers had for the author of *The Pilgrim's Progress*:[21]

Oh thou, whom, borne on fancy's eager wing

Back to the season of life's happy spring,

I pleased remember, and while memory yet

Hold fast her office here, can ne'er forget;

Ingenius Dreamer, in whose well told tale

Sweet fiction and sweet truth alike prevail;

Whose humorous vein, strong sense, and simple style,

May teach the gayest, make the gravest smile;

Witty, and well-employed, and, like thy Lord,

Speaking in parables his slighted word;

I name thee not, lest so despised a name

Should move a sneer at thy deserved fame;

Yet e'en in transitory life's late day,

That mingles all my brown with sober gray,

Revere the man, whose PILGRIM marks the road,

And guides the PROGRESS of the soul to God.[22]

Cowper's unwillingness to name Bunyan, despite his admiration for the author and his love for *The Pilgrim's Progress* as both a child and a mature adult, illustrates how despised Bunyan was as an author at that time. Southey uses Cowper's verse in order to argue that Bunyan's achievement has at last been recognized, although how that recognition occurred represents a reversal of the usual pattern:

In Bunyan's case this [not naming Bunyan] could hardly have been needful forty years ago; for though a just appreciation of our elder and better writers was at that time far less general than it appears to be at present, the author of the Pilgrim's Progress was even then in high repute. His fame may literally be said to have risen; beginning among the people it had made its way up to those who are called the public. In most instances the many receive gradually and slowly the opinions of the few respecting literary merit; and some-

times in assentation to such authority profess with their lips an admiration of they know not what, they know not why. But here the
opinion of the multitude had been ratified by the judicious. The
people knew what they admired. It is a book which makes its way
through the fancy to the understanding and the heart; the child per-
uses it with wonder and delight; in youth we discover the genius
which it displays; its worth is apprehended as we advance in years,
and we perceive its merits feelingly in declining age.[23]

Southey's differentiation between the "people" and the "public"
illustrates that class distinctions still affected the reception of *The
Pilgrim's Progress*; because the "people" embraced the book, the
lettered society rejected it. But Southey proclaims that the achievement of Bunyan's book has now been "ratified" by the "judicious,"
who have found "literary merit" in *The Pilgrim's Progress*; hence,
Bunyan deserves a place among "our elder and better writers." His
description of the appeal *The Pilgrim's Progress* holds for different
readers at different stages of life bears considerable similarity to
Gilpin's dual profile as a reader, and his biography of Bunyan betrays
a similar discomfort with Bunyan's class as well as with his status as a
dissenter.

How Southey construes the fabric of *The Pilgrim's Progress*
constitutes an interpretation in itself: "the history of his [Bunyan's]
own soul."[24] As we shall see in chapter 7, this identification of
Bunyan with his protagonist, Christian, occurred almost immediately
after the publication of the work. Southey begins his biography
proper by declaring that "Bunyan has faithfully recorded his own
spiritual history" in *The Pilgrim's Progress*, as if that were Bunyan's
motive for producing the work. In fact, Southey laments that so few
details of Bunyan's life are known, and he assumes that if Bunyan had
known how successful his book would be he would have included
more biographical material in his work:

Had he dreamed of being "for ever known," and taking his place
among those who may be called the immortals of the earth, he
would probably have introduced more details of his temporal circumstances and the events of his own life. But glorious dreamer as

he was, this never entered into his imaginations; less concerning him than might have been expected has been preserved by those of his own sect, and it is now not likely that any thing more should be recovered from oblivion.[25]

The lettered lens that Southey looks through focuses on the author and his stature. He assumes that Bunyan would have, or at least should have, been interested in the question of fame and in becoming one of the "immortals of the earth." But before Southey can demonstrate the "literary merit" of *The Pilgrim's Progress* that resulted in its phenomenal success, he must rehabilitate Bunyan's stature as an author for a lettered audience.

His strategy is to illustrate the distance Bunyan journeyed to "overcome" his background and become the great author of *The Pilgrim's Progress*. Drawing mostly on the materials in *Grace Abounding*, he proclaims that a knowledge of Bunyan's religious experience and of his age is absolutely necessary if we are to comprehend his achievement:

> But Bunyan's character would be imperfectly understood, and could not be justly appreciated, if this part of his history were kept out of sight. To respect him as he deserves, to admire him as he ought to be admired, it is necessary that we should be informed not only of the coarseness and brutality of his youth, but of the extreme ignorance out of which he worked his way, and the stage of burning enthusiasm through which he passed,—a passage not less terrible than that of his own Pilgrim in the Valley of the Shadow of Death. His ignorance, like the brutal manners from which he had now been reclaimed, was the consequence of his low station in life, but the enthusiasm which then succeeded was brought on by the circumstances of an age in which hypocrisy was regnant, and fanaticism rampant throughout the land.[26]

Southey's language here, in such words as "coarseness," "brutality," and "ignorance," demonstrates that Bunyan's class presented a problem to him. His comparison of Bunyan's "stage" of "burning enthusiasm" to Christian's passage through the Valley of the Shadow of Death documents his distaste for Bunyan's religious experience as it is reflected in *Grace Abounding*.[27] Another measure of his discomfort with Bunyan's class is also reflected in his labelling Bunyan a "blackguard" before his conversion, noting that "such he might have expected to be by his birth, breeding, and vocation, scarcely indeed by possibility could he have been otherwise; but he was never a vicious man."[28]

In Bunyan's passage from "blackguard" to author, Southey focuses on two "beneficial" influences on his literary development: his encounter with the Baptists and his stay in jail. Bunyan's religious affiliation helped him overcome his station in life: "Had it not been for the encouragement which he received from them he might have lived and died a tinker; for even when he cast off, like a slough, the coarse habits of his early life, his latent powers could never without some such encouragement and impulse have broken through the thick ignorance with which they are incrusted."[29], Bunyan's jail sentence made possible his tenure as an author: "The fever of his enthusiasm had spent itself; the asperity of his opinions was softened as his mind enlarged; and the Pilgrim's Progress was one of the fruits of his imprisonment."[30]

When Southey turns to the "fruit of that imprisonment," *The Pilgrim's Progress*, his attention is squarely on the book as artifact. The second part of the "Life of Bunyan" begins with a discussion of various editions, including their illustrations, in order to establish an authoritative text. Southey announces that collating the first part with the earliest copies has enabled him "to restore good old vernacular English which had been injudiciously altered, or carelessly corrupted."[31] Establishing a correct text is crucial to his critical enterprise, for he argues that it is Bunyan's style that elevates his work to the status of literature. In doing so, he must situate *The Pilgrim's Progress* in the history of English literature: "If it is not a well of English undefiled to which the poet as well as the philologist must repair, if they would drink of the living waters, it is a clear stream of current English, — the vernacular speech of his age, sometimes indeed in its rusticity and coarseness, but always in its plainness and its strength."[32] For lettered readers, comparisons with other writers in terms of quality are required. Bunyan is no Chaucer in terms of his language, but his language does have merit.

For Southey, the style of *The Pilgrim's Progress* renders Bunyan an important literary figure, even though it is also its "simplicity" that is responsible for its popularity among the "people":

> His is a homespun style, not a manufactured one. . . . To this natural style Bunyan is in some degree beholden for his general popularity;—his language is everywhere level to the most ignorant reader, and to the meanest capacity: there is a homely reality about it; a nursery tale is not more intelligible, in it's manner of narration, to a child. Another cause of his popularity is, that he taxes the imagination as little as the understanding. The vividness of his own, which, as his history shows, sometimes could not distinguish ideal impressions from actual ones, occasioned this. He saw the things of which he was writing, as distinctly with his mind's eye as if they were indeed passing before him as a dream. And the reader perhaps sees them more satisfactorily to himself, because the outline only of the picture is presented to him, and the author having made no attempt to fill up the details every reader supplies them according to the measure and scope of his own intellectual and imaginative powers.[33]

The emphasis in this passage falls on Bunyan's "homely realism" through the use of simple language and on his vivid imagination, but the terms in which Southey describes these qualities are couched in language that undermines Bunyan's stature as a writer. *The Pilgrim's Progress*'s narration is like a "nursery tale" in its intelligibility, and Bunyan's inability to "distinguish ideal impressions from actual ones" results in his capacity to "see the things of which he is writing" as if they were a dream passing before him. Moreover, because Bunyan does not fill in all the details, both unlettered and lettered readers can supply them according to their own "intellectual and imaginative powers." There is a curious note of elitism here, as if Bunyan himself were not responsible for this effect.

Having traced Bunyan's evolution as a writer and discussed his distinctive style, Southey turns to the predictable literary activity of locating the origins of *The Pilgrim's Progress*. At other points in the

"Life" he had used Bunyan's own writings to trace the growth of his idea for the subject of his narrative. Southey points to the passage about the dream in *Grace Abounding* that we discussed in chapter 2, as well as one of Bunyan's tracts, *The Heavenly Footman*, for the "germ" of *The Pilgrim's Progress*,[34] language that circumscribes a view of books as artifacts. In the second part of the "Life," he confronts the issue of sources in terms of Bunyan's own reading. Citing earlier speculations such as Whitney's emblems or *The Voyage of the Wandering Knight* as well as defending Bunyan against the charge of influence from other quarters,[35] Southey nonetheless concludes: "But original as Bunyan believed his own work to be, and as in the main undoubtedly it is, the same allegory had often been treated before him, so often indeed that to notice all preceding works of this kind would exceed all reasonable limits here. Some of these may have fallen Bunyan's way, and modified his own conception when he was not aware of any influence."[36] Despite Southey's acute awareness of Bunyan's status as a lower-class mechanick preacher and his declarations on the topic of indebtedness, he is incapable of assuming that Bunyan was not influenced by other works of a similar nature. Because he approaches *The Pilgrim's Progress* with a particular orientation towards the value and use of books and with distinct ideas about how authors work, Southey is certain that other texts must have helped Bunyan shape his narrative. For example, evoking Richard Bernard's *Isle of Man*, he concludes that it had "considerable effect upon the style of Bunyan's invention."[37]

Southey's revealing "Life of Bunyan" provides a paradigm for a lettered reader's response to the fabric of *The Pilgrim's Progress*. When this lettered reader peers through the lens provided by a set of literary expectations, he cannot help but assess the qualifications of the author as a writer of literature or situate the work in the context of other examples of its kind. Nor can he believe that authors stumble upon ideas for books; at the center of a lettered reader's expectations about authorship is the notion that books beget other books. Thus, although Bunyan's language does not offer "a well of English undefiled," Southey proclaims that he is nonetheless the "Prince of allegorists in prose."[38] The responses to Southey's attempt to reclaim Bunyan as a literary figure and his work as a classic of literature can be seen in the reviews the edition received from Sir Walter Scott and Thomas Babington Macaulay. These reviews display the same defining characteristics of the lettered reader's response to literature in terms of ideas about authorship and about what constitutes literary merit.

Sir Walter Scott applauds Southey's endeavor in his edition to fulfill his mission as a poet laureate by "illustrating the antiquities and peculiarities of our national literature," and he praises him for his choice of subject, John Bunyan, who "in spite of a clownish and vulgar education, rose in degree of popularity scarce equalled by any English writer."[39] Like Southey, Scott is interested in the question of literary models for *The Pilgrim's Progress*. He endorses Southey's effort to dismiss the charge of Bunyan's plagiarism, but he cannot stop himself from mentioning another possibility overlooked by Southey, Simon Patrick's *Parable of the Pilgrim*. Though he raises the prospect, he "acquits the dean of Peterborough and the tinker of Elstow from copying a thought or idea from each other":

> If Dr. Patrick had seen *The Pilgrim's Progress* he would, probably, in the pride of academic learning, have scorned to adopt it as a model; but, at all events, as a man of worth, he would never have denied the obligation if he had incurred one. John Bunyan, on his part, would in all likelihood have scorned, "with his very heels," to borrow anything from a dean; and we are satisfied that he would cut his hand off rather than written the introductory verses we have quoted [the Advertisement appended to *The Holy War*], had not his Pilgrim been entirely his own.[40]

Scott's stance on the issue of literary "influence" documents the class issues raised by Bunyan's peculiar position as a writer of literature. Patrick, the "man of worth," would have scorned Bunyan's production given his academic background, but he would certainly have acknowledged it if he had used it. Bunyan's witness on this issue emanates from another source, his religious reputation; he would not have written the "Advertisement" if it were not the absolute truth. One final measure of the role class played in the politics of Bunyan's literary reputation was the bizarre debate, initiated by Scott in this review, about Bunyan's possible gypsy origins.[41] Scott's speculation about Bunyan's background betrays a wish to make it more exotic, if it can not be of a more respectable English pedigree.

Like Southey before him and Macaulay after him, Scott attempts to rank Bunyan and his book in the literary canon. Having noted earlier in the review that D'Israeli had proclaimed Bunyan the "Spenser of the people,"[42] Scott awards the higher honor to Bunyan: "In a style of composition, rendered thus venerable by its antiquity, and still more so by the purposes to which it has been applied, John Bunyan, however uneducated, was a distinguished master. For our part, we are inclined to allow him, in the simplicity of his story, and his very shrewdness, and if the reader pleases, homely bluntness of style, a superiority over the poet to whom he has been compared by D'Israeli."[43] Thomas Babington Macaulay's review of Southey's edition shows the same interest in establishing Bunyan as one of England's great writers. He ends his review by alluding to the verses by Cowper with which Southey had begun his biography of Bunyan:

> Cowper said, forty or fifty years ago, that he dared not name John Bunyan in his verse, for fear of moving a sneer. To our refined forefathers, we suppose, Lord Roscommon's Essay on Translated Verse and the Duke of Buckinghamshire's Essay on Poetry, appeared to be compositions infinitely superior to the allegory of the preaching tinker. We live in better times; and we are not afraid to say, that, though there were very clever men in England during the latter half of the seventeenth century, there were only two minds which possessed the imaginative faculty in a very eminent degree. One of those minds produced the Paradise Lost, the other the Pilgrim's Progress.[44]

For Macaulay, as for Southey and Scott before him, The Pilgrim's Progress is an allegory, a literary work of the imagination. Macaulay also finds Bunyan to be a better allegorist than Spenser, even though the allegory is sometimes inconsistent. Bunyan "puts into the mouth of his pilgrims religious ejaculations and disquisitions, better suited to his own pulpit in Bedford or Reading than to the Enchanted Ground or the Interpreter's Garden."[45] Macaulay would dispense with the aspects of the The Pilgrim's Progress that Bunyan counted on to convey his meaning.

The lens a lettered readership brings to a text, as it is repre-sented by readers like Southey, Scott, and Macaulay, magnifies the formal characteristics of literary works. Their activity as lettered readers results in speculations about sources and influences, as they attempt to situate as well as rank the work in a literary taxonomy. It is worth noting that Scott was perfectly aware of the politics of Southey's edition, but he feared that Southey's attempt to make Bunyan and his book more appealing to the upper classes was futile:

> We must not omit to mention, that this edition of *The Pilgrim's Progress* is adorned with a great variety of woodcuts, designed and executed with singular felicity, and with some highly finished en-graving after the rich and imaginative pencil of John Martin. Thus decorated and recommended by the taste and criticism of Mr. Southey, it might seem certain that the established favourite of the common people should be well received among the upper classes; as, however, it contains many passages eminently faulty in point of taste, (as, indeed, from the origin and the situation of the author, was naturally to be expected,) we should not be surprised if it were more coldly accepted than its merits deserve. A dead fly can cor-rupt a precious elixir—an obvious fault against taste, especially if it be of a kind which lies open to lively ridicule, may be enough, in a critical age like the present, to cancel the merit of wit, beauty, and sublimity.[46]

Dressing *The Pilgrim's Progress* up with woodcuts and engravings and having the poet laureate of England espouse its virtues might help sell the volume but, according to Scott, Bunyan's "illiterate" style would clash with the tastes of a lettered, upper-class society of readers and would result in ridicule for the author and the rejection of the work "in this critical age."

Lettered readers and later critics of *The Pilgrim's Progress*, looking through the lens of a literary set of expectations, have oscillated between a response to the work's literary qualities, which seems to demand discussion in the context of other works, and Bunyan's own emphatic denial that *The Pilgrim's Progress* owed its existence to any source but the Bible. Samuel Johnson's response to Bunyan's work was not an isolated phenomenon; a number of later readers addressed the issue of Bunyan's reading from the eighteenth century on. Other influences were put forth by early critics of the work. Dr. Dibkin in his *Typographical Antiquities* described Caxton's *Pilgrimage of the Soul* as a work that "laid the foundation of John Bunyan's *The Pilgrim's Progress*"; Adam Clarke in his postscript to the *Life of Bunyan* chose Richard Bernard's *Isle of Man* and Spenser's *Faerie Queene* as works that "gave birth to *The Pilgrim's Progress*"; James Montgomery in *Christian Poet* speculated that the print and verses entitled "The Pilgrim" in Whitney's *Emblems* "might perhaps have inspired the first idea of this extraordinary work."[47] Like Southey's use of the word *germ* to locate the origins of *The Pilgrim's Progress,* the terms in which these critics assert a connection between works, such as laying a foundation or giving birth, telegraph a particular set of ideas about the nature of books and authors. At the center of this literary supposition about the origin of a text is the idea that writers read in order to write, that they see themselves as participating in a literary tradition.

As we saw in chapter 1, Henry Stebbing's response to the issue of Bunyan's reading is a quintessentially lettered one. In his edition of Bunyan's works, he eagerly contemplated the prospect of what in Bunyan's reading might have fired his imagination. Stebbing's approach was to dominate, with or without apologetic references to Bunyan's own denials, until the end of the century.[48] James Blanton Wharey in his source study definitively put to rest ideas about literary sources, especially candidates such as Deguileville's *Pilgrimage of the Life of Man,* by comparing various proposed models in detail with Bunyan's narrative, but he too reflects uneasiness with his end re-sult—a literary work without literary models. He is the first of several to devise a formula for harmonizing these contradictory elements:

> The most reasonable supposition seems to be that the idea of an al-legorical pilgrimage had become common property and the treat-ment of it conventional by the middle of the seventeenth century, and that Bunyan knowing that others had treated the same theme determined to try his hand at a similar allegory. In doing so, he adopted the framework which had been handed down from De-

guileville through other allegorists, relying for the details of the allegory, however, not upon the works of his predecessors, but upon
his own invention.[49]

In other words, Bunyan somehow picked up the idea by osmosis.
Notice that Wharey's ideas about the way authors write, reflected in
such language as "to try his hand" and "adopted," are from a lettered
perspective. Bunyan must have known "that others had treated the
same theme," even if he generated the details of *The Pilgrim's
Progress* from his own imagination, rather than relying on the works
of predecessors. The discomfort over the connection between Bunyan's presentation of himself and his fictive expression has persisted.
We see its dynamics surfacing in G. R. Owst's proposal in *Literature
and Pulpit in Medieval England* that it is in "the mediation of the
pulpit that we may best be able to find a way of explaining this
medieval contact without havng to accuse the Puritan of deliberate
dishonesty, or conscious misstatement."[50] The same curious mixture
of disdain and disapproval figures in an article by Harold Golder
entitled "John Bunyan's Hypocrisy," which attempts to show a debt
to the romance tradition that Golder sees Bunyan as denying.[51]

Because it seemed impossible to locate sources for *The Pilgrim's
Progress* in the literary tradition, literary critics of Bunyan's narrative
were forced to turn to other sources to explain the origin of the work.
They advanced on two fronts: one to Bunyan's life as a gloss on *The
Pilgrim's Progress*, the other to the Puritan culture of which he was a
member. The predominant critical trend until quite recently has
been to approach *The Pilgrim's Progress* in terms of Bunyan's personal history. F. M. Harrison's observation that "*The Pilgrim's Progress* is
but another version of Bunyan's spiritual autobiography"[52] is pursued by Roger Sharrock and Henri Talon who, in their respective
studies of Bunyan, use the framework of Bunyan's life to explain the
fabric of *The Pilgrim's Progress*. For example, Roger Sharrock finds
that "the internal experience recorded in *Grace Abounding* is translated into allegorical terms, the Puritan psychology of conversion
giving way stage by stage to concrete incidents and characters."[53]
This approach to *The Pilgrim's Progress* locates Bunyan's achievement in his ability to embody his own life in fictional terms. Critics of
the second type turn to Bunyan's milieu to explain the incidents of

The Pilgrim's Progress. Q. D. Leavis begins this line of inquiry: "It is not fantastic to assert that it was the Puritan culture as much as Bunyan that produced *The Pilgrim's Progress.*"[54] This approach develops the Puritan context for Bunyan's work in terms both of doctrine and of Bunyan's status as a dissenter. In *John Bunyan, Mechanick Preacher*, William York Tindall was the first to attempt a full-scale study of this topic. N. H. Keeble's *Literary Culture of Nonconformity in Later Seventeenth-Century England* and Christopher Hill's *Tinker and a Poor Man: John Bunyan and His Church* are two of the most recent examples of this approach.

Both the biographical and historical approaches provide important contexts through which to view the work, but in their extreme forms they devalue both the book and its author. The biographical approach implies that Bunyan either deliberately or unconsciously turned his life into one of the most popular books in history. One of the most blatant examples of this error occurs in John Brown's biography of Bunyan, where he attempts to establish in which of Bunyan's two imprisonments *The Pilgrim's Progress* was written. He points to the break in the dream as a key piece of evidence for assuming that the work was written during Bunyan's first imprisonment: "This is the only break in that occurs in the First Part of the book. It is not artistically required by the plot of the story; indeed it somewhat interferes with it; and the more probable conclusion is that Bunyan's dream was broken by Bunyan's release from the den, and that the remainder of the story, which amounts to nearly a third of the First Part, was written after he was at large."[55] Details in Bunyan's narrative are identified exclusively in terms of the experiences of his life. The historical approach, in its exploration of Bunyan's milieu, also excludes Bunyan's creativity by explaining everything in the text as derived from a set of beliefs and a class-determined role. For example, William York Tindall barely masks his contempt when trying to place Bunyan alongside his contemporaries and show that he was no different from them. He argues that "if we are to understand the meaning of Bunyan's works, we must approach them neither as astonishing departures from the modes of polite or respectable literature, with which we are familiar and by which alone we are tempted to judge them, nor as the products of solitude and the Scriptures, but as representative expressions of Bunyan's inelegant, restless, and now unremembered class."[56]

One offshoot of the historical approach that has supplied a necessary corrective to responses such as Tindall's has been Marxist criticism. Precisely because of his unlettered status and his links to popular culture, Bunyan has received a good deal of attention from critics interested in recovering the social and material basis of literary production. Although early Marxist criticism, such as Jack Lindsay's *John Bunyan: Maker of Myths*,[57] attempted to secularize Bunyan's work (to the point of denying *The Pilgrim's Progress's* relationship to the Bible in terms of style),[58] more recent critics, especially Christopher Hill in *A Tinker and a Poor Man*, locate Bunyan's revolutionary tendencies in the intersection of politics and religion in the period. Here also, attitudes towards Bunyan's class, negative in Tindall's response, positive from a Marxist perspective, determine how *The Pilgrim's Progress* is assessed.

What has followed from these two approaches, one primarily focused on Bunyan's personal life, the other on his culture, is an emphasis on quasi-literary influences that Bunyan, given his personal history and his religious affiliation, might have encountered, and that contributed to the fabric of *The Pilgrim's Progress*. The Bible is put forward as the central influence on Bunyan's narrative, but chapbook romances, spiritual autobiographies, popular sermons or treatises, expository dialogues like that found in Arthur Dent's *Plaine-Mans Pathway to Heaven*, emblem books, and Puritan meditative practices have been put forward as possible candidates for influence.[59] Useful as these contexts for *The Pilgrim's Progress* are, they do not explain how the book came into being or why it was so successful. If we change our lens from a literary to a religious one, the effect of Bunyan's reading on his book seems less important than his book's intended effect on its first readers. What is important is not what Bunyan read but how he conceived of the activities of reading and of writing.

A Protestant Paradigm for Reading and Writing

> but yet let Truth be free
> To make her Salleys upon Thee, and Me,
> Which way it pleases God. For who knows how,
> Better then he that taught us first to Plow,

To guide our Mind and Pens for his Design?

And he makes base things usher in Divine.

("Apology," lines 181–86)

The reception of *Piers Plowman* by a Protestant readership offers a lens through which to view how Bunyan might have conceived of his project in *The Pilgrim's Progress*. As we saw at the close of chapter 4, Bunyan's understanding of the origin of books, as well as their value and use, is fundamentally Protestant. God, through the Holy Ghost, directs both writing and reading for his "Design." Thus the Holy Ghost, to use Crowley's terms, is the "autor of bokes" because he is involved in both their production and their reception by individual readers. He guided the "Mind" and "Pens" of the human authors of Scripture, as well as those writers who wrote, in Bale's terms, "holy" works to further the Reformation, and he provided the impetus for *The Pilgrim's Progress*. He is also the author because he writes books in the reader. This version of reading posits an active role in reading for the Bible in particular and for books in general.[60] As we will see in the third section of this chapter, *Grace Abounding* provides the most obvious example of the way the Holy Ghost through a variety of scriptural texts makes "Salleys," that is, assaults, on Bunyan as a reader, but other works clearly had a similar effect. Bunyan's experience of Martin Luther's *Commentary on Galatians* demonstrates how Bunyan conceived of the relationship between book and reader: "I found my condition in his experience, so largely and profoundly handled, as if his Book had been written out of my heart."[61] So too, in *The Pilgrim's Progress*, he asks readers to find themselves reflected in the text, by laying "my Book, thy Head and Heart together." [62] As in Langland's scene in passus 12 involving Imaginatif, books are mirrors in which to see one's self. But the mirror speaks to the reader more directly and forcefully than one might guess. Crowley had invited his readers to "amende thyne owne misse, which thou shalt fynd here charitably rebuked" (°2v), and, as we have seen, readers read Langland's poem in such a way that they gleaned the moral and applied it to the self. Such a view of reading redefines our sense of what Sir Philip Sidney meant by poetry as a "speaking picture." As literary critics, we have gravitated to the word *picture* as in painting and presumed that a work's verbal texture was configured in *speaking*. Perhaps we should emphasize *speaking* more and assume that the Renaissance reader in general, and the Protestant reader in particular, construed texts in far more intimate and active terms than we have hitherto appreciated.

For the Protestant reader, reading is not merely recreational but requires hard work and diligence.[63] One Protestant figure for reading, perhaps as a happy accident of the infinite interplay of cultural codes, was *plowing*. The Holy Ghost taught the Protestant reader first to "Plow," that is, to read the Bible, and then guided "Mind" and "Pens" to explore not only Scripture but one's experience of grappling with it, "stooping" and seeking "to find out what by pins and loops . . . God speaketh to him" ("Apology," lines 116, 119). Bunyan's conception of the activity of reading as plowing is confirmed in his preface to *The Holy War*, where he points at its close to his marginal notations:

> Nor do thou go to work without my Key,
>
> (In mysteries men do soon lose their way)
>
> And also turn it right if thou wouldst know
>
> My riddle, and wouldst with my heifer plough.[64]
>
> (lines 155–58)

The "heifer," (a figure Bunyan derives from Judges 14.18), is a help for plowing, that is, reading and understanding the allegory.

The sense of intimacy and active engagement that Protestant readers brought to books originated in their encounters with Scripture. Two of the "Scripture-metaphors" explored by Benjamin Keach in *Tropologia: A Key to Scripture-Metaphors*, "The Word of God compared to a Glass" and "Professing the Gospel Compared to the Plough," help shed light on the Protestant reader's distinctive orientation towards the Bible.[65] In the first scriptural trope, to which we will return in the third section of this chapter, Keach points out that Scripture is like a looking-glass because the reader can see both a "clear sight of God" as well as "what man is before Grace"[66] by reading the Bible, a formula that might explain why texts are viewed as mirrors for the self by the Protestant reader. But it is Keach's exploration of the metaphor of plowing that is the most illuminating for our purposes. Constructing his comparison out of Jesus' pronouncement in Luke 9.62, ("No man having put his hand to the plough, and looking backe, is fit for the Kingdome of God"), Keach interprets his words as meaning "preaching, owning, and professing the Gospel,"[67] and proceeds to document the dimensions of the metaphor and its "Parallels" in two columns. The basis of his analysis is the idea that the Gospel itself is a "Plough": "the Gospel is an Instrument, prepared and made fit by the Almighty, to break or plow up the fallow Ground of our Hearts."[68] As these parallels suggest, reading the gospel is like plowing one's heart and preaching is like plowing the hearts of one's field, the congregation.

Noting that the plough "must be held or drawn," that is, "believed in and professed by us," Keach teases out all the ways in which the figure of the plough as the gospel is an apt similitude. Among the more interesting observations under the headings of "Simile" and "Parallel": plowing is "hard work," and so is plowing with the plough of the gospel because of the hard and obdurate heart of the sinner; the plough "pierces" deep into the earth, and the gospel "pierces" the heart of the sinner with "powerful convictions"; plowing is preparative activity for sowing, and the reading of the gospel is preparative for sowing the seed of grace in the heart; and finally, the plough turns up roots and kills "rank weeds" that grow in the field, and the gospel as a plough kills sin at the root in the heart of the reader.[69] Thus, the Protestant reader's encounter with Scripture was an active rather than a passive experience and, in defining the reading process, was one of violent transformation.

Keach appended a poem to his discussion of how plowing was related to professing the gospel that offers a gloss on the connection between plowing and preaching. Labeled only "Mr. John Flavel's Poem Upon the Plough," it begins by talking about skill in plowing, and then explains the fitness of the figure:

> This, as a lively Emblem, fitly may
>
> Describe the Blessed Spirit's Work and Way
>
> Whose Work on Souls with this doth symbolize;
>
> Betwixt them both the Resemblance lies:
>
> Souls are the Soil, the Gospel is the Plow;
>
> God's Workmen hold, the Spirit shews them how.[70]

Here we have another formula of how the Holy Ghost teaches the Christian writer to plow for truth in reading as well as for souls in writing. Holding the "plough," Scripture, according to directions given by the Holy Ghost, "God's Workmen" prepare his field for sowing. The concept of plowing, then, subsumes both the writer's search for the truth contained in Scripture as it applies to the world and to the self, and the end result, a book that is designed to plow the hearts of readers by delivering a picture that speaks to them of their spiritual condition.

Thus, the strategies the Protestant reader brought to texts emerged out of a sense of books and their function that was derived directly from the new religion of the Book, Protestantism. It conditioned their conception of where books came from as well as the role they were expected to play in the spiritual life of the individual reader. Moreover, the figure of the human author was very differently understood in terms of *genius*. Those authorized by the Holy Spirit to write were seen as "God's workmen." According to the prescription set forth in 1 Corinthians, they were "base things," a plowman, perhaps, or a tinker. The Holy Ghost is "he that taught us first to Plow," but human authors could be seen as providing a model of how to "Plow" in their attempts to make sense of the Christian experience of the world and God's promises to his people as they are reflected in Scripture. Both *Piers Plowman* and *The Pilgrim's Progress* can and should be seen in this light. And using the Renaissance version of *Piers Plowman* as it was perceived by a Protestant readership helps us to redefine Bunyan's agenda for *The Pilgrim's Progress*.

At the core of the religious genres of prophecy, exhortation, and spiritual autobiography that comprised the reception of Langland's poem is the figure of the author, participant rather than distant maker, actively engaged in seeking truth and enacting the quest for holiness. The author's activity accounts for a Protestant readership's close identification of the figure of Piers with the dreamer-narrator and sometimes with Langland himself. The Lollards and English reformers saw in the figure of Piers and his metaphorical activity three distinct kinds of action: the prophet ploughing for Christian truth by the violent action of attacking the thorns and briars that were choking Christendom; the preacher exhorting his church and his society to reform; and the plain man, an innocent common laborer who knows better than any priest the way to truth. All three of these versions of Piers rest on his ability to read Scripture. The crucial scene in *Piers Plowman* for the Protestant reader might well have been passus 7, where Piers must rely on a priest to read his pardon for him, a pardon which he tears "in pure tene." Then, suddenly literate, Piers quotes from a psalm in Latin. By the close of the poem he is portrayed as plowing his field with four "stout beasts" who are called Matthew, Mark, Luke, and John, in addition to other "beasts" representing the church fathers.

Even the most casual of readers of Langland, especially given the Crowley annotations, would have recognized the poem itself as saturated with Scripture.[71] And even Crowley, who makes a clear distinction between author and narrator (though not between the narrator and Piers), takes great care to annotate the poem in terms of Langland's reading of Scripture, often undermining the prophetic aspects of the text by calling attention to Langland's biblical sources. Thus, for Crowley, Langland's prophetic status derives from the poet's reading of Scripture in the light of his own time, for his portrayal of a church in crisis correctly forecast its fall. From the perspective of the Protestant reader, then, the metaphor of plowing in the poem had three aspects. First, it evoked the bitter prophetic voice of the poet weeding God's field in order to identify and eliminate the corruptions in society and in the church of his own day. Second, the equation of plowing with preaching defined the role of the book in reforming the reader, rooting out vices such as those reflected in the confessions of the seven deadly sins in passus 5 and elsewhere. And finally, the metaphor of plowing defined the anguished personal search for truth reflected in the text.

Thus, for Protestant readers such as John Bale and Robert Crowley, Langland was one of "God's workmen," using the tools afforded him by the Holy Ghost. Bale, insisting that Langland was a disciple of Wyclif, portrays him as being against the "blasphemies of the papists."[72] Being in God's service takes the form of employing "delightful embellishments and figures" to root out and make clear the corruption in the church, an activity that stamps Langland's work as holy. Crowley's vision of the poem also aligns Langland with Wyclif and links writer and narrator even more closely by describing the poem as "crying out agaynst the works of darknes." The means to cry out chosen by the Holy Ghost involves "reportynge certain visions and dreames, that he fayned himselfe to have dreamed," whose function was to "moste christianlye enstruct the weake, and sharply rebuke the obstinate blynde." But in addition to articulating the urgent need for reform in the church, the book also spoke to the individual reader: "There is no maner of vice, that reigneth in anye estate of men, whiche this wryter hath not godly, learnedlye, and wittlye rebuked" (*2r). For these two readers, the figure of the author empowered by the Holy Ghost to speak out dominates their understanding of the action of the poem.

When we turn to Bunyan's "Apology," we encounter the same emphasis on the active figure of an author doing God's work by speaking out:

> I. I find not that I am denied the use
>
> Of this my method, so I no abuse
>
> Put on the Words, Things, Readers, or be rude
>
> In handling Figure, or Similitude,
>
> In application; but, all that I may,
>
> Seek the advance of Truth, this or that way:
>
> Denyed did I say? Nay, I have leave,
>
> (Example too, and from them that have
>
> God better pleased by their words and ways,
>
> Then any Man that breatheth now adays,)
>
> Thus to express my mind, thus to declare
>
> Things unto thee that excellentest are.
>
> (lines 165–76)

Not only does Bunyan emphasize the "words and ways" of these figures, he also underscores the tools they used to please God, the application of "Figures" and "Similitudes" to seek the "advance of Truth." Moreover, the example these authors in a distant past provide is a legitimate way to declare "Things" that are "excellentest" to the reader. Here again we see the utter confidence of the Protestant reader in the ability of figures and similitudes to speak directly to the reader. We also see that these models Bunyan cites advance Christian "Truth" as well as calling for individual reformation. Instead of merely seeing *The Pilgrim's Progress* as "a version of Bunyan's spiritual autobiography,"[73] we can explore the book's designs on the reader in terms of a more comprehensive vision. *The Pilgrim's Progress* circumscribes the immense changes in religious experience that the Reformation brought into being.

   Piers Plowman and *The Pilgrim's Progress* are prophecies in the sense that they both diagnose as well as predict the fate of the world through their reading of Scripture. But they also prophesy by rendering a reading of the current state of Christendom.[74] Langland's is an all-inclusive vision where the field of the world is based on the conception of the "estates of men" and the premise of a universal Catholic church. He depicts utter chaos as people wander without direction because of institutional corruption in both church and state, and he "weeds God's Field" by locating the sins of the people (especially in the B-text, passus 5), as well as those of the morally bankrupt religious, particularly the friars. His prediction is that Antichrist will reign unless the church reforms itself; after all, it is the friars who make possible the assault by Antichrist at the close of the poem. The picture of "God's field" had shrunk considerably by the seventeenth century, however. The people Christian meets are an exclusively Protestant version of the "fayre felde full of folke" (A1r). With the possible exception of Vanity Fair, his equivalent of Mede and society, Bunyan includes only "professors," those who believe they are among the elect. The seven deadly sins have been replaced by errors of various denominations. All of the characters that Christian meets claim to know the way to heaven and how to get there. Most do not arrive, and the narrative usually makes clear why they fail to do so. As Christopher Hill has pointed out, "Behind *The Pilgrim's Progress* are the literal wanderings of intinerant craftsman or beggars, as well as the spiritual pilgrimage of seekers passing through whole sects."[75] This somewhat restricted vision of society reflects the sectarian fragmentation of Bunyan's time as well as his perception of the world in terms of class.[76]

   Just how precarious the world had become in the seventeenth century can be measured by comparing the versions of society reflected in the two works. In *Piers Plowman*, the salvation of the society is linked to the reformation of the individual, though equal weight is given to both. Bunyan felt that no such solution was at hand. The time for the establishment of Jerusalem on earth had passed.

Writing after the Restoration, Bunyan's intention is to enact reformation for the individual Christian.[77] Society as portrayed throughout *The Pilgrim's Progress*, and in particular in the example of Ignorance, cannot be changed. Bunyan's prophecy is that the City of Destruction, the world, will be burnt. The only possibility for redemption resides in the individual and is possible only, as we are shown in the opening scene, if one leaves the world behind. Christian, putting his fingers in his ears, abandons his family and cries, "Life, Life, Eternal Life."[78] Setting the works side by side illuminates the end results of shifting the responsibility for salvation from holy church to the individual Christian: the proliferation of multiple perspectives on salvation and, ultimately, the sectarian fragmentation of society.

Langland's poem acknowledges that prospect at its close. *Piers Plowman* ends with society on the brink of ruin, the quest failed. Conscience resolves that he will become a pilgrim and start over again. Bunyan closes his narrative, with its sharply restricted focus on the individual, with the quest at least foreshadowing success; Christian is a type that the reader must complete. Langland pictured a world where society could be saved by each individual becoming better, though he acknowledged the unlikeliness of the prospect; Bunyan jettisoned society to save the individual.

Seen as prophecies rather than dream-visions, both Langland's poem and Bunyan's narrative bear considerable structural resemblance to the description found in "Of Prophecy" by John Smith, which was cited in chapter 2:

But for a more distinct understanding of this business, we must remember what hath been often suggested, *That the Prophetical scene* or *Stage upon which all apparitions were made to the Prophet, was his Imagination;* and that there all those things which God would have revealed unto him were acted over *Symbolicallie,* as in a *Masque,* in which divers persons are brought in, amongst which the Prophet himself bears a part: And therefore he, according to the exigencie of this Dramatical *apparatus,* must, as the other Actors, perform his part, sometimes by speaking and reciting things done, propounding questions, sometimes by acting that part which in the *Drama* he was appointed to act by some others; and so not only by

> Speaking, but by Gestures and Actions come in in his due place
> among the rest; as it is in our ordinarie *Dreams*.[79]

The dreamer in these two works is the observer of an action dominated by another character, who is the one who evolves. Twentieth-century readers of *Piers Plowman* would correctly argue that Langland actually combines both kinds of structure. The dreamer-narrator, Will, is the central structuring device, but we find Piers the Plowman also developing throughout the poem. However, Renaissance readers of the poem did not generally construe the structure that way. They ignored any development in Will himself and assumed that Piers was the dreamer-narrator, although we should note that in general they did not follow the plot, as we do. As a result, the dreamer-narrator can be seen in each work as projecting himself into the poem and charting his own spiritual autobiography through the experience of a character formally distinct from himself.

As prophets, Langland and Bunyan are worlds apart in tone. And again, this is a function of their very different perspectives on the problems of the world and their solution. Langland's bitter diatribes against abuses in religion are designed to bring about its reform. Bunyan does not envision the world becoming better, only individuals, and only if they truly leave the world. As a result, his critique of the various "abuses" in his portrait of a religious community takes the form of gentle mockery, as he simply demonstrates that most of the Christian seekers will fail to achieve heaven. William York Tindall was the first to notice that Bunyan "gave literary finality to what may appear to be undeserving of commemoration, his obscure quarrels with Baptists and Anglicans, who supplied material as well as heat for the creation of By-ends, for example, and Ignorance."[80] And other critics have followed up his leads in exploring the satire of *The Pilgrim's Progress*, but pointing to the satire obscures Bunyan's agenda in his narrative.[81]

Bunyan's invitation to his readers, "Would'st read thy self, and read thou know'st not what / And yet know whether thou art blest or not," demonstrates that he conceived of his book not just as rebuke but as instruction. He had clearly signaled earlier in the "Apology" what he expected his readers to pay attention to:

This Book it chaulketh out before thine eyes,
The man that seeks the everlasting Prize:
It shews you whence he comes, whither he goes,
What he leaves undone; also what he does:
It also shews you how he runs, and runs,
Till he unto the Gate of Glory comes.

It also shews too, who sets out for life amain,
As if the lasting Crown they would attain:
Here also you may see the reason why
They loose their labour, and like fools do die.

This Book will make a Travailer of thee,
If by its Counsel thou wilt ruled be;
It will direct thee to the Holy Land,
If thou wilt its Directions understand.

(lines 197–210)

The characters in *The Pilgrim's Progress* are object-lessons for re-forming the self. The reader is expected to view the characters, both those who succeed and those who fail, as delivering instruction. In a way a twentieth-century reader of literature finds hard to fathom, they exhort the reader to examine her- or himself, the portrayal of a particular character perhaps piercing the hard, obdurate heart of the sinner by delivering a vision that speaks to his or her condition.

In *The Pilgrim's Progress*, the characters are labelled as allegorical through their names, but they assume human shape through dialogue.[82] Thus a pilgrim who will not get to heaven is clearly labeled; more than that, his discourse expands the sin that he exemplifies. A character like By-ends is allowed to speak out of his distinctive nature: "'Tis true, we somewhat differ in religion from those of the stricter sort, yet but in two small points: First, we never strive against Wind and Tide. Secondly, we are always most zealous when Religion goes in his Silver Slippers; we love much to walk with him in the Street, if the Sun shines, and the people applaud it" (219). Each of the insincere wayfarers Christian meets is allowed to confess in this way.

From the perspective of the Protestant reader, then, these characters have a functional role that extends beyond satire. In *The*

Pilgrim's Progress, such characters as Mr. Worldly-Wiseman, Talkative, By-ends, and Ignorance offer a warning about religious errors in the reader as well as a critique of them. Bunyan's readers are invited to decode the speech and actions of various characters for an explanation of why they "loose their labour, and like fools do die" (line 206). Thus, the minor characters provide instruction as well as rebuke; they represent one stage in the reader's search for the answer to whether he or she "is blest or not." But, of course, the reader's attention in *The Pilgrim's Progress* would focus primarily on the image of Christian that Bunyan "chaulketh out," for his image provides both instruction and "Direction." There, particularly, readers would plow with the plough of the text in order to chart their own spiritual development.

    The Pilgrim's Progress has often been described as another version of Bunyan's spiritual autobiography, but this reflection deserves some qualification. The experience recorded in *Grace Abounding* certainly receives poignant recreation in Bunyan's narrative, but Bunyan's intention was to present not a fictionalized account of his own experience but a generalized paradigm based on those struggles that would be useful for the reader. Readers are expected to fasten their attention on Christian as they follow him from his first anguished cry to his entrance into the Celestial City. Bunyan creates two other successful pilgrims, Faithful and Hopeful, who represent other avenues for progress in the religious life. Faithful achieves heaven through martyrdom and Hopeful becomes a pilgrim because of that martyrdom. The creation of other successful pilgrims also allows Bunyan to point out that the road one travels and the particular difficulties one encounters depend on the individual. Christian fell into the Slough of Despond, while Faithful avoided it. Both characters were at first turned out of the way towards the Wicket-Gate; Christian encountered Worldly Wiseman while Faithful met Wanton, who tempted him to turn out of the way. Christian lost his roll and had to go back for it, whereas Faithful met with Adam the First and was punished by Moses for his secret inclining. Faithful did not stop at House Beautiful as Christian did; Bunyan uses a different device to underscore Faithful's militancy. Finally, in the Valley of Humiliation, Christian battled with Apollyon while Faithful met Discontent and Shame. Emerging after Faithful's martyrdom, Hopeful illustrates that examples of martyrdom can bring people to the faith.[83] But the figure of Christian himself presents the most comprehensive vision of such progress.

The most striking difference between *Piers Plowman* and *The Pilgrim's Progress* resides in their perspectives on individual reformation. Each work asks at its outset "What shall I do to be saved?" and proposes a plan of action. But Langland's poem offers no definitive solution, whereas Bunyan's narrative clearly delineates a "Way." *Piers Plowman* sends its dreamer on a quest for Do-Well, Do-Better, and Do-Best. The meaning of these formulations, however, is multiple and enigmatic. Scriptural history and abstractions such as Learning, Study, and Holy Church are evoked as offering possible solutions, but they are ultimately jettisoned. "Having" Piers Plowman, whatever that means, emerges as the only possible hope. For Bunyan, no such tenuous proposals are required. To be saved, Christian moves through a well-defined verbal landscape where the steps toward salvation are clearly differentiated.

How did salvation come to be defined so unambiguously in the three centuries between the two works? We can see in *Piers Plowman* and *The Pilgrim's Progress* the cultural matrix of the Reformation movement; *The Pilgrim's Progress* is the final product of an intellectual revolution of which we can see early signs in *Piers Plowman*. Langland's poem can be said to be proto-Protestant in the extent to which it insists that individuals must work out their own salvation, however important sacraments, history, and the church as an institution may be to that process. Bunyan's narrative, on the other hand, documents how this can actually be done. Obviously these two works are only convenient landmarks in the process of Reformation history, but they exemplify the key shift in perspective that began to take place in the fourteenth century and found its final expression in the later seventeenth century.

The Individual Before the Biblical Text

Piers Plowman and *The Pilgrim's Progress*, when we place them on a historical continuum of the kind we have been charting, take on historical and cultural significance beyond their literary meanings. Seen from this perspective, the most illuminating points to be made about the two works involve exploring their differences, and doing so helps us to chart how far Bunyan and his age had moved from that first fourteenth-century call for reform. Though Langland stresses over and over again that individual reform is essential, his work as a whole is curiously ambiguous about the means to bring it about. Do-Well, Do-Better, and Do-Best remain problematic in spite of the fact that there are passages where the matter seems quite clear, as when Piers tells the folk that the way to Truth's house involves simply obeying the Ten Commandments. Langland brings to bear on the question a number of formulas; he buttresses his arguments with scriptural texts, glosses, patristic commentary and even proverbs, but almost all these formulas break down when coping with the real world. As we have noted, Bunyan's narrative displays no like ambiguity about the way to salvation. By the seventeenth century, a new means had emerged to harmonize scriptural truth and individual experience.

One striking witness to this changed perspective can be seen in the opening passage of *The Pilgrim's Progress*, where we see Christian for the first time: "I dreamed, and behold *I saw a Man clothed with Raggs standing in a certain place, with his face from his own House, a Book in his hand, and a great burden upon his Back.* I looked, and saw him open the Book, and Read therein; and as he read, he wept and trembled: and not being able longer to contain, he brake out with a lamentable cry; saying what shall I do?" (146). The starting point for Christian's journey is not something he sees, but rather something he reads.[84] Scripture, through its verbal texture, delivers to the sinner a vision of his spiritual state and acts as a goad to set him on his journey. For Bunyan, the impetus for the journey is not a problem about the world but a problem about the state of the individual soul as it is reflected in Scripture.

Such reflections of the self in Scripture are discussed by Keach in the section of *Tropologia* entitled "The Word of God compared to Glass." Just as "a true Glass shews or represents unto a Man his own natural Face," so that "by looking therein he may see what manner of Man he is . . . whether fair or deformed," so Scripture shows both "what Man is before Grace, how wretched, blind, naked, deformed, polluted! and also after Grace through Christ, how happy, adorned, beautiful and glorious!"[85] Keach's exposition of this metaphor encapsulates the entire progress of Bunyan's hero, from his original rags to his final adornment in shining raiment. All states of his soul are thus reflected in the mirror of Scripture.

How did it come about that Scripture could be accorded this kind of power? The question is most fully explored in Barbara K. Lewalski's *Protestant Poetics and the Seventeenth-Century Religious Lyric*. Two aspects of her argument about a Protestant poetics are particularly relevant to an understanding of Bunyan's achievement: "Besides looking to the Bible as source and model for the presentation of sacred truth as art, Protestant poetics also calls for the treatment of another kind of truth in religious lyric poetry—the painstaking analysis of the personal religious life.[86] The focus here will be on the significance of the Bible's role in assessing the individual life and the consequences of that role for *The Pilgrim's Progress* from a cultural perspective rather than a literary one. The purpose of this section is not to propose a new interpretation of Bunyan's use of the Bible but to use scholarship on this topic to illuminate the distance travelled by the Protestant readership I have described from its fourteenth-century inception to Bunyan's seventeenth-century response to it.[87]

The Reformation changed the terms in which one's spiritual life was negotiated; the right understanding of Scripture emerged as the one sure way to gain heaven. William Whittaker, in a Latin treatise published in 1588, defended the new Protestant emphasis on Scripture. He insists that its message is accessible to everyone: "We confess that all have not the gift of publicly interpreting the scriptures; but in private all the faithful, taught by the Holy Ghost, can understand the scriptures and recognize the true sense of scripture."[88] To complement the idea that Scripture is accessible to all because the Holy Ghost worked through it, the Protestant reformers argued for a method of interpreting Scripture different from the medieval one, which had been based on a belief that the Bible had four levels of meaning. They insisted that there was only "one sense of scripture": "We affirm that there is but one true, proper and genuine sense of scripture, arising from the words rightly understood, which we call the literal; and we contend that allegories, tropologies, and anagogues are not various senses, but various collections from one sense, or various applications and accomodations of that one meaning."[89] The ramifications of this distinction are described by Lewalski: "It makes for a different sense of the Bible as a unified poetic text, and for a much closer fusion of sign and thing signified, type and antitype."[90] By collapsing the fourfold method of interpreting Scripture into one whole sense, the individual's recognition of Scripture's message as it related to him or her came to be seen as contained in the literal terms that Scripture spelled out.

As Lewalski notes, the Reformers "exalted . . . typological symbolism."[91] The individual was urged to think in these terms: "Christians were invited to perceive the events and personages of Old and New Testament salvation history not merely as exemplary to them but as actually recapitulated in their lives, in accordance with God's vast typological plan of recapitulations and fulfillments."[92] Scripture became the grid through which experience was perceived; biblical, figurative language conditioned the way people processed their experiences. The flowering of religious lyric based on a Protestant poetics in the seventeenth century is one result of this new emphasis on Scripture, as Lewalski conclusively demonstrates. *The Pilgrim's Progress* represents another way in which the scriptural text came to be seen as personal history.

The Pilgrim's Progress is the necessary result of this typological focus on Scripture. U. Milo Kaufmann is on the verge of this point when discussing the idea that for the Puritan "all scripture could be reduced to a consistent body of doctrine": "The susceptibility of Scripture to such a reduction meant that it could be seen simultaneously as a *fait accompli*, one complete thought in the mind of God, and as a dynamic unfolding, and this superimposition of stasis and cursus is a paradigm for *The Pilgrim's Progress*."[93] Bunyan's narrative consciously works toward that "dynamic unfolding" of scriptural truth by constructing a universe where scriptural terms are applied to the individual self. The narrative of *The Pilgrim's Progress* is woven out of biblical texts, and the work as a whole attempts a synthesis of scriptural truth from the perspective of the individual Christian. As Damrosch points out, "Bunyan sees the Bible as a collection of one-sentence *texts*," each of which "has a direct and specific meaning, and the chief goal of *The Pilgrim's Progress* is to exhibit those meanings in narrative guise."[94]

The way biblical tropes were applied to individual experience is well documented in *Protestant Poetics*. In addition, as we saw in chapter 2, a number of tracts had explicated the metaphor of pilgrimage and in the process caused the metaphor to become inextricably tied to the way people perceived their lives. John Bunyan's *Grace Abounding*, however, provides the most eloquent witness to the way Scripture dominated personal experience.[95] Jesus's command, "Search the scriptures" (John 5.39), was taken by seventeenth-century Protestants as an invitation to find evidence of personal election in the Bible. *Grace Abounding* testifies to the power accorded Scripture both to indict and to save the individual Christian. Bunyan's comment toward the close of the work, "Wo be to him against whom the Scriptures bend themselves" (79) would make a fitting epigraph to *Grace Abounding*, for Scripture does indeed bend and shape Bunyan's conversion experience.

The overall drama of *Grace Abounding* includes a tempter who causes Bunyan to doubt whether he is saved, but this tempter has unusual powers and can manipulate Scripture to demoralize his subject: "the Tempter came in with this delusion, That there was no way for me to know I had Faith, but by trying to work some miracle, urging those *Scriptures* that seem to look that way, for the enforcing and strengthening his Temptation" (20). Scripture looks a certain way and provides a mirror for the sinner; Bunyan sees a reflection of himself within it. In fact, the role of Scripture as an active agent is the predominant theme of *Grace Abounding*. Roger Sharrock has noted that the quotations from Scripture are already, even within the limits of autobiography, becoming personified ideas about justification[96] and that the Bible is a physical presence (or, to use Stranahan's terminology, an "event").[97] But the role of Scripture is more specialized than that and is portrayed with an immediacy that demonstrates how personified it had become.[98] The one scriptural text, above all, that torments Bunyan is as follows:

141. And withal, that Scripture did seize upon my Soul, *Or profane person, as Esau, who for one morsel of meat sold his Birth-right; for you know how that afterwards when he would have inherited the blessing, he was rejected, for he found no place of repentance, though he sought it carefully with tears*. Heb. 12.16, 17

142. Now was I as one bound, I felt myself shut up unto the Judgment to come; nothing now for two years together would abide with me, but damnation, and an expectation of damnation: I say, nothing now would abide with me but this, save some few moments for relief, as in the sequel you will see.

143. These words were to my Soul like Fetters of Brass to my Legs, in the continual sound of which I went for several months together. (45–46)

So complete is Bunyan's identification with the Esau passage that the scriptural text imprisons him. Different passages from Scripture war within him: "for this about the sufficiency of grace, (Heb. 7.25) and that of Esau's parting with his Birth-right, would be like a pair of scales within my mind, sometimes one end would be uppermost, and sometimes again the other, according to which would be my peace or trouble" (67). What is ultimately being weighed is the truth of a passage of Scripture as it applies to him. Scripture is the place where one looks for oneself: "Then began I with sad and careful heart, to consider of the nature and largeness of my sin, and to search in the word of God, if I could in any place espy a word of Promise, or any encouraging Sentence by which I might take relief" (47). But at times, Scripture plays a more active role and pursues Bunyan:

> But blessed be his grace, that scripture, in these flying fits would call as running after me, *I have blotted out as a thick cloud thy transgressions, and, as a cloud thy sins: Return unto me, for I have redeemed thee*, Isa. 44.22. This, I say, would come in upon my mind, when I was fleeing from the face of God; for I did flee from his face, that is, my mind and spirit fled before him; by reason of his highness, I could not endure; then would the text cry, *Return unto me, for I have redeemed thee.* (54)

What is so distinctive about the characterization of Scripture in *Grace Abounding* is Bunyan's certainty that a given scriptural passage speaks directly to him. The scriptural citations in the work are treated as if they self-evidently involved his personal history.[99]

So direct is the applicability of Scripture to the individual life that it can be described as barring one from eternal life:

> 208. Thus I went on for many weeks, sometimes comforted, and sometimes tormented, and, especially at some times my torment would be very sore, for all those Scriptures forenam'd in the

Hebrews would be set before me, as the only sentences that would keep me out of Heaven. Then, again, I should begin to repent, that ever that thought went thorow me; I should also think thus with myself, why, How many Scriptures are there against me? there is but three or four, and cannot God miss them, and save me for all of them? Sometimes again I should think, O if it were not for these three or four words, now how might I be comforted! and I could hardly forbear at some times, but to wish them out of the Book. (68)

Sentences, not sacraments, can now bar or open the way to heaven.

The importance of this response to Scripture can best be seen if we return briefly to the larger issue of the radical shift reflected when we set *Piers Plowman* beside *The Pilgrim's Progress*. *Piers Plowman* demonstrates a similar grappling with scriptural quotations, but the application of them to the individual is radically different. It should be noted at the outset that Langland does not differentiate Scripture from the writings of the church fathers and the cumulative tradition of Christian culture. They all have authority, the Bible, creeds, and liturgy radiating authority outward to confer a derived authority on the texts that explain and transmit them, so that all are similarly treated. But *Piers Plowman* is marked by the same kind of questioning about whether a given text can be applied to the self. The most famous instance occurs in the pardon scene in passus 7, where Piers "in pure tene" tears the pardon that proclaims only, in a Latin text that a priest must translate, "Et qui bona egerunt ibunt in vitam eternam / Qui vero mala in ignem eternam."[100] As he tears the pardon, Piers, now able to use Latin, quotes Ps. 22.4: "Si ambulavero in medio umbre mortis / Non timebo mala quoniam tu mecum es."[101] He then proclaims:

I shal cease of my sowinge quod pierce, swinke not
    so hard
Ne about my bealy joy, so busy be no more
Of prayers & penaunce, my plowe shalbe hereafter.

                (K2r)

Here is not the place to probe what Piers's tearing of the pardon means. Instead, we should note that the pardon, the text, provokes a reaction that sets Piers on a different course, which he marks by appropriating another text to himself, its language no longer an obstacle. The transformation occurs because Piers has been presented with two possibilities by a text that lies across his path as both a sign and an obstacle; armed with the Twenty-second Psalm, he will now pursue his own salvation. Significantly, this puts him into confrontation with the priest who translated the original text and who challenges his right, as an ignorant man, to quote and interpret Scripture. Still, this is a very different kind of identification with a given text than we find in *Grace Abounding*. Furthermore, the scene was clearly both difficult and shocking in its own time; Langland omitted much of it from the more conservative C-text, and its meaning is the subject of controversy still.

An even more telling instance to illustrate the two works' different approaches to Scripture, even where they are most parallel, occurs in passus 10. There the dreamer encounters the figure of Scripture herself and asks about Do-Well, Do-Better, and Do-Best, clearly expecting a definitive answer. We must first note the different valuation given Scripture: she is Clergie's (Learning's) wife, and Langland clearly uses her to mean not only the Bible but all traditionally associated writings. Scripture glosses a biblical text ("To me belongeth vengeance, and recompense," Deut. 32.35), provoking a violent reaction from the Dreamer:

> For I shall punyshe hem in purgatorye, or in the pyt of hell
>
> Every man for hys misdedes, but if mercy it let,
>
> This is a longe lesson quod I, and litle I the wyser
>
> Where dowell is or dobet, darkely ye shewen,
>
> Many tales ye tell, that Theology lerneth,
>
> And that I man made was, and my name entred
>
> In the legend of lyfe, longe er I were,
>
> Or els unwryten for some wyckednes, as holy wryte manaceth.
>
> (N3r)

The dreamer's anger is provoked by the same message that Piers was given: the mystery of election and damnation. He actually sees the holy text menace him. So serious is the crisis for the dreamer that the first version of the poem actually ends with this confrontation. The B-text introduces here a period of rebellion in which the dreamer refuses to learn any more about Do-Well, Do-Better, and Do-Best. The dreamer's frustration at the ambiguity of whether he is included in the "Book of Lyfe" comes about because no one can tell him how to do well.

After a recognition of his own mortality, a confrontation with the Friars, and a meeting with Justice that gets him started again on his search for Do-Well and on the writing of the poem, the dreamer is put back into his encounter with Scripture. Scripture begins preaching on the same subject, predestination, that caused his rebellion in the first place:

> He sayth soth quod scripture tho, & scypte up and preached
>
> And the matter that she meaned, if lewde men it knew,
>
> The lesse as I leve, loven it they woulde.
>
> This was hyr theme & her text, I toke ful gode hede
>
> *Multi* to a mangery, and to the mete were sumpted
>
> Whan the people were plener come, the porter unpind the gate
>
> And plucked in *pauci*, prively, & let the remnaunt go
>
> All for tene of her text trembled my herte,
>
> And in a were gan I wexe, & with my selfe to dispute
>
> Whether I wer chose or not, on holi kirke I thought
>
> That underfonged me at the font for one of gods chosen.
>
> (O2v)

As the dreamer makes clear, Scripture's message about predestination would not be well received by "lewde men," an ominous foreshadowing of the difficulties that were to follow once the uneducated were indeed to be confronted with this document. The portrayal of a banquet to which many are summoned but to which only a few are admitted causes the dreamer to wonder again if he is among the saved, and his train of thought epitomizes the shift we are charting. There are similarities to Bunyan: the crisis is provoked by a scriptural text that the individual applies to himself, and the anxiety is about whether one is saved, not about spiritual progress. But the dreamer turns to Holy Church and remembers his baptism. External sacraments and the mediation of the church are invoked to help solve the problem of predestination and to free the individual from solitary grappling with the text.

We see in this scene Langland dramatizing a crucial, personal encounter between an individual and a text. But the images he uses to describe this ("scypte up and preached," for example, and the reference to how other possible listeners, "lewde men," would react) reinforces his viewpoint. The private experience leads into and, at least here, is ultimately subsumed by a communal one, liturgical and institutional. Similarly, the dreamer's own vision of the Crucifixion and the harrowing of hell, his interior experience of the biblical and historical event, gives way to a waking scene in which he and his family take part in Easter Mass. Langland is clearly on the borderline between the two views of Scripture. Toward the end of the poem, he might be seen as tipping toward the interior and personal, since the poem ends with the now solitary Conscience setting off on a search to "have" Piers Plowman. Yet even here the image of Conscience, in the ruins of Unity, on the great field where the poem began, has an implied publicness and communal relevance that are very different from the context in which Bunyan pictures himself as wrestling with Scripture in *Grace Abounding*. The Reformation changed the terms in which one's spiritual life was negotiated as, with the emphasis on the Bible as the one sure guide to salvation, a new relationship between the individual and Scripture came into being. This tradition of appropriating Scripture to one's own experience and self-exploration reached its fruition in *The Pilgrim's Progress*. The events that *The Pilgrim's Progress* allegorically portrays are derived from this unusual typological focus on Scripture.

Christian's physical progress through the narrative documents his and our developing ability to look through the lens Scripture offers as we decode the meaning of various episodes.[102] Keach's comparison of Scripture to a looking-glass records one dissimilarity that is crucial to an understanding of Bunyan's appropriation of the Bible. Under the heading of Simile, he notes that "one Glass hath not all the Properties which we have here mentioned." Under Disparity, he writes that "the Gospel or Word of God is a spiritual Perspective Glass, as well as a Looking-Glass."[103] Embedded in *The Pilgrim's Progress* is a figure for this aspect of Scripture, the Perspective Glass of the Shepherds. Up to that point in the narrative, Bunyan had used Scripture as a mirror in which to see the self (in rags) and the world (Vanity Fair). Significantly, Christian and Hopeful cannot see the prospect of heaven until they reach the Delectable Mountains, and even then, they can only see "something like the Gate, and also some of the Glory of the place" (238). Thus, *The Pilgrim's Progress* is the inevitable result of an attitude towards Scripture as a lens through which to see the self as well as "a clear sight of God." Even more importantly, the narrative itself provides a lens for its readers to apprehend the applicability of Scripture to their own experience.

The scriptural citations affixed to the margins of *The Pilgrim's Progress* testify to the work's scriptural underpinnings.[104] And, as we have noted before, this kind of glossing is not analytical or explanatory; rather, the scriptural glosses identify the narrative's building blocks and provide a key to understanding the fictive expression of a "gospel truth."[105] The opening scene, introducing the image of Christian, exemplifies the process by which Bunyan built his narrative: "I dreamed, and behold *I saw a Man clothed with Raggs standing in a certain place, with his face from his own House, a Book in his hand, and a great burden upon his Back.* I looked, and saw him open the Book, and Read therein; and as he read, he wept and trembled: and not being able longer to contain, he brake out with a lamentable cry; saying, *what shall I do?*" (146). The scriptural citations attached to this passage both document the biblical borrowing and illuminate what is meant by the visual image:

> Isa. 64.6: But we are al as an unclean thing, and all our righteousnesses are as filthy ragges; and we all doe fade as a leafe; and our iniquities like the wind have taken us away.

> Luke 14.33: So likewise, whosoever he be of you, that forsaketh not all that he hath, he cannot be my disciple.

> Ps. 38.4: For mine iniquities are gone over mine head: as an heavy burden they are too heavie for me.

Hab. 2.2: And the Lord answered me and said, Write this vision, and make it plain upon tables, that he may runne that readeth it.

Acts 16.31: And they saide, Beleeve on the Lord Jesus Christ, and thou shalt be saved, and thy house.

Two of the scriptural citations, Isa. 64.6 and Ps. 38.4, identify landmarks associated with the visual picture being presented: the rags the sinner is clothed in and the burden on his back. The citation of Luke 14.33 provides a gloss on why the figure is placed with "his face from his own house": unless the sinner is willing to forsake everything, he cannot be saved. The citation of Hab. 2.2 has a dual role. It specifically explicates the role of the Book, the Bible, which makes plain to the sinner his own spiritual condition so that he might run to obtain salvation. But the citation also by extension refers to the book the reader is reading, *The Pilgrim's Progress*. It can be described, and in fact is described in the "Apology," as having a similar role to the Bible: "this Book will make a Travailer of thee" (line 207). Finally, the function of the last citation, Acts 16.31, is not to gloss any explicit part of the text. Rather, it provides an answer to Christian's question and a forecast of what the action of the work will involve. Christian, in order to be saved, must believe in the New Testament preachings of Jesus Christ.

Thus the biblical citations function as both explication and sanction for the fiction-making. But the dimensions of *The Pilgrim's Progress*'s relationship to the Bible go far beyond this kind of marginal glossing of fictive expressions. The work's texture is built out of biblical details and the work as a whole attempts to be an epitome of the Bible's message.

As we discussed earlier, the biblical metaphor of pilgrimage provides the central structural action for *The Pilgrim's Progress*. Imagery associated with the pilgrimage metaphor provides some of the features of the landscape, such as the "strait gate." For instance, the term "City of Destruction" can be traced to Heb. 13.14: "Here have we no continuing citie, but we seeke one to come," though Bunyan does not actually cite this text. Bunyan translates the idea of having no continuing city into a concrete place, the City of Destruction, from which Christian must depart. A landscape feature like the

Slough of Despond at first sight seems to reflect a purely personal experience without scriptural precedent until we see the action of Help glossed with the biblical citation from Ps. 40.2: "He brought me up also out of an horrible pit, out of the mirie clay, and set my feete upon a rock, and established my goings." The episode is created both to signal that despondency is part of the conversion process and to provide a visual narrative equivalent to the biblical passage. Other biblical passages provide features of the landscape: Christian witnesses the fury of Mount Sinai and fears that it will fall on his head; the highway that Christian must take is lined with a wall named Salvation and glossed with Isa. 26.1 ("salvation will God appoint for walles and bulwarkes"),[106] and the River of Life comes directly out of Scripture.

Similarly, landscapes that involve larger episodes are created through biblical allusion. The Valley of the Shadow of Death (the Twenty-third Psalm) is stripped of its metaphoric connotations and becomes a landscape Christian walks through. Its description is taken whole cloth from Jer. 2.6: "Now at the end of this Valley, was another, called the Valley of the *Shadow of Death*, and *Christian* must needs go through it, because the way to the Celestial City lay through the midst of it. Now this Valley is a very solitary place: The Prophet *Jeremiah* thus describes it, A *Wilderness, a Land of desarts, and of Pits, a Land of drought, and of the shadow of death, a Land that no Man* (but a Christian) *passeth through, and where no man dwelt"* (188). Bunyan's interjection ("but a Christian") in the middle of the passage demonstrates his concern to adopt scriptural motifs and reshape them to typify the experience of every Christian.

The creation of Vanity Fair represents another reshaping of scriptural material. The origins of Vanity Fair and the Town of Vanity are to be located in Isa. 40.17 ("All nations before him are as nothing; and they are counted to him less than nothing and vanity") and Eccles. chapters 2, 11, and 17, all of which sound the preacher's theme: "all is vanity." Bunyan chooses a title for his representation of the world that is meant to evoke these biblical pronouncements; the things of this world are as nothing to God.

Scriptural borrowings are not confined to the landscape features of *The Pilgrim's Progress*. Bunyan also sets biblical personages into the world of his narrative. For instance, although the episode is not directly presented, Faithful relates his encounter with Moses. Lot's wife is placed in the landscape as a "wayside memorial," to use U. Milo Kaufman's terms. The figure Demas, who occurs only as a name in 2 Tim. 4.10 ("Do your best to join me soon, for Demas has deserted me because his heart is set on the world"), is developed by Bunyan into a minor figure, appropriately associated with Hill Lucre. His role is to tempt pilgrims into wanting the things of this world; By-ends and his companions follow Demas and are never seen again.

The figure of the flatterer represents another kind of reworking of scriptural allusions. Christian and Hopeful meet a man "black of flesh, but covered with a very light Robe" (246), who leads them into a net. Bunyan developed this episode from several scriptural sources:

Prov. 29.5: A man that flattereth his neighbour, spreadeth a net for his feet.

Dan. 11.32: And such as doe wickedly against the covenant, shall he corrupt by flatteries: but the people that do know their God, shall be strong and doo *exploits*.

2 Cor. 11.13, 14: For such are false Apostles, deceitfull workers, transforming themselves into the Apostles of Christ. And no mer-veile for Sathan himselfe is transformed into an angel of light.

The first citation explains the action of entrapping the pilgrims in a net. The citation from Daniel does not explicitly gloss any features of the episode; rather, it explains the theological reason for the scene. The final quotation from 2 Corinthians both explicates the visual details of the figure and identifies the character. To make the episode absolutely clear, Bunyan has the "shining one" explain to Christian and Hopeful who it is that they have met: "It is *Flatterer*, a false Apostle, that hath transformed himself into an Angel of Light" (247). This episode illustrates the process by which Bunyan reshaped scriptural allusions to create a generalized image of the Christian experience.

Thus Bunyan creates a world where individual experience can be charted. He makes that world out of Scripture and peoples it not only with pilgrims but with figures from biblical history. The landscape is a universal Christian one, and one that, as Christian is told in Vanity Fair, Christ himself has had to walk through: "The Prince of Princes himself, when here, went through *this Town*, to his own Countrey" (211). Moreover, Christian at House Beautiful is shown "Engines with which some of his Servants had done wonderful things" (183). The engines are part of biblical history, and among them we find Moses's rod and David's sling. The allusions to biblical history define the world where Christian walks as one that combines individual with biblical history: all are part of the same experience.

Christian's story is set forth to delineate "the Way" of the Christian. The events that befall him along the way are events that are mapped out metaphorically in Scripture and are literalized and objectified in *The Pilgrim's Progress*. Thus we see Christian being armed according to the prescription in Eph. 6.11 ("Put on the whole armour of God, that ye may be able to stand against the wiles of the devill"). When Christian sights the cross, three "shining ones" come to him. Their actions toward him follow a pattern marked out in the Bible: "Now as he stood looking and weeping, behold three shining ones came to him, and saluted him, with *Peace be to thee*; so the first said to him, *Thy sins be forgiven*. The second stript him of his Rags, and cloathed him with a change of Raiment. The third also set a mark in his fore-head, and gave him a Roll with a Seal upon it, which he bid him look on as he ran, and that he should give it in at the Celestial Gate" (169–70). The text of Mark 2.5 ("Thy sinnes be forgiven thee") is spoken directly to him. He is given new clothing according to the prescription in Zech. 3.4 ("And unto him he said, Behold, I have caused thine iniquity to passe from thee, and I wil clothe thee with change of raiment"). He is given a seal that originates in Eph. 1.13 ("In whom ye also trusted after that ye heard the word of trueth, the Gospel of your salvation: in whom also after that yee beleeved, yee were sealed with that holy Spirit of promise").[107] Bunyan, through a careful collating of different scriptural passages, portrays a universal Christian experience.

Not only is Scripture all around, making a world in which the pilgrim can move, it is also something the pilgrims use within that world.[108] It is quoted and encountered throughout *The Pilgrim's Progress*. Evangelist gives Christian a parchment roll containing Matt. 3.7 ("flee from the wrath to come"). And it is featured in the dialogues between pilgrims, especially towards the latter part of the work.

By applying scriptural truths to the individual Christian and creating a world in which they can be enacted, Bunyan provides a reformulation of scriptural truth from the perspective of the individual person rather than God.[109] Through a skillful use of allegorical and biblical materials, he creates a character with biblical and universal experience. When Christian announces his name at House Beautiful, we find a perfect blending of allegorical, personal, and biblical history: "My name is, now, *Christian*; but my name at the first was *Graceless*: I came of the race of *Japhet*, whom God will perswade to dwell in the Tents of *Shem*" (176). When Bunyan, in his "Apology," claims that by reading his book the reader can "read thy self . . . / And . . . know whether thou art blest or not, / By reading these same lines" ("Apology," lines 233–35), he is announcing that his book, like the Bible, can provide a mirror and a goad to set the reader on a spiritual journey. As Damrosch notes, "The reader's work . . . must be to meditate on scriptural truth so deeply that heart and head, life and text merge into unity."[110] *The Pilgrim's Progress* portrays a life made out of Scripture and bound by Scripture; it gives its readers a new type by which to chart their spiritual lives. In the last chapter, we will see that later readers have used *The Pilgrim's Progress* just as Bunyan used the Bible, though in an increasingly secular fashion.

7

"Would'st read thy self?"
The Pilgrim's Progress as a "Perspective Glass" for Readers

> "But then so many readers are fools," said Lily. "And yet they get something out of their reading. Mrs. Crump is always poring over the Revelations, and nearly knows them by heart. I don't think she could interpret a single image, but she has a hazy, misty idea of the truth. That's why she likes it,—because it's too beautiful to be understood; and that's why I like Pilgrim's Progress."
>
> Anthony Trollope, *The Small House at Allington*

 Lily Dale's comment while searching for reading matter to cure a broken heart has profound significance for this study of what readers get out of reading. The juxtaposition of Revelation with *The Pilgrim's Progress* as two books "too beautiful to be understood," but that nevertheless deliver "a hazy, misty idea of the truth," is an apt one, for *The Pilgrim's Progress* became a second Scripture for its readers, although sometimes a secularized one. *The Pilgrim's Progress* was the most popular prose work in the seventeenth century,[1] and it has until comparatively recently remained popular. But why and how readers read it varied enormously. Noting that Bunyan's works "provide a fascinating case study of cultural assimilation," Richard Greaves has pointed out that in it "writers as disparate as evangelicals and atheists, revolutionaries and imperialists have found support for their views."[2] His comment underscores the fact that texts do not change, but readers do. Perhaps "readers are fools," as Lily Dale claims, but their responses to texts are at least as interesting as the texts themselves in what they tell us about how and why readers read and the cultural effects of those readings.

Tracing the history of the reception of *The Pilgrim's Progress* would require several volumes, but we can chart its immediate afterlife by focusing on the same kinds of "opaque documents" that we used to assess the reception of *Piers Plowman*.[3] One certain yardstick to its popularity is printing history; *The Pilgrim's Progress* was enormously successful. It went through eleven editions before Bunyan's death and was translated into other languages in his lifetime, something quite unprecedented for the period.[4] But changes in various editions, spurious versions, appropriations of both author and text, and imitations are also reliable barometers of its popularity as well as its varied meanings for the culture as a whole. Even more fascinating is the fact that it speaks to other cultures. *The Pilgrim's Progress* has been translated into over two hundred languages and, next to the Bible, is perhaps the second best-selling book in the world.[5] As for English readers, as Q. D. Leavis has pointed out, for two centuries after its publication "even the grimmest and poorest Puritan household owned a copy of the Bible and *The Pilgrim's Progress*."[6] How did *The Pilgrim's Progress* come to be seen as a work as necessary to human life as the Bible? We can begin to answer by briefly sketching the later reception of *The Pilgrim's Progress* in order to frame what has happened to it over time.

The association of *The Pilgrim's Progress* with the Bible, made by readers as different as Q. D. Leavis and Trollope's fictional Lily Dale, has been an important aspect of the book's reception throughout its history. As we saw in chapter 6, this equation of the two texts is not surprising given the status of *The Pilgrim's Progress* as a reformulation of Scripture. At least three different kinds of audience have regarded it as a sacred text of sorts. For the Protestant reader, Bunyan's narrative hardly seemed to be fiction at all, for two reasons. First, it was regarded as the autobiography of a Protestant saint, John Bunyan himself. And second, because of its relationship to the Bible, it was specifically opposed to mere fiction by certain devout Christians. For example, a young Quaker woman, dying at the age of twenty-five in the year 1810, read *The Pilgrim's Progress* a short time before her illness. On her deathbed, she sent a message to a friend on the subject of reading, "which at that awful period she saw required great caution, and lamented that much precious time was often wasted perusing works of the imagination. 'Tell her' said she 'to read the Holy Scriptures,' intimating the more she did so, the less she would feel disposed for perusing books of an unprofitable tendency."[7] The implications of this passage are clear: if the two poles are Scripture and works of the imagination, *The Pilgrim's Progress* more closely resembles the former. Imaginative works are unprofitable because they do not enlist the reader in a search for salvation the way both the Bible and *The Pilgrim's Progress* do.

A second group of more lettered readers, without abandoning the text's religious connotations, also admitted that it was a work of the imagination and emphasized form over content. *The Pilgrim's Progress* was described often as a "theological romance" or a "religious romance,"[8] and one anonymous critic in 1765 illustrates the process of sorting out genre and content: "As a work of imagination, however, illustrating a particular set of religious principles, the *Pilgrim's Progress* is certainly a work of original and uncommon genius. . . . In a word, it contains a most excellent epitome and illustration of a *Calvinistic* divinity, under an allegory highly entertaining and affecting."[9] The dominant terminology used to define what *The Pilgrim's Progress* represents is here literary rather than religious. This critic assigns it, as a work of the imagination, to the genre of allegory, and emphasizes the aesthetic effects of the narrative. The discussion of the work's content, an illustration of a "particular set of religious principles" and an "excellent epitome and illustration of *Calvinistic* divinity," is subordinated to the consideration of the author as a genius for his skill in creating a "sugared pill" of religious doctrine.

This dual vision of the fabric of *The Pilgrim's Progress* received its most cogent expression from Coleridge:

With the same illusion that we read any tale known to be fictitious, as a novel,—we go on with the characters as real persons, who had been nicknamed by their neighbours. . . .

This wonderful work is one of the very few books which may be read over repeatedly at different times, and each time with a new and a different pleasure. I read it once as a theologian—and let me assure you that there is great theological acumen in the work—once with devotional feelings—and once as a poet. I could not have believed beforehand that Calvinism could be painted in such exquisitely delightful colours.

I know of no book, the Bible excepted, as above all comparison, which I, according to my judgment and experience, could so safely recommend as teaching and enforcing the whole saving truth according to the mind that was in Christ Jesus, as in the Pilgrim's Progress. It is, in my conviction, incomparably the best *Summa Theologiae Evangelicae* ever produced by a writer not miraculously inspired.[10]

Coleridge recognizes that it is the reader who changes, not the text; depending on how it is read, *The Pilgrim's Progress* is both story and sacred writing. Like the anonymous reader above, Coleridge praises Bunyan's ability to "paint" Calvinism in "exquisitely delightful colors," but he also provides a succinct statement about the pleasures of the narrative as a novel. As we will see, even some of the book's earliest readers were attracted to it by its characters rather than its doctrine.

Coleridge's reference to teaching also hints at the nature of a subset of this more lettered readership. Suggesting that the work can legitimately be read as fiction also allows it to be seen as suitable entertainment for children. In *The English Common Reader*, Richard Altick has pointed out that "the familiar assumption that Bunyan's book figured in the imaginative awakening of countless children is entirely correct," citing as proof the responses of Joseph Barker, the future religious controversialist ("I had no idea that it was a parable or an allegory"), and Thomas Burt ("Not as a dream or allegory but as solid literal history did it present itself").[11] The problematic nature of this phenomenon is demonstrated by George Burder, who wrote *Bunyan's Pilgrim's Progress Versified* for children in 1804. In a revealing preface, Burder justifies his inclusion of explanatory notes that he declares are "intended as a key to the author's spiritual design, that so the work may not be considered as a Novel, intended only to amuse, but as a correct representation of Christian experience."[12] Burder registers the Protestant reader's fear that the religious aspects of the book are being lost because of its appeal as fiction and as story. Even the Protestant divine Adam

Clarke in his autobiography admitted that his childhood reading of *The Pilgrim's Progress* predisposed him to seeing it as a romance, as George Offor reports: "At this early age he read the 'Pilgrim's Progress,' as he would read a book of chivalry. Christian was a great hero, by whom the most appalling difficulties were surmounted, the most incredible labours performed, powerful enchantments dissolved, giants conquered, and devils quelled. It was not likely that he would see it as a *spiritual allegory.*"[13] Like Joshua Gilpin, Clarke discovered the work's religious implications in his adulthood. The descriptive tags Coleridge and Clarke assign to *The Pilgrim's Progress* when they view it purely as entertainment are also instructive. They demonstrate that even within the same lettered readership, different lenses brought to the text refract different experiences of it. Coleridge delights in the characters and labels the work as a novel, whereas Clarke is attracted to the adventures and therefore defines Bunyan's narrative as a romance.

Other readers, however, have used it as a secular rather than as a religious model for their lives. John Buchan, for example, entitles his autobiography *Pilgrim's Way*, and records how his early experiences of life were mediated by Bunyan's narrative:

The Pilgrim's Progress became my constant companion. Even today I think that, if the text were lost, I could restore most of it from memory. My delight in it came partly from the rhythms of its prose, which, save in King James's Bible, have not been equalled in our literature; there are passages, such as the death of Mr. Valiant-for-Truth, which all my life have made music in my ear. But its spell was largely due to its plain narrative, its picture of life as a pilgrimage over hill and dale, where surprising adventures lurked by the wayside, a hard road with now and then long views to cheer the traveller and a great brightness at the end of it. John Bunyan claimed our woods as his own. There was the Wicket-Gate at the back of the colliery, where one entered them; the Hill Difficulty—more than one; the Slough of Despond—various specimens; the Plain called Ease; Doubting Castle—a disused gravel-pit; the Enchanted Land—a bog full of orchises; the Land of Beulah—a pleasant grassy place where tinkers made their fires. There was no River at the end, which was fortunate, perhaps, for otherwise my brothers and I might have been drowned in trying to ford it.[14]

Once again, *The Pilgrim's Progress* is compared to the Bible, but now it has become a secular and mythic Scripture. And that first childhood encounter with *The Pilgrim's Progress* is never lost. Buchan defines his life in terms of it in his title, and, as we have seen in chapter 1, soldiers in World War I also used it, without reference to its religious allegory, as a paradigm for their adult experience.[15]

As the early Protestant readings of *The Pilgrim's Progress* degenerated into Lily Dale's "hazy, misty idea of the truth," truth itself became multiple and enigmatic: sometimes sacred, sometimes personal or mythic, and sometimes even political. Just as Christian used a perspective glass to find an unsteady vision of his goal, so readers used *The Pilgrim's Progress* itself to attain a hazy idea of their own goals. Readers still saw "something like the Gate, and also some of the Glory of the place" (238)—but the "place" had changed. As we have noted, *The Pilgrim's Progress* emerged as "one of the two foundation texts of the English working-class movement"; according to E. P. Thompson, readers found in *The Pilgrim's Progress* a "slumbering Radicalism which was preserved through the 18th century and which breaks out again and again in the 19th."[16] That readership is epitomized by Thomas Cooper, the Chartist, who commented that *The Pilgrim's Progress* was his "book of books."[17] It is no longer the Bible that plays this archetypal role in the reader's consciousness, but *The Pilgrim's Progress* in its secular, political context. The social ideology of the figure of Bunyan as Christian, like the figure of Piers Plowman, is thus appropriated for increasingly secular ends. And *The Pilgrim's Progress* appears to be eminently adaptable to almost any political and societal situation. Christopher Hill notes that the leader of the nineteenth century Taiping Christian sect that almost took over all of China, Hong Xiuquan, named his capital the New Jerusalem and declared that his "two favorite books were the Bible and *The Pilgrim's Progress*."[18] Vera Brittain, writing a biography of Bunyan shortly after World War II, demonstrates the process by which a contemporary reader uses a politically and religiously marginalized seventeenth-century work as an allegory of her own political present:

The epic story of Christian's creator is hence not merely dramatic and absorbing in itself. The fact that it is a mirror of seventeenth-century England in the quality and direction of its spiritual adventure gives it a special relevance for our own epoch, in which the same struggle is taking place in a different form. It brings the challenge of hope and courage to all who are fighting for the integrity of the human soul against totalitarian philosophies and spiritual demoralization.[19]

These reactions to *The Pilgrim's Progress* were determined by the work's varied reception by different segments of the culture in the decades immediately following its original publication. Within those early responses are the vestiges of both the Protestant and the lettered readings, as well as the first stirrings of another kind of reader. That readership was not exclusively interested in interpretation from either a religious or a literary perspective. Its position on the value and use of books is epitomized by Lily Dale's remark with which this chapter began. All three kinds of readers thought they understood the book, and all three reacted to it. The Protestant readership saw *The Pilgrim's Progress* as a salvational text and elevated its author to the stature of a Protestant saint. A lettered readership also viewed Bunyan's narrative as a literary artifact, accused Bunyan of plagiarism, and felt licensed to rewrite the text. But ordinary readers saw *The Pilgrim's Progress* as the story of a man and were shocked by the fact that Christian left his family behind. These three evolving audiences illustrate how very different readers can shape and be shaped by the same text.

Protestant Readers of *The Pilgrim's Progress*

The lens the Protestant reader brought to *The Pilgrim's Progress* magnified the content rather than the form of Bunyan's narrative. Because it was perceived as containing a "correct representation of Christian experience," it was defined as a salvational text that contained the truth and was therefore not a fiction. That lens also accentuated the book's designs on readers and made them aware that the text required their active engagement.[20] One measure of its power to enlist readers in a search for their own salvation is signaled by an anonymous comment made in 1729 that appeared in *A Dis-*

course of Ridicule and Irony: "Bunyan's *Pilgrim's Progress* had infinitely outdone the *The Tale of the Tub*; which, perhaps had not made one convert to *infidelity*, whereas *Pilgrim's Progress* had converted many sinners to Christ."[21] *The Pilgrim's Progress*, like the Bible, was not an object to be admired but a potentially rigorous experience to be undergone. Moreover, for a Protestant readership, books did not reflect the skill of the artificer so much as the ultimate source of inspiration: God, who, through the Holy Ghost, directed both writing and reading for "his Design" ("Apology," line 144). Thus, the figure of the author as God's servant was emphasized. Spurious versions as well as imitations and adaptations of *The Pilgrim's Progress* illustrate how the fabric of Bunyan's narrative was construed by this kind of reader. Appropriations of the figure of the author, as well as prefaces to editions of *The Pilgrim's Progress* itself, shed light on which aspects of that figure this readership found attractive. Finally, the machinery of later editions, such as notes and keys, allows us to chart shifts in this audience.

Before turning to the spurious versions of *The Pilgrim's Progress*, we should set in place the contours of meaning put forth by a hypothetical Protestant reader such as the one we originally discussed in our investigation of Bunyan's "Apology." Interestingly, the issues we found reflected in that paradigm for reading reappear in their entirety in a 1685 French translation of *The Pilgrim's Progress*.[22] The translator comments on what the reader should look for in the text, gives the religious credentials of the author, states the author's aim in producing the work, provides a description of what readers will find, invites them to recognize themselves, justifies the work's style, and closes with a wish for the reader's salvation. This preface reverses the order of the concerns as they appear in Bunyan's "Apology," beginning with the book's designs on the reader before turning to the question of style, perhaps because the translator was a careful reader of the "Apology."

The translator defines Bunyan's objectives for his works in a way that demonstrates his understanding of the narrative as an accurate portrayal of the various states of Christian professors:

The aim of our Author is simply to take the case of a penitent soul who is seeking God as he journeys towards Eternity. We learn how he turns away from evil and destruction, his former state, leaves his father's house, and directs his face and his steps towards the new *Jerusalem* that stands on high, what he meets on his journey, and how he finally accomplishes his pilgrimage, says farewell to the world, and arrives safely on the hither side of death among the joys of eternity. And at the same time the book deals also with some of the divergencies from the proper route, and with many of those persons who travel in a different fashion, who seek their own road which is no good one, and how they finally discover that their steps lead them down into hell, and that none of the pleasures they have found can preserve them from death.[23]

The translator also returns to Bunyan's concern with putting the book together with the reader's "head and heart." The book itself emerges as a kind of test for its readers; if they read "the pages of this book in a pious frame, there will be some who will recognise themselves in some places, their hearts' fashion painted true like a portrait before their eyes, as they behold their own conduct in the carriage of another."[24] This process is another version of what Bunyan called "chaulking" out "the man that seeks the everlasting prize" ("Apology," line 198). Those who "like fools die" are also alluded to: "Alas, if a worldly man, a hypocrite, a soul without grace, could only have the eyes of his understanding sufficiently opened, how often would he not behold himself here under another name? how often would he not behold here the destruction of those foolish imaginings which he had conceived by studying the desires of his own heart for the ground of his salvation! They would see their hopes and all their efforts brushed away like a spider's web."[25] For this Protestant reader, *The Pilgrim's Progress* presents, to use a later succinct formulation of its content, "a map of the Christian profession in its current mixed state."[26] As we saw in chapter 6, the readers are expected to decipher what both, using U. Milo Kaufman's terms, the "sincere" and the "insincere" wayfarers represent, and then scan themselves for evidence of this phenomenon. Readers are here encouraged to use Bunyan's book in just the same way that Keach encouraged earlier readers to use the Bible: as an image of the self, whether before or after the reception of grace.

The last section of this preface, while still keeping the focus squarely on the book's effect on the reader, discusses the style. The translator notes that Bunyan struggled over whether he should publish his work and proclaims that he finally allowed the work to be printed as "an offering destined to win souls."[27] However, the translator is more honest than Bunyan in his discussion of this "Novelty," labelling it a "pious fraud" that can result in the addition of souls to "Christ's flock."[28] The preface next provides justification for the allegorical mode by summarizing Bunyan's arguments on the topic. First, the manner was chosen "so that divine truths may penetrate to the inmost heart."[29] Secondly, this practice does not need to be defended because "several theologians and spokesmen of God's people" and "the great and sovereign doctor Jesus" himself have "set out grave and lofty truths in a figurative way."[30] Finally, the translator closes by noting that if his translation meets with success, he will translate another "treatise" by Bunyan: "A second part describing the whole sinful career of a reprobate person, from his childhood through his whole life and conduct to his death, under the title of *The Life and Death of Badman in the Form of Dialogue*."[31] The anonymous translator clearly views, just as Bunyan had, *The Pilgrim's Progress, Part I*, and *Mr. Badman* as companion pieces.

This preface demonstrates that at least some portion of his Protestant readership was indeed reading the text as Bunyan had intended, and within the very parameters of meaning he had specified. Labelling the work a treatise defines its preaching function. The preface's main concern is squarely with readers' search for themselves through an encounter with the figures in the text. But spurious versions of *The Pilgrim's Progress*, as well as imitations, adaptations, and appropriations of the figure of the author, provide potential readings of his text that Bunyan might not have recognized.

The profit motive must be considered in assessing the existence of these texts, but these works were also attempts to duplicate Bunyan's success in addressing a new audience of Protestant readers who viewed *The Pilgrim's Progress* itself as an epitome of the Christian experience and its function as promoting the spiritual welfare of the reader. These works provide evidence that readers read Bunyan's narrative in terms of the Protestant genres of prophecy, exhortation, and spiritual autobiography discussed in chapter 6. There were three spurious versions of *The Pilgrim's Progress*. Two positioned themselves in opposition to Bunyan's paradigm for salvation, thus reading Bunyan's narrative as an exhortation or treatise that set forth the way to salvation, by their lights, incorrectly. The first spurious edition, entitled *The Second Part of The Pilgrim's Progress*, appeared in 1682 and was printed again in 1683.[32] It was written by one T. S., believed to be Thomas Sherman. As Roger Sharrock has noted, this edition registers the objections of at least one particular religious community, the General Baptists. The work was designed to correct the "defects" of the original, which included Bunyan's stress on a particular call, his neglect of church life and the sacraments, and the frivolous style.[33] Sherman read *The Pilgrim's Progress* as a religious tract that set forth a paradigm for salvation that he disagreed with; he did not think it gave accurate weight to tradition and to doctrine in its portrayal of a Christian's experience. He also thought it lacked seriousness. In his preface he claims that he tried to "deliver the whole in such serious and spiritual phrases that may prevent the lightness and laughter which the reading of some passages therein may occasion in some vain and frothy minds."[34]

Sherman's idea of what the proper style for a discourse on this topic should be is immediately evident in the opening scene. After an extended meditation on the beauties of spring, the narrator turns to the business at hand:

> I one day took a walk in the fields to feast my eyes with the variety of delightful objects which that season of the year wherein the universe bears the nearest resemblance to the happy state wherein the immortal God at first created it liberally offers to the view of the admiring beholders, and thereby lays an irresistible obligation upon heavenly minds to spiritualize the several objects they behold, and satiate their happy souls with heavenly meditation, by affording them such innumerable occasions of contemplating the divine goodness.[35]

In this work we find ourselves from the outset in a verbal universe totally different from the starkly simple one of Bunyan's original. In addition to correcting the particular flaws he perceived, Sherman is also clearly displaying his own learned background and denigrating Bunyan's lack of education.

The next spurious version chronologically, *The Pilgrim's Progress, The Third Part* (1693), does not provide a corrective to Bunyan's paradigm. Instead, it borrows it in order to feature the adventures of other pilgrims. It is a clear attempt to profit from Bunyan's phenomenal success, but it also correctly diagnoses what readers were hungering for. It appropriates both the title and the name of the author as well as Bunyan's strategy of showcasing various kinds of Christians in Part II of *The Pilgrim's Progress*. *The Third Part* concerns the pilgrimage through life of four pilgrims named Tender-Conscience, Spiritual Man, Seek-Truth, and Convert. Its title page also revises Bunyan's formula in response to what readers must have loved best; it shows "the Several Difficulties and Dangers he met with, and the many Victories he obtained over the World, the Flesh, and the Devil."[36] The title page also reflects an understanding of *The Pilgrim's Progress* in terms of Bunyan's personal history: *"To which is added The Life and Death of John Bunyan, Author of the First and Second Part; compleating the whole Progress."*[37] The title page is designed so that readers will assume Bunyan wrote it; his name receives the second largest type ("Dream" is in the largest). An "Advertisement" prefixed to a 1693 edition of *The Pilgrim's Progress* illustrates that *The Third Part* fared far better than Sherman's attempt: "The Pilgrims Progress; The Third Part; in a Dream: Printed in 1692, is an impostor, thrust into the World by a Nameless Author, and would insinuate to the *Buyers*, that 'tis *John Bunyan's* by adding a false Account of His Life and Death, not compleating the Work, as is said, &c. The Skeleton of *his* Design, and the Main of the Book Done by him, As a third Part, remains with *Nath. Ponder*; which when con[ve]nient time serves, shall be published."[38] Notice that Nathaniel Ponder is himself searching for a way to assemble a sequel to Parts I and II, unsuccessfully, we may safely assume. The shift in this spurious version to a focus on characters as models for living rather than object-lessons in reforming the self is a change first "authorized" by Bunyan himself in Part II in 1684.

The unknown author of *The Third Part* does not include an "Apology," but his preface, which is signed J. B., describes the content of the work and comments on several of the issues Bunyan had dealt with in his "Apology" to Part I. "The Preface to the Christian Reader" notes that "in this Book is set forth a tedious Pilgrimage through the many dangerous hazards of the Wilderness of this World, to the Heavenly *Canaan* of Eternal Rest and Peace: In which, though under the Similitude of a Dream, is Lively represented the state of our Christian warfare,"[39] an indication that romance elements in the portrayal of the Christian struggle will predominate in the work, just as they do in *The Pilgrim's Progress,* Part II. The use of a feigned dress receives comment in ways reminiscent of Bunyan's "Apology" as well:

> This has been in the former, as well as the present Age, a way
> of writing that has been extreamly taking, representing to the mind
> things that command our most serious Thoughts and Attentions,
> and work more upon the minds of Men, than if delivered in plainer
> terms; however, to the discerning Christian there is nothing in this
> that is obscure, or difficult to be understood, nothing but what is
> grounded upon Sacred Truths, and the Mercies of God in Jesus
> Christ, held forth to us by his assured Word.[40]

This writer is more explicit about past models, but he too sees them as engaging the minds of his readers in terms similar to those we found in the "Apology" to Part I. He also must assure the reader that the work is sound in terms of Christian doctrine.

The Third Part is an obvious attempt to mimic Bunyan's strategy in Part II by creating additional characters, but the final spurious version of *The Pilgrim's Progress* represents a return to a reading of the content of Bunyan's narrative in terms of a religious paradigm, for it "corrects" the original and rewrites it in terms of Catholic spiritual experience. *The Progress of the Christian Pilgrim*[41] changes the names and places slightly: for example, Christianus for Christian, Fidelius for Faithful, Mr. Director for Evangelist, House of the Instructor for Interpreter's House, and Grace-Hall for House Beautiful. It is also rewritten in terms of religious denominations. In a typically Catholic visual meditation on the Crucifixion, Christianus encounters three crosses instead of one, one of which is labeled "Jesus of Nazareth, King of the Jews." Similarly, at Grace-Hall Christian is presented with food that is reminiscent of the sacrament: "They set Bread and Wine before me, one of them saying, Come eat of my Bread, and Drink of the Wine that I have mingled."[42] There is also one major change that may reflect the author's casual appropriation of Bunyan's narrative: *The Progress of the Pilgrim* does not separate the Dreamer and the protagonist. The journey proper begins when the narrator falls asleep and sees himself covered in rags. The work includes "The Author's Apology to the Reader," which is a shorter rewritten version of Bunyan's defenses for his fiction, but without its depth.

There are also countless imitations and adaptations of *The Pilgrim's Progress* that register readings of the work in terms of prophecy and spiritual autobiography. Some of these are Joseph Morgan's *History of the Kingdom of Basaruah, Containing a Relation of the Most Transactions, Revolutions, and Heroick Exploits in That Kingdom* (1715), an attempt to apply the structures of *The Pilgrim's Progress* and *The Holy War* to the "American colonial world"; an anonymous work entitled *A New Pilgrim's Progress, Shewing the Many Discoveries Which Christian had in the Town of Formality* (1760); William Shrubsole's *Christian Memoirs: or a Review of the Present State of Religion in England. In the Form of a New Pilgrimage to the Heavenly Jerusalem* (1776); and Mary Ann Burges's *Progress of the Pilgrim of Good-Intent, in Jacobinical Times* (1800). These works reflect readings of the *The Pilgrim's Progress* as a prophecy that can diagnose the current state of Christendom. Other imitations and adaptations represent readings of *The Pilgrim's Progress* in terms of spiritual autobiography. Stephen Crisp's *Short History of Long Travel, from Babylon to Bethel* (1691), which describes a Quaker's search for peace, and Francis Bugg's *Pilgrim's Progress From Quakerism to Christianity*,[43] which depicts a Quaker convert returning to the Anglican church, illustrate how Bunyan's paradigm for spiritual autobiography could be appropriated to describe any individual's spiritual journey. Even more typical are imitations that focus on the accounts of single travelers like John Mitchell's *Female Pilgrim: or the Travels of Hepzibah, under the Similitude of a Dream* (1762) and an anonymous work entitled *The Christian Pilgrim: Containing an Account of the Wonderful Adventures and Miraculous Escapes of a Christian* (1811).[44] Reading *The Pilgrim's Progress* as a realistic version of Bunyan's struggle with himself and with the world inspired versions of other travelers in the wilderness. This process continues into the nineteenth century with such works as *The Pilgrim's Progress in the Nineteenth Century* (1824), a Puritan attack on liberalism by

William Raymond Weeks, writing under the pseudonym of "Bun-yanus"; Joseph Ivimey's *Pilgrims of the Nineteenth Century* (1827), which includes a visit to the town of Toleration; and *The Adventures of Search for Life: A Bunyanic Narrative, as Detailed by Himself* (1838), a Universalist tract.[45] Eventually this paradigm for experience becomes completely secularized and begins to surface in the characters and structures of the nineteenth-century novel.[46]

Two other works appropriate the figure of Bunyan in order to capitalize on his fame in selling their books. In doing so they register two distinct aspects of readers' perceptions of Bunyan in the first few decades after his death. Both works appeared in 1725. In *Rest for the Wearied Soul: or, the Pilgrim at his Journey's End. Being the Last Legacy of Mr. John Bunyan of Bedfordshire*,[47] the emphasis is on Bunyan as a godly man and as the "Pilgrim" of *The Pilgrim's Progress*. The work claims to contain the admonitions, verses, and meditations that Bunyan gave to his children on his deathbed. The second work delivers a very different legacy. *The Visions of John Bunyan, Being his Last Remains. Giving an Account of the Glories of Heaven and the Terrors of Hell, and of the World to Come*,[48] is a Dantesque vision of heaven and hell. The protagonist, Epenetus, after conversing with a friend who claims that hell and heaven do not exist, resolves to commit suicide, but he is stopped by an angel who takes him away to see both heaven and hell and meet the inhabitants. The damned soul he converses with in hell turns out to be Thomas Hobbes, who had almost convinced Epenetus "to be of my opinion."[49]

The Visions of John Bunyan focuses on the figure of Bunyan as prophet rather than as godly man. The preface, which bears Bunyan's initials, stresses that the work is to the reader's "Spiritual Advantage" because it will engage the heart and mind. The substitution of "vision" for "dream" suggests how the author arrived at his decision to appropriate the mantle of Bunyan:

> Nor let any one be stumbled that this is delivered under the Similitude of a *Vision*: For so long as the Truths herein convey'd are according to the Analogy of Faith, the Dress, in which they are put may be very well dispensed with. I have done herein like the Physicians, who put their Physick in some pleasant Vehicle, to make it go down the easier with their Patients. And since the way to Heaven

has been so taking under the Similitude of a *Dream*, why should not the Journey's End be as acceptable under the Similitude of a *Vision*?[50]

Dreams are the acceptable mode for a description of the way to take in this world; the mode of vision is for the exploration of other worlds.

These two attempts to capitalize on Bunyan's fame represent popular ideas about the author. Prefaces to later editions of Bunyan's works document more learned and legitimate ways to engineer his reputation. The charge of plagiarism we explored in chapter 1 was really about social class. Bunyan's class, while a virtue from a religious perspective, was a grave fault from a literary one because *The Pilgrim's Progress* seemed far too sophisticated, too literary, to be the work of a mechanick preacher. But even a learned, religious readership was uncertain about the legitimacy of his writing, enough so to address the charge in the preface to the first edition of Bunyan's works in 1692. Addressed to the "Serious, Judicious, the Impartial Reader,"[51] the "Epistle to the Reader" deals explicitly with the issue of learning, but it also responds to the issue of authorship as it attempts to depict Bunyan as a Puritan divine:

> The Author indeed had a Peculiar Phrase to himself in expressing the Conceptions of his Mind; his words were his own, as well as his Matter. The Matter and Contexture of that which is New (never before printed) in this Volume, will easily induce any who know the Author, to believe that it was his own; and we may say as much his own, as any mans Works that ever came into Publick, he not having those Helps, that others have been or are, bless'd withall: Like the Spider, all came from his Bowels; what the Spirit of God gave in to him, by Prayer and Study, that he freely gave out, and communicated to others, cloathed in a familiar Style.[52]

The editors feel sufficiently skittish about enshrining Bunyan as an important figure by printing his *Works*, despite his lack of learning, to make the traditional disclaimer of the Protestant readership about where books come from. But in locating readers as serious, judicious, and impartial, they ask them to withhold judgment on the issue of learning. They point specifically to the "Words" and "Matter," thus alluding to the charge of plagiarism, and invite readers to compare the style of various of Bunyan's writings. They also justify his activity as a writer by noting that he was restrained from preaching and therefore spent his time composing "that which might be useful and beneficial to the Church of God, when in Person he could not do so."[53] Later prefaces to Bunyan's *Works* will see in his lack of education an example of the workings of God.

A preface to Bunyan's works by George Whitefield that first appeared in 1767 and was appropriated numerous times by later editors will suffice as a demonstration that the Protestant reader's understanding of the role of the author persisted well into the eighteenth century.[54] Towards the beginning of his address to the "Christian reader," he summons the passage from 1 Corinthians that played such a major role in the reception of *Piers Plowman*:

The Great Apostle of the Gentiles, [says] "God hath chosen the foolish things of this world to confound the wise: and God has chosen the weak things of the world, to confound the things which are mighty; and base things of the world, and things which are despised hath God chosen, yea, and things that are not to bring to nought things that are." . . . And why? . . . That no flesh should glory in his presence. Perhaps, next to the first publishers of the Gospel of the blessed God, these sayings were never more strongly exemplified in any single individual (at least in this or the last century) than in the conversion, ministry and writings of that eminent servant of Jesus Christ, Mr. John Bunyan, who was of the meanest occupation, a notorious sabbath-breaker, drunkard, swearer, blasphemer, &c. by habitual practice: And yet, through rich, free, sovereign, distinguishing Grace, chosen, called, and afterward formed, by the all-powerful operations of the Holy Ghost, to be a scribe ready instructed to the Kingdom of God. The two volumes of his works previously published, with the great success that attended them in pulling down Satan's strong-holds in sinners hearts, when sent forth in small detach'd parties, are pregnant proofs of this. Some of them have gone through a variety of editions. His Pilgrim's Progress in particular, hath been translated into various languages, and to this day is read with the greatest pleasure, not only by the truly serious, of divers religious persuasions, but likewise by those, to whom pleasure is the end of reading. Surely it is an original.[55]

Bunyan's life and work are merged to produce a powerful example of the mysterious workings of God, and his role as author is defined as that of a mere "scribe" who is directed by the Holy Spirit. In fact, Whitefield's emphasis on Bunyan's transformation by the Holy Spirit emphasizes his life as reader and writer rather than the conversion from sinner to saint. He is "formed" into a scribe "ready instructed" in scriptural truth. Whitefield illustrates that Bunyan's elevation to the status of a Protestant saint comes about through the powerful effect of his book on readers; the book pulls down "Satan's stronghold in sinners."

The last great expression of the connection between Bunyan's life and *The Pilgrim's Progress* from the perspective of a Protestant readership occurs in George Offor's edition of Bunyan's works. Offor's table of contents to volume 3 begins with a statement that defines his view of the relationship between the life and the works: "The author's religious experience and knowledge of the way to salvation, first published in a treatise on the covenants, and enlarged in *Grace Abounding To the Chief of Sinners*; was completed in an Allegory, showing the Christian's journey from time to eternity, under the title of THE PILGRIM'S PROGRESS FROM THIS WORLD TO THAT WHICH IS TO COME.[56] For a Protestant reader such as Offor, an important part of the depiction of Bunyan's life was that it allowed *The Pilgrim's Progress* to be seen outside of a literary tradition and as a part of a miraculous story. The work reflected back on the life and was seen exclusively as part of Bunyan's personal history.

Offor saw *The Pilgrim's Progress* as a thoroughly divine achievement.[57] The chapter headings of Offor's *Life of Bunyan*, in his single-volume edition of *The Pilgrim's Progress*, read like stages in a saint's life:

I. His Birth, Youthful Depravity, and Marriage.
II. The Internal Conflict or New Birth.

III. Manner of Preaching—Committed to Prison.
IV. His Remarkable Deliverance from Prison.
V. Bunyan's Pastoral Duties, Works, Popularity, and Death.[58]

As a nineteenth-century Protestant reader, Offor must contend with a lettered audience in the ascendant:

> It is absurd to suppose that learned men read to him old monkish manuscripts, or the allegories of the previous age; for his design was unknown, he had formed no plan, nor had he any intention to have written such a book, until it came upon him suddenly. His first idea was inspired from his own works while composing it, and then the whole story flowed into his mind as quick as he could write it. Every attempt has been made to tarnish his fair fame; the great and learned, the elegant poet and the pious divine have asserted, but without foundation in fact or probability, that some of his ideas were derived from the works of previous writers.[59]

As we have seen, the origin of texts from the perspective of the Protestant reader came from God.

The prefaces by Whitefield and Offor, separated by a century, offer evidence that the way *The Pilgrim's Progress* was read was changing dramatically. The strategies for reading the book in terms of a Protestant interpretive paradigm become increasingly strident as the suspicion that the book is being read as a novel grows. For example, Whitefield's "Recommendatory Preface" to a volume of Bunyan's works begins by attempting to locate the reader: "Christian reader, if such thou art in reality; or indeed if only a bare outward professor . . ."[60] The inclusion of notes to various editions of *The Pilgrim's Progress*, such as Thomas Scott's "Original Notes" (1801) and William Mason's "Notes Explanatory, Experimental, and Practical" (1813) are typical of a Protestant readership's attempt to steer the reader towards a religious response to Bunyan's narrative. As a Protestant reader, Scott is struck by the applicability of Bunyan's portrayal of a society of "professors":

Indeed, the accurate observer of the church in his own days, and
the learned student of ecclesiastical history, must be equally sur-
prised to find, that hardly one remarkable character, good or bad,
or mixed in any manner or proportion imaginable; or one fatal delusion, by-path, or injurious mistake, can be singled out, which may
not be paralleled in the PILGRIM'S PROGRESS; that is to the
grand outlines. . . . For every part of this singular book *exclusively*
suits the different descriptions of such that profess these doctrines;
and relates the experiences, mistakes, recoveries, distresses, temptations, and consolations of serious persons of this class in our own
times, as exactly as if it had been penned from the observation of
them, and for their immediate benefit; while, like the sacred Scriptures, it remains a sealed book to all who are strangers to evangelical religion.[61]

Here again, *The Pilgrim's Progress* is compared to the Bible in terms
of its ability to locate its readers in terms of religious experience.
Scott is particularly interested in decoding the characters; William
Mason's attention gravitates to the book's effect on the reader.

Mason explains in a preface what he intends the function of the
notes to be: "to cause the reader of this work to attend to more
closely, and to understand more clearly, the spiritual end and design
of the author."[62] The gloss of the opening scene epitomizes his
method of forcing the reader to "plow" his soul with the "plough of
the book." Discussing Christian's cry of "What shall I do," Mason
comments:

As he reads, he weeps and trembles to think what will become of
him. Reader, was this ever your case? Did you ever see your sins,
and feel the burden of them, so as to cry out, in the anguish of your
soul, What must I do to be saved? If not, you will look on this precious book as a romance or history which no way concerns you; you
can no more understand the meaning of it, than if it were wrote in
an unknown tongue: for you are yet carnal, dead in your sins, lying
in the arms of the wicked one in false security. But this book is spir-

itual; it can only be understood by spiritually quickened souls, who have experienced that salvation in the heart which begins with a sight of sin, a sense of sin, a fear of destruction, and a dread of damnation. Such, and only such, commence Pilgrims from the city of destruction to the heavenly kingdom.[63]

Unlike Crowley, who seemed to have utter confidence that the visual scene of *Piers Plowman* would speak directly to the reader, Mason clearly feels he must restate and situate the readers in terms of doctrine before he can grab their attention by directly addressing a series of questions to them. Interestingly, the understanding of Bunyan's narrative becomes a test for the readers, as in the French preface cited above. If they cannot identify themselves with the opening portrait of Christian, their minds are "carnal," not spiritual, and therefore the book will be a romance or a history rather than a salvational treatise.

   Mason sets up literary and historical genres in opposition to religious ones, but other attempts to provide keys for understanding *The Pilgrim's Progress* do not jettison the literary perspective in favor of the religious. For example, the full title of one of the first keys to Bunyan's narrative shows that some readers of the text found no discrepancy between reading the work for entertainment and reading it for spiritual enlightenment: "A Key To the Pilgrim's Progress Designed To assist the Admirers of that Excellent Book to read it with understanding and profit, as well as pleasing entertainment. In a Series of Letters To a Friend."[64] Choosing as his pseudonym Andronicus, the author of the notes specifically singles out history as a necessary adjunct to understanding the meaning of *The Pilgrim's Progress*. The work is both salvational and a cultural document in need of decoding:

   The Allegory often alludes to the Times in which the Author lived, and those which preceded it: also to the Maxims, Manners, Prejudices, and Bigotry of those Times, and the Sufferings of godly consciencious Persons from these Sources. Readers who lived in, or soon after the Author's Day, could much better understand such Parts of his Allegory, than modern Readers can, unless it be those who have read and studied the History of those Times alluded to: to those who have not had these Advantage[s], it may be pleasing and profitable to be able to enter into the Author's Meanings.[65]

Another key in an edition of Bunyan's narrative is oriented more towards the lettered community. The title of the edition suggests that the notes will focus on Bunyan's life and on the contemplation of the beauties of *The Pilgrim's Progress*: "The Pilgrim's Progress to which is prefixed 'The Life of the Author' With a Key to the Allegory and A Critique on Its Beauties."[66] The author states that he will consider Bunyan's narrative from two points of view, as a literary composition and as a theological one. The order is significant, for a lettered readership emphasized the contemplation of the text over the book's designs on the reader.

Responses from a Lettered Readership

Initially, Bunyan's readers were mostly lower class, which had the predictable effect on the more "lettered" society of readers. We have already explored Gilpin's attempt in 1811 to appeal to an upper-class community of readers by making the prose more "literate,"[67] but poetic translations of portions of *The Pilgrim's Progress* appear within the first few decades of its publication. They fail as spectacularly as Thomas Sherman's *Second Part*, and for similar reasons: the starkness and desperation reflected in the figure of the lowly Christian simply cannot be rendered in the poetic structures of the upper classes. Two examples of these early poetic renditions of Christian illustrate the impossibility of turning Bunyan's narrative into an epic poem with an epic hero. The first attempt occurs in 1687. Written by one M. S., and entitled *The Heavenly Passenger, Or The Pilgrim's Progress From This World to that Which Is to Come*, it begins with the dreamer falling asleep beside a tree and dreaming that he sees a man:

I dreamed, and behold! I thought I see

A man with Tears, in sad extremity,

With careful Visage, looking too and fro,

As if he'd run, but knew not where to go,

And in his Hand behold he held a Book,

Then in the same he did carefully look;

Upon his back a burden he did bear,

Which seem'd to drive him almost to dispair.[68]

The repetition of *behold* and such elevated terms as *extremity* seem totally foreign to the substance of Bunyan's image of Christian.

Ager Scholae's two poetic installments also reflect, even in their titles, the issue of class: *The Pilgrim's Passage in Poesie: to the Palace Beautiful, in the Chamber of Peace* (1697) and *The Pilgrim's Passage, in Poesie, from the Palace Beautiful, to the Meeting with Faithful* (1698).[69] The hard work of a "Progress" has been translated into a "Passage"; House Beautiful has become a Palace. Another class marker can be observed at Christian's entrance into the Palace Beautiful. In Bunyan's original version, Christian is invited in. He bows his head and enters: "So when he was come in, and set down, they gave him somthing to drink" (177). Scholae's poetic version is considerably more class-bound: "They call'd the *Butler*, Christian being dry, / And bid the *Cook* get Supper speedily."[70] Scholae's overcivilized image of Christian joining his hosts for cocktails while the servants prepare dinner markedly alters the impact of Bunyan's version of Christian hospitality after an arduous journey.

His version of the opening scene suffers from similar dislocations in terms of content and mode:

Through this World's Wilderness, poor Pilgrim, I

Wandering, at length a Den I did espy;

Where lying down, I dream'd, and thought I see

A Man in Raggs, full of Perplexity,

Some distance from his house: a Book in hand,

A great *Back-burthen*, there I found him stand,

Reading, and weeping, shaking, trembling too:

Still crying out, *Sirs! Sirs! what shall I do?*[71]

Here again the use of such terms as *perplexity* strips away the stark power of the image of Christian. Scholae, to his credit, admits that he had doubts about his attempt to take "the *Pilgrim* to my own Glass": "Art so often failed me, that I was ready to throw up All; as looking far better in his plain Cloathes, than by all the Lacing, Pricking, and Pinning, that I could afford him."[72] The remembrance of a verse by Herbert ("A Verse may find him / That a Sermon flies") allows him to persevere in his endeavor. Wishing he had "but more of the Rare Spirit of that Divine Man," he nonetheless presents the reader with the fruit of his labors: "I present thee then, Christian Reader! tho in mean Ornaments, a person of most Noble Extract, the Christian Pilgrim."[73]

The preface to Scholae's second poetic installment, addressed to the "Unprejudic'd Reader," takes up where the first had ended by expostulating on Bunyan's "translation" into a nobleman in God's kingdom. He begins by reflecting on God's use of both learned and unlearned men as prophets to do his work when his kingdom is "under Siege":

> For now and then, being but a *Blockade*, there Sallies forth a
> Prophet; either as *Elijah* from the Schools, or as *Amos*, from
> amongst the Herdsmen. . . . In all the Gospel Days our Forefathers
> have seen, never was there yet a close Siege, but some or other
> have ventur'd forth (*having the Everlasting Gospel to Preach*) either
> on Horse-back, or on Foot, or both. Either great Scholars, as the
> most *useful Bishop Usher*, or Men of less Learning, yet great Parts,
> as he whose Pen powered forth so liberally, the Pilgrim's Progress.[74]

Continuing his metaphor of Bishop Usher and Bunyan as Christian warriors, Scholae finds "the Infantry to be as useful as the Cavalry in our Christian Warfare; and the Foot have not been so despised by the Horse, as of late."[75] Turning his attention exclusively to Bunyan, Scholae delivers a poetic meditation on what is represented by the phenomenon of Bunyan's status as God's servant in terms of class:

> There is sometimes a Season, wherein the *Field-flower* has the
> honour to be brought into the *Inclosed Garden*, by some Noble or

Royal hand; and by that Grace and Favour to be planted in the
Flower Garden of the Palace.

The Composer of this *Progress*, tho' he was a Flower in the
Field, it pleased the King to bring him to the Palace, which yet
smells sweetly of the *Odours* and *Perfumes* of that Royal hand
which plac'd him there.[76]

A clue to Scholae's fascination with Bunyan's achievement, despite
his tinker's status, is reflected in his comment concerning Bunyan's
style: "That so many Metaphors, Tropes, and figures, should in such
Abundance flow from a Person of such mean Education; Is not this a
call from God to the Learned, to *consider what they are*?"[77] Scholae
demonstrates a genuine appreciation for Bunyan's gifts as a writer, as
well as a sense of profound cultural dislocation at their assault on his
preconceived ideas about the lower classes. Not surprisingly, the
final installment of his version never appeared.

Although these poetic re-visionings are dismal failures, they
represent an attempt to turn *The Pilgrim's Progress* into literature.
That they fail illustrates the untenable nature of their task, for
Bunyan's narrative resisted conforming to their standards for an
artistic production. But as late as 1809, despite countless attempts
and failures, Adam Clarke still bemoans the fact that no one has
elevated *The Pilgrim's Progress* to the status of an epic:

I shall beg leave, in concluding, to express an *opinion*, which has indeed the form of a *wish* in my mind, that the Pilgrim's Progress
would be more generally read, and more abundantly useful to a particular class of readers, were it turned into decent *verse*. The whole
body of the dialogue and description might be preserved perfect
and entire; and the task would not be difficult, as the work has the
complete form of an *epic poem*, the lack of versification alone excepted. But a *poet*, and a poet only can do this work; and such a
poet, too, as is *experimentally* acquainted with the work of God on
his own soul. Even a *laureat*; and a *poetaster*, however pious, would
degrade by his *bouts rimees* the sublime though rugged original.[78]

The failure to turn the fabric of *The Pilgrim's Progress* into a work of literature resulted (as we have seen in the example of Gilpin) in the narrative being relegated to the status of a children's book for an upper-class audience.

But even as a children's book, a verse translation of *The Pilgrim's Progress* still seemed a necessity. George Burder, whose preface contrasting views of the book as novel and as "a correct representation of Christian experience" is quoted above, was a literary reader in his opening passage, though an Evangelical in the notes to his poetic version:

> 'Twas in the silent watches of the night,
>
> When airy visions please us, or affright,
>
> Fast lock'd in sleep's embrace, I dreamt a dream;
>
> The Pilgrim's journey was the fruitful theme.
>
> I thought I saw him in a certain place;
>
> From home he turn'd his pale, affrighted face;
>
> Trembling with fear and cloth'd with rags he stood,
>
> His weeping eyes pour'd forth a briny flood;
>
> His bending back a heavy burden bore,
>
> While guilt and grief his bursting bosom tore.
>
> At times, when able, in his book he read,
>
> He wish'd for refuge, — gladly would have fled.
>
> "O that my soul," he cried, "a refuge knew, —
>
> "But ah, I'm lost! I know not what to do!"

The notes take a very different view of this scene than the verse does: "This is a figurative description of a convinced sinner. Sensible of his guilt, he is afraid of the wrath of God; sees that his own righteousness is as filthy rags; and weeps on recollection of his iniquities. The burden on his back denotes that 'the remembrance of his sins is grievous, and the burden of them intolerable.' In this condition he exclaims, with the Phillippian jailer, — 'What shall I do to be saved?'"[79]

The reading of the work as an artistic production does not really begin again until the nineteenth century discovers Bunyan's natural genius and probes for its sources in other literary works, as we have seen in chapter 6. But there is one final manifestation of interest in the book among the upper classes. *The Pilgrim's Progress*, perhaps because of its perceived simplicity and its religious subject, made it an ideal book for children. Its success has been attested by such lettered readers as Joshua Gilpin, William Cowper, and Robert Southey. And its usefulness, even for the most casual of readers, was endorsed by such evangelicals as Thomas Scott:

> The pious Christian, in proportion to "his growth in grace and in the knowledge of Jesus Christ," derives more and more instruction from repeated perusals of this remarkable book; while his enlarged experience and extended observation enable him to unfold, with progressive evidence, the meaning of the agreeable similitudes employed by its ingenious author: and even the careless reader is fascinated to attention, by the simple and artless manner in which the narrative is arranged. Nor should this be represented as mere amusement; for it has been observed, by men of great discernment and acquaintance with the human mind, that young persons, having perused the PILGRIM as a pleasing tale, often retain a remembrance of its leading incidents, which, after continuing perhaps in a dormant state for several years, has at length germinated, as it were, into the most important and seasonable instruction; while the events of their own lives placed it before their minds in a new and affecting point of view.[80]

The work of *The Pilgrim's Progress* goes on even if read at a young age; like Scripture, as one grows in life and in knowledge, one discovers its application to one's personal experience of the world and of the self in terms of a religious paradigm. As we will see in the next section, this observation remains true, although Bunyan's narrative is increasingly appropriated by more secular readers.

The testimony of such readers as Adam Clarke, Joseph Barker, and Thomas Burt cited at the beginning of this chapter, however, indicates that the religious import of *The Pilgrim's Progress* was not coming through at a tender age. In response to this problem, a number of writers set themselves the task of adapting or appropriating Bunyan's narrative for children. Such works as an *Explanation of the Pilgrim's Progress, Abridged and Adapted to the Capacities of Chidren, In a Dialogue Between a Child, and His Mother, By a Lady* (1808)[81] and Isaac Taylor's *Bunyan Explained to a Child; Being Pictures and Poems, Founded Upon The Pilgrim's Progress* (1825)[82] attempt to make the religious dimensions of Bunyan's book transparent. Like Scott, the anonymous "Lady" believes her book will plant the seed for future exploration of the Bible:

> This little abridgement of the Pilgrim's Progress is intended solely for children, and meant to amuse and as well as inculcate in their young minds, a serious and ardent *desire* of searching the Sacred Scriptures at a future period in their lives; when, as their comprehension increases, they will find to be a sure guide to everlasting truth, and comfort in their old age: and by adhering to the precepts therein contained, they will, in another world, reap Eternal Reward.[83]

For this writer, the "sound and honest Gospel-strains" of *The Pilgrim's Progress*, if properly heightened, represent a means of making Scripture attractive to young minds, an attitude very close to Bunyan's own in producing *The Pilgrim's Progress*. The Protestant attitude toward the usefulness of books survived among the upper classes in their search for suitable reading matter for their children.[84]

The paradigm of human experience Bunyan offered in *The Pilgrim's Progress* proved to be eminently adaptable for children's fiction. Mrs. Sherwood's *Infant's Progress From the Valley of Destruction to Everlasting Glory* (1821) provides a graphic illustration of what the structure of Bunyan's narrative offered for the writer of books for children.[85] Although she creates new protagonists and villains, she borrows many of the features of the landscape of *The Pilgrim's Progress*, such as Interpreter's House, House Beautiful, the Valley of Humiliation, and the Enchanted Ground, and she translates some of Bunyan's "insincere wayfarers" into recognizable types for

children, such as schoolteachers. In her attempt to turn Bunyan's
narrative into an educative experience suited to children, Mrs.
Sherwood demonstrates that the Protestant attitude towards the
nature and function of books persisted in the nineteenth century,
even though its target audience had changed.

Mrs. Sherwood's introduction to *The Infant's Progress* bears
considerable similarities to those of Robert Crowley and John Bunyan in its perspective on the role of the book in awakening readers to
religion. Interestingly enough, she never mentions Bunyan or his
book despite her indebtedness to it, a measure of how much *The
Pilgrim's Progress* became part of the fabric of one's experience in the
nineteenth century. Her opening statement provides a succinct
formulation of the good such a work can provide: "My little Children,
The intention of this book is to make you acquainted, in an agreeable
manner, with many of those awful mysteries of our holy Religion, the
knowledge of which is necessary to your salvation."[86] Like Bunyan,
she acknowledges that the "Dialect" ("Apology," line 146) of an
allegorical fiction can reach a greater audience ("listless men" for
Bunyan, children for Mrs. Sherwood) and, like Bunyan, she is
extremely explicit about her subject and her handling of it:

You do not yet know, what it is that has separated you from
your God: nor do you fully understand what it was that induced the
Lord our Redeemer to descend from heaven for the purpose of assuming our nature, and dying upon the cross. You have, perhaps,
never yet been informed, that the Sin of man's heart is very great,
very prevalent and very hateful; and that, except it be overcome, it
will subject him to everlasting perdition.

Many long sermons have been preached, and many learned volumes have been written, in order both to describe the nature of this
Sin, and to guard us against its influence: but little children cannot
understand these grave and elaborate discourses. I have therefore
written for your instruction on this subject, a story about some little
children, who, like yourselves, were born in a state of sin. And in
this story I have personified the Sin of our nature, and introduced it
as the constant companion of these children.[87]

The child readers are given three figures in which to locate themselves: Humble-Mind, who is ten, and his two younger sisters Playful and Peace. Like Faithful in *The Pilgrim's Progress*, Peace dies in the town of Vanity. The villain who attempts to deter the children on their pilgrimage through life is called In-Bred Sin (i.e., Original Sin). Indeed, he is an ever-present source of trouble for the children, never leaving them, "dwelling in their house, lying in their bosoms, walking out with them when they went abroad, and sitting down with them at all their meals."[88] In many ways he fills the role of the Tempter in *Grace Abounding*, sometimes deterring Humble-Mind from reading Scripture, other times forcing him to read passages which proclaim his sinfulness. Many of the divine agents are the same as those in Bunyan's narrative, such as Evangelist and the shepherds at the Delectable Mountains, but some are specifically created for the child reader, such as Discipline, who beats the children because of their stay at the House of Indulgence. (Predictably, the children kiss Discipline's rod.)[89]

In the preface, Mrs. Sherwood provides her audience with explicit directions about how to read her story:

> The relation is given under the form of a Dream, the various incidents of which are so contrived, as to shew how incessantly sin assaults even those who are truly devoted to God, and what unhappiness it causes them from the beginning to the end of their days.
>
> Through the whole of this dream, the present life is compared to a *Pilgrimage*, which signifies a journey undertaken for some pious purpose. And in every part of it especial care has been taken, distinctly to mark the straight and only way to the Kingdom of Heaven, namely, the Lord Jesus Christ, who himself hath said, *I am the way, the truth, and the life; no man cometh unto the Father but by me.*[90]

Using the same figures Crowley and Bunyan employed to describe the relationship between form and content, Mrs. Sherwood invites her readers to decode and apply the lessons of her story: "Now as nuts and almonds are hidden under rough shells, and as honey is concealed in the bells and cups of flowers; so there is a hidden meaning in every part of my allegory, which I hope you will be enabled to draw forth for your profit. In the mean time, my dear children, I pray God to seal instruction upon your hearts, and fill you with that heavenly wisdom, whose price is far above rubies."[91] Like Bunyan, she claims that her "dark and cloudy words" enclose a heavenly wisdom more precious than rubies: "The Truth, as Cabinets inclose the Gold" ("Apology," lines 127–28).

Like *The Pilgrim's Progress*, Mrs. Sherwood's story provides a "reading" of the world in terms of religious experience, as well as various markers to indicate her religious affiliation. From the vantage point of an adult educating a child, she explores the secular dangers that lie in wait for the unsuspecting Christian. She begins by appropriating Bunyan's role as the Dreamer. As her narrative opens, she tells us that she dreamed one night in bed that she saw herself sitting in a cloud, looking down at the Plain of Destruction, "containing all the towns, and villages, and dwelling-places of the children of men, with the kings' houses and the temples of their gods."[92] She sees storms of thunder and lightning afflict some of the travellers and reports Evangelist's appearance at the door of many houses, warning people to flee from wrath. At one house he tells a couple that they must flee without their three children, for it is the will of God. The parents go off and cross the River of Death, leaving their children behind, dwelling with their companion, In-Bred Sin. Evangelist shows the children where the wicket-gate is, inviting them to start their pilgrimage to heaven. The story depicts their struggles with In-Bred Sin as they journey towards the Celestial City.

Many of the landmarks are derived from *The Pilgrim's Progress*, but the adventures the children have differ from those of Christian. For example, they are so absorbed by their reading that they pass by the "stile and path leading to the ruined castle of giant *Despair*,"[93] who was defeated by Christian. Mrs. Sherwood also creates specific landscapes suited to the experience of children, such as the pasture where the shepherd Sincerity watches over them and the House of Indulgence, presided over by In-Bred Sin. At the close of the story, Humble-Mind and another character, Martha, enter the River of Death where they are separated from In-Bred Sin by Christ and enter heaven. The narrator awakes and resolves to write down her vision.

As in *The Pilgrim's Progress*, Mrs. Sherwood's narrative is studded with scriptural citations, but she also indicates her denomination by citing the Articles of the Faith from the Book of Common Prayer. Another measure of her faith is the fact that she names as the only good characters in the town of Vanity Mr. Orthodox and his wife, Mrs. Bountiful, who live in the suburbs of the town. Mr. Orthodox lectures Humble-Mind on the centrality of Scripture:

> Then I saw that Mr. *Orthodox* took one of the books in his hand, and said, "This Holy Volume, my dear children, containeth all things the knowledge of which is necessary to salvation: so that whatsoever is not read therein, nor may be proved thereby, ought not to be required of any man to be believed as an article of the faith, or be thought requisite or necessary to salvation. And here you must carefully note that by that term, Holy Scriptures, we understand those Canonical Books of the Old and New Testament, of whose authority there was never any doubt in the Church." *(See 6th Article of the Church.)*[94]

Mrs. Sherwood's translations of Bunyan's characters and events are often specifically oriented toward the issue of learning and the right use of books. Mr. Worldly-Wiseman, who turns Christian out of the Way, is made into the schoolteacher, Mr. Worldly Prudence, who tells Humble-Mind to put aside the book that Evangelist had given him and to read "certain heathen writers of ancient date."[95] Evangelist rebukes Humble-Mind for abandoning Scripture and locates the errors in Mr. Worldly-Prudence's pedagogy:

> I heard then that Evangelist spake of Mr. *Worldly-Prudence* and his followers. "These are the men," said he, "who think themselves wiser than their Maker, and who turn aside many young persons from the right way, in order to fill them up with such knowledge as only puffeth up, and tendeth to destruction. They take the sling and the stone from the hand of the youthful pilgrim, and put on him the armour of Saul; they rob him of his Bible, and fill his mouth with the words of man's wisdom: so that more young pilgrims are destroyed by this *Worldly-Prudence*, than by thousands of the open enemies of our Lord."[96]

A Mr. Lover-of-Novelty had sent Humble-Mind to Mr. Worldly-Prudence's school, and he later reappears to direct him to the new House of Interpreter, where scripture is viewed as not "hidden." Humble-Mind, however, consulting his book, chooses the correct Interpreter's House, the old one, and there encounters another school-master with considerably more authority named Law, who teaches the children the Ten Commandments. In House Beautiful, the children are taught what was wrong about Mr. Worldly-Prudence's method :"He did not make the Book of God the basis and groundwork of his plan, using heathen authors only as auxiliary lights, and their works as books of reference."[97] His mistake was to not understand the correct relationship between divine and human knowledge.

The instruction at House Beautiful also includes a "reading" of the secular values of the society. Prudence lets the children look at a magic glass, given to her by one Spiritual Man, where they see an old man on a plain where rubbish is scattered all about. Heaven is above the plain, and Satan stands at his right hand. The old man begins to gather the rubbish together frantically, until Law, the schoolmaster, beats him and he sits on the heap. Suddenly Satan, who we are told is the old man's father, makes "a great bustle" and ushers in his servants: Art, who covers over the old man's wounds and sores; Fashion, who puts "gaudy garments" over his rags; and Light-Mind and her train of teachers of "elegant accomplishments." The children are instructed to notice that none of these embellishments remove the wounds and rags the old man has. The old man is then given books by many "learned professors." Having read the books, he rises up "inflated with vanity" and is led to the top of the heap where he is crowned and where people bow before him. One of the flatterers strikes him and he falls into a pit and disappears while Satan laughs.[98] This emblem rather graphically critiques both the values of polite society and the monarchy.

The Infant's Progress demonstrates that a Protestant attitude towards the nature and right use of books persisted among more lettered readers in the nineteenth century, although those assumptions about books surfaced only in terms of educating children. However, later attempts to adapt Bunyan's narrative for children increasingly stripped away the theological underpinnings and turned it into pure story.[99] Mrs. Sherwood's narrative also illustrates just how adaptable Bunyan's paradigm of human experience proved to be, as well as the extent to which the structures embedded in *The Pilgrim's Progress* had established themselves in the minds of its readers. We must now turn to more secular readers to see how they adapted the experience of *The Pilgrim's Progress* to their own lives.

"Would'st read thy self?": Some Secular Readers

Bunyan's invitation to his readers at the close of the "Apology," "Would'st read thy self, and read thou know'st not what?" (line 233) undergoes a radical revision as an exclusively Protestant readership disappears in the nineteenth and twentieth centuries. Readers are no longer necessarily looking to books for a transcendent spiritual meaning but rather for an understanding of the lives they really lead. Once again, Fussell's World War I soldiers' use of *The Pilgrim's Progress* to understand their real-life experiences provides an instructive example:

> Christian's burden drops away when he beholds the Cross; Private Anthony French's when his equipment is blown off by the shell that wounds him in the thigh: "I had ceased to be a soldier. . . . Only my helmet remained. . . . I found myself without a waterbottle, iron rations, gasmask. My watch had lost cover and glass. . . . Then an enormous burden of responsibility seemed to roll away as if this were the end of a pilgrim's progress. There was no pain. I felt at rest."[100]

The experience is salvational, but secular; and it is *The Pilgrim's Progress* that allows Private French to see being wounded as a redemption, although from psychological rather than spiritual pain. Whereas the book had acted upon Protestant readers, secular readers act upon the book, appropriating its structures to organize their own experience, whatever that experience may be. There are as many truths as there are readers. Hence it is, in Lily Dale's terms, "hazy," "misty," and above all "beautiful," because it is what the reader makes it. This secularization and fragmentation of universal experience begins, surprisingly, with some of Bunyan's earliest readers. His response to them is reflected in changes he made in his book after its first printing and in his "re-visioning" of the narrative in Part II. It ends with the novel. Bunyan's changes and the subsequent afterlife of *The Pilgrim's Progress* demonstrate that the relationship between books and readers is an interactive one.

Bunyan made most of the major changes in the second printing.[101] The most significant are the addition of the passage where Christian returns home and attempts to explain to his wife and children what he feels; the Worldly-Wiseman episode, where one of the temptations for turning out of the way is that Christian can live in the Town of Morality with his family; and Charity's discourse with Christian about them (154). All three additions involve a significant "revisioning" of his text. And all three are quite probably the result of readers responding negatively to the fact that Christian leaves his wife and family behind, crying "Life, Life, Eternal Life" (148).[102]

The Pilgrim's Progress was an attempt to reformulate scriptural truth from the perspective of the individual Christian in order to "chaulk" out the way Christians must go to gain salvation. But some of Bunyan's readers took Christian to be not a type but a literal character who had a wife and children. Although the biblical injunction had insisted that the world must be left behind to attain salvation, readers read the text on some level as if it were a realistic story of a man. As Christopher Hill has pointed out, allegorically the scene where Christian abandons his family is instructive, "but taken literally it is horrifying": the scene is "unpleasantly true to the life of the poor in the seventeenth century. Many men fled from a poverty in which wife and children had become burdens."[103] The placement of the addition in the second edition is significant. It follows directly after the opening vision of Christian reading his book and crying out "what shall I do?" (146). Christian returns to his family and tells them what is wrong, but they fail to understand the problem and deride him. After a while, he goes out into the field and reads his book again. This time, however, he says "What shall I do to be saved?" (147). The revision of the question is an attempt to justify why Christian must leave his family behind.

The same point is made by the Worldly-Wiseman episode, where Mr. Worldly-Wiseman attempts to dissuade him from pursuing the most "dangerous and troublesome way in the world" (153). Mr. Worldly-Wiseman is not inherently a villain, such as Apollyon, although he does turn Christian out of the "way" temporarily. He is associated with the village of Carnal Policy, near another village named Morality, where Legality and Civility live. When they meet,

Mr. Worldly-Wiseman asks two questions before he offers advice. The first concerns why Christian is walking in such a "burdened manner," and the second is "hast thou a wife and children?" (153). Mr. Worldly-Wiseman promises him "safety, friendship, and content" and tells him that he can send for his wife and children and live in the Town of Morality (154). Christian sets out for Mr. Legality's house, but he becomes afraid that the hill next to it will fall on his head. Evangelist must rescue Christian and define his error by explicating in a passage added to the third edition what Mr. Worldly-Wiseman represents in terms of the Christian profession: "He favoureth only this Doctrine of the World therefore he always goes to the Town of *Morality* to Church and partly because he loveth that Doctrine best, for it saveth him from the Cross, and because he is of this carnal temper, therefore he seeketh to prevent my ways, though right" (156–57). The message is clear: one cannot live in the world and save one's soul.

Bunyan returns to the issue of Christian's abandonment of his wife and children in a conversation between Charity and Christian added to the second edition. (Charity does not speak at all in the first edition.) It occurs just after Christian rehearses his experience of the Cross and the loss of his burden. Charity asks him if he has a wife and children and then why they did not come along. Christian recounts the opening scene with his family in such a way that he becomes the abandoned one: "Why, my Wife was afraid of losing this World; and my Children were given to the foolish delights of youth; so what by one thing, and what by another, they left me to wander in this manner alone" (180). Charity responds by bringing up the example of Abel and Cain, and declares that *"if thy Wife and Children have been offended with thee for this, they thereby shew themselves to be implacable to good; and thou has delivered thy soul from their blood"* (181). Lest we fail to understand what has been decided here, the marginal note makes it clear that Christian is absolved of responsibility for their souls: "Christian *clear of their blood if they perish.*" Bunyan must have encountered enough significant comment about Christian's desertion to cause him to heighten and emphasize the doctrinal point being made in the scene.

In *The Pilgrim's Progress*, Part II, Bunyan capitulates to the will of his readers and returns to the question of Christian's wife and children. This concern with character rather than doctrine signals the shift from allegory to novel, from religion to literature. This shift can be seen even more clearly in Part II itself. For example, its "Apology" is in marked contrast to the one we encountered in Part I. This time, instead of arguing for the method of such a work, Bunyan sends his text into the world in literary fashion with an envoy to the book and anticipates its reception. Organized in terms of a dialogue with the book itself, with "Objects" and "Answers," this "Apology" is playful and confident. In the first section, the book professes itself afraid that the audience will think it counterfeit, a detail that testifies to Bunyan's awareness of the existence of the spurious version of Part II by Thomas Sherman. Bunyan answers that, although some have his "Title set" and his name as well "stitched to their Book," everyone will recognize that by their "Features" these works declare themselves as frauds. In the second objection, the book "worries" that if he mentions the first part of *The Pilgrim's Progress* some will "rage" at him. In his answer, Bunyan assures his book that it is welcomed everywhere, pointing specifically to France, Holland, Scotland, Ireland, and New England, singling out specific readers, "Brave Galants," "Young Ladys, and young Gentle-women too," as well as children, who loved the first part. Bunyan assures his book that it

> com'st after with a Second store,
>
> Of things as good, as rich, as profitable,
>
> For Young, for Old, for Stag'ring and for stable.
>
> (lines 116–18)

The third objection focuses on the negative perceptions about authors who use this method in ways reminiscent of Part I:

> But some there be that say he laughs too loud;
>
> And some do say his Head is in a Cloud.
>
> Some say, his Words and Storys are so dark,
>
> They know not how, by them, to find his mark.
>
> (lines 119–22)

Bunyan answers these objections by appealing to the arguments of

Part I. He notes

> Whereas some say a Cloud is in his Head,
>
> That doth but shew how Wisdom's covered
>
> With its own mantles.

(lines 129–31)

This formula harks back to the views on Scripture metaphors and on prophecy discussed in chapters 2 and 6. As for the charge of "darkness," Bunyan declares:

> And to stir the mind
>
> To a search after what it fain would find,
>
> Things that seem to be hid in words obscure,
>
> Do but the Godly mind alure;
>
> To study what those Sayings should contain,
>
> That speak to us in such a Cloudly strain.

(lines 131–36)

This is another version of "stooping" to find out what God speaks to the reader in Scripture, only this time his own book is the object that the reader must "plow." In the fourth and final objection, Bunyan returns again to the issue of his method but, whereas in Part I he strenuously defends it, in Part II he dismisses it almost instantly in favor of listing a catalogue of characters that readers will meet. The "Object" describes how some have reacted to the method of *The Pilgrim's Progress*: "But some love not the method of your first, / Romance they count it, throw't away as dust . . ." (lines 149–50). Bunyan declares the matter to be one of taste; he no longer is afraid of the label of "romance." He then sends the book forth and advertises what the reader will find in the pages of Part II. He catalogues a number of pilgrims, some of whom will achieve salvation despite certain weaknesses: Christiana, Mercy, Honest, Master Fearing, Master Feeblemind, Master Ready-to-halt, Master Valiant-for-Truth, and even Master Despondancie and Much-a-fraid, his daughter. This catalogue of characters and the "Apology" to Part II are witness to a change in Bunyan's perception of his book. No longer is he trying to give abstract directions to readers willing to decode the significance of various characters. Instead he is creating characters with whom readers can identify themselves, for the sake of encouragement, not instruction.

We are also in another world when we turn to the opening of Part II. Part I simply introduces the Dreamer in one poignant, compressed, and alliterative sentence: "As I walk'd through the wilderness of this world, I lighted on a certain place, where was a Denn; And I laid me down in that place to sleep: and as I slept I dreamed a dream" (146). The dream proper receives center stage in the narrative. Part II opens with an address to readers as "Courteous Companions," an excursus on what the author has been doing, and an encounter with a Mr. Sagacity who fills him in on what has transpired since he dreamed last. After he has been given the details of Christiana's decision, which goes on for several pages, he simply announces, "And now Mr. *Sagacity* left me to Dream out my Dream by my self" (293). In Part I, Bunyan went to great lengths to justify his feigned dream as a means of reformulating scriptural truth from the Christian's perspective. By the time he writes Part II, that skittishness has disappeared, and in its place we have an acknowledgment of the first dream as an actual event in itself and more attention paid to the figure of the dreamer. These changes represent another way in which the book's first readers reshaped the fabric of *The Pilgrim's Progress* for, in their reading, the relationship between the Dreamer and Christian was a central part of the story, and both were identified emphatically as versions of the author. It is thus his family, both in terms of a Christian community and in terms of his children in a novelistic sense, that receive attention in Part II.[104] A measure of how successful this strategy of presenting characters rather than doctrine is the production of *The Third Part*. Despite Ponder's denunciation of this edition, it was published with Parts I and II until well into the nineteenth century.[105] It obviously seemed of a piece with Parts I and II because it satisfied some readers' need for realistic models of experience. However, in the shift to a focus on characters as models of experience rather than as object lessons in reforming the self and in the heightening of the romance elements, these "revisionings" by Bunyan and in the spurious *Third Part* already reflect the tensions that will ultimately result in the secularization of this religious paradigm for experience. Forrest and Greaves note that one nineteenth-century *History of Fiction* still "faults Bunyan for having Christian leave his wife and children behind" and depicts him "as selfish, narrow, and illiberal," and "Bunyan's poetry as execrable and his taste coarse."[106] A subtler response is Mark Twain's ironic account of Huckleberry Finn's failure to recognize his own pilgrimage in Bunyan's book, which Huck sees only as a story "about a man that left his family it didn't say why."[107] Thus, I wish to add to the mountain of scholarship on the relationship of *The Pilgrim's Progress* to the origins of the novel the possibility that readers as well as writers contributed to it.

We have journeyed a long distance in this study, (one might well say from the "Wicket Gate" of the "Apology" to the "Delectable Mountains" of a new form, the novel). Perhaps we can find a "Perspective Glass" wherein we can see "something like the Gate, and also some of the Glory of the place" (238), of *The Pilgrim's Progress*'s final destination in the consciousness of three centuries of readers. Such a Glass can be found in Macaulay's review of Southey's edition:

> That wonderful book, while it obtains admiration from the most fastidious critics, is loved by those who are too simple to admire it. Doctor Johnson, all whose studies were desultory, and who hated, as he said, to read books through, made an exception in favour of the Pilgrim's Progress. That work was one of the two or three works which he wished longer. It was by no common merit that the illiterate sectary extracted praise like this from the most pedantic of critics and the most bigoted of Tories. In the wildest parts of Scotland the Pilgrim's Progress is the delight of the peasantry. In every nursery the Pilgrim's Progress is a greater favourite than Jack the Giant-killer. Every reader knows the straight and narrow path as well as he knows a road in which he has gone backward and forward a hundred times. This is the highest miracle of genius, that things which are not should be as though they were, that the imaginations of one mind should become the personal recollections of another. And this miracle the tinker has wrought.[108]

Indeed.

Notes

Bibliography

Index

Notes

1. Introduction: Tracing the History of Reading Through the History of Books

1. See Barbara K. Lewalski, *Protestant Poetics and the Seventeenth-Century Religious Lyric* (Princeton: Princeton University Press, 1979); John N. King, *English Reformation Literature: The Tudor Origins of the Protestant Tradition* (Princeton: Princeton University Press, 1982); David Norbrook, *Poetry and Politics in the English Renaissance* (London: Routledge & Kegan Paul, 1984). See also Andrew Weiner, *Sir Philip Sidney and the Poetics of Protestantism* (Minneapolis: University of Minnesota Press, 1978); Alan Sinfield, *Literature in Protestant England, 1550–1660* (Totowa, N.J.: Barnes & Noble, 1983); and Ritchie D. Kendall, *The Drama of Dissent: The Radical Poetics of Nonconformity, 1380–1590* (Chapel Hill: University of North Carolina Press, 1986).

2. I use the word *lettered* rather than literary to define a set of readers who are often highly educated and well read and who typically approach texts as imaginative productions and as art.

3. That *The Pilgrim's Progress* plays a role in the history of the novel is something of a commonplace, but two recent studies explore the topic in more depth. Leopold Damrosch, Jr., focuses on Puritan individualism and its relationship to the origins of the novel in *God's Plot and Man's Stories: Studies in the Fictional Imagination from Milton to Fielding* (Chicago: University of Chicago Press, 1985). See especially chapter 4, "Experience and Allegory in Bunyan," 121–86. Michael McKeon locates the origins of the novel in romance in *The Origins of the English Novel 1600–1740* (Baltimore: Johns Hopkins University Press, 1987). See chapter 8, "Romance Transformations (II): Bunyan and the Literalization of Allegory," 295–314.

4. Raymond Williams, *Keywords: A Vocabulary of Culture and Society* (New York: Oxford University Press, 1976), 150–54.

5. Thomas Warton, *History of English Poetry*, 1774; reprint, New York: Johnson Reprint Corporation, 1968, 3:187.

6. Warton, 1:266.

7. Warton specifically faults Langland's choice of verse form, which he labels as "perpetual alliteration": "But this imposed constraint of seeking identical initials, and the affectation of obsolete English, by demanding a constant and necessary departure from the natural and obvious forms of expression, while it circumscribed the power of our author's genius, contributed also to render his manner extremely perplexed and to disgust the reader with obscurities" (1:266–67).

8. For a fuller discussion of the term itself and Bunyan's relationship to the other "mechanicks" who preached, see William York Tindall's *John Bunyan, Mechanick Preacher* (New York: Columbia University Press, 1934).

9. Joshua Gilpin, "To the Reader," in *The Pilgrim's Progress* (London, 1810), xiii. Hereafter all references to this preface will be indicated by page numbers in the body of the text.

10. E. P. Thompson, *The Making of the English Working Class* (1963; reprint, New York: Vintage Books, 1966), 31. The other text is Thomas Paine's *Rights of Man*. Ellen Cantarow ("A Wilderness of Opinions Confounded: Allegory and Ideology," *College English* 34 [1972]: 215–52) links Bunyan's lower-class social status to his readers' active identification with the text; see especially 237–52. Other useful investigations of Bunyan's class identity are Joan Bellamy, "John Bunyan and the Democratic Tradition," *Zeitschrift für Anglistik und Amerikanistik* 27 (1979): 218–24, and Thomas Metscher, "Subversive, Radical and Revolutionary Traditions in European Literature Between 1300 and the Age of Bunyan: Some Comments," *Zeitschrift für Anglistik und Amerikanistik* 29 (1981): 12–20.

11. John Bunyan, "The Author's Apology for his Book," in *Grace Abounding to the Chief of Sinners and The Pilgrim's Progress From This World to that Which is to Come*, ed. Roger Sharrock (London: Oxford University Press, 1966), 139–45. All quotations from the "Apology" will hereafter be cited by line number in the body of the text. All quotations from *Grace Abounding* or *The Pilgrim's Progress* will come from this edition unless otherwise noted.

12. For useful surveys of reader-response criticism see Susan R. Suleiman and Inge Crosman, eds., *The Reader in the Text* (Princeton: Princeton University Press, 1980), and Jane Tompkins, ed., *Reader-Response Criticism* (Baltimore: Johns Hopkins University Press, 1980). For an analysis and a history of the field, see Elizabeth Freund, *The Return of the Reader: Reader-Response Criticism* (London: Methuen, 1987).

13. Jonathan Culler, *Structuralist Poetics: Structuralism, Linquistics, and the Study of Literature* (Ithaca: Cornell University Press, 1975), 118.

14. Stanley Fish, *Is There a Text in This Class?: The Authority of Interpretive Communities* (Baltimore: Johns Hopkins University Press, 1978), 169.

15. Jane Tompkins, "The Reader in History: The Changing Shape of Literary Response," in *Reader-Response Criticism*, 205–6.

16. Tompkins, 225. Tompkins defines texts as "instruments" in earlier periods in terms of a public sphere of experience. I argue in this study that texts are "instruments" for Protestant readers on a private, personal, and spiritual level of experience.

17. Warton, 1:209.

18. For a detailed discussion of their role in promoting an English Protestant tradition see King, *English Reformation Literature*, especially 56–75, 319–57, and 434–43.

19. Warton, 1:ii.

20. Warton, 1:iii.

21. Wolfgang Iser, *The Act of Reading: A Theory of Aesthetic Response* (Baltimore: Johns Hopkins University Press, 1978), 169.

22. Hans Robert Jauss, *Toward an Aesthetics of Reception*, trans. Timothy Bahti (Minneapolis: University of Minnesota Press, 1982), 5.

23. Jauss, 21.

24. Jauss, 19.

25. See Hans-Georg Gadamer, "The Universality of the Hermeneutical Problem" and "On the Scope and Function of Hermeneutical Reflection," in *Philosophical Hermeneutics*, ed. and trans. David E. Linge (Berkeley: University of California Press, 1976), 3–17 and 18–43.

26. Jauss, 22–24.

27. N. H. Keeble, *The Literary Culture of Nonconformity in Later Seventeenth-Century England* (Athens: The University of Georgia Press, 1987). My quarrel is not with his discussion of this culture, which is extremely useful, but with his categorization of nonconformist texts as "literary" in an aesthetic sense. Keeble gives a synchronic description of this culture whereas I am tracing its ancestry and historical development.

28. Paul Fussell, *The Great War and Modern Memory* (1975; reprint, New York: Oxford University Press, 1979), 142; see also 137–44, 152, 160, 168, 169.

29. Fussell, ix.

30. See Kenneth E. Carpenter, ed., *Books and Society in History* (New York: R. R. Bowker, 1983), especially Robert Darnton's "What is the History of Books?" (3–26), for a useful introduction to the field. See also Lucien Fèbvre and Henri-Jean Martin, *The Coming of the Book*, trans. David Gerard (London: NLB, 1976), and G. Thomas Tanselle, *The History of Books as a Field of Study* (Chapel Hill: University of North Carolina, Rare Book Collection, 1980).

31. Natalie Zemon Davis, *Society and Culture in Early Modern France* (Stanford: Stanford University Press, 1975; reprint, 1985), 190, 192.

32. Carlo Ginsberg, *The Cheese and the Worms: The Cosmos of a Sixteenth-Century Miller,* trans. John and Anne Tedeschi (1980; reprint, New York: Penguin Books, 1982).

33. As we will see in chapter 3, John Foxe believed that God invented printing to bring about the reformation of His church. In a section entitled "The Benefit and Invention of Printing," Foxe cites the year 1450 as "memorable" and "famous" because of the "divine and miraculous inventing of printing" (John Foxe, *Acts and Monuments* [London, 1684], 1:803).

34. Robert Darnton, *The Literary Underground of the Ancien Regime* (Cambridge: Harvard University Press, 1982), viii.

35. Robert Darnton, *The Business of Enlightenment: A Publishing History of the Encyclopedie, 1775–1800* (Cambridge: Harvard University Press, 1979), 2.

36. Robert Darnton, *The Great Cat Massacre and Other Episodes in French Cultural History* (New York: Vintage Books, 1984), 5.

37. Robert Darnton, "Towards a History of Reading," *Princeton Alumni Weekly,* 8 Aug. 1987, 19–32.

38. Darnton, "Towards a History of Reading," 24. A recent book by Cathy N. Davidson, *Revolution and the Word: The Rise of the Novel in America* (New York: Oxford University Press, 1986), also combines the methodologies of reader-response and reception theory and *l'histoire du livre* to trace the origins of the novel in America. See especially chapter 1, "Introduction: Towards a History of Texts," 3–14. Focusing on the responses of actual readers, her objective and her conclusions with respect to how readers respond to texts are similar to my own here. She proposes "a way of reading texts in response to a specific set of circumstances that not only created both texts and ways of reading them, but also that those texts, in turn, created" (4). Both *Piers Plowman* and *The Pilgrim's Progress* participate in this process.

39. Darnton, "Towards a History of Reading," 21.

40. Darnton, "Towards a History of Reading," 23.

41. "He that wrote the Satyr of Piers Ploughman, seemed to have bene a malcontent of that time, and therefore bent himselfe wholy to taxe the disorders of that age, and specially the pride of the Romane Clergy, of whose fall he seemeth to be a very true Prophet, his verse is but loose meetre, and his termes hard and obscure, so as in them is little pleasure to be taken" (George Puttenham, *The Arte of English Poesie, A Facsimile Reproduction,* ed. Edward Arber [1906; reprinted with an introduction by Baxter Hathaway, Kent, Ohio: Kent State University Press, 1970], 76).

42. Harvey J. Graff, *The Legacies of Literacy: Continuities and Contradictions in Western Culture and Society* (Bloomington: Indiana University Press, 1987), 77.

43. Margaret Aston, *Lollards and Reformers: Images and Literacy in Late Medieval Religion* (London: Hambledon Press, 1984); Anne Hudson, *Lollards and Their Books* (London: Hambledon Press, 1985), and her *Premature Revolution: Wycliffite Texts and Lollard History* (Oxford: Clarendon Press, 1988).

44. Graff, 156.

45. Keeble notes that "literacy rates were higher amongst noncomformists than in other sections of society. Not only did they write copiously, confident of noncomformist readers, but they were heirs to the educational drive of Puritanism and . . . continued to be enthusiastic advocates of the benefits of literacy, encouraging all classes of society, and especially children, to learn to read and to write and to be diligent practitioners of these skills" (*Literary Culture*, 136–37).

46. For this conjecture, see E. Talbot Donaldson, *Piers Plowman: The C-Text and Its Poet* (New Haven: Yale University Press, 1949), 108–9.

47. Damrosch makes a similar point when he notes that "whatever the novel may later have become, its origins—as our reflections on Puritan inwardness suggest—lie in the private experience of the individual who was faced not so much with the society as with the ultimate order of the universe, of which society may or may not be a faithful mirror" (*God's Plot and Man's Stories*, 13). Keeble notes that nonconformist writing created "personal and intimate literature in which people count for more than politics, a literature fascinated by people's lives (the conversations in *The Pilgrim's Progress* nearly always turn on the pilgrims', or someone else's, experience) and convinced of the value of the individual self" (*Literary Culture*, 212).

48. John Bunyan, "An Advertisement to the Reader," in *The Holy War*, ed. Roger Sharrock and James F. Forrest (Oxford: Clarendon Press, 1980), 251. Line numbers for the "Advertisement" will be indicated in the body of the text.

49. James Boswell, *The Life of Samuel Johnson*, ed. C. B. Tinker (1904; reprint revised by R. W. Chapman, London: Oxford University Press, 1960), 529.

50. George Offor, ed., *The Complete Works of John Bunyan* (1853; reprint, New York: AMS, 1978), 3:30.

51. Offor, section 5 of Introduction, 3:29–55.

52. Offor, 3:30.

53. Henry Stebbing, ed., *The Complete Works of John Bunyan* (London, 1859), 2:2.

54. Stebbing, Notes, 2:134–35.

55. Hunting for sources for *The Pilgrim's Progress* is a favored sport for critics of Bunyan. See James Blanton Wharey, *A Study of the Sources of Bunyan's Allegories, with Special Reference to Dequilleville's Pilgrimage of*

Man (1904; reprint, New York: Gordian Press, 1968) for a comprehensive survey of the earlier suggested sources put forward for *The Pilgrim's Progress*. Recent criticism of Bunyan has become far more sophisticated in its handling of this vexed issue. U. Milo Kaufmann's groundbreaking study, *The Pilgrim's Progress and Traditions of Puritan Meditation* (New Haven: Yale University Press, 1966), was the first to usher in a "renaissance" in Bunyan studies. N. H. Keeble's *Literary Culture of Nonconformity* and Christopher Hill's *Tinker and a Poor Man: John Bunyan and His Church, 1628–1688* (1988; reprint, New York: Alfred A. Knopf, 1989) place the writer definitively in his culture, and three anthologies, Vincent A. Newey, ed., *The Pilgrim's Progress: Critical and Historical Views* (Totowa, N.J.: Barnes & Noble, 1980); N. H. Keeble, ed., *John Bunyan: Conventicle and Parnassus* (Oxford: Clarendon Press, 1988); and Robert G. Collmer, ed., *Bunyan in Our Time* (Kent, Ohio: Kent State University Press, 1989), provide a enlightening range of contexts for assessing Bunyan's achievements as a writer.

56. William Haller provides a useful summary of the publishing history of this remarkable book: "Foxe published two preliminary versions of his book on the Continent in 1554 and 1559, the first English version in 1563, a much revised and larger version in 1570, and two editions in 1576 and 1583 with some further revisions and additions, but no significant changes. In the century after his death five more editions, based on the text of 1583, appeared in 1596, 1610, 1631–2, 1641 and 1684" (William Haller, *The Elect Nation: The Meaning and Relevance of Foxe's Book of Martyrs* [New York: Harper & Row, 1963], 9). I have used for the most part the 1632 edition in this study as representative of seventeenth-century Foxe.

57. John Foxe, *Acts and Monuments* (London, 1632), 1:510. Here and elsewhere in this book I have silently expanded abbreviations and have normalized the usage of i/j and u/v.

2. Bunyan as First Reader of *The Pilgrim's Progress:* Puritan and Protestant Paradigms for Reading

1. See John Bunyan, *The Pilgrim's Progress as Originally Published by John Bunyan, Being a Facsimile Reproduction of the First Edition* (1875; reprint, Old Woking, Surrey: The Gresham Press, 1978). For the title pages of subsequent editions see *The Pilgrim's Progress*, ed. James B. Wharey and rev. Roger Sharrock (Oxford: Clarendon Press, 1960).

2. Thomas Tuke, *The Highway to Heaven: Or the Doctrine of Election, Effective Vocation, Justification, Sanctification, and Eternal Life* (London, 1609).

3. Christopher Lever, *The Holy Pilgrime, Leading the Way to Heaven: Or a Divine Direction in the Way of Life* (London, 1618).

4. J. M., *The Soul's Pilgrimage to Celestial Glory: Or a Perfect Way to Heaven and to God* (London, 1634).

5. John Reading, *A Guide to the Holy City: Or Directions and Helps to a Holy Life* (London, 1651).

6. Many more titles could be cited here. A whole series of tracts dwell on the related metaphor of "walking" such as E. Bury's *Help to Holy Walking, or a Guide to Glory* (London, 1627) and Christopher Nesse's *Christian's Walk and Work on Earth Until He Attain Heaven* (London, 1678). Countless sermons take up the metaphor of an arduous journey to heaven such as Z. Crofton's *Hard Way to Heaven Explained and Applied* (London, 1664). And still other tracts refer to landscape features to garner the reader's attention. Abraham Fleming's two works use the metaphor of a footpath: *The Footpath of Faith and the Highway to Heaven* (London, 1581) and *The Footpath to Felicitie, Which everie Christian must walk in* (London, 1581). One T. I. describes a "pathway": *The Pathway to the Pleasant Pasture of delightsome and Eternal Paradyse* (London, 1577).

7. George Keith, *The Way to the City of God Described* (London, 1669).

8. Keith, "To the reader," in *The Way to the City of God Described*, 2d ed. (London, 1678), 2.

9. Leopold Damrosch states that it "would be wrong to suppose that Puritans distrusted fictions per se" (*God's Plot and Man's Stories*, 69), but I would argue that this is true only after the phenomenal success of *The Pilgrim's Progress*. This survey and the dynamics of the "Apology" testify to the severe strictures against the writing of fiction for a Puritan readership.

10. David Lindsay, *The Godly Man's Journey: Containing Ten Several Treatises* (London, 1625).

11. Samuel Denny, *Pelecanicidium: Or the Christian Advisor Against Self-Murder. Together with a Guide, and the Pilgrim's Pass to the Land of the Living* (London, 1653).

12. Simon Patrick, *The Parable of the Pilgrim: Written to a Friend* (London, 1665). The work was immensely popular and was issued seven times between 1665 and 1687.

13. Patrick, A3r. Of course, a modesty topos is being used in the address, but its effect depends on the writer's having correctly diagnosed the reader's expectations.

14. Patrick, A3v.

15. My discussion of Patrick's work is confined to the preface. For views of the relationship between *The Parable of the Pilgrim* and *The Pilgrim's Progress*, see Stuart Sim, "'Vertuous Mediocrity' and 'Fanatick Conventicle': Pilgrimage Styles in John Bunyan and Bishop Simon Patrick," *English Studies* 68 (1987): 316–24, and Jackson I. Cope, "The Progresses of Bunyan and Symon Patrick," *ELH* 55 (1988): 599–614.

16. Patrick, A4r.

17. Biblical quotations follow the 1611 King James Version unless otherwise noted.

18. Henri Talon, for example, stresses Bunyan's "instinctive art" in *John Bunyan: The Man and His Works,* trans. Barbara Wall (London: Rockcliff, 1951), 217, while Roger Sharrock notes his "supremely unsophisticated attitude to the literary product" in "Personal Vision and the Puritan Tradition in Bunyan," *Hibbert Journal* 56 (1957–58): 47.

19. William York Tindall, theorizing that *The Pilgrim's Progress* was a controversial pamphlet for Bunyan and his readers (43), recognizes that the "Apology" is an "essay in criticism" (*Mechanick Preacher*, 181–82). U. Milo Kaufman calls it an "aesthetic brief" in *Traditions in Puritan Meditation*, 8. Pointing to the speaker's claim that the work had a will of its own, Kaufmann argues that this confession of intent is "the inadvertent witness to a radical irresolution on Bunyan's part" (4). He argues that there is tension existing in Bunyan's aesthetic between "the didactic and literalist methods widespread in Puritanism and the imaginative methods native to the grand traditions of literature" (5). I argue that that tension is far from inadvertent, but that it is resolved in the "Apology" itself through an appeal to a tradition of writing that was not conceived of as literary but as reformist. See also the discussion of the "Apology" in John Knott's *The Sword of the Spirit: Puritan Responses to the Bible* (Chicago: University of Chicago Press, 1980), 139–40. Knott argues, with Kaufmann, that Bunyan was "uncomfortable with the Puritan habit of reducing biblical metaphor to doctrine," and he focuses on the depth of Bunyan's commitment to biblical similitudes (139).

20. John Steadman, *The Lamb and the Elephant: Ideal Imitation and the Context of Renaissance Allegory* (San Marino: Huntington Library, 1974), 72.

21. Kenneth B. Murdock, *Literature and Theology in Colonial New England* (Cambridge: Harvard University Press, 1956), 49.

22. For the changes in typeface which emphasize the change of speaker, I follow the third edition (1679), where it first occurred. Wharey and Sharrock both print "satisfied" rather than *"satisfy'd,"* for reasons that are unclear.

23. Lawrence A. Sasek, *The Literary Temper of the English Puritans* (Baton Rouge: Louisiana State University Press, 1961), 64.

24. Puttenham, *The Arte of English Poesie*, 196.

25. Puttenham, 197.

26. Puttenham, 197.

27. Puttenham, 166.

28. Edmund Spenser, "A Letter of the Authors," in *Poetical Works*, ed. J. C. Smith and E. de Selincourt (Oxford: Oxford University Press, 1912; reprint, 1977), 407.

29. Arthur Dent, *The Plain Mans Path-way to Heaven* (London, 1601). See *Grace Abounding*, 10. Bunyan's wife brought him this book and Lewis Baylie's *The Practice of Pietie* (London, 1627).

30. See Dayton Haskin's *"The Pilgrim's Progress* in the Context of Bunyan's Dialogue with the Radicals," *Harvard Theological Review* 77:1 (1984): 73–94, for a provocative argument about the meaning of this line in terms of Bunyan's reading of the Bible.

31. John Bunyan, *The Life and Death of Mr. Badman*, ed. Roger Sharrock and James F. Forrest (Oxford: Clarendon Press, 1988), 1.

32. Bunyan, *Mr. Badman*, 1.

33. As John Knott observes, "in the terms of Bunyan's narrative one can gain entrance to heaven only by learning to understand the visible world of ordinary experience in the metaphoric terms established by the Word: as an alien, and ultimately insubstantial country through which God's people must journey until they attain the ultimate satisfaction of communion with God" (*The Sword of the Spirit*, 153). Jacques Blondel makes a similar point: "l'allègorie, loin d'estomper le réèl, cherche à le traduire, donc à le recréer, parcequ'il est apparu trop riche, trop insaisissable, pour être épuisé soit par l'observation directe, soit par un inlassable recours aux 'similitudes'" ("Allégorie et Réalisme dans *The Pilgrim's Progress* de Bunyan," Etudes de Critique et d'Histoire Littéraire, no. 28[61–63], *Archives des Lettres Modernes* 3 [1959]: 5). This sheds light on Bunyan's peculiar position in literary history, between the death of one dominant form and the birth of another, the novel: "Bunyan nous paraît donc avoir recouru à l'allégorie d'abord par souci de réalisme, si l'on veut bien momentanémeant laisser au terme son ancienne signification scolastique. . . . Mais l'allégorie, d'autre part, a suscité un autre réalisme, celui-là même par lequel on désignera ce que fera bientôt DeFoe" (9).

34. Bunyan, *Grace Abounding*, 21–22.

35. Lewalski, *Protestant Poetics*, 6–7. For a much fuller discussion of the wealth of rhetoric books and manuals that extolled the poetic nature of Scripture, see Lewalski, 72–86. See also, for a discussion of contexts for Bunyan's style in terms of the debate, Roger Pooley, "Plain and Simple: Bunyan and Style," in *John Bunyan: Conventicle and Parnassus*, ed. N. H. Keeble, 91–110.

36. John Smith, *The Mysterie of Rhetorique Unvailed* (London, 1657), A5r–5v.

37. Smith, *Mysterie*, A6r.

38. John Prideaux, *Sacred Eloquence: Or, the Art of Rhetorick, As it is layd down in Scripture* (London, 1659), A2r.

39. Robert Ferguson, *The Interest of Reason in Religion; With the Import and Use of Scripture-Metaphors; and the Nature of the Union Betwixt Christ & Believers* (London, 1675), 367. The *DNB* notes Ferguson's influence

on dissenters and his role in the Popish Plot and the Monmouth Rebellion.

40. Ferguson, 278.

41. Ferguson, 342.

42. Ferguson, 281–82.

43. John Smith, "Of Prophecy," in *Select Discourses* (London, 1660), 172. This John Smith, who died in 1652, cannot be the same as the author of the 1656 *Mysterie*. The Smith who wrote "Of Prophecy" was a Puritan divine, Cambridge Platonist, and orientalist, associated with Emmanuel and Queen's Colleges, Cambridge.

44. Smith, "Of Prophecy," 222.

45. Smith, "Of Prophecy," 222.

46. Tindall lists some of the authors we can surmise that Bunyan had read: "The spiritual integrity of his sixty works could not be injured, however, by the casual mention of a dozen men: John Fox, Luther, Tindall, Campian, Ainsworth, Owen, Baxter, Jessey, Dent, Bayley, Samuel Clarke, and the author of *Francis Spira*; nor even more casual references, apparently at second hand, to Machiavelli, Origen, Cranmer, and the Koran, nor by the detestable names of his controversial enemies" (193).

47. Offor, *Works*, 3:464.

48. Offor, 1:392.

49. Tindall, 209.

50. Offor, 1:1v.

51. Quoted in Margaret Aston, *Lollards and Reformers*, 235.

52. "Foxe strewed his own text and margins thick with references to his sources and came near to snowing his readers under with primary documents" (Haller, *The Elect Nation*, 159).

53. Foxe, *Acts and Monuments*, (1632), 1:512.

54. Foxe (1632), 1:520.

55. Foxe (1632), 1:520.

56. As we will see in chapter 5, *Piers Plowman* was seen as a historical record by some Protestant readers.

57. See Margaret Spufford, "First Steps in Literacy: The Reading and Writing Experiences of the Humblest Seventeenth-Century Autobiographers," in *Literacy and Social Development in the West: A Reader*, ed. Harvey J. Graff (Cambridge: Cambridge University Press, 1981), 125–50, for a discussion of Bunyan's reading and writing in this context.

58. See *Discourse on The House in the Forest of Lebanon*, which first appeared in Charles Doe's folio volume of Bunyan's works in 1692: "This as I said, is part of a letter writ by Pomponious Algerius, an Italian martyr, who, when he wrote it, was in prison, in, as he calls it, his delectable orchard, the prison of Leonine, 12 calend. August anno 1555. As it is to be seen in the second volume of the book of martyrs" (Offor, 3:532).

3. Whom God Hath Chosen: Lollards, Reformers, and the Figure of Piers Plowman

1. Thomas Fuller, *The History of the Worthies of England*, ed. John Nichols (London, 1811), 261. Although the text of *Piers Plowman* clearly indicates the author's first name as William, John Bale and others were led to believe that Langland's first name was Robert. See Skeat's two-volume edition of the parallel texts for a discussion of the confusion over Langland's first name. See William Langland, *The Vision of Piers Plowman* . . ., ed. W. W. Skeat (1886; reprint, Oxford: Oxford University Press, 1968), 2:xxvii–xxxii.

2. See Aston, *Lollards and Reformers*, 243–72.

3. Most of these works and other contemporary references to *Piers Plowman* were listed by W. W. Skeat in his nineteenth-century edition of the three versions of the poem: William Langland, *The Vision of William Concerning Piers Plowman* . . ., ed. W. W. Skeat, Part 4, Section 2, E.E.T.S. o.s. 81 (London: N. Trubner & Co., 1884), 863–74. They have been exhaustively catalogued by Myrta Ethel McGinnis, "'Piers the Plowman' in England, 1362–1625: A Study in Popularity and Influence," (Ph.D. diss., Yale, 1932). McGinnis makes no attempt to interpret this material — popularity and influence are, in fact, just what she does not study — but her catalogue is invaluable, especially the chronological list of references, 240–351. See also Kitty Marx, *Das Nachleben von Piers Plowmann bis zu Bunyan's: The Pilgrim's Progress (1678)* (Ph.D diss., Albert-Ludwigs-Universität, 1931) for many of the same references. Many are also discussed in George Roush, "The Political Plowman: The Expression of Political Ideals in 'Piers Plowman' and its Successors" (Ph.D. diss., Berkeley, 1966). I make no attempt to survey this material exhaustively but rather am concerned with the implications of some uses to which the poem and the plowman figure were put. Helen C. White was the first to declare these texts as representing "a tradition of social-religious criticism," in *Social Criticism and Religious Literature* (New York: Macmillan, 1944), 2. See in general chapter 1, "The Piers Plowman Tradition." She focuses on the social issues embodied in *Piers Plowman* and articulated by Wyclif and then points to the texts as evidence that the sixteenth-century reformers called upon that tradition to speak for social and religious concerns. Hallett Smith examines *Piers Plowman* and some of the apocrypha to establish a native source for the genre of satire in *Elizabethan Poetry* (Cambridge: Harvard University Press, 1952), 194–256. Alvin Kernan develops the link with satire further as he locates the medieval satiric persona in "the mask of the plowman" and shows how this mask was transformed by Renaissance satirists in *The Cankered Muse* (1954; reprint, Hamden, Conn.: Archon Books, 1976), 16–17, 34–36, and 37–65; see especially "The Mask of the Plowman," 40–54. John King's

study of Crowley's editions of *Piers Plowman* notes the earlier "meta-morphosis" of Langland's figure into a "harsh anticlerical spokesman" in "Robert Crowley's Editions of *Piers Plowman*: A Tudor Apocalypse," *Modern Philology* 73 (1976): 343.

4. Pamela Gradon, "*Piers Plowman* and the Ideology of Dissent," *Proceedings of the British Academy* 66 (1980), 179–205, reprinted in *Middle English Literature: British Academy Gollancz Lectures,* ed. J. A. Burrows, (Oxford: Oxford University Press, 1989), 196.

5. Gradon, 221.

6. Christina von Nolcken, "*Piers Plowman*, the Wycliffites, and *Pierce the Plowman's Creed*," *Yearbook of Langland Studies* 2 (1988): 72–73.

7. D. A. Lawton, "Lollardy and the 'Piers Plowman' Tradition," *Modern Language Review* 76 (1981): 793. See also Russell A. Peck, "Social Conscience and the Poets," in *Social Unrest in the Middle Ages,* ed. Francis X. Newman (Binghamton, N.Y.: Medieval and Renaissance Texts and Studies, 1986), 112–48.

8. von Nolcken, 97.

9. See Anne Hudson's *Premature Revolution* for an illuminating discussion of this issue, 398–408. Hudson argues that Langland is orthodox in his understanding of the Eucharist as well as the legitimacy of the religious orders and is silent on the matter of oral confession, but on the "question of clerical temporalities and endowments, he is most closely in accord with Wyclif" (405). She also notes that the line between heterodoxy and orthodoxy had not been drawn until after Langland's three versions had appeared: "It seems to me that the answer to the problem of *Piers Plowman* lies in the recognition that unusually, perhaps uniquely, it is a poem whose impact became more unorthodox as time passed" (404).

10. Hudson notes that early editions of Langland's poem are "often annotated with references to Wyclif or Wycliffite texts" (*The Premature Revolution,* 401). In this chapter, I have adopted Hudson's practice in *The Premature Revolution* of treating "Lollard" and "Wycliffite" as synonymous terms (2).

11. Anne Hudson, "Epilogue: The Legacy of *Piers Plowman*," in *A Companion to Piers Plowman,* ed. John A. Alford (Berkeley: University of California Press, 1988), 253.

12. Hudson, "Epilogue," 254.

13. Hudson, "Epilogue," 255.

14. Hudson, "Epilogue," 257.

15. According to one recent editor, Derek Pearsall, "The three versions of *Piers Plowman* are extant in 51 manuscripts (excluding fragments). Of these, 16 are of the A-text (including 6 with C-text conclusions), 13 of B, and 18 of C, and the rest are scribal composites of other kinds" (*Piers Plowman:*

An Edition of the C-text, by William Langland [London: Edward Arnold, 1978], 20). As Hudson points out, "Only *The Prick of Conscience* and *The Canterbury Tales* significantly exceed" *Piers Plowman* in number of surviving manuscripts ("Epilogue," 252).

16. Gotthard Victor Lechler commented on the difference quite early, in *John Wyclif and His English Precursors*, trans. Peter Lorimer (London: Kegan Paul, Tench, 1881), 69–70. See William Langland, *Piers Plowman: The A-Version*, ed. George Kane (London: Athlone Press, 1960); and *Piers Plowman: The B-Version*, ed. George Kane and E. Talbot Donaldson (London: Athlone Press, 1975). Compare Geoffrey Chaucer, *The Text of the Canterbury Tales*, ed. John M. Manly and Edith Rickert, vol. 1, *Descriptions of the Manuscripts* (Chicago: The University of Chicago Press, 1940). See also George Kane, *Piers Plowman: The Evidence for Authorship* (London: Athlone Press, 1965).

17. J. A. Burrow, "The Audience of *Piers Plowman*," *Anglia* 75 (1957): 373–84; reprinted, with corrections and postscript, in *Essays on Medieval Literature* (Oxford: Clarendon Press, 1984), 102–16.

18. Anne Middleton, "The Audience and Public of *Piers Plowman*," in *Middle English Alliterative Poetry and its Literary Background*, ed. D. A. Lawton (Cambridge and Totowa, N.J.: D. S. Brewer, 1982): 101.

19. Middleton, 104.

20. Hudson notes that the mere ownership of books among the Lollards was evidence of heresy; considerable caution was required (*The Premature Revolution*, 166–67).

21. Janet Coleman, *English Literature in History, 1350–1400: Medieval Readers and Writers* (London: Hutchinson, 1981), 22. She thinks the author of *Pierce the Ploughman's Crede* and John Ball are "'proletariat' members of that middle group" (62).

22. As Hudson notes, "Social insignificance, or even poverty, was evidently no bar to Lollard access to books. A major factor in answering the practical problems of access seems to have been group ownership" (*The Premature Revolution*, 205).

23. Coleman, 170.

24. Aston, 199.

25. Anne Hudson notes that Lollard writings "reveal a community of ideas and assumptions between texts of very different types" in Anne Hudson, ed., *Selections from English Wycliffite Writings* (Cambridge: Cambridge University Press, 1978), 9.

26. Aston, 207. See also Ritchie D. Kendall, *The Drama of Dissent: The Radical Poetics of Noncomformity, 1380–1590* (Chapel Hill: University of North Carolina Press, 1986), 14–49, for an analysis of Lollard "aesthetics" and the importance of reading.

27. See Brian Stock, *The Implications of Literacy: Written Language and Models of Interpretation in the Eleventh and Twelfth Centuries* (Princeton: Princeton University Press, 1983), 88–92.

28. Stock, 88.

29. Aston, 198.

30. Aston, 206.

31. Quoted in Aston, 198. On the issue of Lollard anti-intellectualism, see Hudson, *The Premature Revolution*, 224–27, and Kendall, 70.

32. Kendall, 14–49. Kendall attempts to define a Lollard "aesthetic." He focuses on Lollard writings and the writings of later nonconformists as "displaced drama."

33. Hudson, *The Premature Revolution*, 274.

34. Aston, summarizing and quoting Pecock, 206.

35. See Hudson, *Lollards and Their Books*, especially the chapter entitled "Some Aspects of Lollard Book Production," 181–91.

36. Aston, 211.

37. Aston, 44.

38. Coleman, 17.

39. See *The Vision and Creed of Piers Ploughman*, ed. Thomas Wright (1842; 2d ed., rev. London, 1856) 1: xxxiv–xxxv.

40. See R. B. Dobson, ed., *The Peasants' Revolt of 1381* (New York: St. Martin's Press, 1970), 381. These letters are preserved in Thomas Walsingham's *Historia Anglicana* and Henry Knighton's chronicle. Anne Hudson argues that the leaders of the Revolt must have known Langland's poem in some form; see "Epilogue," 251–52.

41. Dobson, 380.

42. Dobson, 382.

43. Quoted in Dobson, 380.

44. Dobson, 380.

45. Prologue, *Piers Plowman: The B Version*, ed. Kane and Donaldson, lines 146–208.

46. The Chronicle's account of 1381–1404 is printed by M. V. Clarke and V. H. Galbraith, "The Deposition of Richard II," *Bulletin of the John Rylands Library* 14 (1930): 164–89.

47. See Aston, 1–47, for an examination of the connection between Lollardy and the Peasants' Revolt. She concludes that Wyclif himself never advocated rebellion, but some of his followers pursued the implications of his statements on a political and social level. The established church, of course, saw the political usefulness of drawing a direct parallel between the two events.

48. Coleman, 60. Her description of *Piers Plowman* is apt: "Langland's subject matter is centered on man's spiritual disorientation amidst social crisis" (295 n.12).

49. Hudson demonstrates the extent to which Lollard works of the fifteenth and early sixteenth centuries echo *Piers Plowman* ("Epilogue," 254–58).

50. *Piers Plowman*, B-version, 5.557–629.

51. Elizabeth D. Kirk, "Langland's Plowman and the Recreation of Fourteenth-Century Religious Metaphor," *Yearbook of Langland Studies* 2 (1988): 1–21. I am indebted to Kirk's article throughout the following discussion of perceptions of plowmen up through Langland.

52. Jill Mann, *Chaucer and Medieval Estates Satire* (London: Cambridge University Press, 1973), 67–74.

53. Kirk, "Langland's Plowman," 13. See also Stephen A. Barney, "The Plowshare of the Tongue: The Progress of a Symbol from the Bible to *Piers Plowman*," *Mediaeval Studies* 35 (1973): 261–93, and Margaret E. Goldsmith, *The Figure of Piers Plowman: The Image on the Coin* (Cambridge: D. S. Brewer, 1981), for somewhat different views.

54. It should also be noted that although Barney's article is an attempt to show that the meaning of Langland's plowman is traditional, most of his evidence concerns other kinds of agricultural laborers: farmers, sowers, oxen, planters, and so on. Very few of the traditional images he cites actually concern plowmen. As Kirk points out in her generally more convincing article, "the farming process itself is one thing and plowmen are another" (3).

55. See John Gower, *Le Mirour de l'omme*, lines 26482–506, in *The Complete Works of John Gower*, ed. G. C. Macaulay (Oxford: Clarendon Press, 1899–1902), 1:293–94, and his *Vox clamantis*, Book 1, lines 880–936, in *Complete Works*, 4:46–48. Dobson gives English versions of these passages, 97–98 and 387–89, respectively.

56. Quoted in Bertie Wilkinson, *The Later Middle Ages in England 1216–1485* (London: Longmans, Green, and Co., 1969), 202; cited by Kirk, "Langland's Plowman," 8.

57. *Reliquae Antiquae*, ed. T. Wright and J. Holliwell (London, 1841), 43–47.

58. Donaldson, *C-text*, 110–11. See also Peck, 121–25, for a discussion of this point.

59. Judith Anderson, *The Growth of a Personal Voice: Piers Plowman and the Faerie Queene* (New Haven: Yale University Press, 1971), 1.

60. See King, *English Reformation Literature*, 4, 323.

61. *Pierce the Ploughman's Crede . . . to which is appended God Speed the Plough*, ed. W. W. Skeat, E.E.T.S. o.s. 30 (1867; reprint, New York: Greenwood Press, 1969). See also McGinnis, 203–7.

62. On this point, see Hudson, "Epilogue," 255.

63. Hudson, "Epilogue," 257. Hudson gives further reasons for dating the text to the fifteenth century: "The balance of probability is against the

likelihood that the strongly archaic language of the *Praier and complaynte* was composed by a sixteenth-century forger, but this cannot be formally proved. . . . In subject matter there seems to be nothing in the *Praier* that would be out of place in a Lollard tract of the early fifteenth century" (*Lollards and Their Books*, 246–47). As Hudson notes, Lollard texts are notoriously difficult to date; much of this evidence is speculative.

64. See McGinnis, 207–10. Foxe attributes to Tyndale the anonymous preface to the 1531 edition which dates the poem in 1300.

65. *Foxe, Acts and Monuments* (1632), 1:520.

66. Foxe (1632), 1:524.

67. Foxe (1632), 1:525.

68. Aston, 227.

69. *The Praier and complaynte of the plowman unto Christe: written not longe after the yere of oure Lord A thousand and three hundred*, ed. William Tyndale? (Antwerp?, 1531?).

70. "To the Christen reader," in *Praier and complaynte, 1531*.

71. Alan G. Chester, "'The New Learning': A Semantic Note," *Studies in the Renaissance* 2 (1955), 142. Chester demonstrates that the term was never used to refer to the revival of classical learning.

72. *A Proper Dialogue Between a Gentilman and a Husbandman eche complayning to the other their miserable calamitie, through the ambition of the clergy. An ABC of Spirituality* (London, 1530). See Aston, 220–21. Furnival lists the books banned by the Bishop of London in 1530, which include two books made up from two Lollard texts each, of which this is one (*Political, Religious and Love Poems*, ed. Frederick J. Furnival, E.E.T.S. o.s. 15 [London: Kegan Paul, Tench, Trubner, 1866; reprint, 1903]).

73. Hudson notes that although the dialogue frame of this text is a sixteenth-century production, the fragment introduced at this point comes from a medieval Lollard text known as *The Clergy may not hold Property*, which exists in two different versions, one surviving in a single medieval manuscript, the other in three medieval manuscripts and one from the sixteenth-century (*Lollards and Their Books*, 233–34).

74. According to Hudson, this text was also published separately—i.e., without the framework provided by the *Proper Dialogue*—in 1530 and in 1538, under the title *A compendious olde treatyse, shewynge, howe that we ought to haue ye scripture in Englysshe* (*Lollards and Their Books*, 229); like the *Proper Dialogue*, it also survives in medieval manuscript versions (242–44). It includes "a version of a short Lollard text defending biblical translation" (229).

75. P. L. Heyworth, ed., *Jack Upland, Friar Daw's Reply and Upland's Rejoinder* (London: Oxford University Press, 1968).

76. Foxe (1632), 1:340.

77. Foxe (1632), 1:339–40.

78. The date of this work is a particularly vexed issue. Andrew N. Wawn has demonstrated that most of it is early, but that the mentions of the plowman are probably later additions; see his "Genesis of *The Plowman's Tale*," *Yearbook of English Studies* 2 (1972): 21–40, and "Chaucer, *The Plowman's Tale*, and Renaissance Propaganda: The Testimonies of Thomas Godfray and *I playne Piers*," *Bulletin of the John Rylands Library* 56 (1973): 174–92. Hudson, "Epilogue," suggests an early fifteenth-century date.

79. Francis Thynne, *Animadversions upon the Annotations and corrections of Some Imperfections of Impressions of Chaucer's Workes* . . ., ed. F. J. Furnival, Chaucer Society, 2d series 13 (London, 1875).

80. See W. W. Skeat, *The Chaucer Canon* (Oxford: Clarendon Press, 1900), 99–100. See also McGinnis, 220–23. "The Plowman's Tale" was printed separately, probably in 1532–35. It was added to Thynne's edition in 1542, placed separately after the end of the *Canterbury Tales*. It was reissued separately in 1547–48. The third Thynne edition integrated it into the *Canterbury Tales* by printing it just before the final tale, the Parson's. See Geoffrey Chaucer, *The Workes of Our Ancient and learned English Poet Geoffrey Chaucer, newly printed* . . ., ed. William Thynne, 2d edition (London, 1542).

81. Foxe (1632), 2:55-56.

82. Foxe (1632), 2:56.

83. Foxe (1684), 1:803.

84. Foxe (1684), 1:803.

85. Foxe (1684), 1:803.

86. Foxe (1684), 1:803.

87. *The Plowman's Tale* (London, 1606).

88. The place and date are not known. McGinnis, 262, speculates that *I playne Piers* was written c. 1540 and *A godlye dyalogue and dysputacyon betwene Pyers Plowman and a popish preest/concernyng the supper of the lorde* between 1547 and 1553 but gives no evidence for her choices. Hudson, "Epilogue," suggests dates of around 1550 for both.

89. *A godlye dyalogue*, A3r.

90. *The Bankett of Johan the Reve, Unto piers ploughman/Laurens laborer/Thomlyn Tailyor/And Hobbe of the hille/with other*, (British Museum MS Harley 207). McGinnis dates the manuscript c. 1532 but gives no basis for doing so (223, 261). Hudson thinks this date may be too early ("Epilogue," 260).

91. There is no date or printer named. McGinnis speculates that 1549 is a possible date given references to contemporary references in the work. She gives the whole text, 262–309.

92. *I playne Piers*, B7r.

93. *I playne Piers*, E7v.

94. *I playne Piers*, F4v.

95. *Pyers the plowmans exhortation, unto the lordes, Knightes and burgoysses of the Parlyamenthouse* (London, 1550).

96. *Pyers plowmans exhortation*, B4r.

97. See Leland H. Carlson, *Martin Marprelate, Gentleman: Master Job Throkmorton Laid Open in His Colors* (San Marino: Huntington Library, 1981). Carlson (376, n.65) refers to an edition of *Piers Plowman* of this date, but the work is actually this Marprelate tract. The last half of the original tract is missing, suggesting that the printers may have been interrupted.

98. George Gascoigne, *The Steele Glas A Satyre compiled by George Gascoigne Esquire. Togither with the Complainte of Phylomon. An Elegie . . .* (London, 1576). Signature numbers are indicated in the body of the text.

99. "The Plow-Mans Complaint, The Free-Holder's Proposition, And, The High-shoes Resolution" (London, 1678; Bodleian Library, Firth Collection, b.20 [f.54]).

100. "The Plow-mans Prophesie, Or, The Country-mans Calculation" (Bodleian Library, Rawlinson Collection, 566 [120]). The *S.T.C.* suggests a date of 1680.

101. Foxe (1632), 1:654.

102. See Robert L. Kelly, "Hugh Latimer as Piers Plowman," *Studies in English Literature 1500–1900* 17 (1977): 13–26.

103. Hugh Latimer, *Selected Sermons of Hugh Latimer*, ed. Allan G. Chester (Charlottesville: The University of Virginia Press, 1968), 29.

104. Kendall argues that the Bible became the Lollard's "sacrament" because it was the "ritual cornerstone of the reformed church" (17, 23), but the use of language such as "sacrament" and "ritual" is problematic, given the Lollard stance toward both as they were represented in the traditions of the church.

105. Thomas Delaune and Benjamin Keach, *Tropologia, or, a Key to Open Scripture-Metaphors* (London, 1681).

106. Delaune, *Tropologia*, 1:142.

107. Delaune, 1:143.

108. Delaune, 1:143.

109. Tindall, *Mechanick Preacher*, 6.

110. Tindall, 71. For a detailed examination of nonconformist attitudes toward the issue of education and "humane" learning, see Keeble, *Literary Culture*, chapter 5, especially section 1, "Education and the Spirit," 156–62, and section 2, "Humane Learning," 162–70.

111. Cited in Eric C. Walker, *William Dell, Master Puritan* (Cambridge: W. Heffer & Sons, 1970), 170.

112. William Dell, *Several Sermons and Discourses of William Dell Minister of the Gospel* (London, 1652; reprint, 1709), 484.

113. Dell, Preface, A2r.

114. Dell, 354.

115. Dell, 619–20.

116. J. B. Bockett, Preface, *The Poor Mechanick's Plea Against the Rich Clergy's Oppression* (London, 1700), A2r.

117. Bockett, 36.

4. The Holy Ghost Is the Author of Books: A Protestant Reader Reads *Piers Plowman*

1. All quotations from Crowley, unless otherwise noted, follow the facsimile edition edited by J. A. W. Bennett of the Magdalen College copy: *The Vision of Pierce Plowman, now fyrst imprinted by Robert Crowley* . . . (London, 1550; facsimile reprint, David Paradine Developments, 1976). This copy, which belonged to Samuel Pepys, has two different states of the front matter; I have quoted from the version nearest the front which uses an asterisk. The synopsis is for the most part unpaginated, so I have simply carried on the use of the asterisk in referring to pages. All abbreviations are silently expanded. Marginal glosses added to later editions are quoted from a copy of the third edition in the British Library, C. 122 d. 9. This copy was used by Kane and Donaldson for their collation of the third edition, and its readings appear as C3 in their collation of the B-text (see Kane and Donaldson, 6–7). Material on the Owen Rodgers reprint of 1561 follows the copy that belonged to Richard Harvey and is in the Beinecke Library at Yale.

2. See John King's chapter, "Robert Crowley: A Tudor Gospeller," in *English Reformation Literature*, 319–57. His earlier article, "Robert Crowley's Editions of *Piers Plowman*: A Tudor Apocalypse," 342–52, offers invaluable information about Crowley's enterprise, and any subsequent work is greatly in its debt. Much of the information in this article has been reprinted in *English Reformation Literature*, 319–57. King briefly summarizes the steps leading to the publication of Crowley of *Piers Plowman* and argues that Crowley "transformed" the work into a "Tudor Apocalypse."

3. King, "Crowley's Editions," 342.

4. See Kane and Donaldson, 6–7. For a study of the precise text of each edition and its relationship to the manuscripts, see William Crawford, "Robert Crowley's Editions of *Piers Plowman*: A Bibliographical and Textual Study" (Ph.D. diss., Yale, 1957).

5. King, "Crowley's Editions," 346. See Crawford, "Editions," especially 28–60.

6. King, "Crowley's Editions," 347.

7. For complete details of the alterations, see Crawford, "Editions," and the account in King, "Crowley's Editions," 347–48. King notes that the omission was necessary to "what was for Crowley a central prophecy of *Piers Plowman*, the vision of a reforming monarch who will punish the religious orders. Crowley's marginal interpretation of this as a prophecy of the 'Suppression of Abbayes' (N2r) would have been negated had he retained the omitted passages; what was originally a call for monastic reform has been transformed into a destructive attack on the very principles of monasticism" (346). Crawford demonstrates how unpolemical most of Crowley's changes were.

8. "The Printer to the Reader" is included in all three Crowley editions, but not in the Rodgers reprint.

9. "He wrote altogyther in miter: but not after the maner of our rimers that write nowe adays (for his verses ende not alike) but the nature of hys miter is, to have thre wordes at the leaste in every verse whiche beginne with some one letter" (°1v).

10. Anderson, *The Growth of a Personal Voice*, 2.

11. Thynne, Preface, A2r.

12. King notes in his article on the Crowley editions of *Piers Plowman* that the authorities found Chaucer acceptable as an author of fiction, but they agreed with the reformers that Langland's work was an account of real history. "The Plowman's Tale" was allowed into print in the 1542 edition of Chaucer, though another apocryphal tale, "The Pilgrim's Tale", was disallowed because Chaucer's works were seen as fables. See King, "Crowley's Editions," 343, and Francis Thynne's *Animadversions*, 5–12.

13. The different tactics of the two prefaces probably also have a practical function, reflecting the contrasting situations at the court of Henry VIII, who considered himself a connoisseur of literature, an artist, and a patron of the arts, and the Puritan Protectorate of Edward VI. According to Francis Thynne, Henry took a great personal interest in William Thynne's editions and promised to protect him against Wolsey. Even so, the proto-first edition was scrapped because it contained a "Pilgrim's Tale" deemed too radical, and the "Plowman's Tale" jeopardized the second edition.

14. Robert Crowley, *The Voyce of the Last Trumpet . . . calling al estats of men to the right path of their vocation* (London, 1550).

15. See King, "Robert Crowley: A Tudor Gospeller" in *English Reformation Literature*, 319–357.

16. King, "Crowley's Editions," 342.

17. King, "Crowley's Editions," 350.

18. King accounts for Crowley's millenarian application of *Piers Plowman* by bringing three specific kinds of evidence to bear on the problem. First, he points briefly to the apocryphal plowman texts as evidence of the

transformation of Piers into a radical spokesman ("Crowley's Editions," 342–45). Second, he sees John Bale's commentary on Revelation, *The Image of Both Churches* (1548), which interprets Revelation as a prophecy of the English Reformation, as an influence on Crowley's other writings (344). Finally, King claims that *"Piers Plowman's* reputed connection with John Wyclif, the prototype of the English reformer, supplied its claim to authority as a Protestant prophecy" (344). It should be noted that King appears to have modified his position somewhat: in *English Reformation Literature,* he acknowledges that *Piers Plowman* itself is "tinged with Lollardry" (4). See also Lawton, "Lollardy and the 'Piers Plowman' Tradition," 780–93, which implies a similar connection.

19. The classic study of this problem is Morton W. Bloomfield, *Piers Plowman as a Fourteenth-Century Apocalypse* (New Brunswick, N.J.: Rutgers University Press, 1961).

20. This is not to say that Crowley never sees connections between Langland's text and actual events. The reference in the preface to the suppression of abbeys is the best known and most obvious instance. Another instance can be found in the last part of the prologue. Crowley glosses one of Langland's scriptural quotations: "Woe to the land where the king is a child," by inserting a comment in Latin declaring the passage to mean when the king is childish, not when the king is a child, lest it be taken as an attack on Edward VI (see A3v).

21. Critics of *Piers Plowman* have failed to achieve agreement on the meaning the pardon scene had for Langland. Not only is the scene enigmatic but Langland's own ambivalence about it is indicated by the excision of major elements of it in the C-text revision. Crowley's interpretation of it is no less tenable than many suggested by more recent scholars.

22. William Perkins, *Works* (Cambridge, 1608), 2:762.

23. Skeat, 4:866.

24. For a discussion of the radical implications of this scene and of its uniqueness in the context of medieval literary theory, see Elizabeth D. Kirk, *The Dream Thought of Piers Plowman* (New Haven: Yale University Press, 1972), 139–45.

5. "Peres became a protestande": Renaissance Readings of *Piers Plowman*

1. I deliberately use this modern term for rhetoricians such as Puttenham in order to emphasize the fact that their ideas about what constituted literature resulted in a theory of literature.

2. William Crawford believes that Crowley had at least one copy of the A-text, two copies of the B-text, and one copy of the C-text ("Editions," 60).

3. John Bale, *Illustrium Maioris Britanniae Scriptorum . . . Summarium*, (Wesel, 1548), 525.

4. John Bale, *Scriptorum Illustrium, maioris Brytanniae . . . Catalogus* (Basel, 1557-59), 474. "Robert Langland, priest, as it appears, was born in the county of Shropshire in a town commonly called Mortymers Clibery, in a muddy land, an eighth of a milestone from Malvern Hills. Nevertheless I cannot affirm with certainty whether or not he was educated continuously in this rude and rural place in good letters to a mature age, or whether he mingled with those at Oxford or Cambridge: when among the masters of those places studies principally flourished. Truly, nevertheless, it is certainly agreed that he was one of the disciples of John Wycliffe, and in a fervent spirit against the open blasphemies of the papists against God and his Christ, under delightful embellishments and figures he had brought forth a holy work in English speech worthy of the reading of good men which he called *The Vision of Peter Plowman*. Book I. *In a somer seson, when softe was the sonne.* I know nothing else brought forth by him. In this learned work, aside from various delightful similitudes, he foretold prophetically more things, which we have seen in our days fulfilled. He completed his work in the year of our Lord 1369, while John Chicester was mayor of London." Translation by Sara Thorne-Thomsen. See also *Index Britanniae Scriptorum . . . John Bale's Index of British and Other Writers*, ed. R. Lane Poole with Mary Bateson (Oxford, 1902).

5. *A Petition directed to her most excellent Majestic . . .* , Middleburg, 1592? The *S.T.C.* dates it 1590 and attributes it to Henry Barrow. For a date of 1592 and an attribution to Job Throckmorton, see Carlson, 117–20. Carlson considers the work Presbyterian. Note that Carlson refers (376 n.65) to an edition of Langland later than that of Rodgers. This is an error; the work to which Carlson refers is actually the Marprelate version of *I playne Piers*.

6. *Petition*, 34.

7. *Petition*, 34.

8. *Petition*, 35. We have noted in chapter 4 that the first Thynne edition of Chaucer's works dedicated to Henry VIII did not contain the "Plowman's Tale" and that the second edition, which did, was authorized by Parliament only on the grounds that the "Plowman's Tale" was a mere fiction, not a part of pre-Reformation polemic.

9. Puttenham, *Arte of English Poesie*, 41.

10. Puttenham, 74.

11. Puttenham, 76.

12. It is difficult to be sure to what extent sixteenth-century readers were aware of this connection; Puttenham presumably was not, since he dates the poem later. But the Peasants' Revolt was an aspect of late fourteenth-century attempts at reform that was viewed unsympathetically by

such Reformation historians as John Foxe; social criticism as radical as Langland's, as opposed to the criticism of the Catholic Church, was generally regarded as dangerous.

13. Reprinted in G. G. Smith, *Elizabethan Critical Essays* (Oxford: Clarendon Press, 1904), 1:242.

14. Smith, *Elizabethan Critical Essays*, 2:314.

15. Smith, *Elizabethan Critical Essays*, 2:320.

16. John Stowe, *The Annales of England* (1580 and 1592; reissued London, 1600), 372.

17. John Stowe, *A Survey of London* (London, 1603) 159.

18. William Camden, *Remains Concerning Britain* (London, 1603), 218.

19. Skeat, *The Vision of William Concerning Piers Plowman*, Part 4, section 2, 868–69. Selden's annotations for the first eighteen songs appeared in 1612, the rest in 1622.

20. John Weever, *Ancient Funeral Monuments* (London, 1631), 72–73.

21. Edmund Spenser, *Poetical Works*, ed. J. C. Smith and E. de Selincourt (London: Oxford University Press, 1912; reprint, 1970), 467. Oddly enough, Spenser's use of the name Piers in the May eclogue, where he is describing the Protestant minister, has not been regarded as an unambiguous allusion, a point to which we will return below.

22. Commenting on this passage, Skeat says "Spenser does not show any very close acquaintance with 'Piers Plowman,' but probably alludes to his own Eclogues for May, July, and September, in which he treats of the evils caused by unworthy pastors" (Skeat, *Vision*, Part 4, section 2, 867).

23. Anderson, 2.

24. Kernan places Skelton's Colin Clout, at least, if not Spenser's, among the "plowman" figures of native satire (*The Cankered Muse*, 43–45).

25. As we will see below, a copy of the Rodgers edition belonging to Gabriel Harvey's brother Richard has annotations illustrating the extent to which an admittedly exceptionally sophisticated reader could move beyond the interpretation offered by the Crowley annotations on this point.

26. Michael Drayton, *The Works of Michael Drayton*, ed. J. William Hebel (Oxford: Basil Blackwell, 1932), 2:451–75. Quotations taken from the poem are identified in the body of the text.

27. The fact that Piers is a shepherd, not a plowman, is a necessity of the genre, not a denial of the connection. As we observed in chapter 3, Latimer's linking of the ministry with plowing with his assertion in the "Sermon of the Plough" that "preachers are plowman" represents one development of the plowman image that Spenser clearly evokes in the May Ecologue.

28. John Milton, "An Apology Against a Pamphlet," in *Complete Prose Works of John Milton*, ed. Don M. Wolfe (New Haven: Yale University Press, 1953), 1:915–16.

29. Skeat thought that Milton might also have known the poem in manuscript as well: "But the most remarkable parallel is the employment of guns by the rebel angels (P. L. vi. 484–91, 571–94, as compared with P. Pl. C. xxi. 283–96). As this remarkable passage only occurs in the C-text, it would seem as if Milton had access to a Ms" (Skeat, *Vision*, Part 4, section 2, 868). As we will see in the next section, the poem was being read in manuscript well into the seventeenth century.

30. William Prynne, *Histrio-Mastix* (London, 1633), 833–34.

31. Fuller, 261–62.

32. William Greaves, *The History of the Church of Great Britain* (London, 1667), 113–14.

33. John Strype, *Ecclesiastical Memorials* (London, 1721), ix.

34. Strype, 266.

35. I have examined all the copies of the Crowley and Rodgers editions in the British Library (4), the Bodleian Library (9, including the Bostock copy referred to by King), Cambridge University Library (7), and the Beinecke Library at Yale (8). I am grateful to Professor Suzanne Woods for information about the marginalia in the two copies in the Huntington Library.

36. See Yale copy Id/L26/550c.

37. Suzanne Woods, in a letter, 9 July 1982.

38. Bodl. Douce L. 205.

39. See King, "Crowley Editions," 51. The following commentary is quoted from King's footnote 39:

Bostock calls into question the premises of Crowley's revisionist interpretation by repudiating the . . . attribution of authorship to a disciple of John Wyclif: "Wickliffe was a corruptor of truth and the Master of a sect of Rebels who being led by Sr. John Oldcastle rose against the Soviraign and the cheif of them executed as they deserved, as our chronicles read and these were men that this Printer says had their eyes open and so they had, [not] upon truth but rapine and plunder, and their mouth open not to cry out against the works of darkness, but vent [*sic*] heresie and sedition" (sig. °2r). Bostock undercuts Crowley's central assertion that the "Abbayes shoulde be suppressed," arguing correctly that "this is false, for the Author speaks against abuses onely" (sig. °4v). He qualifies Crowley's attack on "The fruites of Popishe penaunce" by noting, "Not the fruits but abuse of Penance" (sig. C4v, B.3.52–60). In answering the editor's gloss, "Note howe he scorneth the auctority of Popes," the sweeping implications of Bostock's reply call into question the whole of Crowley's interpretation: "No Catholick

Doctor can be shewd to have writ or ever taught that the Pope hath power to pardon without any penance or obligation to live well. The Pope's Bull or pardons are for remitting of canonical penances, or temporal punishment, which remains to be suffered after the sin as far as it incurred eternal damnation is forgiven by the Sacrament of penance. And the pardons or Indulgences ever suppose a fit disposition in the persons to whom they are applied. And that must be a sincere resolution of forsaking evil and of doing good. And the Author must not be understood to scorn the Authority of the Cheif Pastor, as the Heretical margin would suggest, but to reprove those who must, or presume upon such pardons whilst they live viciously." (sig. K3r, B.7.170–86)

This material constitutes the whole of the Bostock marginalia.

    40. The copy is C. 122 d.9.

    41. For convenience sake, I will refer to the reader here as "he."

    42. I have been unable to locate the line "in a day will apear."

    43. This passage represents an interesting change from Langland's text which reads "But holy churche and hi" (i.e., "they"). At first sight, this looks like a simple mistake on Crowley's part. But the effects of that mistake are significant. The Renaissance reader assumed that the speaker of the work was Piers and that the dream was a record of his spiritual growth. Given that fact, the reader must have seen in this line a portent of Piers's break with the established church.

    44. King, *English Reformation Literature*, 350.

    45. The copy is at Yale in the Beinecke Library, Id/L26/550f.

    46. Carlson, 68–69.

    47. Curione, Celio Seconde, *Pasquine in a Traunce* (London, 1566).

    48. For Pasquin and Pasquil, see Kernan, especially 53.

    49. Since Rodgers had eliminated the Crowley preface, Harvey had to date the work for himself and turn to other sources of information about authorship. He cites 1342 on the first page, but later picks up the date of 1350 (T2r).

    50. The British Museum *Additional Manuscript Catalogue*, 16:192–93. Signatures in the manuscript are those of Arthur Surteys (fol. 124r), Francis Aiscough of Cottam (fol. 1r, 124r, 124v), Thomas Thyrnbeke, clarke (fol. 124v), and Maurice Johnson, Ayscoughfe Hall, Spalding, 1735. The catalogue describes the marginalia as by "various hands of the sixteenth and seventeenth centuries." The manuscript was discovered after Skeat's great edition. Derek Pearsall discusses the manuscript briefly in his edition of the *C-Text*, 20–21. Quotations from the C-text will be taken from that edition and will be

cited by passus and line number in the body of the text. The annotations written on the manuscript will be indicated by folio number, and recto or verso.

51. The reverse does not hold; some small additions of text to the second edition show that Crowley knew both the A and C versions of the poem. See Crawford, "Editions," 60, and King, "Crowley's Editions," 346–47.

52. The commentator is apparently not aware at this point that "Kytte" is identified much later (passus 20 of the C-text) as the dreamer's wife; hence his confusion as to whether Kit is short for Christopher or for Katherine. It is not clear why the annotator confused Cornhill (in London) with Cornwall.

53. Pearsall in his *C-Text* edition notes that "*lollare* means 'loller, idler, vagabond,' but during the 14th c. the word is confused, perhaps deliberately, with a new borrowing, *lollard* (from Dutch *lollaert*, a pious layman who mutters his prayers, from *lollen*, 'to mumble'), which is used to refer perjoratively to the followers of Wyclif" (97). The term is usually pejorative in Langland.

54. See *C-Text*, lines 108–45.

6. "The excellent, though illiterate, Bunyan": Reconfiguring Bunyan and His Book Within a Protestant Paradigm for Reading

1. Darnton, "Towards a History of Reading," 23.

2. John Brown, *John Bunyan: His Life, Times, and Work,* 3d ed. (London, 1887), 459.

3. Brown cites Charles Doe's comment that over one hundred thousand copies were printed in Bunyan's lifetime (458).

4. Brown, 439.

5. In *The Pilgrim's Progress,* (2d ed.), J. B. Wharey notes that this edition was considered the standard one until Robert Southey's appeared (vii).

6. Brown, 460. He notes as well that the engravings were printed together, four on a page, and inserted in the folio editions of 1736–37 and 1767.

7. Preface to *The Pilgrim's Progress, Adorned with Curious Sculptures by J. Sturt* by John Bunyan (London, 1757), viii.

8. For a further discussion of the reception of *The Pilgrim's Progress* by a lettered readership in the eighteenth century, see Keeble, "'Of him thousands daily Sing and Talk,'" in *Conventicle and Parnassus*, 246–48 (a section entitled "The Augustan Bunyan").

9. Preface, iii.

10. Preface, iv–v.

11. Preface, v–vi.

12. Preface, vi.

13. Preface, vi–vii.

14. Preface, vii.

15. A twelve-page advertisement for both current and forthcoming publications is at the back of the edition; the advertisement for the edition of *The Pilgrim's Progress* elucidates the publisher's strategy for appealing to a lettered audience. Unlike many of the other listings, which cite authorities who recommend the work, the notice for *The Pilgrim's Progress* requires no commendation. The advertisement puts the most emphasis on the embellishments of the edition:

> The Pilgrim's Progress. With a corrected text, considerably amplified marginal references, and an original Life of John Bunyan, by Robert Southey, Esq. LL. D., &c. &c. &c. The Embellishments of this work consist of a Series of large Vignettes, engraved on Wood by the first Artists, from original Designs by Mr. Harvey; a fine Portrait of the Author, and Two Principal Designs of the Valley of the Shadow of Death and of the Celestial City, painted by John Martin, Esq. These admired compositions are engraved in the *line manner* on *Copper*, by Mr. Smith as Frontispieces to Parts I. and II. of the work. The Designs of Mr. Harvey (twenty-seven in number) portray the main incidents of the Pilgrim's Journey, to an extent hitherto unattempted. (Southey edition, "Works Published During the Last Season," 12)

16. According to the *DNB*, Barton was a minor Quaker poet who was a friend of Southey and Lamb.

17. See Wharey's 2d edition, "Appendix: The Sleeping Portrait," 353–54, for its history.

18. John Bunyan, *The Pilgrim's Progress, with a Life of John Bunyan by Robert Southey, poet laureate* (London, 1832), ci.

19. Southey edition, ci.

20. Southey edition, lxxxiv.

21. See Richard Greaves, "Bunyan Through the Centuries: Some Reflections," *English Studies* 64 (1983): 113–21, for a discussion of the ways Bunyan fell out of favor with the educated public until Southey's "scholarly" edition (114–15).

22. Southey edition, iv. The verse is from Cowper's *Tirocinium, or a Review of Schools* (1784), lines 131–46.

23. Southey, "Life of John Bunyan," v–vi.

24. Southey, xxv.

25. Southey, vi.

26. Southey, xiv.

27. At one point, in talking about a passage in Bunyan's spiritual autobiography, Southey reveals his distaste for Bunyan's spiritual experience: ". . . and when it seemed to his *diseased imagination* that this text called audibly and loudly after him . . ." (xxxi–xxxii; italics mine).

28. Southey, xlii.

29. Southey, xlii. As an example of that thick crust of ignorance, Southey points to verses allegedly by Bunyan affixed to the margins of an edition of Foxe and comments that "the coarseness of that incrustation could hardly be conceived, if proofs of it were not preserved in his own handwriting" (lxii). He labels them "miserable doggerel" and rhetorically asks: "How is it possible that the man who wrote such illiterate and senseless verses in the margins of his Book of Martyrs, could have composed a treatise like this [*Some Gospel Truths Opened*], about the same time, or shortly afterward?" (xlix). His answer is that Bunyan had neither the knowledge nor aptitude for "versifying, . . . but in prose he wrote as he conversed and as he preached, using the plain straightforward language of the common life" (xlix).

30. Southey, xxii. Southey disputes claims that Bunyan deserved the status of martyr for his faith: "Bunyan has been, and no doubt will continue to be, most wrongfully represented as having been the victim of intolerant laws and prelatical oppression," arguing that Bunyan did not need to go to jail, for he did not differ with the Church of England except in the matter of "Infant-Baptism" (lxx).

31. Southey, lxxxviii.

32. Southey, lxxxviii.

33. Southey, lxxxvii.

34. Southey, xix, xc.

35. He discusses the "Advertisement" in some detail (lxxxix).

36. Southey, xc.

37. Southey, xcii.

38. Southey, xcvi.

39. Sir Walter Scott, "*The Pilgrim's Progress*, with a Life of John Bunyan, by Robert Southey," *Quarterly Review* 43 (1830), reprinted in *Sir Walter Scott: On Novelists and Fiction,* ed. Ioan Williams (London: Routledge & Kegan Paul, 1968), 379–80.

40. Scott, 393.

41. Responding to Southey's query about why Bunyan's craft was esteemed as "mean," Scott writes, "We believe the reason to be that the tinker's craft is, in Great Britain, commonly practiced by gypsies; and we surmise the probability that Bunyan's own family, though reclaimed and settled, might have sprung from this caste of vagabonds" (380). For the full scope of this debate, see

the many listings on the topic in James F. Forrest and Richard L. Greaves, *John Bunyan: A Reference Guide* (Boston: G. K. Hall & Co., 1982).

42. Scott, 380. D'Israeli's remark is in *Essays on the Literary Character* (1795). See Scott, 488 n.2.

43. Scott, 397.

44. Thomas Babington, Lord Macaulay, "*The Pilgrim's Progress, with a Life of John Bunyan.* By Robert Southey, Esq., LL.D. Poet Laureate. Illustrated with Engravings. 8vo. London: 1831," *Edinburgh Review,* Dec. 1830; reprinted in *Critical and Historical Essays,* ed. Hugh Trevor-Roper (New York, McGraw-Hill, 1965), 143–44.

45. Macaulay, 137.

46. Scott, 405.

47. For the complete listing from which these comments were taken see the introduction to *The Pilgrim's Progress* in Offor, 3:29–30.

48. See, for example, Nathaniel Hill's *The Ancient Poem of Guillaume de Guileville entitled the Pelerinage de L'Homme compared with the The Pilgrim's Progress of John Bunyan* (London, 1858), and L. A. H., "The Poet and the Dreamer. 1. *The Faerie Queene* by Edmund Spenser, 2. The *The Pilgrim's Progress* by John Bunyan," *The Methodist Quarterly Review* 40 (1858): 209–27.

49. James Blanton Wharey, *A Study of the Sources of Bunyan's Allegories, with Special Reference to Deguilleville's Pilgrimage of Man* (1904; reprint, New York: Gordian Press, 1968), 136.

50. G. R. Owst, *Literature and Pulpit in Medieval England* (Cambridge: Cambridge University Press, 1933), 98.

51. Harold Golder, "John Bunyan's Hypocrisy," *North American Review* 223 (1926): 323–32.

52. Quoted in Sharrock, *John Bunyan,* 72–73.

53. Sharrock, 74. See also Talon, *The Man and His Works,* 141–224.

54. Leavis, *Fiction and the Reading Public,* 87. See also L. D. Lerner, "Bunyan and the Puritan Culture," *Cambridge Journal* 7 (1954): 221–42, for an expansion of this thesis.

55. Brown, 262. This explanation of the break in the dream is almost universally accepted by Bunyan critics.

56. Tindall, *Mechanick Preacher,* viii.

57. Jack Lindsay, *John Bunyan: Maker of Myths* (London: Methuen Press, 1937).

58. See David Herreshoff, "Marxist Perspectives on Bunyan," in Collmer, 165.

59. For general discussions of the problem of sources and influence, see Talon, 166–72, and Hill, *Tinker and a Poor Man,* 197–209. In addition to arguing for Bunyan's religious experience as the best source for *The Pilgrim's*

Progress, Sharrock, in *John Bunyan*, proposes three "literary forms evolved by the Puritans" (95): the spiritual autobiography, the popular sermon or treatise, and the expository dialogue, and, as lesser influences, chapbook romances and emblem books (94–101). On emblem books as possible sources, see also Sharrock, "Bunyan and the English Emblem Writers," *Review of English Studies* 21 (1945): 105–116, and David J. Alpaugh, "Emblem and Interpretation in *The Pilgrim's Progress*," *ELH* 33 (1966): 299–314. On Bunyan's possible use of chapbooks, see Margaret Spufford, *Small Books and Pleasant Histories: Popular Fiction and its Readership in Seventeenth-Century England* (Cambridge: Cambridge University Press, 1981), 6–8, 156, 249, and 259. On other possible sources in popular literature, see several articles by Harold Golder: "Bunyan's Valley of the Shadow," *Modern Philology* 27 (1929): 55–72; "Bunyan's Giant Despair," *Journal of English and Germanic Philology* 30 (1931): 361–79; and "John Bunyan's Hypocrisy." On various aspects of folk culture as possible influences, see George W. Walton, "Bunyan's Proverbial Language," in Collmer, 7–34; Sharrock, "Life and Story in *The Pilgrim's Progress*," in Newey, *Critical and Historical Views*, 49–68; Nick Davis, "The Problem of Misfortune in *The Pilgrim's Progress*," in Newey, *Critical and Historical Views*, 182–204; Nick Shrimpton, "Bunyan's Military Metaphor," in Newey, *Critical and Historical Views*, 205–24; and S. J. Newman, "Bunyan's Solidness," in Newey, *Critical and Historical Views*, 225–50. On the possible influence of the dialogue and debate genres, see David Seed, "Dialogue and Debate in *The Pilgrim's Progress*," in Newey, *Critical and Historical Views*, 69–90. On sermons and satire, see Owst, 97–109, and Brean Hammond, "*The Pilgrim's Progress*: Satire and Social Comment," in Newey, *Critical and Historical Views*, 118–30. On Puritan meditation, see Kaufman, *Traditions in Puritan Meditation*.

60. For a very different view, one emphasizing the reader's passivity, see Thomas H. Luxon, "The Pilgrim's Passive Progress: Luther and Bunyan on Talking and Doing, Word and Way," *ELH* 53 (1986): 73–98.

61. Bunyan, *Grace Abounding*, 43.

62. "Apology," line 236.

63. See James F. Forrest, "Allegory as Sacred Sport: Manipulation of the Reader in Spenser and Bunyan," in Collmer, 93–112.

64. Bunyan, "To the Reader," *The Holy War*, 5.

65. There were a number of different figures used to describe the action of Scripture on the human heart, such as a hammer, for example. Here I am particularly interested in the figure of the plough because Bunyan himself uses it to describe both the action of the Holy Spirit and the reader's use of the book as an instrument. For other figures, see Lewalski, *Protestant Poetics*, chapter 6: "Protestant Emblematics and Religious Lyrics," 179–212, and John Knott, Jr., *The Sword of the Spirit*.

66. Delaune and Keach, *Tropologia*, 3:63.

67. Delaune and Keach, 3:65.

68. Delaune and Keach, 3:65.

69. Delaune and Keach, 3:65–66.

70. Delaune and Keach, 3:66.

71. John A. Alford makes this point in "The Role of the Quotations in *Piers Plowman*," *Speculum* 52 (1977): 80–99. He argues that Langland began with the scriptural texts and derived the substance of the poem from them.

72. Bale, *Scriptorum*, 474.

73. Roger Sharrock, "Spiritual Autobiography in *The Pilgrim's Progress*," *Review of English Studies* 24 (1948) 102–20.

74. Keeble, *Literary Culture*, makes a similar point: "*The Pilgrim's Progress* is 'about' Christian; but it is also about Bunyan himself, is, indeed, a reworking of *Grace Abounding*; it is about the state of England during the Restoration period, to which topical and satirical reference is several times made; it is about the Old Testament experience of similar circumstances; and it is about the new Testament resolution of both Israel's earlier and England's later history" (264).

75. Hill, *Tinker and a Poor Man*, 211–12.

76. Hill has pointed out that "Running through *The Pilgrim's Progress* is a strong sense of the superiority of the poor to the rich" (*Tinker and the Poor Man*, 211), and that all the "undesirable characters are almost obsessively labelled as lords and ladies, gentlemen and gentlewomen" (215).

77. Hill claims that Bunyan was a "passive millenarian" (*Tinker and a Poor Man*, 343).

78. Sharrock, ed., *Grace Abounding and The Pilgrim's Progress*, 148. Hereafter all quotations from *Grace Abounding* and *The Pilgrim's Progress* will be from this volume unless otherwise noted and will be indicated by page number in the body of the text.

79. Smith, "Of Prophecy," in *Select Discourses*, 222.

80. Tindall, 44. As Tindall suggests, Mr. Ignorance has typically been regarded as the image of one sectarian error or another; see, for example, Maurice Hussey, "Bunyan's 'Mr. Ignorance,'" *Modern Language Review* 44 (1949): 483–89, and John W. Draper, "Bunyan's Mr. Ignorance," *Modern Language Review* 22 (1927): 15–21. For a more sophisticated reading of this character, see James F. Forrest, "Bunyan's Ignorance and the Flatterer: A Study in the Literary Art of Damnation," *Studies in Philology* 60 (1963): 12–22. See also Keeble, *Literary Culture*, 207–8.

81. For a discussion of contemporary religious politics and class issues reflected in *The Pilgrim's Progress*, see Hill, *Tinker and a Poor Man*, 209–26.

82. Kaufmann offers the most illuminating discussion of Bunyan's conception of character, 89–105. I have adopted his categories of sincere and insincere

wayfarers and wayside memorials. See also Maureen Quilligan, *The Language of Allegory* (Ithaca and London: Cornell University Press, 1979), 128–29.

83. The compositional nature of Faithful's martyrdom is another indicator that Bunyan intended to present a generalized pattern of Christian experience derived from Scripture and from Foxe rather than a fictionalized presentation of his own life: "They therefore brought him out, to do with him according to their Law; and first they Scourged him, then they Buffetted him, then they Lanced his flesh with Knives; after that they Stoned him with Stones, then prickt him with their Swords, and last of all they burned him to Ashes at the Stake. Thus came *Faithful* to his end" (218). The different kinds of execution inflicted on Faithful recapitulate the different fates of traditional martyrs, rather than offering a realistic program for the execution of one individual.

84. See Dayton Haskin, "The Burden of Interpretation in *The Pilgrim's Progress*," *Studies in Philology* 79 (1982): 256–78.

85. Delaune and Keach, 3:63.

86. Lewalski, 13. See also Jacques Blondel, "Bunyan et la Bible dans *The Pilgrim's Progress*," *Les Langues Modernes* 67 (1973): 57–66.

87. Scholarship on the relationship between Scripture and *Grace Abounding* and *the Pilgrim's Progress* has journeyed quite a distance from the tentative theses put forward by Talon and Sharrock on how Biblical images come to life in *The Pilgrim's Progress*. Talon remarks that "Bunyan thought in images. He never really grasped his idea until he saw it personified; and so biblical metaphors came to populate—literally—the universe he created" (182). Sharrock claims that "in his attitude towards the Bible, Bunyan is like a child or a man of little reading not far from childhood, who interprets a poem or story by an old illustration which fills his mind and excludes fresh impressions" (*John Bunyan*, 99). My discussion of these issues has benefited from more recent research on Protestant hermeneutics in the following areas: first, the relationship between the Protestant self and the Bible; second, the role of the reader and problems of interpretation; third, the place of Scripture in Protestant ideology; and finally, Bunyan's use of specific scriptural sources. On the self and the Biblical text, see John Knott, Jr., "'Thou must live upon my Word': Bunyan and the Bible," in Keeble, *Conventicle and Parnassus*, 153–70; Forrest, "Allegory as Sacred Sport" in Collmer, 91–112; and Brainerd P. Stranahan, "Bunyan's Special Talent: Biblical Texts as 'Events' in *Grace Abounding* and *The Pilgrim's Progress*," *English Literary Renaissance* 11 (1981): 329–43. Knott also discusses Bunyan's gift for exploiting "the dramatic potential of biblical metaphors" in *Grace Abounding*, *The Pilgrim's Progress*, and *The Holy War* in *The Sword of the Spirit*, 131–63. On the reader's role in interpretation, see three articles by Dayton Haskin: "Bunyan's Scriptural Acts," in Collmer, 61–92, "*The Pilgrim's Prog-*

ress in the Context of Bunyan's Dialogue with the Radicals," and "The Burden of Interpretation," as well as Valentine Cunningham, "Glossing and Glozing: Bunyan and Allegory," in Keeble, *Conventicle and Parnassus*, 217–41. For an unusual, ahistorical view of the reader's role, see Stanley E. Fish, "Progress in *The Pilgrim's Progress*," in his *Self-Consuming Artifacts: The Experience of Seventeenth Century Literature* (Berkeley: University of California Press, 1972), 224–64. On the Bible in Protestant ideology, see two articles by Thomas H. Luxon: "Calvin and Bunyan on Word and Image: Is There a Text in Interpreter's House?," *English Literary Renaissance* 18 (1988): 438–59, and "The Pilgrim's Passive Progress," as well as Dayton Haskin, "Bunyan, Luther, and the Struggle with Belatedness in *Grace Abounding*," *University of Toronto Quarterly* 50 (1981): 300–313. On Bunyan's use of specific Biblical sources, see two articles by Brainerd P. Stranahan: "'With Great Delight': The Song of Solomon in *The Pilgrim's Progress*," *English Studies* 68 (1987): 220–27, and "Bunyan and the Epistle to the Hebrews: His Source for the Idea of Pilgrimage in *The Pilgrim's Progress*," *Studies in Philology* 79 (1982): 279–96, as well as N. H. Keeble, "The Way and the Ways of Puritan Story: Biblical Patterns in Bunyan and His Contemporaries," *English* 33 (1984): 209–32, and his *Literary Culture*, 263–82.

88. William Whittaker, *A Disputation on Sacred Scripture*, trans. William Fitzgerald (Cambridge: Parker Society, 1849), 433.

89. Whittaker, 404.

90. Lewalski, 117.

91. Lewalski, 117.

92. Lewalski, 131.

93. Kaufmann, 108.

94. Damrosch, *God's Plot and Man's Stories*, 154.

95. The following articles are useful discussions of Bunyan's view of the Bible in *Grace Abounding*: Margaret Olofson Thickstun, "The Preface to Bunyan's *Grace Abounding* as Pauline Epistle," *Notes and Queries* 32 (1985): 180–82; Felicity A. Nussbaum, "'By These Words I was Sustained': Bunyan's *Grace Abounding*," *ELH* 49 (1982): 18–34; Rebecca S. Beal, "*Grace Abounding to the Chief of Sinners*: John Bunyan's Pauline Epistle," *Studies in English Literature 1500–1900* 21 (1981): 147–60; and Peter J. Carlton, "Bunyan: Language, Convention, Authority," *ELH* 51 (1984): 17–32.

96. Sharrock, "Spiritual Autobiography," 102–20.

97. Sharrock, "Spiritual Autobiography," 109. See also Stranahan, "Bunyan's Special Talent."

98. See Stranahan, "Bunyan's Special Talent": "Since his verbal memory was so accurate, and his sensitivity to the predicaments of biblical personages was so keen, both Bunyan's own journey of faith and that of his fictional characters constitute a kind of literal reenactment of the truth of

Scriptural language" (343); "*Grace Abounding* also contains a notable example of another technique that was to become important for the composition of *The Pilgrim's Progress*. This is the ability to visualize a text of Scripture, to flesh it out with setting, characters, and action so that it becomes a little drama" (334).

99. For some further implications of this relationship between the Bible and the individual Christian reader, see Stranahan, "Bunyan's Special Talent," and Haskin, "The Burden of Interpretation."

100. "And those who have done well shall go into eternal life; but those who have done evil (will go) into eternal fire."

101. "For though I should walk in the midst of the shadow of death, I will fear no evils, for thou art with me."

102. John Knott is on the verge of this point when he argues that "Bunyan's narrative works by establishing the credibility of an entire world of spiritual experience, based upon the Word and opposed to the actual world," whose topgraphy "is determined largely by Bunyan's experience of Scripture, and the key to understanding Christian's progress through it is his understanding of the Word" (Knott, *The Sword of the Spirit*, 144, 147).

103. Delaune and Keach, *Tropologia*, 3:64.

104. All the biblical passages discussed below are cited by Bunyan in the margins of the first edition, unless otherwise noted.

105. On the marginalia, see Keeble, *Literary Culture*, 146–52, and Carolynn Van Dyke, *The Fiction of Truth: Structures of Meaning in Narrative and Dramatic Allegory* (Ithaca: Cornell University Press, 1985), 157–66.

106. This gloss was not in the first edition.

107. Only the Zech. 3.4 passage was cited in the first edition.

108. John Knott observes that Christian uses the Word as a "means of spiritual survival" (*The Sword of the Spirit*, 149).

109. Dayton Haskin in "*The Pilgrim's Progress* in the Context of Bunyan's Dialogue with the Radicals" approaches *The Pilgrim's Progress* as a conscious attempt on Bunyan's part to provide an analogue to the Bible, one which finds individual moral relevance in Biblical history: "Bunyan, like the radicals thought the real meaning of Scripture lies in its capacity for teaching moral and religious lessons, not in its record of historical truths. A fictional story can re-present the Bible's meaning, and the author presents his allegory as a reiteration of gospel-truth" (93).

110. Damrosch, 157.

7. "Would'st read thy self?": *The Pilgrim's Progress* as a "Perspective Glass" for Readers

1. C. C. Mish, "Bestsellers in Seventeenth-Century Fiction," *Papers of the Bibliographical Society of America* 47 (1953): 358–59.

2. Greaves, "Bunyan Through the Centuries," 113.

3. See Forrest and Greaves, *John Bunyan: A Reference Guide* cited hereafter as *Reference Guide*. Any subsequent scholarship on Bunyan's reception is greatly in their debt. Two essays give a comprehensive but succinct summary of the topic: the essay by Greaves cited above and an essay by N. H. Keeble, "'Of him thousands daily Sing and talk'" in Keeble, *Conventicle and Parnassus*, 241–63. See also Roger Sharrock, ed. *The Pilgrim's Progress: A Casebook* (London: Macmillan Press, 1976), cited hereafter as *Casebook*.

4. Keeble, in *Literary Culture*, notes that "the 22 seventeenth-century editions of *The Pilgrim's Progress* probably represent over 30,000 copies" (128). For an exploration of the profile of the nonconformist writers and readers, see chapter 4, "'Fit Audience Though Few'? Nonconformist Writers and their Readers," 127–55. Keeble speculates about Bunyan's initial intended readership: "The folk tale conventions and romance motifs of Part I, besides telling us something of Bunyan's own youthful reading, imply an originally intended readership rather below the level of yeomen, the people who bought chapbooks and popular romances. The milieu of Part II is more realistically social and sociable, that of a country town" (143).

5. Joyce Godber, *John Bunyan of Bedfordshire* (Bedford: Bedford County Council, County Records Office, 1972), 9, cited in Christopher Hill, *Tinker and Poor Man*, 375. For a fuller discussion of the topic, see chapter 29, "Bunyan and the World," 367–80.

6. Leavis, *Fiction and the Reading Public*, 87.

7. This example was given to me by the late Helen G. Hole. See *Friends Family Library* 6 (Philadelphia, 1842): 291.

8. Anonymous comment in *The Gentleman's Magazine* 11 (September, 1741): 488, cited in *Casebook*; Daniel and Samuel Lysons, *Magna Britania*, vol. 1, Part 1 (1813), 82, cited in *Reference Guide*.

9. Review of *Some Account of the Imprisonment of Mr. John Bunyan*, in *The Gentleman's Magazine* 35 (April, 1765), 168, quoted in *Casebook*, 50–51.

10. Roberta Florence Brinkley, ed., *Coleridge on the Seventeenth Century* (Duke University Press, 1955), 475–76, cited in *Casebook*, 53.

11. Richard Altick, *The English Common Reader: A Social History of the Mass Reading Public 1800–1900* (Chicago: University of Chicago Press, 1957), 255.

12. George Burder, *Bunyan's Pilgrim's Progress Versified*, 2d ed. (London, 1804), iii–iv, quoted in *Reference Guide*, 26.

13. Adam Clarke, *An Account of the Infancy, Religious and Literary Life, of Adam Clarke, LL.D.F.A.S.* (London, 1833), cited by Offor, 3:67.

14. John Buchan, *Pilgrim's Way: An Autobiography* (1940; reprint, New York: Carroll & Graf, 1984), 7–8.

15. For a fuller discussion of how World War I revived interest in Bunyan, see Greaves, "Bunyan Through the Centuries," 118.

16. Thompson, 31. For a discussion of other political implications of the text, see Herreshoff, "Marxist Perspectives on Bunyan," in Collmer, 161–85.

17. Thompson, 31, quoting Leavis, 97.

18. Hill, *Tinker and a Poor Man*, 375.

19. Vera Brittain, *Valiant Pilgrim: The Story of John Bunyan and Puritan England* (New York: Macmillan, 1950), 15.

20. Keeble, *Literary Culture*, 135, notes that explicit declarations of designs upon the reader are a hallmark of nonconformist writing.

21. See *Reference Guide*, 13.

22. Preface to *Voyage d'un Chrestien vers l'Eternite. Ecrit en Anglois, par Monsieur Bunjon, F.M. en Bedtfort; Et nouvellement traduit en Francois*, trans. Roger Sharrock, in *Casebook*, 44–46.

23. Preface, 44.

24. Preface, 44–45.

25. Preface, 45.

26. John Newton, Preface to Bunyan's *Works* (London, 1776), A3r.

27. Preface, 45.

28. Preface, 45.

29. Preface, 45.

30. Preface, 45–46.

31. Preface, 46.

32. T[homas] S[herman], *The Second Part of The Pilgrim's Progress* (London, 1682).

33. Sharrock, *John Bunyan*, 139. Sharrock regards the work as an "honest attempt to improve" *The Pilgrim's Progress*.

34. Quoted in Sharrock, 139.

35. Quoted in James Turner, "Bunyan's Sense of Place," in Newey, *Critical and Historical Views*, 91. Turner's essay is a superb reading of the cultural contrasts represented by the two opening passages.

36. Title page, *The Pilgrim's Progress From This World to that Which Is to Come: The Third Part* (London, 1693).

37. The *Reference Guide* dates *An Account of the Life and Actions of Mr. John Bunyan* as 1692, 7.

38. *The Pilgrim's Progress*, 13th ed. (1693), facing the title page.

39. *The Third Part*, A3r.

40. *The Third Part*, A4r.

41. *The Progress of the Christian Pilgrim* (London, 1705). Forrest and Greaves in the *Reference Guide* list the work as destroyed (10), but it was available in the British Library in the summer of 1985.

42. *The Progress of the Christian Pilgrim*, 27, 34.

43. Titles are taken from *Reference Guide*, 20, 25, 7, 17.

44. *Reference Guide*, 17, 29.

45. *Reference Guide*, 35, 37, 45.

46. For example, Charlotte Bronte's *Jane Eyre*: see Sandra M. Gilbert, "Plain Jane's Progress," *Signs* 2 (1977): 779–804. See also Gayle Edward Wilson, "'As John Bunyan Says': Bunyan's Influence on *Uncle Tom's Cabin*," *American Transcendental Quarterly* n.s. 1 (1987): 157–62; two articles by Vincent A. Newey, "Dorothea's Awakening: The Recall of Bunyan in *Middlemarch*," *Notes and Queries* 31 (1984): 497–99, and "The Disinherited Pilgrim: *Jude the Obscure* and *The Pilgrim's Progress*," *Durham University Journal* 80 (1987–88): 59–61; and Ronald R. Thomas, "The Novel and the Afterlife: The End of the Line in Bunyan and Beckett," *Modern Philology* 86 (1988–89): 385–97. For more comprehensive discussions, see also Keeble, "'Of him thousands daily Sing and talk,'" 256–57, and David E. Smith, *John Bunyan in America* (Bloomington: Indiana University Press, 1966), which discusses, among other topics, Bunyan's influence on Hawthorne, Louisa May Alcott, and e. e. cummings.

47. *Rest for the Weary Soul: or, the Pilgrim at his Journey's End. Being the Last Legacy of Mr. John Bunyan of Bedfordshire* (London, 1725). It is attributed to James Handley, who is the author of the preface. See the *Reference Guide*, 12.

48. *The Visions of John Bunyan, Being his Last Remains. Giving an Account of the Glories of Heaven and the Terrors of Hell, and of the World to Come* (London, 1725). The *Reference Guide* attributes the work to George Larkin, 13.

49. *Visions*, 132.

50. *Visions*, A3v.

51. Ebenezer Chandler and John Wilson, "Epistle to the Reader," in Bunyan's *Works* (London, 1692), 1:A1v.

52. Chandler and Wilson, A2r.

53. Chandler and Wilson, A2r.

54. See Greaves, "Bunyan Through the Centuries," 115, and Keeble, "'Of him thousands daily Sing and Talk,'" 248–51, for a more comprehensive discussion of the Evangelical reception of *The Pilgrim's Progress*.

55. George Whitefield, "Recommendatory Preface" to Bunyan's *Works*, 3d ed. (London, 1767), iii.

56. Offor, *Works*, 3: table of contents.

57. "Shut up for twelve years with his Bible, all the rags of popery and heathenism were stripped off, and he came out a living body of divinity, comparatively free from mere human doctrines or systems. The spirit of the prophets breathes in his language" (Offor, 3:9). Note the similarity to Whitefield's discussion of Bunyan's transformation by God through the operation of the Holy Ghost.

58. *The Pilgrim's Progress*, ed. Offor (London, 1856), xv–xxxi.

59. Offor, 3:30.

60. Whitefield, "Recommendatory Preface," iii.

61. Thomas Scott, Preface, *Original Notes to the Pilgrim's Progress* (London, 1801; reprint, Hartford, 1828), iv–v.

62. Mason, "Notes" to *The Pilgrim's Progress* (London, 1813), iii–iv.

63. Mason, 2.

64. Andronicus, *Key* (London, 1790), title page.

65. Andronicus, iv–v.

66. *The Pilgrim's Progress* (London, 1816), title page.

67. It should be noted that, according to Roger Sharrock ("'When at the first I took my Pen in hand': Bunyan and the Book," in Keeble, *Conventicle and Parnassus*, 71–90), even Bunyan's printers tried to make his language more "genteel" in later editions of *Grace Abounding* by regularizing his grammar and eliminating colloquialisms, and that such efforts were "certainly not resisted by Bunyan" (88–89).

68. M. S., *The Heavenly Passenger, Or The Pilgrim's Progress From This World to that Which Is to Come*, London, 1687, A2r.

69. Ager Scholae, *The Pilgrim's Passage in Poesie: to the Palace Beautiful, in the Chamber of Peace* (London, 1697); *The Pilgrim's Passage, in Poesie, from the Palace Beautiful, to the Meeting with Faithful* (London, 1698). I will designate these two installments as I and II in the notes.

70. Scholae, I:32.

71. Scholae, I:1.

72. Scholae, "To the Charitable Reader," I:A2r.

73. Scholae, I:A2r.

74. Scholae, II:A2r–2v.

75. Scholae, II:A2v.

76. Scholae, II:A3v.

77. Scholae, II:A3r–3v.

78. Adam Clarke, in a postscript to *The Pilgrim's Progress*, ed. by David M'Nicoll (London, 1809), xxx–xxxi.

79. Burder, A1r–1v.

80. Scott, Preface, iii.

81. *Explanation of the Pilgrim's Progress, Abridged and Adapted to the Capacities of Children, In a Dialogue Between a Child, and His Mother, By a Lady* (London, 1808).

82. Isaac Taylor, *Bunyan Explained to a Child; Being Pictures and Poems, Founded Upon The Pilgrim's Progress* (London, 1825).

83. *Lady*, A2r.

84. For a comprehensive survey of the afterlife of Bunyan's text in American children's books, see Ruth K. MacDonald, *Christian's Children:*

The Influence of John Bunyan's "The Pilgrim's Progress" on American Children's Literature, American University Studies Series 25, vol. 10 (New York: Peter Lang, 1989), a book that should be used with caution.

85. Mrs. Sherwood, *The Infant's Progress From the Valley of Destruction to Everlasting Glory* (London, 1821). I wish to thank my colleague Mary Burgan for calling Mrs. Sherwood's book and its relevance to my interests to my attention. Mrs. Sherwood also wrote another version of *The Pilgrim's Progress* for a somewhat different audience. *The Indian Pilgrim; or, the Progress of the Pilgrim Nazareenee, (Formerly called Goonah Purist, or the Slave of Sin,) From the City of the Wrath of God to the City of Mount Zion* (London, 1818), written during her stay in India, was intended to appeal "to the taste, the manners, and the peculiar prejudices of Hindoostann" (vi), although she was unable to publish it until her return to England.

86. Mrs. Sherwood, *Infant's Progress*, Preface, iii.

87. Preface, iii–iv.

88. Sherwood, 7.

89. Sherwood, 104–6.

90. Preface, iv–v.

91. Preface, iv.

92. Sherwood, 1.

93. Sherwood, 205.

94. Sherwood, 171–72.

95. Sherwood, 19.

96. Sherwood, 23.

97. Sherwood, 122.

98. Sherwood, 113–15.

99. See, for example, Mary Godolphin's *The pilgrim's progress, in words of one syllable* (New York: G. Routledge and Sons, n.d.). For a detailed discussion of children's editions see MacDonald, chapter 6: "'The Stripling of the Day': Children's Editions of *The Pilgrim's Progress* in America," 137–69.

100. Fussell, 138.

101. See J. B. Wharey, *The Pilgrim's Progress*, 2d ed., for a complete listing of substantive additions, xiii.

102. See Hill, *Tinker and a Poor Man*, 26–27.

103. Hill, *Tinker and a Poor Man*, 227.

104. On Part II, see Hill, *Tinker and a Poor Man*, 226–30. See also James F. Forrest, "Vision, Form, and the Imagination in the Second Part of *The Pilgrim's Progress* (1684)," *The Journal of Narrative Technique* 13 (1983): 109–16; John R. Knott, Jr., "Bunyan and the Holy Community," *Studies in Philology* 80 (1983): 200–225; and Thickstun, 439–53.

105. Keeble, "'Of him thousands daily Sing and Talk,'" 246.

106. John Colin Dunlop, *The History of Fiction: Being a Critical Account of the Most Celebrated Prose Works of Fiction* . . ., 2d ed. (London, 1814), 2:293, cited in *Reference Guide*, 30.

107. Mark Twain, *Adventures of Huckleberry Finn* (1885; rev. ed. Berkeley: University of California Press, 1985), 137.

108. Macaulay, 132–33.

Bibliography

Primary Sources

Editions of *Piers Plowman*

Bennett, J. A. W., ed. *The Vision of Pierce Plowman, now fyrst imprinted by Robert Crowley.* . . . London, 1550. Facsimile reprint. David Paradine Developments, 1976.

Crowley, Robert, ed. *The Vision of Pierce Plowman,* by William Langland. 3 eds. London, 1550.

Kane, George, ed. *Piers Plowman: The A-Version,* by William Langland. London: Athlone Press, 1960.

Kane, George, and E. Talbot Donaldson, eds. *Piers Plowman: The B-Version,* by William Langland. London: Athlone Press, 1975.

Langland, William. *The Vision of Piers the Ploughman, with Do-well, Do-bet, and Do-best* (Manuscript of C-Text). British Museum, MS Add. 35157.

Pearsall, Derek, ed. *Piers Plowman: An Edition of the C-Text,* by William Langland. London: Edward Arnold, 1978.

Rodgers, Owen, ed. *The Vision of Pierce Plowman, Printed from the author's old copy. With Pierce the Ploughman Crede.* London, 1561.

Skeat, W. W., ed. *The Vision of William Concerning Piers the Plowman.* . . . by William Langland. E.E.T.S. o.s. 81. London: N. Trubner & Co., 1884.

Skeat, W. W., ed. *The Vision of William Concerning Piers the Plowman . . . Together with Richard the Redeless,* by William Langland. Oxford: Oxford University Press, 1886. Reprint. Oxford: Oxford University Press, 1968.

Wright, Thomas, ed. *The Vision and Creed of Piers Ploughman.* 2d ed., rev. London, 1856.

Apocryphal *Plowman* Texts

The Bankett of Johan the Reve, Unto piers ploughman / Laurens Laborer / Tomylyn Tailyor, and Hobbe of the hille / with other. British Museum, MS Harley 207.

A godlye dyalogue and dysputation betwene Pyers plowman and a popish preest / concernyng the supper of the lorde. Antwerp?, 1540?–1553?

I playne Piers which can not flatter. Antwerp?, 1540?

Pierce the Ploughmans Crede. London, 1553.

Pierce the Ploughman's Crede . . . to which is appended God Speed the Plough. Edited by W. W. Skeat. E.E.T.S. o.s. 30, 1867. Reprint. New York: Greenwood Press, 1969.

"The Plow-Mans Complaint, The Freeholders Proposition, And, The High-shoes Resolution." London, 1678. Bodleian Library. Firth Collection, b.20 (f.54).

"The Plow-mans Prophecie, Or, The Country-mans Calculation." London, 1680. Bodleian Library. Rawlinson Collection, 566 (120).

The Plowman's Tale. Showing by the doctrine and lives of the Romish Clergy, that the Pope is AntiChrist and they his Ministers. London, 1606.

The Praier and complaynte of the plowman unto Christe: Written not longe after the year of oure Lord A thousand and three hundred. Edited by William Tyndale? Antwerp, 1531?

A Proper Dialogue Between a Gentilman and a Husbandman eche complayning to the other their miserable calamitie, through the ambition of the clergy. An ABC of Spirituality. London, 1530.

Pyers the plowmans exhortation, unto the lordes, knightes and burgoysses of the Parlyamenthouse. By Robert Crowley? London, 1550.

Read me, for I am of great Antiquitie. / I plaine piers which cannot flatter . . . I am the Grandsier of Martin mareprelitte. London? 1590.

Editions of Bunyan's Works

Bunyan, John. *Grace Abounding to the Chief of Sinners and The Pilgrim's Progress From This World to that Which is to Come.* Edited by Roger Sharrock. London: Oxford University Press, 1966.

———. *The Holy War.* Edited by Roger Sharrock and James F. Forrest. Oxford: Clarendon Press, 1980.

———. *The Life and Death of Mr. Badman.* Edited by Roger Sharrock and James F. Forrest. Oxford: Clarendon Press, 1988.

———. *The Pilgrim's Progress as Originally Published by John Bunyan, Being a Facsimile Reproduction of the First Edition.* 1875. Reprint. Old Woking, Surrey: The Gresham Press, 1978.

————. *The Pilgrim's Progress. By John Bunyan.* Edited by James B. Wharey. Revised by Roger Sharrock. Oxford: Clarendon Press, 1960.

————. *The Pilgrim's Progress From This World To that Which is to Come.* London, 1678.

————. Preface. *The Pilgrim's Progress, Adorned with Curious Sculptures by J. Sturt.* London, 1757.

Chandler, Ebenezer, and John Wilson. "Epistle to the Reader." In *Works of John Bunyan.* London, 1692.

Gilpin, Joshua, ed. "To the Reader." In *The Pilgrim's Progress.* London, 1810.

Mason, William. "Explanatory Notes." In *The Pilgrim's Progress.* London, 1813.

M'Nicoll, David, ed. "The Life of John Bunyan." In *The Pilgrim's Progress.* London, 1809.

Newton, John. Preface. *The Works of John Bunyan.* London, 1776.

Offor, George, ed. *The Complete Works of John Bunyan.* 3 vols. Glasgow, 1853. Reprint. New York: AMS, 1978.

————. ed. "Memoir of John Bunyan." In *The Pilgrim's Progress . . . A New Edition with a Memoir and Notes,* by John Bunyan. London, 1856.

Scott, Thomas, ed. "Life" and "Original Notes." In *The Pilgrim's Progress.* London, 1801.

Southey, Robert., ed. "The Life of John Bunyan." In *The Pilgrim's Progress, with a Life of John Bunyan by Robert Southey, poet laureate.* London, 1832.

Stebbing, Henry, ed. *The Complete Works of John Bunyan.* 4 vols. London, 1859.

Whitefield, George. "Recommendatory Preface." In *Works of John Bunyan.* 2 vols. 3d ed. London, 1767.

Adaptations, Transformations, Keys, and Bunyan Apocrypha

Andronicus [pseud.]. *A Key to The Pilgrim's Progress . . . in a Series of Letters to a Friend.* London, 1790.

Burder, George. *Bunyan's Pilgrim's Progress Versified.* 2d. ed. London, 1804.

Godolphin, Mary. *The pilgrim's progress, in words of one syllable.* New York: G. Routledge and Sons, n.d.

[Handley, James]. *Rest for the Weary Soul: or, The Pilgrim at his Journey's End. Being the Last Legacy of Mr. John Bunyan of Bedfordshire.* London, 1725.

[Larkin, George.] *The Visions of John Bunyan, Being his Last Remains. Giving an Account of the Glories of Heaven and the Terrors of Hell, and of the World to Come.* London, 1725.

The Pilgrim's Progress From This World to That which is to come: The Third Part. London, 1693.

The Progress of the Christian Pilgrim. London, 1705.

S., M. *The Heavenly Passenger, Or, The Pilgrim's Progress From This World to that Which Is to Come.* London, 1687.

Scholae, Ager. *The Pilgrim's Passage, in Poesie, from the Palace Beautiful, to the Meeting with Faithful.* London, 1698.

———. *The Pilgrim's Passage in Poesie, to the Palace Beautiful, in the Chamber of Peace.* London, 1697.

S[herman], T[homas]. *The Second Part of The Pilgrim's Progress.* London, 1682.

Sherwood, Mrs. *The Infant's Progress From the Valley of Destruction to Everlasting Glory.* London, 1821.

Reference Works, 1500–1800

Bale, John. *Illustrium Maioris Britanniae Scriptorum . . . Summarium.* Wesel, 1548.

———. *Index Britanniae Scriptorum . . . John Bale's Index of British and Other Writers.* Edited by Lane R. Poole and Mary Bateson. Oxford: Clarendon Press, 1902.

———. *Scriptorum Illustrium maioris Brytanniae . . . Catalogus.* 2 vols. Basel, 1557–59.

Camden, William. *Remains Concerning Britain.* London, 1603.

Foxe, John. *Acts and Monuments.* 3 vols. London, 1632.

———. *Acts and Monuments.* 3 vols. London, 1684.

Fuller, Thomas. *The History of the Worthies of England.* Edited by John Nichols. London, 1811.

Greaves, William. *The History of the Church of Britain.* London, 1667.

Puttenham, George. *The Arte of English Poesie, A Facsimile Reproduction.* Edited by Edward Arber. 1906. Reprint with an introduction by Baxter Hathaway. Kent, Ohio: Kent State University Press, 1970.

Smith, G. G. *Elizabethan Critical Essays.* 2 vols. Oxford: Clarendon Press, 1904.

Stowe, John. *The Annales of England.* 1580 and 1592. Reprint. London, 1600.

———. *A Survey of London.* London, 1603.

Strype, John. *Ecclesiastical Memorials.* London, 1721.

Warton, Thomas. *History of English Poetry.* 4 vols. 1774. Reprint. New York: Johnson Reprint Corporation, 1968.

Weever, John. *Ancient Funeral Monuments.* London, 1631.

Religious Tracts

Baylie, Lewis. *The Practice of Pietie: Directing a Christian how to walk That He Might Please God.* London, 1627.

Bockett, J. B. *The Poor Mechanick's Plea Against the Rich Clergy's Oppression.* London, 1700.

Bury, E. *A Help to Holy Walking, or a Guide to Glory.* London, 1627.

Crofton, Z. *The Hard Way to Heaven Explained and Applied.* London, 1664.

Crowley, Robert. *The Voyce of the Last Trumpet . . . calling al estats of men to the right path of their vocation.* London, 1550.

Delaune, Thomas, and Benjamin Keach. *Tropologia, or, A Key to Open Scripture-Metaphors.* London, 1681.

Dell, William. *Several Sermons and Discourses of William Dell Minister of the Gospel.* London, 1652. Reprint. 1709.

Denny, Samuel. *Pelecanicidium: Or the Christian Advisor Against Self-Murder. Together with a Guide, and the Pilgrim's Pass to the Land of the Living.* London, 1653.

Dent, Arthur. *The Plaine Man's Path-Way to Heaven. Wherein every man may clearly see whether he shall be saved or damned. Set forth dialogue-wise, for the better understanding of the simple.* London, 1601.

Ferguson, Robert. *The Interest of Reason in Religion; With the Import and Use of Scripture-Metaphors; and the Nature of the Union Betwixt Christ & Believers.* London, 1675.

Fleming, Abraham. *The Footpath of Faith and the Highway to Heaven.* London, 1581.

———. *The Footpath to Felicitie, Which everie Christian must walk in.* London, 1581.

I., T. *The Pathway to the Pleasant Pasture of delightsome and Eternal Paradyse.* London, 1577.

Keith, George. *The Way to the City of God Described.* London, 1669.

———. "To the reader." In *The Way to the City of God Described.* 2d. ed. London, 1678.

Lever, Christopher. *The Holy Pilgrime, Leading the Way to Heaven: Or a Divine Direction in the Way of Life.* London, 1618.

Lindsay, David. *The Godly Man's Journey: Containing Ten Several Treatises.* London, 1625.

M., J. *The Soul's Pilgrimage to Celestial Glory: Or a Perfect Way to Heaven and to God.* London, 1634.

Nesse, Christopher. *A Christian's Walk and Work on Earth Until He Attain Heaven.* London, 1678.

Patrick, Simon. *The Parable of the Pilgrim: Written to a Friend.* London, 1665.

Perkins, William. *Works.* 3 vols. Cambridge, 1608.

A Petition directed to her most excellent Majestie. . . . Middleburg, 1592?.

Prideaux, John. *Sacred Eloquence: Or, the Art of Rhetorick, As it is layd down in Scripture.* London, 1659.

Prynne, William. *Histrio-Mastix.* London, 1633.

R., M., Gent[leman]. *The Pilgrim's Pass to the New Jerusalem: Or the Serious Christian his Enquiries after Heaven.* London, 1659.

Reading, John. *A Guide to the Holy City: Or Directions and Helps to a Holy Life.* London, 1651.

Smith, John. *The Mysterie of Rhetorique Unvailed.* London, 1657.

Smith, John. *Select Discourses.* London, 1660.

Tuke, Thomas. *The Highway to Heaven: Or the Doctrine of Election, Effective Vocation, Justification, and Sanctification, and Eternal Life.* London, 1609.

Whittaker, William. *A Disputation on Sacred Scripture.* Translated by William Fitzgerald. Cambridge: Parker Society, 1849.

Miscellaneous Editions

Buchan, John. *Pilgrim's Way: An Autobiography.* 1940. Reprint. New York: Carroll & Graf, 1984.

Boswell, John. *The Life of Samuel Johnson.* Edited by C. B. Tinker. 1904. Reprint revised by R. W. Chapman. Oxford: Oxford University Press, 1960.

Chaucer, Geoffrey. *The Workes of Our Ancient and learned Poet Geoffrey Chaucer, newly printed.* . . . Edited by William Thynne. 2d. ed. London, 1542.

Dobson, R. B. *The Peasants' Revolt of 1381.* New York: St. Martin's Press, 1970.

Drayton, Michael. *The Works of Michael Drayton.* Edited by William J. Hebel. 5 vols. Oxford: Basil Blackwell, 1932.

Friends Family Library. vol. 6. Philadelphia, 1842.

Furnival, Frederick J., ed. *Political, Religious and Love Poems.* E.E.T.S. o.s., no. 15. London: Kegan Paul, Tench, Trubner, 1866. Reprint. 1903.

Gascoigne, George. *The Steele Glas A Satyre compiled by George Gascoigne Esquire. Togither with the Complainte of Phylomon. An Elegie.* . . . London, 1576.

Gower, John. *The Complete Works of John Gower.* Edited by G. C. Macaulay. 4 vols. Oxford: Clarendon Press, 1899–1902.

Heyworth, Peter L., ed. *Jack Upland, Friar Daw's Reply and Upland's Rejoinder.* London: Oxford University Press, 1968.

Latimer, Hugh. *Selected Sermons of Hugh Latimer.* Edited by Allan G. Chester. Charlottesville: The University of Virginia Press, 1968.

Manley, John M., and Edith Rickert, eds. *The Text of The Canterbury Tales,* by Geoffrey Chaucer. 8 vols. Chicago: University of Chicago Press, 1940.

Milton, John. "An Apology Against a Pamphlet." In *The Complete Prose Works of John Milton.* Vol. 1. Edited by Don M. Wolfe. New Haven: Yale University Press, 1953.

Spenser, Edmund. "A Letter of the Authors." In *Poetical Works.* Edited by J. C. Smith and E. de Selincourt. Oxford: Oxford University Press, 1912. Reprint. 1970.

Thynne, Francis. *Animadversions upon the Annotations and corrections of Some Imperfections of Impressions of Chaucer's Workes. . . .* Edited by F. J. Furnival. Chaucer Society, 2d series, no. 13. London, 1875.

Trollope, Anthony. *The Small House at Allington.* Oxford: Oxford University Press, 1970.

Twain, Mark. *Adventures of Huckleberry Finn.* 1885. Rev. ed. Berkeley: University of California Press, 1985.

Wright, T., and J. Halliwell, eds. *Reliquae Antiquae.* London, 1841.

Secondary Materials

Alford, John A. "The Role of the Quotations in *Piers Plowman.*" *Speculum* 52 (1977): 80–99.

————, ed. *A Companion to Piers Plowman.* Berkeley: University of California Press, 1988.

Alpaugh, David J. "Emblem and Interpretation in *The Pilgrim's Progress.*" *ELH* 33 (1966): 299–314.

Altick, Richard. *The English Common Reader: A Social History of the Mass Reading Public 1800–1900.* Chicago: University of Chicago Press, 1957.

Anderson, Judith. *The Growth of a Personal Voice: Piers Plowman and The Faerie Queene.* New Haven: Yale University Press, 1971.

Aston, Margaret. *Lollards and Reformers: Images and Literacy in Late Medieval Religion.* London: Hambledon Press, 1984.

Babington, Thomas, Lord Macaulay. Review of *The Pilgrim's Progress, with a Life of John Bunyan.* Edited by Robert Southey. *Edinburgh Review,* December 1830. Reprinted in *Critical and Historical Essays.* Edited by Hugh Trevor-Roper. New York: McGraw Hill, 1965.

Barney, Stephen A. "The Plowshare of the Tongue: The Progress of a Symbol from the Bible to *Piers Plowman.*" *Mediaeval Studies* 35 (1973): 261–93.

Beal, Rebecca S. "*Grace Abounding to the Chief of Sinners*: John Bunyan's Pauline Epistle." *Studies in English Literature 1500–1900* 21 (1981): 147–60.

Bellamy, Joan. "John Bunyan and the Democratic Tradition." *Zeitschrift für Anglistik und Amerikanistik* 27 (1979): 218–24.

Blondel, Jacques. "Allégorie et Réalisme dans *The Pilgrim's Progress* de Bunyan." Etudes de Critique et d'Histoire Littéraire, no. 28[61–63], *Archives des Lettres Modernes* 3 (1959): 3–48.

———. "Bunyan et la Bible dans *The Pilgrim's Progress.*" *Les Langues Modernes* 67 (1973), 57–66.

Bloomfield, Morton W. *Piers Plowman as a Fourteenth-Century Apocalypse.* New Brunswick, N.J.: Rutgers University Press, 1961.

Brittain, Vera. *Valiant Pilgrim: The Story of John Bunyan and Puritan England.* New York: Macmillan, 1950.

Brown, John. *John Bunyan: His Life, Times, and Work.* 3d. ed. London, 1887.

Burrow, J. A. "The Audience of *Piers Plowman.*" *Anglia* 75 (1957): 373–84. Reprinted with corrections and a postscript in his *Essays on Medieval Literature*, 102–16. Oxford: Clarendon Press.

Cantarow, Ellen. "A Wilderness of Opinions Confounded: Allegory and Ideology." *College English* 34 (1972): 215–52.

Carlson, Leland H., ed. *Martin Marprelate, Gentleman: Master Job Thockmorton Laid Open in His Colors.* San Marino: Huntington Library, 1981.

Carlton, Peter J. "Bunyan: Language, Convention, Authority." *ELH* 51 (1984): 17–32.

Carpenter, Kenneth E., ed. *Books and Society in History.* New York: R. R. Bowker, 1983.

Chester, Allan G. "'The New Learning': A Semantic Note." *Studies in the Renaissance* 2 (1955): 138–47.

Clarke, M. V., and V. H. Galbraith. "The Deposition of Richard II." *Bulletin of the John Rylands Library* 14 (1930): 164–89.

Coleman, Janet. *English Literature in History, 1350–1400: Medieval Readers and Writers.* London: Hutchinson, 1981.

Collmer, Robert G., ed. *Bunyan in Our Time.* Kent, Ohio: Kent State University Press, 1989.

Cope, Jackson I. "The Progresses of Bunyan and Symon Patrick." *ELH* 55 (1988): 599–614.

Crawford, William. "Robert Crowley's Editions of *Piers Plowman*: A Bibliographical and Textual Study." Ph.D. diss., Yale, 1957.

Culler, Jonathan. *Structuralist Poetics: Structuralism, Linquistics, and the Study of Literature.* Ithaca: Cornell University Press, 1975.

Cunningham, Valentine. "Glossing and Glozing: Bunyan and Allegory." In *John Bunyan: Conventicle and Parnassus*, edited by N. H. Keeble, 215–40. Oxford: Clarendon Press, 1988.

Damrosch, Leopold, Jr. *God's Plot and Man's Stories: Studies in the Fictional Imagination from Milton to Fielding.* Chicago: University of Chicago Press, 1985.

Darnton, Robert. *The Business of Enlightenment: A Publishing History of the*

Encyclopedie, 1775–1800. Cambridge: Harvard University Press, 1979.

————. *The Great Cat Massacre and Other Episodes in French Cultural History*. New York: Vintage Books, 1984.

————. *The Literary Underground of the Ancien Regime*. Cambridge: Harvard University Press, 1982.

————. "Towards a History of Reading." *Princeton Alumni Weekly*, 8 Aug. 1987.

————. "What is the History of Books?" In *Books and Society in History*, edited by Kenneth E. Carpenter, 3–26. New York: R. R. Bowker, 1983.

Davidson, Cathy N. *Revolution and the Word: The Rise of the Novel in America*. New York: Oxford University Press, 1986.

Davis, Natalie Zemon. *Society and Culture in Early Modern France*. Stanford: Stanford University Press, 1975. Reprint. 1985.

Davis, Nick. "The Problem of Misfortune in *The Pilgrim's Progress*." In *The Pilgrim's Progress: Critical and Historical Views*, edited by Vincent A. Newey, 182–204. Totowa, N.J.: Barnes & Noble, 1980.

Donaldson, E. Talbot. *Piers Plowman: The C-Text and Its Poet*. New Haven: Yale University Press, 1949.

Draper, John W. "Bunyan's Mr. Ignorance." *Modern Language Review* 22 (1927): 15–21.

Fèbvre, Lucien, and Henri-Jean Martin. *The Coming of the Book*. Translated by David Gerard. London: NLB, 1976.

Fish, Stanley E. *Is There a Text in This Class?: The Authority of Interpretive Communities*. Baltimore: Johns Hopkins University Press, 1978.

————. "Progress in *The Pilgrim's Progress*." In *Self-Consuming Artifacts: The Experience of Seventeenth-Century Literature*. 224–64. Berkeley: University of California Press, 1972.

Forrest, James F. "Allegory as Sacred Sport: Manipulation of the Reader in Spenser and Bunyan." In *Bunyan in Our Time*, edited by Robert G. Collmer, 91–112. Kent, Ohio: Kent State University Press, 1989.

————. "Bunyan's Ignorance and the Flatterer: A Study in the Literary Art of Damnation." *Studies in Philology* 60 (1963): 12–22.

————. "Vision, Form, and the Imagination in the Second Part of *The Pilgrim's Progress* (1684)." *The Journal of Narrative Technique* 13 (1983): 109–16.

Forrest, James F., and Richard L. Greaves. *John Bunyan: A Reference Guide*. Boston: G. K. Hall & Co., 1982.

Freund, Elizabeth. *The Return of the Reader: Reader-Response Criticism*. London: Methuen, 1987.

Fussell, Paul. *The Great War and Modern Memory*. 1975. Reprint. New York: Oxford University Press, 1979.

Gadamer, Hans-Georg. "The Universality of the Hermeneutical Problem"

and "On the Scope and Function of Hermeneutical Reflection." In
Philosophical Hermeneutics, translated and edited by David E. Linge,
3–17 and 18–43. Berkeley: University of California Press, 1976.

Gilbert, Sandra M. "Plain Jane's Progress." *Signs* 2 (1977): 779–804.

Ginsberg, Carlo. *The Cheese and the Worms: The Cosmos of a Sixteenth-
Century Miller.* Translated by John and Anne Tedeschi. 1980. Reprint.
New York: Penguin Books, 1982.

Golder, Harold. "Bunyan's Giant Despair." *Journal of English and Germanic
Philology* 30 (1931): 361–79.

———. "Bunyan's Valley of the Shadow." *Modern Philology* 27 (1929): 55–72.

———. "John Bunyan's Hypocrisy." *North American Review* 223 (1926):
323–32.

Goldsmith, Margaret E. *The Figure of Piers Plowman: The Image on the
Coin.* Cambridge: D. S. Brewer, 1981.

Gradon, Pamela. "*Piers Plowman* and the Ideology of Dissent." *Proceedings
of the British Academy* 66 (1980): 179–205. Reprinted in *Middle English
Literature: British Academy Gollancz Lectures*, edited by J. A. Burrows,
195–221. Oxford: Oxford University Press, 1989.

Graff, Harvey J., *The Legacies of Literacy: Continuities and Contradictions in
Western Culture and Society.* Bloomington: Indiana University Press, 1987.

———. ed. *Literacy and Social Development in the West: A Reader.* Cambridge: Cambridge University Press, 1981.

Greaves, Richard. "Bunyan Through the Centuries: Some Reflections."
English Studies 64 (1983): 113–21.

H., L. A. "The Poet and the Dreamer. 1. *The Faerie Queene* by Edmund
Spenser. 2. *The Pilgrim's Progress* by John Bunyan." *The Methodist
Quarterly Review* 40 (1858): 209–27.

Haller, William. *The Elect Nation: The Meaning and Relevance of Foxe's Book
of Martyrs.* New York: Harper & Row, 1963.

Hammond, Brean. "*The Pilgrim's Progress*: Satire and Social Comment." In
The Pilgrim's Progress: Critical and Historical Views, edited by Vincent
A. Newey, 118–31. Totowa, N.J.: Barnes & Noble, 1980.

Haskin, Dayton. "Bunyan, Luther, and the Struggle with Belatedness in
Grace Abounding." *University of Toronto Quarterly* 50 (1981): 300–313.

———. "Bunyan's Scriptural Acts." In *Bunyan in Our Time*, edited by Robert
G. Collmer, 61–92. Kent, Ohio: Kent State University Press, 1989.

———. "The Burden of Interpretation in *The Pilgrim's Progress.*" *Studies in
Philology* 79 (1982): 256–78.

———. "*The Pilgrim's Progress* in the Context of Bunyan's Dialogue with the
Radicals." *Harvard Theological Review* 77:1 (1984): 73–94.

Herrshoff, David. "Marxist Perspectives on Bunyan." In *Bunyan in Our
Time*, edited by Robert G. Collmer, 161–85. Kent Ohio: Kent State

University Press, 1989.

Hill, Christopher. *A Tinker and a Poor Man: John Bunyan and His Church, 1628–1688.* 1988. Reprint. New York: Alfred A. Knopf, 1989.

Hill, Nathaniel. *The Ancient Poem of Guillaume de Guileville entitled the Pelerinage de l'Homme compared with The Pilgrim's Progress of John Bunyan.* London, 1858.

Hudson, Anne. "Epilogue: The Legacy of *Piers Plowman.*" In *A Companion to Piers Plowman,* edited by John A. Alford, 251–66. Berkeley: University of California Press, 1988.

————. *Lollards and Their Books.* London: Hambledon Press, 1985.

————. *Premature Revolution: Wycliffite Texts and Lollard History.* Oxford: Clarendon Press, 1988.

————. ed. *Selections from English Wycliffite Writings.* Cambridge: Cambridge University Press, 1978.

Hussey, Maurice. "Bunyan's 'Mr. Ignorance'." *Modern Language Review* 44 (1949): 483–89.

Iser, Wolfgang. *The Act of Reading: A Theory of Aesthetic Response.* Baltimore: Johns Hopkins University Press, 1978.

Jauss, Hans Robert. *Toward an Aesthetics of Reception.* Translated by Timothy Bahti. Minneapolis: University of Minnesota Press, 1982.

Kane, George. *Piers Plowman: The Evidence for Authorship.* London: Athlone Press, 1965.

Kaufmann, U. Milo. *The Pilgrim's Progress and Traditions of Puritan Meditation.* New Haven: Yale University Press, 1966.

Keeble, N. H. *The Literary Culture of Nonconformity in Later Seventeenth-Century England.* Athens: The University of Georgia Press, 1987.

————. "'Of him thousands daily Sing and Talk'." In *John Bunyan: Conventicle and Parnassus,* 241–63. Oxford: Clarendon Press, 1988.

————. "The Way and the Ways of Puritan Story: Biblical Patterns in Bunyan and His Contemporaries." *English* 33 (1984): 209–32.

————, ed. *John Bunyan: Conventicle and Parnassus.* Oxford: Clarendon Press, 1988.

Kelly, Robert L. "Hugh Latimer as Piers Plowman." *Studies in English Literature 1500–1900* 17 (1977): 13–26.

Kendall, Ritchie D. *The Drama of Dissent: The Radical Poetics of Nonconformity, 1380–1590.* Chapel Hill: University of North Carolina Press, 1986.

Kernan, Alvin. *The Cankered Muse.* 1954. Reprint. Hamden, Conn.: Archon Books, 1976.

King, John N. "Robert Crowley: A Tudor Gospeller." In *English Reformation Literature: The Tudor Origins of the Protestant Tradition,* 319–57. Princeton: Princeton University Press, 1982.

————. "Robert Crowley's Editions of *Piers Plowman*: A Tudor Apocalypse." *Modern Philology* 73 (1976): 342–52.

Kirk, Elizabeth D. *The Dream Thought of Piers Plowman.* New Haven: Yale University Press, 1972.

————. "Langland's Plowman and the Recreation of Fourteenth-Century Religious Metaphor." *Yearbook of Langland Studies* 2 (1988): 1–21.

Knott, John R., Jr. "Bunyan and the Holy Community." *Studies in Philology* 80 (1983): 200–25.

————. *The Sword of the Spirit: Puritan Responses to the Bible.* Chicago: University of Chicago Press, 1980.

————. "'Thou must live upon my Word': Bunyan and the Bible." In *John Bunyan: Conventicle and Parnassus,* edited by N. H. Keeble, 153–70. Oxford: Clarendon Press, 1988.

Lawton, D. A. "Lollardy and the 'Piers Plowman' Tradition." *Modern Language Review* 76 (1981): 780–93.

Leavis, Q. D. *Fiction and the Reading Public.* 1932. Reprint. London: Peregrine Books, 1979.

Lechler, Gotthard Victor. *John Wyclif and His English Precursors.* Translated by Peter Lorimer. London: Kegan Paul, Tench, 1881.

Lerner, L. D. "Bunyan and the Puritan Culture." *Cambridge Journal* 7 (1954): 221–42.

Lewalski, Barbara K. *Protestant Poetics and the Seventeenth-Century Religious Lyric.* Princeton: Princeton University Press, 1979.

Lindsay, Jack. *John Bunyan: Maker of Myths.* London: Methuen Press, 1937.

Luxon, Thomas H. "Calvin and Bunyan on Word and Image: Is There a Text in Interpreter's House?" *English Literary Renaissance* 18 (1988): 438–59.

————. "The Pilgrim's Passive Progress: Luther and Bunyan on Talking and Doing, Word and Way." *ELH* 53 (1986): 73–98.

MacDonald, Ruth K. *Christian's Children: The Influence of John Bunyan's "The Pilgrim's Progress" on American Children's Literature.* American University Studies Series 25, vol. 10. New York: Peter Lang, 1989.

McGinnis, Myrta Ethel. "'Piers the Plowman' in England, 1362–1625: A Study in Popularity and Influence." Ph.D. diss., Yale, 1932.

McKeon, Michael. *The Origins of the English Novel 1600–1740.* Baltimore: Johns Hopkins University Press, 1987.

Mann, Jill. *Chaucer and Medieval Estates Satire.* London: Cambridge University Press, 1973.

Marx, Kitty. *Das Nachleben von Piers Plowmann bis zu Bunyan's: The Pilgrim's Progress (1678).* Ph.D. diss., Albert-Ludwigs-Universität., 1931.

Metscher, Thomas. "Subversive, Radical and Revolutionary Traditions in European Literature Between 1300 and the Age of Bunyan: Some

Comments." *Zeitschrift für Anglistik und Amerikanistik* 29 (1981): 12–20.

Middleton, Anne. "The Audience and Public of *Piers Plowman.*" In *Middle English Alliterative Poetry and its Literary Background*, edited by David Lawton, 101–23. Cambridge and Totowa, N.J.: D. S. Brewer, 1982.

Mish, C. C. "Bestsellers in Seventeenth-Century Fiction." *Papers of the Bibliographical Society of America* 47 (1953): 358–59.

Murdock, Kenneth B. *Literature and Theology in Colonial New England.* Cambridge: Harvard University Press, 1956.

Newey, Vincent A. "The Disinherited Pilgrim: *Jude the Obscure* and *The Pilgrim's Progress.*" *Durham University Journal* 80 (1987–88): 59–61.

―――. "Dorothea's Awakening: The Recall of Bunyan in *Middlemarch.*" *Notes and Queries* 31 (1984): 497–99.

―――, ed. *The Pilgrim's Progress: Critical and Historical Views.* Totowa, N.J.: Barnes & Noble, 1980.

Newman, S. J. "Bunyan's Solidness." In *The Pilgrim's Progress: Critical and Historical Views*, edited by Vincent A. Newey, 225–50.

Norbrook, David. *Poetry and Politics in the English Renaissance.* London: Routledge & Kegan Paul, 1984.

Nussbaum, Felicity A. "'By These Words I was Sustained': Bunyan's *Grace Abounding.*" *ELH* 49 (1982): 18–34.

Owst, G. R. *Literature and Pulpit in Medieval England.* Cambridge: Cambridge University Press, 1933.

Peck, Russell A. "Social Conscience and the Poets." In *Social Unrest in the Middle Ages*, edited by Francis X. Newman, 112–48. Binghamton, N.Y.: Medieval and Renaissance Texts and Studies, 1986.

Pooley, Roger. "Plain and Simple: Bunyan and Style." In *John Bunyan: Conventicle and Parnassus*, edited by N. H. Keeble, 91–110. Oxford: Clarendon Press, 1988.

Quilligan, Maureen. *The Language of Allegory.* Ithaca and London: Cornell University Press, 1979.

Roush, George. "The Political Plowman: The Expression of Political Ideals in 'Piers Plowman' and its Successors." Ph.D. diss., Berkeley, 1966.

Sasek, Lawrence A. *The Literary Temper of the English Puritans.* Baton Rouge: Louisiana State University Press, 1961.

Scott, Sir Walter. Review of *"The Pilgrim's Progress*, with a Life of John Bunyan by Robert Southey." *Quarterly Review* 43 (1830). Reprinted in *Sir Walter Scott: On Novelists and Fiction*, edited by Ioan Williams. London: Routledge & Kegan Paul, 1968.

Seed, David. "Dialogue and Debate in *The Pilgrim's Progress.*" In *The Pilgrim's Progress: Critical and Historical Views*, edited by Vincent A. Newey, 69–90. Totowa, N.J.: Barnes & Noble, 1980.

Sharrock, Roger. "Bunyan and the English Emblem Writers." *Review of English Studies* 21 (1945): 105–16.

———. *John Bunyan.* London: Macmillan; New York: St. Martin's Press, 1968.

———. "Life and Story in *The Pilgrim's Progress.*" In *The Pilgrim's Progress: Critical and Historical Views,* edited by Vincent A. Newey, 49–68. Totowa, N.J.: Barnes & Noble, 1980.

———. "Personal Vision and the Puritan Tradition in Bunyan." *Hibbert Journal* 56 (1957–58): 47–60.

———. "Spiritual Autobiography in *The Pilgrim's Progress.*" *Review of English Studies* 24 (1948): 102–20.

———. "'When at the first I took my pen in hand': Bunyan and the Book." In *John Bunyan: Conventicle and Parnassus,* edited by N. H. Keeble, 71–90. Oxford: Clarendon Press, 1988.

———, ed. *The Pilgrim's Progress: A Casebook.* London: Macmillan, 1976.

Shrimpton, Nick. "Bunyan's Military Metaphor." In *The Pilgrim's Progress: Critical and Historical Views,* edited by Vincent A. Newey, 205–24. Totowa, N.J.: Barnes & Noble, 1980.

Sim, Stuart. "'Vertuous Mediocrity' and 'Fanatick Conventicle': Pilgrimage Styles in John Bunyan and Bishop Simon Patrick." *English Studies* 68 (1987): 316–24.

Sinfield, Alan. *Literature in Protestant England 1550–1660.* Totowa, N.J.: Barnes & Noble, 1983.

Skeat, W. W. *The Chaucer Canon.* Oxford: Clarendon Press, 1900.

Smith, David E. *John Bunyan in America.* Bloomington: Indiana University Press, 1966.

Smith, Hallett. *Elizabethan Poetry.* Cambridge: Harvard University Press, 1952.

Spufford, Margaret. "First Steps in Literacy: The Reading and Writing Experiences of the Humblest Seventeenth-Century Autobiographers." In *Literacy and Social Development in the West: A Reader,* edited by Harvey J. Graff, 125–50. Cambridge: Cambridge University Press, 1981.

———. *Small Books and Pleasant Histories: Popular Fiction and its Readership in Seventeenth-Century England.* Cambridge: Cambridge University Press, 1981.

Steadman, John. *The Lamb and the Elephant: Ideal Imitation and the Context of Renaissance Allegory.* San Marino: Huntington Library, 1974.

Stock, Brian. *The Implications of Literacy: Written Language and Models of Interpretation in the Eleventh and Twelfth Centuries.* Princeton: Princeton University Press, 1983.

Stranahan, Brainerd P. "Bunyan and the Epistle to the Hebrews: His Source for the Idea of Pilgrimage in *The Pilgrim's Progress.*" *Studies in Philology* 79 (1982): 279–96.

——. "Bunyan's Special Talent: Biblical Texts as 'Events' in *Grace Abounding* and *The Pilgrim's Progress.*" *English Literary Renaissance* 11 (1981): 329–43.

——. "'With Great Delight': The Song of Solomon in *The Pilgrim's Progress.*" *English Studies* 68 (1987): 220–27.

Suleiman, Susan R., and Inge Crossman, eds. *The Reader in the Text.* Princeton: Princeton University Press, 1980.

Talon, Henri. *John Bunyan: The Man and His Works.* Translated by Barbara Wall. London: Rockcliff, 1951.

Tanselle, G. Thomas. *The History of Books as a Field of Study.* Chapel Hill: University of North Carolina, Rare Book Collection, 1980.

Thickstun, Margaret Olofson. "From Christiana to Standfast: Subsuming the Feminine in *The Pilgrim's Progress.*" *Studies in English Literature 1500–1800* 26 (1986): 439–53.

——. "The Preface to Bunyan's *Grace Abounding* as Pauline Epistle." *Notes and Queries* 32 (1985): 180–82.

Thomas, Ronald R. "The Novel and the Afterlife: The End of the Line in Bunyan and Beckett." *Modern Philology* 86 (1988–89): 385–97.

Thompson, E. P. *The Making of the English Working Class.* 1963. Reprint. New York: Vintage Books, 1966.

Tindall, William York. *John Bunyan, Mechanick Preacher.* New York: Columbia University Press, 1934.

Tompkins, Jane. "The Reader in History: The Changing Shape of Literary Response." In *Reader-Response Criticism,* 201–32. Baltimore: Johns Hopkins University Press, 1980.

——, ed. *Reader-Response Criticism.* Baltimore: Johns Hopkins University Press, 1980.

Turner, James. "Bunyan's Sense of Place." In *The Pilgrim's Progress: Critical and Historical Views,* edited by Vincent A. Newey, 91–110. Totowa, N.J.: Barnes & Noble, 1980.

Van Dyke, Carolynn. *The Fiction of Truth: Structures of Meaning in Narrative and Dramatic Allegory.* Ithaca: Cornell University Press, 1985.

von Nolcken, Christine. "*Piers Plowman,* the Wycliffites, and *Pierce the Plowman's Creed.*" *Yearbook of Langland Studies* 2 (1988): 71–102.

Walker, Eric C. *William Dell, Master Puritan.* Cambridge: W. Heffer & Sons, 1970.

Walton, George W. "Bunyan's Proverbial Language." In *Bunyan in Our Time,* edited by Robert G. Collmer, 7–34. Kent, Ohio: Kent State University Press, 1989.

Wawn, Andrew N. "Chaucer, *The Plowman's Tale,* and Renaissance Propaganda: The Testimonies of Thomas Godfray and *I playne Piers.*" *Bulletin of the John Rylands Library* 56 (1973): 174–92.

————. "The Genesis of *The Plowman's Tale*." *Yearbook of English Studies* 2 (1972): 21–40.

Weiner, Andrew. *Sir Philip Sidney and the Poetics of Protestantism*. Minneapolis: University of Minnesota Press, 1978.

Wharey, James Blanton. *A Study of the Sources of Bunyan's Allegories, with Special Reference to Deguilleville's Pilgrimage of Man*. 1904. Reprint. New York: Gordian Press, 1968.

White, Helen C. *Social Criticism and Religious Literature*. New York: Macmillan, 1944.

Williams, Raymond. *Keywords: A Vocabulary of Culture and Society*. New York: Oxford University Press, 1976.

Wilson, Gayle Edward. "'As John Bunyan Says': Bunyan's Influence on *Uncle Tom's Cabin*." *American Transcendental Quarterly* n.s. 1 (1987): 157–62.

Index